JEWISH ETHICS AND HALAKHAH FOR OUR TIME:

Sources and Commentary

by

BASIL F. HERRING

KTAV PUBLISHING HOUSE
YESHIVA UNIVERSITY PRESS
NEW YORK

Published by
KTAV PUBLISHING HOUSE
527 Empire Blvd.
Brooklyn, NY 11225
www.ktav.com | orders@ktav.com
(718) 972-5449

Library of Congress Cataloging in Publication Data

Herring, Basil.
Jewish ethics and Halakhah for our time.

(The Library of Jewish law and ethics ; vol. 11)
Includes bibliographical references.
1. Ethics, Jewish—Addresses, essays, lectures.
2. Jewish law—Addresses, essays, lectures. 3. Orthodox
Judaism—Addresses, essays, lectures. I. Title.
II. Series
BJ1285.H38 1984 296.3'85 84-5699

ISBN: 978-1-60280-157-8

MANUFACTURED IN THE UNITED STATES OF AMERCIA

To Sherri:
Eshet Ḥayil,
Source of Blessing,
—and True Friend.

Contents

An Appreciation

Dr. David Shatz
Professor of Philosophy, Yeshiva University,
and editor of *The Torah u-Madda Journal*

Rabbi Dr. Basil Herring is well known for his communal roles, first as a practicing rabbi, then as chair of the Orthodox Caucus, and now as the vigorous and oft-quoted Executive Vice President of the Rabbinical Council of America. But Rabbi Herring has long combined this leadership with scholarly research and writing, producing an unusual fusion of philosophy and Halakhah. (Philosophers would say he lives both the active and the contemplative life.) On the one hand, he authored a valuable book on the philosopher-exegete Joseph ibn Kaspi and has taught Jewish philosophy on the university level; on the other, he has been closely involved in halakhic matters and has produced the present volume.

The republication of *Jewish Ethics and Halakhah for Our Time* (the original appeared in 1981) is an event that many pedagogues and researchers have long wished for. It is, to begin with, a wonderful book to use in classes and an excellent choice for an introduction to key issues and sources. The judicious and appealing arrangement of primary texts that begin each chapter, the use of scenarios to motivate discussion, and the crisp exposition of issues—all these give readers a strong grasp of key ethical challenges facing decisors and instill an appreciation of the subtlety, challenge, and richness of the halakhic tradition. Readers familiar with the issues will still benefit from the clear, organized analyses.

The processes of Jewish law, its stress on *masorah* (Jewish tradition), call for a rigorous understanding of ancient texts and later commentary and decisions. For this reason, Rabbi Herring's discussions remain foundational even given the explosion of literature in Jewish ethics in recent times and the ever increasing complexity of medical, economic, and social realities. *Zil gemor*—go and learn from this erudite and rewarding volume.

Author's Preface to the Augmented Edition

Twenty five years is by most measures a significant passage of time in the life of the printed word.

That after such a lapse there should still be some interest in a two volume publication that presumed to speak to the interface of halakhah and ethics "for our time," as it was then titled, says more about the undiminished timelessness of halakhah and the rabbinic tradition than it does about any presumed virtues that the volumes in question may have had.

And thus it is more out of a heightened sense of the ever-fresh value and appeal of fundamental halakhic principles and texts, than of any author's achievement, that we can now contemplate this reissue, in a chapter-selective one-volume edition, of the two volumes of Jewish Ethics and Halakhah For Our Time.

The chapters that have been chosen in this edition were chosen on the basis of their ongoing relevance to ethical and societal issues that continue to be widely-discussed. Nonetheless attentive readers might find certain contemporary references to, or formulations of, social issues to appear dated. And of course the secondary halakhic literature itself has grown considerably over the intervening years. There has been no attempt to incorporate that new literature—instead the reader is urged to regard this volume as a useful presentation and grounding in the basic halachic literature until recent decades, and a foundation on which to further study the dynamic halachic process as it has continued to unfold year after year, into the 21st Century.

I express my deep gratitude to Bernard Scharfstein of Ktav Publishing, for his initiative in this reissuance—not to speak of his indispensable role in their original appearance. And I want to thank my dear friend and colleague Professor David Shatz, not only for his gracious words of preface, but for his having shared the original volumes with so many of his students over the years—and brightened my day on so many occasions with his uncritical appreciation of their educational value.

May Hashem grant that this edition help to bring the beauty and profundity of the ethical moment within halakhah to a new generation of readers.

Basil Herring
Woodsburgh, New York.
February 2010

Preface

In recent years there has been a veritable explosion of books, courses, and public debate dealing with "ethics." The educational process, from kindergarten through postgraduate work, has come to incorporate a concern with, and teaching of, public and professional ethics. In part this is attributable to the fact that society at large is going through a phase in history where it is reexamining many basic beliefs and values. Many question the values once taken for granted, as a result of a new ethical relativism, or of specific developments in public life, such as the Watergate scandals, revolutionary changes in medical technology and procedures affecting the definition and possibilities of life itself, and a judicial system that raises many questions of ethical and moral import.

Within Jewish life, similar interests have emerged, out of a concern to clarify a specifically Jewish perspective on many of these issues. This concern is found among traditionalists and nontraditionalists alike, and it extends beyond academe to the less formal settings of discussion groups, study circles, synagogue gatherings, and family settings. The process of establishing "the Jewish view" is complicated by several factors: often there is no single Jewish view, but many; many views that purport to speak for Judaism are molded more by personal preference or questionable Jewish sources than by what is reasonably and objectively "Jewish"; much of the basic material dealing with the issues at hand is not available in English, or else presumes a measure of technical expertise often lacking in the reader; and often authors fail to draw a line between analysis and apologetics, leaving the reader with a sense of being "talked down at."

The present volume is an attempt to fill part of the need for a work that can address itself to clarifying Jewish values and practices relating to some of the more familiar social and professional dilemmas facing us presently. It is admittedly partial, in that it presents what might be called the traditional focus and perspective. It has tried to avoid both polemics and apologetics, while striving for clarity and comprehensiveness. In that respect it does not assume an ethical neutrality, and does not subscribe to the philosophy that one ethical system is no better or worse than other such systems, but simply "different." A system of ethics based on revelation simply cannot subscribe to such total ethical relativism; it must assume certain objective truths and moral principles, and attempt to identify its own values as embodying those truths and principles. Some may call this "moral indoctrination," yet traditional Jewish ethics has not hesitated to imbue specific values leading to concrete action both by the individual and the community.

There is one important caveat: this volume makes no consistent attempt to describe how the Halakhah would expect a non-Jewish society to deal with Gentiles on any given issue. Our focus and concern is to present the Halakhah as a prescription for Jewish life and a normative Jewish society. It is of course possible to generalize from these discussions to articulate broad halakhic values and principles that could be applied to the goal of establishing a just and moral society for all men. But such applications would have to be undertaken with care and precision.

In this book, the issues dealt with, fall under three broad headings: bioethics, legal ethics, and the ethics of the behavioral and social sciences. It does not deal directly with the fourth area of professional training, business ethics, as that has been dealt with at length in another volume in this series, by Aaron Levine, entitled *Free Enterprise and Jewish Law: Aspects of Jewish Business Ethics.*

The introductory chapter of the book attempts to clarify certain philosophical, methodological, and historical issues underlying the body of the work. The subsequent chapters are devoted to a thorough examination of various ethical issues confronting Jews in the modern world. Each chapter begins with a presentation of some of the major views of its subject found in society at large. By way of focusing the discussion, the issue is then introduced in the form of a case history posing specific questions and problems to be clarified. Certain fundamental Jewish sources relevant to the issue then follow in precise translation, and these sources (referred to with capital letters) form the basis for the discussion and analysis of the issue in the main body of the chapter. To facilitate reference to these sources, they have been reproduced as an insert on the inside back cover of the book. In this way the reader can evaluate the views presented against the basic texts themselves. All Hebrew terms are defined as they appear in each chapter, and essential information (e.g. acronym, dates) is provided about the halakhic authorities cited. There is no appended bibliography added, as the footnotes on each chapter include whatever references to the literature on the topic are considered useful or important.

It is hoped that the work herein presented will make a modest contribution to the ongoing clarification and understanding of what is uniquely Jewish in "Jewish ethics."

Introduction

This volume deals with the interaction of Jewish law (Halakhah) and certain contemporary ethical issues confronting Western society. It is not a philosophical or ethical work, as these terms are generally understood, but rather an attempt to present certain perspectives emanating from the corpus of Jewish law as they relate directly or indirectly to these issues. The book does not attempt any "apologetics" or "rationalization" on behalf of any of these perspectives. What is attempted is a fair treatment of the texts, opinions, and arguments that characterize the many views found therein. This necessarily entails careful textual study and analysis of the classic sources of Jewish law, as well as of the subsequent codes, responsa, and occasional writings of halakhic authorities over the centuries. Accordingly, the volume could more accurately be described as a literary history of the treatment of these issues at the hands of the leading halakhists of each generation, our own included.

Yet, because "ethics" is concerned with values, and in part deals with normative behavior, this book can also be said to be concerned with ethics. For the discussions involved do not only reveal many of the values and principles inhering in Jewish law, they also attempt to prescribe (and proscribe) attitudes and actions in human relations.

To appreciate more fully the nature of the relation between these halakhic discussions and ethics, it would be helpful to examine traditional views on the interaction of Jewish law and ethics. The problem has been formulated in a variety of ways, but for our purposes we may put it as follows: To be a truly ethical person in practice, is it sufficient to follow the dictates of the Halakhah as formulated by halakhic authorities, or is it necessary in addition to subscribe to purely voluntary ethical principles that are a matter of personal conscience? Does the Halakhah include its own ethical principles, and if so do they differ in any fundamental way from other systems of ethics and ethical behavior?

In modern, "postemancipation," times this question has been of great interest to Jewish scholars and laymen alike. For it goes to the heart of the critical issue of the centrality of Jewish law and observance in the definition of the "good Jew." At the same time it is really part of the philosophical debate over the relation between Faith and Reason that has been ongoing since the Middle Ages: What does the revelation of the Torah teach us that we would not in any case be able to derive from our intellect and experience?

With regard to ethical principles, there are some contemporaries who argue that the Halakhah, in its texts and their interpretation, incorporates all of Jewish ethics.[1] In this view, Jewishly sanctioned behavior and Jewish ethical positions must always find some justification in a legally binding halakhic rule. Furthermore, the Halakhah by itself is sufficient to produce a truly ethical personality. Such a view takes support from the writings of Rabbi A. I. Karelitz (known as Ḥazon Ish, d. 1953), which state that "punctilious observance of the law [*din*] is the only path to the perfection of moral virtue."[2] Proponents of this view likewise point to certain writings of Maimonides (R. Moses b. Maimon, known as Rambam; 1135–1204) that deny that man can achieve a full knowledge of the rules of morality by way of rational reflection.[3] Maimonides, according to this view, regards secular or autonomous morality as no more than a set of social conventions which may be useful or in good taste, but not "true" or rationally necessary. Only a divine law, i.e., Halakhah, possesses the means to bring man to perfection of both body and soul in a just society of men,[4] and man can come to an appreciation of the wisdom imbedded in that law by careful examination and study thereof.

Opposed to such views of an all-inclusive Halakhah is the view that sees large areas of human behavior as being beyond the strict purview of the Halakhah. According to this, the Halakhah does not pretend to legislate rules to cover every situation, especially in those areas where so much depends on particular circumstances or conflicting principles. Certainly the Halakhah provides extensive and detailed laws covering many areas of human relations—

but it does leave other mundane and existential choices to man's reasoned decision, based on man's own moral sense of right and wrong. Just because certain moral perceptions cannot be buttressed by explicit, formal rules of Halakhah, they should not be dismissed as invalid or inferior.[5]

This view takes support from the writings of Rabbi A. I. Kook, a past Chief Rabbi of Israel. In a notable passage, this authority wrote the following regarding the relationship of Torah to morality:

> Morality, in its naturalness, in all the depths of its splendor and power of its strength, must be determined in the soul, and will be receptive to those noble influences deriving from the force of the Torah. Every word of the Torah must be preceded by worldliness. If it is a matter with which reason and natural honesty agree, it must directly traverse the tendency of the heart and the agreement of the pure will imprinted in man. The Torah was given to Israel, so that the gates of her light—clearer, more extensive, and holier than all the gates of light of man's natural wisdom and natural moral spirit—will open before us, and through us, to the rest of the world. But if we deafen our ears so that we cannot hear the simple call of the Lord which is potentially proclaimed through all the natural gates of light, which are in every man's reach, because we think that we will find the light of the Torah in a Torah which is severed from all the light of life spread over the world and planted in the splendid soul of man, then we have not understood the value of the Torah. Of this it has been said: "foolish people and unwise" (Deut. 32:6), which is translated by Targum Onkelos: "A people who received the Torah and did not grow wiser."[6]

These words of Rav Kook, taken in juxtaposition to the view of the Ḥazon Ish, are understood to leave significant room for a universal morality that derives from extra-Torah sources, without necessarily contradicting the letter or the spirit of the Torah.

In philosophical terms this debate revolves around the issue of natural law versus positive law. Fundamentally the question is whether moral principles can be known to man without divine revelation specifying them. Can uncommanded man be ethical merely by deriving the rules of morality from "nature," i.e., either by observing the world around him or by his own thought processes? Or should we say that there is no natural morality that can help man choose right from wrong, so that man depends entirely on a divine law or revelation (in this case, the Halakhah) to determine moral behavior. In the history of Jewish thought, both views have had their supporters, including a number in the present.[7] The view propounding natural law is historically identified with the tenth-century Saadya Gaon, who posited the distinction between rational laws and revelational laws, the former constituting a kind of naturally derived imperative. The opposing view is identified with Judah Halevy (1075–1141), who insisted on revelation as the exclusive source of Jewish law and morality. An ambivalent role is played by Maimonides, but on balance he too seems to recognize the realm of uncommanded morality, i.e., natural law, rationally derived whether by Gentile or Jew.[8] Of course conflicting views of Maimonides' doctrines are not uncommon, given his own sometimes conflicting statements on these issues.

This discussion has its roots in talmudic literature. The Gemara speaks on numerous occasions of virtues that man can learn through observation of the animal world,[9] and quite clearly recognizes the notion of *derekh ereẓ* (common moral decency) as separate from Torah per se.[10] But the crucial discussion and texts on this issue occur in the context of the notion of *lifnim mi-shurat ha-din*, literally "behavior that goes beyond the letter of the law," with the connotation of action that is legally open and unspecified in any halakhic text—but morally desirable.[11] Naḥmanides (R. Moses b. Naḥman, known as Ramban; 1194–1270) in several places elaborates on this principle, explaining that the Torah could not possibly have legislated every conceivable situation—instead it laid down certain paradigmatic rules, and then generalized them to require the Jew to follow his conscience in all such cases. This is the meaning of doing "that which is right and good in the sight of the Lord" (Deut. 6:18).[12] From the formulation of Naḥmanides it appears that moral behavior of this kind is not simply optional but is required of every Jew.[13]

The view of Maimonides is somewhat more complex. In his early *Commentary on the Mishnah* he discusses the question of ethical motivation and concludes that in areas where ethical behavior is required, a "noble soul has absolutely no desire for any such crimes and experiences, no struggle in refraining from them."[14] Ethical behavior, inasmuch as its dictates are universally appreciated, is the better expressed when it is completely autonomous, i.e., freely desired and undertaken out of one's own inclination. Clearly, morality according to Maimonides is not dependent on revelation as a source.[15] As to the notion of *lifnim mi-shurat ha-din*, in the same work Maimonides limits its desirability, saying that it should only be undertaken as a temporary means to perfecting the "golden mean" that is represented by *din* (the letter of the law). Does this contradict his preference for moral autonomy? One answer would deny this, arguing that Maimonides simply subsumes supralegal behavior and ethical sensitivity under a different rubric; that of *imitatio dei*, the imitation of God.[16] This is borne out in the *Mishneh Torah*, where Maimonides states that "we are commanded to walk in these median paths, and they are the right and the good paths, as it is written, 'and ye shall walk in His ways' (Deut. 6:18)."[17]

Further examination of the *Mishneh Torah* reveals that Maimonides came to view heteronomy, or divinely commanded morality, to be superior to morality freely undertaken. Thus he states that a heathen who observes the seven so-called Noahide Laws, including fundamental laws of morality and justice, is indeed a "righteous heathen"—but only if he accepts them and performs them because they are commanded by God.[18] Likewise the repentant sinner is in some ways superior to one who has never sinned, the reason being that "the former has had to put forth greater effort to subdue his passions than the latter."[19] Thus Maimonides insists that a moral personality can well come to a rational appreciation of ethical laws and principles, but this in no way substitutes for the ethical laws of the Torah and Halakhah that draw their sanction from revelation.[20]

In one further passage in the *Mishneh Torah*, Maimonides speaks of *lifnim mi-shurat ha-din* as a standard voluntarily subscribed to by "one who is great in Torah and well known for his piety [*ḥasidut*]," but which at the same time embraces the "golden mean." Thus he says,

> And if that wise man[21] has been scrupulous in his conduct, gentle in his conversation, pleasant toward his fellow creatures, affable in manner when receiving them, not retorting even

> when confronted, but showing courtesy to all, even to those who treat him with disdain, conducting his commercial affairs with integrity, not readily accepting the hospitality of the ignorant nor frequenting their company, not seen at all times, but devoting himself to study of the Torah, wrapped in the tallit and crowned with the phylacteries, and doing more than his duty [*lifnim mi-shurat ha-din*] in all things, but avoiding extremes and exaggerations—such a man has sanctified God . . . [22]

While it is not entirely clear how one can go beyond the letter of the law while at the same time avoiding extremes and exaggerations,[23] the major thrust of the passage is that the halakhic ideal is a personality that incorporates adherence to the law so that it may enhance his perception of the "good" and "true," inducing behavior which transcends the letter of the law.[24] Whether this ideal is purely voluntary or required by the Halakhah is a matter of debate among medieval authorities generally,[25] but it would appear that for Maimonides it is not a legal obligation, merely that to which the righteous aspire.[26]

A recent typological analysis of Maimonides' classification of ethical personalities, as developed both in the Introduction to the *Commentary on the Mishnah* and in the *Mishneh Torah*, yields the following four types:[27]

1. Natural Man: He acts instinctively toward his fellows, albeit with good intentions, yet bereft of any objective or substantive code of moral action that might anchor his moral personality.
2. The Functional Ethicist: He subscribes to the Aristotelian type of moral rationalism that develops the intellectual model of the golden mean. He avoids extremes, controls his passions, and seeks to find correct behavior without any reference to a transcendental source.
3. The Imitator of God: He adopts God as his model; through a knowledge of God's ethical ways he comes to develop his entire character. In Maimonides' terminology he is a *ḥakham*, a man of wisdom, capable of making careful distinctions so that he knows which of God's attributes to adopt, which extremes might be desirable. His is a transcendental ethic, albeit one that is legally (i.e, halakhically) enforceable.
4. The Ḥasid: His is the highest morality. While he too starts with

the obligation to imitate God, his moral framework is characterized by the search for personal holiness. This he achieves by aspiring to entirely voluntary selflessness and "giving." In the process his "self" is overcome, going far beyond the formalism of the golden mean to a selflessness that is expressed typically in behavior that is *lifnim mi-shurat ha-din*, beyond the letter of the law.

If we have dealt with the principle of *lifnim mi-shurat ha-din* at some length, it is because the principle is illustrative of the more general interrelationship of law and ethics in rabbinic literature. Historically Judaism has been accused of inordinate legalism, of lacking in sensitivity to moral concerns. In reality, however, normative Judaism has always viewed law as a branch of ethics, constituting the minimal requirements of ethical behavior that are necessary for a well-functioning society. Beyond the necessary realm of such laws is the whole spectrum of ethical behavior to which man should aspire, and which the law attempts to make possible. The law simply encompasses those areas of ethics which it is possible to enforce; beyond this, it attempts in a variety of ways to bring people to their own observance of behavior that is ethically desirable, and which they themselves should appreciate as a matter of conscience.[28] The relationship is not a static one, in that over time the law will come to incorporate ethical principles or aspirations that were initially purely voluntary—and vice versa.

In those cases where ethical principles that were initially voluntary later became legally binding, the reason was generally that the sages of later generations perceived the masses as having failed to maintain the voluntary standards set by earlier generations. A good example is that of charity. In biblical times charity was purely voluntary, but by the time of the Second Temple things had changed, as a result of Roman influences that denigrated charity, as well as changing socioeconomic realities. Consequently the giving of charity became legally enforceable, as when the Talmud records the law that a community can force a recalcitrant minority to participate in fund-raising activities. Likewise, in biblical times a father could not be forced to provide sustenance for his minor children; it was assumed that such ethical behavior would occur rather spontaneously. But again in later generations this began to change under outside influences, so that it became necessary to require a father to make such provisions, and with the passage of time these obligations became more and more explicit and binding. Similar processes took place in other areas, such as support of elderly parents, preferential consideration in the sale of property to abutting landowners, or for that matter the semilegal treatment of *lifnim mi-shurat ha-din* on numerous occasions.[29]

Where the process worked in the opposite direction—i.e., the evolution of obligatory behavior into the "merely" supererogatory—the process was generally the result of changed attitudes and social realities. Thus, for example, by law a thief who repented was required to return everything he had stolen. But at a later time this obligation was found to be a major obstacle preventing many thieves from changing their errant ways; thus *mipnei takkanat ha-shavim* (i.e., to facilitate rehabilitation) it was decreed that it would no longer be necessary to return stolen goods. But while this was not legally required, there was a moral onus placed upon erstwhile criminals to "do the right thing" and voluntarily return what they had improperly taken. Similarly, the mandatory punishments laid down in the Torah for certain transgressions were seen in subsequent generations to be self-defeating or manifestly inapplicable, and thus they were not imposed or legally enforced, but left to the good conscience of the people. These included the execution of the gluttonous minor, the destruction of idolatrous Israelite cities, capital punishment in general, and the so-called bitter waters administered to the suspected adulteress that led to physical disfigurement.[30] In cases such as these, improper behavior was "decriminalized," coercive punishment was suspended—but moral exhortation was still applied, to the end of attaining a more sensitive and ethical society.

An important statement of this attitude is found in the writings of R. Vidal Yomtov of Tolosa, one of the commentators on the *Mishneh Torah* in the fourteenth century.

> The Torah has laid down general principles concerning the development of man's character and his conduct in the world; . . . likewise it said, "And thou shalt do the right and the good," meaning that one's interpersonal conduct should be good and

> just. With regard to all this, it would not have been proper to command about details. For the Torah's commands apply at all times, in every period and under all circumstances, whereas man's characteristics and his behavior vary, depending upon the time and the individual. The rabbis therefore set down some relevant details subsumed under these principles, some of which they made absolute *din* [law] and others only *le-khatḥilah* [preferred] and by way of *ḥasidut* [special piety]—all, however, ordained by them. And it is with reference to this that they said, "The words of consorts [i.e., the rabbis] are more beloved than the wine of Torah, as it is stated, 'For thy love is better than wine.' "[31]

Thus we can conclude that in addition to the extensive corpus of halakhic material that very carefully articulates acts and beliefs that are commanded or prohibited, pure or impure, proper or improper, there exists a whole dimension of halakhic concern that lies beyond that which can be carefully prescribed or proscribed. This dimension, which we may loosely call "the ethical moment of the Halakhah," covers the infinite variety of day-to-day situations encountered by the individual in his dealings with his social environment, in which he is called upon to make decisions that could not possibly have been precisely described in the corpus of Jewish law. Some of these situations were anticipated in rabbinic writings, and therefore found a legal formulation to either prohibit or permit a given course of behavior. But the vast majority remain a matter of individual judgment based on a sensitivity to the moral thrust of the broad principles of the Halakhah, as well as the existence of specific principles and concepts that relate to the given "problem" in one degree or another. Sometimes the clarification of the proper moral path is made the easier by the presence of an outstanding role model who through word or deed can point the way for a student or follower.[32]

The relationship between Jewish law and morality thus emerges as one demonstrating considerable dynamism, flexibility, and growth. Far from being a negatively-charged "legalism," the Halakhah from biblical times on strove to raise the ethical consciousness of the people, through prescription and exhortation, depending on circumstances and period.[33] Whether or not we include such moral concerns under the rubric of "Halakhah" is a question of semantics and how we define the terms "Halakhah" and "morality," but what is clear is that we are dealing with two realms that are closely interconnected, if not in many ways identical.

A related issue is the attitude of the Halakhah to the non-Jew. If the Halakhah is an ethical system, does it have to treat Jew and Gentile alike? To what extent is the Gentile obligated to follow the principles of the Halakhah, if at all? These questions are important to the concerns of the present volume in that it deals with universal ethical issues from a halakhic perspective that may not be applicable to (Gentile) society at large.

There can be no doubt that as a total system of behavior and belief, Jewish law addresses itself only to the Jewish people. Jewish law is the practical expression of the historic covenant between God and the people of Israel, who voluntarily entered into the covenant of commandment and obligation.[34] Nonetheless the Halakhah does recognize the existence of certain precovenantal imperatives, universal in nature, and binding on all men. These laws are the seven Noahide Commandments, and they include six prohibitions (against idolatry, murder, incest, blasphemy, theft, eating meat from a live animal) as well as one positive obligation (to establish a system of law and justice).[35] These laws are universal in nature, and therefore in one sense to be considered "natural law," mandatory even had they not been revealed or confirmed in Scripture.[36] At the same time the Talmud clearly makes them obligatory on non-Jews living under Jewish sovereignty.[37]

An important, and controversial, statement regarding the obligations of Gentiles under the seven Noahide Laws is the formulation of Maimonides. In the *Mishneh Torah* he states:

> Moses our teacher bequeathed the law and commandments to Israel . . . and to those of the nations who are willing to be converted to Judaism, as it is said, "One law and one ordinance shall be both for you and for the resident alien" [Num. 15:16]. But no coercion to accept the law and commandments is practiced on those who are unwilling to do so. Moreover, Moses our teacher was commanded by God to compel all human beings to accept the commandments enjoined upon the descendants of

> Noah. . . . A heathen who accepts the seven commandments and observes them scrupulously is a "righteous heathen," and will have a portion in the world-to-come, provided that he accepts them and performs them because the Holy One, blessed be He, commanded them in the law and made known through Moses our teacher that the observance thereof had been enjoined upon the descendants of Noah even before the law was given. But if his observance thereof is based upon a reasoned conclusion, he is not deemed a resident alien, or one of the pious of the Gentiles, but one of their wise men.[38]

This statement, quite consistent with Maimonides' view that morality is not dependent on revelation,[39] is based on the *Mishnat R. Eliezer*, written in the eighth century.[40] Later authorities concurred with this ruling.[41] What Maimonides is saying is that the wise Gentile can well live a moral life (in accordance with "natural morality"), but in order to acquire immortality he must accept the Mosaic revelation as the ultimate source of that morality, for it is only the revelation that makes such morality authoritative and binding, i.e., law.[42] The part of Mosaic revelation that is coextensive with universal morality is that which deals with the seven Noahide Laws, and according to Maimonides, the observance of these laws is obligatory on all men. Even so, in carrying out the seven Noahide Laws different procedures apply to Jews and Gentiles,[43] and hence they cannot be said to be treated in an identical manner even regarding these fundamental moral laws.

This discussion leads to the related question of Jewish-Gentile relations as a practical matter: What demands does the Halakhah make on the Jew in his dealings with the non-Jew? The topic is a vast one, requiring detailed analysis and historical perspective.[44] Within the framework of this introduction, however, certain observations are pertinent. Firstly, it is important to appreciate the fact that, in the words of Jacob Katz, the relationship of Jews and Gentiles is at all times a reciprocal one, in that the behavior of Jews toward their neighbors is conditioned by the behavior of the latter toward them, and vice versa.[45] Secondly, there were always clear distinctions drawn between different groups of non-Jews, depending on their specific beliefs, moral behavior, and economic practices. Thirdly, it is particularly difficult to formulate an "authoritative position" that would fairly reflect a normative view within one generation of halakhic authorities, let alone over the course of Jewish history. Attitudes, interpretations of texts, and practical rulings varied widely from place to place and age to age.

In the Talmud, the status of the Gentile, and his treatment, varies widely in many areas, including laws of personal status, marriage and inheritance, proselytization, laws of accession, contract, agency, evidence and damages, purity and impurity, personal property, Temple procedures, food preparation, social contact, religious holidays, and many others. The Gentile is a legal personality in Halakhah, and although sometimes discriminated against, is generally treated equitably.[46] Thus the Talmud relates that once the Romans sent two officials to learn the Jewish law, and after careful study, they said, "We have scrutinized all your laws and found them to be just, except for your law that says that if a Jew's ox gores that of a Gentile, the owner is free from damages, while if a Gentile's ox gores that of a Jew, he is obliged to pay damages."[47]

Where there is legal discrimination against the non-Jew in the Talmud, it is usually based on objective reasoning, such as the failure of the Gentile to subscribe to morally acceptable standards of behavior. As a rule individual Jews suspected of the same faults would likewise encounter discrimination or exclusion. One further factor leading to talmudic wariness of Gentile behavior and contact was the desire to discourage social intimacy that might lead to assimilation and intermarriage. Nonetheless, the Talmud itself recognized the need for sensitive handling of Jewish-Gentile relations, and therefore required of the Jew that he treat the non-Jew wherever possible with compassion and generosity, *mipnei darkei shalom*, "for the sake of peaceful mutual relations," and to prevent the profanation of God's name (*ḥillul Hashem*).

In later times, with the expansion of Jewish communities into closer social and economic contact with the Gentile world, many of these laws and attitudes underwent significant change. Starting in the tenth century, certain important halakhists began a process whereby many of the earlier restrictions were reinterpreted, and redefined, so as to allow easier access to the surrounding societies, as well as a more accepting attitude on the part of the halakhic community. This process, in which the school of Rashi and the Tosafists in France, Germany, and Italy was particularly prominent, reached a climax of sorts in the person of the fourteenth-century Provençal halakhist R. Menaḥem ha-Meiri. It was he who formulated and applied the distinction, long-brewing among the aforementioned authorities, between the pagan world with its assorted heathen faiths, so widespread in antiquity, and the dominant faiths of medieval times, Christianity and Islam. The latter were "nations restricted by the ways of religion"; they were not to be considered heathen, and their social and moral behavior was sufficient to exempt them from the restrictive laws regarding non-Jews in the Talmud.[48] But even Meiri did not apply this dispensation beyond certain social and economic activities. He too was mindful of the need to safeguard ritual sanctity and Jewish separateness, as well as all of the institutions of Jewish community life. He thus was careful not to demolish all social barriers between Jews and Gentiles, for tolerance was one thing, assimilation another.[49]

A famous responsum by the thirteenth-century R. Meir of Rothenburg, one of the great authorities of the Middle Ages, provides a good summary of several principles of medieval halakhic practice vis-à-vis the Gentile world of the time. One of the more universal malpractices in the Middle Ages was the tampering with coins in common usage. In a certain town Jews were required to take an oath not to clip the current coins, something that they hesitated to swear to. They approached R. Meir for permission to swear, but with a *reservatio mentalis* that would effectively annul the oath. In response, R. Meir forbade such action with great moral indignation. He reasoned that Jews should obey the law in accordance with the highest moral sensitivity, for several reasons. Firstly, a law protecting the value of currency is the law of the land, and as such is binding on all Jews under the rubric of *dina de' malkhuta dina* ("the law of the land is the law"). Secondly, debasing a coin is the equivalent of theft, and therefore forbidden equally in respect to a Jew and a non-Jew. Thirdly, an oath given in a just cause is fully valid, and cannot be mentally annulled. Such an act would entail a clear case of *ḥillul Hashem*, the desecration of God's name, in the eyes of the Gentiles. Finally, such a practice would endanger innocent fellow Jews, who could well be held responsible for the malfeasance of those who clipped the coins.[50]

R. Meir's responsum reflects the ambiguities and conflicts confronting many medieval halakhists as they attempted to harmonize the talmudic tradition with contemporary conditions and practices, both of Jew and non-Jew. Similar themes were struck in other halakhic works, including the thirteenth-century *Sefer Ḥasidim* by R. Judah ha-Ḥasid[51] and the *Sefer Miẓvot haGadol* by R. Moses of Coucy (known as Semag),[52] both urging scrupulous moral behavior toward Christians and Moslems.

But while these views could be said to constitute a trend among the medievals, there were others who took a more restrictive, and less universal, attitude toward contemporary faiths. Perhaps the most notable figure in this regard is Maimonides. In his *Mishneh Torah* (according to the uncensored version) he states that the talmudic legislation on heathens remains intact vis-à-vis Christianity and Islam.[53] Both, especially the former, are tainted with elements of idolatry. By implication, therefore, those talmudic laws that put idolaters at a disadvantage, as codified in the *Mishneh Torah*, would apply to the practitioners of these religions. These laws include such areas as lost property,[54] damages, the death penalty, and the commandment to "love your fellow."[55] Maimonides' stance in Jewish-Gentile relations appears to contradict his generally rationalistic approach to ethics. He did, after all, draw on Greek and Islamic sources in formulating much of his own ethical theory, a theory which is included in the *Mishneh Torah* itself.[56]

In clarifying Maimonides' position, several observations are in order. Maimonides accepted a crucial distinction in the Talmud between the idolater (*akum*) and the resident alien (*ger toshav*).[57] The latter is a non-Jew who accepts and lives up to the requirements of the seven Noahide Laws and lives under Jewish sovereignty. In the *Mishneh Torah* Maimonides is quite clear as to the obligations and privileges of the resident alien: If he wishes to observe all the laws of the Torah he may do so; if he finds himself under Jewish jurisdiction, the Jewish court is required to establish proper judicial procedures affecting him, in accordance with the Noahide Laws (even where the opposing litigant is a Jew); furthermore, says Maimonides, "it appears to me that resident aliens are to be treated with civility and compassion, as with an Israelite. For we are commanded to maintain them, as it is said: 'to the stranger that is within thy gate you shall give it to be eaten.' "[58] As far as Maimonides was concerned, the resident alien was a far cry from the idolater, both in matters of dogma and in ethical practice. And yet, it appears that Maimonides could not classify contemporary religions as possessing resident-alien status. This might well have been on doctrinal grounds, in that he perceived their notions regarding God and metaphysics generally to include ideas incompatible with a strict monotheism. Thus, irrespective of their actual moral behavior, he would have no choice but to exclude them from the status of resident alien. This is all the more true in that Maimonides' experience indicated that they did not in fact maintain proper moral and judicial standards. Thus he states, in explaining why the non-Jew is responsible when his ox gores that of a Jew (even though the reverse is not the case), "this is a fine imposed upon heathens, because being heedless of scriptural commandments, they do not remove sources of damage. Accordingly, should they not be held liable for damage caused by their animals, they would not take care of them, and thus would inflict loss on other people's property."[59] Maimonides here adopts a principle of reciprocity, whereby the non-Jew is to be judged in accordance with his own standards and attitudes toward the rights and possessions of others.

It should also be noted in this regard that Maimonides does not stop at the strict letter of the law. As seen earlier, Maimonides makes a particularly strong distinction between what is absolutely required by law and what he considers to be "merely" desirable and praiseworthy (*lifnim mi-shurat ha-din*).[60] This is equally true in the field of Jewish-Gentile relations, both toward the idolater and toward the resident alien, where Maimonides states that "the sages have commanded" the Jew to relate to the idolater by visiting his sick, burying his dead, supporting his poor, and generally pursuing "peaceful relations" (*mipnei darkei shalom*).[61]

Even so, it remains true that for Maimonides the contemporary Christian and Moslem populations were not to be treated under the same halakhic principles as the Jew, except insofar as a Jew might wish to benefit them. This does not mean, however, that for Maimonides nothing of ethical importance can be learned from such nonbelievers. Individuals among them, according to what we have seen Maimonides say,[62] can well attain great wisdom and lead lives that are morally virtuous and exemplary, so that even Maimonides himself could learn from their wisdom.

What emerges from this discussion is that the Halakhah is not a closed system impervious to the non-Jew. Certain fundamental halakhic precepts (the seven Noahide Laws), including the pursuit of justice, are incumbent upon the non-Jew, and others are optional to him. As to the treatment of the non-Jew in Halakhah, there is clearly a divergence of opinion as well as classification, but the predominant strain has been to search for ways to achieve moral equity and justice as these have evolved out of the classical sources themselves. Accordingly, as a general statement it is true that the views treated in this volume can well serve as a model for the clarification of the same issues as they appear in society at large.

THE MAJOR PERIODS, PERSONALITIES, AND WORKS OF JEWISH LAW

To the uninitiated, the history of the Halakhah might appear forbiddingly complex. Yet a rudimentary knowledge of the major periods, personalities, and works of the halakhic corpus is vital to a clear understanding of the halakhic treatment of any given topic. What follows is an attempt to summarize in broad outline the history of the law.[63]

Jewish law has a history that extends over a period of more than three thousand years. We may divide this into two periods: the first covering the time from the Torah until the closing of the Talmud, the second from the post-talmudic period until the present day. This division has no bearing on the matter of the continuing creativity and evolution of the Halakhah. Such creativity not only continued uninterruptedly after the closing of the Talmud, but, as regards volume and literary output, even gathered momentum in certain fields of the law. The significance of the closing of the Talmud as a historic turning point in Jewish law finds expression in the degree of authenticity attributed to the talmudic Halakhah, which was accepted in Judaism as the authoritative expression and rendering of the Oral Law. The talmudic literature became the starting point for any study or discussion of Jewish law, and retained this status even after Jewish law was enriched—in the course of some fifteen hundred years—by many additional literary creations which, in comprehensiveness, orderly arrangement, and convenience of use, overtake the talmudic literature.

The first period can be divided into six eras:

1. The biblical age (up to the time of Ezra and Nehemiah, about the middle of the fifth century B.C.E.).
2. From Ezra and Nehemiah until the age of the *zugot* (approx. 160 B.C.E.), sometimes referred to as the period of the *soferim* ("scribes").
3. The age of the *zugot*, literally "pairs," i.e., the five pairs of leading scholars who headed the courts during this period, the last of which were Hillel and Shammai (from 160 B.C.E. up to the beginning of the common era).
4. The age of the *tannaim* (up to 220 C.E.), which spans the activities of six generations of *tannaim*, from Gamaliel the Elder and his contemporaries to Judah ha-Nasi, the redactor of the Mishnah, Besides the Mishnah, this era also produced collections of halakhic Midrashim (such as the *Mekhilta, Sifra, Sifre)*, the Tosefta, Beraitot, and other tannaitic literary sources.
5. The age of the *amoraim*, embracing the activities of five generations of *amoraim* in Israel (till the end of the fourth century C.E.), and eight generations of *amoraim* in Babylon (up till the end of the fifth century). Extant from this period are the Babylonian Talmud and the Jerusalem Talmud.
6. The age of the *savoraim* (till the end of the sixth century, or according to some scholars the middle of the seventh century). This era was mainly occupied with completing the redaction of the Babylonian Talmud and determining rules of decision.

The second period of the history of Jewish law starts with the age of the *geonim* (from the seventh till the middle of the eleventh century). For most of this period the center of spiritual life was in Babylon, notably the academies of Sura and Pumbedita, led by their respective *geonim*. The *geonim*, as the acknowledged authorities for all of Jewry, including the new communities of North Africa and Spain, were instrumental in cementing the authority of the Babylonian Talmud. The better-known *geonim* are R. Yehudai, R. Amram, R. Saadya, R. Samuel b. Ḥofni, R. Sherira, and R. Hai; others from this time include R. Aḥa of Shabḥa (author of the *Sefer ha-She'iltot*) and R. Simon Kayyara (author of the *Halakhot Gedolot*). During the geonic period literary productions centered on three areas: commentaries and novellae (*ḥiddushim*); responsa (*teshuvot*); and the codes of practical law, systematically presented.

The geonic age was followed by the rabbinic age, which itself can be divided into three eras:

1. The period of the *rishonim*, from the middle of the eleventh century (the time of Isaac Alfasi) till the sixteenth century (the time of Joseph Karo and Moses Isserles). This was the golden period of the rabbinic age, in which were compiled the classic creations in all three branches of the post-talmudic literary sources of Jewish law: Rashi's commentary on the Talmud and the novellae of the Tosafists; the codes of Isaac Alfasi, Maimonides (the *Mishneh Torah)*, Jacob b. Asher (the *Tur)*, Joseph Karo (the *Shulḥan Arukh*), Moses Isserles (the *Mapah*), and others; the responsa collections of R. Solomon b. Adret (Rashba), R. Meir of Rothenburg, R. Asher b. Yeḥiel (Rosh), R. Isaac b. Sheshet Perfet (Rivash), R. Simon b. Ẓemaḥ Duran (Tashbeẓ), R. Joseph b. Solomon Colon (Maharik), and others. The period embraces the rise and decline of Spanish Jewry, and its close saw the initial flowering of several other Jewish centers, particularly in Israel and Poland-Lithuania.
2. The period of the *aḥaronim*, from the middle of the sixteenth till the end of the eighteenth century, with the coming of the Emancipation. The legal creativity in the fields of commentary, codification, and responsa continued during this time, especially in the case of responsa, which reached a peak of activity. Major personalities during this period include R. Joel Sirkes (Baḥ, d. 1640), R. Yair Ḥayyim Bachrach (Ḥavvot Yair, d. 1702), R. Jacob Emden (Ya'aveẓ, d. 1776), R. Ezekiel Landau (*Noda bi-Yehudah*, d. 1793), R. Elijah (Vilna Gaon, d. 1797), R. Akiva Eger (d. 1837), and others. This period also produced various communal enactments, reflecting local custom and legislation.
3. From the beginning of the nineteenth century till the present time. During this period there was a marked abrogation of Jewish judicial autonomy, with Gentile and secular courts assuming jurisdiction over many matters that heretofore had been subject to rabbinic authority in most Jewish communities. Nonetheless great literary output continued, both in the

> field of recodifying and in responsa. Prominent in the former were R. Abraham Danzig (*Ḥokhmat Adam*, d. 1820), R. Abraham Zevi Eisenstadt (*Pitḥei Teshuvah*, d. 1868), R. Joseph Babad (*Minḥat Ḥinukh*, d. 1875), R. Solomon Ganzfried (*Kiẓur Shulḥan Arukh*, d. 1886), R. Yeḥiel Michael Epstein (*Arukh ha-Shulḥan*, d. 1908), and R. Abraham Isaiah Karelitz (Ḥazon Ish, d. 1953). In the field of responsa literature, major works included those of R. Moses Schreiber (Ḥatam Sofer, d. 1839), R. Naphtali Ẓevi Berlin (Neẓiv, d. 1893), R. David Ẓevi Hoffman (*Melamed le'Ho'il*, d. 1921), R. Ḥayyim Ozer Grodzinsky (*Aḥiezer*, d. 1942), and R. Yeḥiel Weinberg (*Seridei Esh*, d. 1966). Contemporary authorities who have published responsa that are widely referred to include R. Moshe Feinstein (*Iggerot Moshe*) and R. Eliezer Waldenberg (*Ẓiẓ Eliezer*).

With the rise of the State of Israel, Jewish law received new impetus, given the opportunity for widespread application of Halakhah in public life. Nonetheless Halakhah has no official place in the Israeli legal system, save in matters of personal status. In Israel such matters are generally entrusted to the rabbinical courts. Outside of Israel halakhic creativity continues, primarily in North America.

Clearly the Halakhah has been characterized by constant growth and evolution. As noted by Menaḥem Elon,[64] the Halakhah is essentially one large unit in which the earlier and the later, the basis and the construction, are all interwoven and arranged according to subject matter with no particular regard for historical distinctions. Halakhists have always united and integrated the various periods of the Halakhah into a single, all-embracing epoch of unitary Halakhah, without distinguishing between different stages and periods. Nonetheless it is true that halakhic authorities themselves frequently emphasized the changes and development through which one or another institution of Jewish law had passed, not only by specific enactments (*takkanot*), but by expressly changing the existing law through reinterpretation of earlier texts. Thus, while Jewish law continued to evolve and give direction to Jewish behavior, it was itself directed and influenced both in form and content by the realities of place and time, even while maintaining intact the central principles and institutions of Jewish law. The chapters of the present volume provide ample illustration of these historical processes as they affected the halakhic corpus that was forced to grapple with the manifold needs of every succeeding generation, down to our own.

Notes

1. See, for instance, Marvin Fox, "Reflections on the Foundations of Jewish Ethics and Their Relation to Public Policy," *Selected Papers*, Society of Christian Ethics, Twenty-first Annual Meeting, 1980, pp. 23–62; Y. Leibowitz, *Torah u-Mizvot* ba-Zeman ha-Zeh (Tel Aviv, 1954).

2. Ḥazon Ish, *Emunah u-Vitaḥon* (Jerusalem, 1954), p. 49.

3. M. Fox, "Maimonides and Aquinas on Natural Law," *Dine Israel* 3 (1972): 5–27.

4. Maimonides, *Guide of the Perplexed*, trans. Shlomo Pines (Chicago, 1963), 3:27.

5. See for instance W. Wurzburger, "Law as the Basis of a Moral Society," *Tradition* 19, no. 1 (Spring 1981): 50.

6. A. I. Kook, *Orot ha-Torah* (Jerusalem, 1961), pp. 69–71. See also his *Orot ha-Kodesh* (Jerusalem, 1964), vol. 2, p. 27. For further analysis of this view, see Ẓ. Yaron, *Mishnato shel ha-Rav Kook* (Jerusalem, 1974), pp. 131–138.

7. For a description of the respective views, and a comprehensive treatment of the whole subject, see N. Lamm and A. Kirschenbaum, "Freedom and Constraint in the Jewish Judicial Process," *Cardozo Law Review* 1, no. 1 (Spring 1979): 99–133, esp. pp. 109–120. A similarly full and most insightful discussion of the issues surrounding natural law and the Halakhah is found in A. Lichtenstein, "Does Jewish Tradition Recognize an Ethic Independent of Halakhah?" in *Modern Jewish Ethics*, ed. M. Fox (Columbus, 1975), p. 60 ff. Likewise see E. Urbach, *Ḥazal: Pirkei Emunot ve'De'ot* (Jerusalem, 1971), pp. 280–290.

8. Lamm and Kirschenbaum, "Freedom and Constraint," pp. 113–120, and also see below, dealing with natural or autonomous morality and the Noahide Code.

9. See for instance in *Eruvin* 100b.

10. *Pirke Avot* 3:17, *Lev. Rabbah* 9:3. Cf. *Tosafot Yeshanim* to *Yoma* 85b.

11. *Bava Mezia* 30b, *Mekhilta Yitro* 2. Urbach, *Ḥazal*, pp. 291–294, shows convincingly that *lifnim mi-shurat ha-din* in the Talmud is not in the category of *din* (requisite behavior) but a matter of individual aspiration.

12. Naḥmanides' *Commentary on the Torah* to Lev. 19:2, 6:18. For further elaboration of these texts, see Lichtenstein, "Jewish Tradition," pp. 69–70.

13. Lichtenstein, "Jewish Tradition," p. 71, who points out that the *Sefer Mizvot Katan* counts this as one of the 613 commandments of the Torah.

14. Maimonides, *Introduction to Ethics of the Fathers* (*Shemonah Perakim*), chap. 6.

15. I. Twersky, *Introduction to the Code of Maimonides (Mishneh Torah)* (New Haven, 1980), pp. 453–454.

16. Lichtenstein, "Jewish Tradition," p. 72.

17. See *M.T. Hil. Deot* 1:5. One problem with explaining Maimonides' view in this manner is that elsewhere Maimonides seems to identify the right and the good paths with *lifnim mi-shurat ha-din*, a problem that Lichtenstein himself is aware of—cf. Lichtenstein, "Jewish Tradition," pp. 86–87 (n. 44). A valuable analysis of the notion of *imitatio dei* as the realm of voluntary behavior involving *lifnim mi-shurat ha-din* is found in N. Lamm, "Notes on the Concept of Imitatio

Dei," in *Rabbi Joseph H. Lookstein Memorial Volume* New York, 1980), pp. 217–229, esp. p. 221. Lamm develops the distinction between image (*ẓelem*) and likeness (*demut*), such that the existence of the former in every human being demands with the power of law that I act properly toward my fellow, whereas the latter is in the realm of supererogatory imitation of God's kindness, i.e., "walking in His ways." This would be quite consistent with Maimonides' appreciation of *lifnim mi-shurat ha-din* as developed here. See below, n. 26.

18. *M.T. Hil. Melakhim* 8:10–11. Cf. Twersky, *Introduction*, p. 455, n. 239. On the problems posed by the text of this passage in Maimonides, see below, n. 38.

19. *M.T. Hil. Teshuvah* 7:4.

20. See below, pp. 10–11.

21. Twersky, *Introduction*, p. 428, has the translation "If a man . . . " This reading seems to miss Maimonides' emphasis in the passage, the whole thrust of which is directed to the exceptional behavior of the outstanding (and atypical) sage.

22. *M.T. Hil. Yesodei ha-Torah* 5:11.

23. The *Kesef Mishnah* (R. Joseph Karo) ad loc. recognizes the problem and suggests Maimonides' intention to be as follows: One should try to go beyond the letter of the law, but even that only in moderation (*be'ofen memuẓah*), so as to win universal admiration.

24. Twersky, *Introduction*, p. 428.

25. See S. Federbush, *ha-Mussar ve'ha-Mishpat beYisrael* (New York, 1944), pp. 102–103, 81–82. See also Lichtenstein, "Jewish Tradition," pp. 74–76, and *Ketuvot* 49a, with the comments of Rashi and Tosafot ad loc. An interesting and instructive discussion of the *Sefer Ḥasidim* with its development of these ideas is found in H. Soloveitchik, "Three Themes in *Sefer Ḥasidim*," *AJS Review* 1 (1976): 311–357, esp. pp. 320–321.

26. *M.T. Hil. Roẓeiaḥ* 13:4. It should be noted that Maimonides uses the terminology of obligation and commandment only in the context of doing "the right and the good" (cf. Lichtenstein, pp. 72–73), that which we can identify with the golden mean. Cf. Urbach, *Ḥazal*, p. 292, nn. 51–52. It also seems to be true that for Maimonides *midat ḥasidut* is coextensive with *lifnim mi-shurat ha-din*, and therefore interchangeable. See *M.T. Hil. Deot* 1:5, and Federbush, *Mussar*, pp. 141–144. Similarly see Azariah Figo, *Binah le-Ittim*, no. 10, as found in Federbush, p. 81.

27. See N. Lamm, "ha-Ḥakham ve'he-Ḥasid be'Mishnat ha'Rambam," in *Samuel Belkin Memorial Volume* (New York, 1981), pp. 11–28.

28. An extensive and insightful description of this interrelationship is to be found in Federbush, *Mussar*, in its general thesis.

29. Federbush, *Mussar*, pp. 88–116. On the process of new decrees and *takkanot*, as well as the formulation of new Halakhah generally, see Menaḥem Elon, "Takkanot," in *Encyclopaedia Judaica* 15:712–728, and *Encyclopaedia Judaica* Index, s.v. "Mishpat Ivri."

30. Federbush, *Mussar*, pp. 117–137.

31. *Maggid Mishnah* to *M.T. Hil. Shekhenim* 14:5, quoting *Avodah Zarah* 14a. Cf. Lichtenstein, "Jewish Tradition," p. 80, and Federbush, *Mussar*, p. 147.

32. Wurzburger, "Law," p. 52. This, according to Rabbi Naphtali Ẓevi Judah Berlin, *Ha'amek Davar* to Gen. 1:1, is the reason for the inclusion of the biblical narratives of the lives of the patriarchs in Scripture: not so much as a source of historical information, but as paradigmatic role models, as explaimed by Wurzburger.

33. See generally *Encyclopaedia Judaica* 10:1480–1484, s.v. "Law and Morality."

34. That the covenant was voluntarily entered into is clearly the majority and normative view, according to the talmudic sources, in spite of the oft-quoted passage to the contrary. Cf. Urbach, *Ḥazal*, pp. 287–290.

35. The major talmudic discussion of these laws is found in *Sanhedrin* 56a–60b; also Tosefta *Avodah Zarah* 8:4, and Maimonides' summary in *M.T. Hil. Melakhim* 8:10, 10:12. There are certain variations in the precise identification of these commandments—see *Encyclopaedia Judaica* 12:1189–1191.

36. *Yoma* 67b, *Sifra Aḥarei Mot* 13:10.

37. *Sanhedrin* 56a–59a.

38. *M.T. Hil. Melakhim* 8:10–11. The reading of the final phrase of this passage has been a matter of some debate, but it would appear that the reading given here is the authoritative one, for this reading of Maimonides is accepted by the preponderance of halakhic authorities and historians. These include the *Responsa Alshakar*, no. 117; *Sefer Kevod Elokim; Sefer Ma'aseh Efod; Responsa Oneg Yomtov, Oraḥ Ḥayyim* 19; and others. See *Encyclopedia Talmudit* 6:290, n. 11. This reading is also accepted by Jacob Katz, *Exclusiveness and Tolerance* (New York, 1962), p. 175; Twersky, *Introduction*, p. 455; and A. Altmann, *Moses Mendelssohn: A Biographical Study* (Philadelphia, 1973), p. 294. Others, however, accept the reading "and not one of their wise men," a reading which caused great difficulties in harmonizing Maimonides' views. Cf. Fox, "Maimonides and Aquinas on Natural Law," pp. 13–14, and *Encyclopaedia Judaica* 12:1191, taking the minority view.

39. Cf. above, n. 14—as opposed to Fox's view.

40. *Mishnat R. Eliezer*, ed. H. Enelow (New York, 1934), p. 121. See Katz, *Exclusiveness*, p. 175, n. 5; *Encyclopaedia Judaica* 16:1515; and *Teshuvot ha-Rambam*, ed. Freimann, p. 370.

41. See *Kesef Mishnah* (by Joseph Karo, author of the *Shulḥan Arukh)* ad loc., as well as R. Jacob Emden, in his personal correspondence, Altmann, *Mendelssohn*, pp. 295, 806.

42. Twersky, *Introduction*, pp. 456–457.

43. See *M.T. Hil. Melakhim* 9–10 generally.

44. See, in general, Katz, *Exclusiveness*, Urbach, *Ḥazal*, and *Encyclopaedia Judaica*, Index, s.v. "Gentiles."

45. Katz, *Exclusiveness*, p. 3.

46. *Encyclopaedia Judaica* 7:411.

47. *Bava Kamma* 38a.

48. See the extensive discussion of Meiri on this topic in Katz, *Exclusiveness*, chap. 10, esp. pp. 114–128, and Ernst Simon, "The Neighbor (Re'a) Whom We Shall Love," *Modern Jewish Ethics*, pp. 47–49.

49. Katz, *Exclusiveness*, pp. 126–128.

50. Ibid., p. 62.

51. Ibid., pp. 93–102; *Encyclopaedia Judaica* 7:413.

52. Katz, *Exclusiveness*, pp. 103–105.

53. *M.T. Hil. Avodah Zarah* 9:4. See G. Tschernowitz, *ha-Yaḥas Ben Yisrael le'Goyyim le'fi ha-Rambam* (New York, 1950), p. 20.

54. The status of Islam is a matter of debate. See the commentaries of R. Joseph Karo and R. Joel Sirkes to the *Tur Sh.A. Ḥ.M.* 149.

55. *M.T. Hil. Nizkei Mamon* 8:5; *Hil. Rozeiaḥ* 2:11, 4:11, and Simon, "The Neighbor," pp. 36, 42, 48, and the rebuttal by H. Fisch, "A Response to Ernst Simon," in the same volume.

56. S. Pines, "The Philosophic Sources of the *Guide of the Perplexed*," *The Guide of the Perplexed* (Chicago, 1963), pp. lvii–cxxxii: and in particular H. Davidson, "Maimonides' *Shemonah Peraqim* and Alfarabi's *Fusul Al-Madani*,"

Proceedings of the American Academy for Jewish Research 31 (1963), reprinted in *Essays in Medieval Jewish and Islamic Philosophy*, ed. A. Hyman, pp. 116–133, particularly pp. 130–131. The same Maimonidean ethical principles are found in *M.T. Hil. Deot* 2:1–2, 1:5.

57. *M.T. Hil. Melakhim* 8:10, *Hil. Issurei Biah* 14:7. Rashi also accepts this—cf. *Avodah Zarah* 24b. The category of resident alien probably served as a model and starting point for Meiri's distinction between the idolaters of old and the contemporary Gentile. See Katz, *Exclusiveness*, p. 121.

58. *M.T. Hil. Melakhim* 10:10–12.

59. *M.T. Hil. Nizkei Mamon* 8:5.

60. Cf. above, pp. 4–6.

61. *M.T. Hil. Melakhim* 10:12, as well as *Hil. Gezeilah ve'Aveidah* 11:3.

62. Cf. above, pp. 10–11.

63. This description is based on Menaḥem Elon, in *Encyclopaedia Judaica* 12:121–123, s.v. "Mishpat Ivri."

64. Ibid., pp. 129–130.

Bio-Ethics

1

Abortion

Introduction

The question of the morality and legality of abortion, i.e., the termination of an unwanted pregnancy, is an ancient one. But the debate received great impetus on January 22, 1973, when the United States Supreme Court ruled, in the famous *Roe* v. *Wade* decision, on the constitutionality of certain state statutes forbidding abortion except to save the life of the mother. The court ruled that because the unborn cannot be included in the definition of "person," the state may not interfere with a woman's right to an abortion during the first trimester of pregnancy; thereafter, and until the fetus is viable, the state may regulate the abortion procedure only for the health of the mother; after the fetus becomes viable the state may prohibit all abortions except those necessary to preserve the health or life of the mother. The ruling was based substantially on the view that a woman's right to privacy enables her to choose whether to have children.

The public debate that has followed this decision has seen three broad positions emerge. First, there is the so-called conservative view, which holds that abortion is never morally justifiable, or at most only in order to save the mother's life. In the public eye this view has come to be identified particularly with the Roman Catholic Church, but there are many others who would support it as well. Essentially this view posits that from the moment of conception there is not only human life but personhood, and that abortion is therefore homicide. In contrast to this view is the so-called liberal view, which considers abortion to be always morally justifiable, regardless of the stage of fetal development or of the reasons for which the abortion is desired by the woman. Most recently this view has been identified with women's-rights advocates, who focus on the woman's right to make decisions that will affect her body, but there are others as well who support the liberal view. The third broad view to emerge is the intermediate or moderate position, which with some variations considers abortion morally acceptable up to a certain point in fetal development, and/or claims that some reasons, not all, provide a sufficient justification for abortion. This intermediate view attempts to balance considerations of fetal life or potential life, the absolute versus relative rights of a woman with regard to her body, and the various criteria adduced to pinpoint viability and other stages of pregnancy.

In the eyes of many people, the "Jewish view" is identified with the Roman Catholic position. At the same time many Jewish leaders have taken a position based on what they consider the "religious traditions" of Judaism, without specific reference to the halakhic tradition, and some of them, especially in the Reform rabbinate, have adopted a relatively liberal view of abortion. The following discussion illustrates the complexity and richness, not to speak of the multiplicity of views, of the halakhic parameters of this issue.

The Question

A woman who is five months pregnant is told by her physician that a continued pregnancy will permanently damage her health, although it will not pose any danger to her life. Can she abort the fetus?

In approaching the issue of abortion, three questions can be considered:

1. Is abortion prohibited, and if it is, what is the nature of the prohibition?
2. At what point during the pregnancy does the prohibition take effect?
3. Under what conditions can the prohibition be suspended so as to permit an abortion?

Sources

A. Exodus 21:22–23

And if men strive together and hurt a woman with child, so that her fruit depart and yet no harm follow, he shall be surely fined, according as the woman's husband shall lay upon him; and he shall pay as the judges determine. But if any harm follow, then thou shalt give life for life.

B. Mekhilta Exodus, Nezikin 8

"Yet no harm follow" refers to harm to the woman; "he shall surely be fined" refers to compensation for the loss of the fetus.

C. Sanhedrin 67b

In the name of R. Ishmael they said: "[A Noahide receives capital punishment] even for destroying a fetus." What is the reason of R. Ishmael? It is the verse "he who sheds the blood of man, in man shall his blood be shed" [Gen. 9:6]. What is the meaning of "man in man"? This can be said to refer to a fetus in its mother's womb.

D. Mishnah, Ohalot 7:6

If a woman in labor has a [life-threatening] difficulty, one dismembers the embryo within her, removing it limb by limb, for her life takes precedence over its life. But once its greater part [Tosefta Yevamot 9: "head"], has emerged it may not be harmed, for we do not set aside one life for another.

E. Sanhedrin 72b

"Once the head has emerged it may not be harmed." Why, is he not a pursuer? The answer is that it is considered to be from heaven that she is pursued.

F. Rashi, Sanhedrin 72b

". . . removing it limb by limb." This is because as long as it has not emerged into the world it is not a human being [*lav nefesh hu*], and therefore it can be killed in order to save its mother.

G. Sanhedrin 84b
It was necessary for the Torah to write "he that smiteth a man [*ish*] so that he dieth shall surely be put to death" [Exod. 21:12]. For had the Torah written only "whoso killeth any person [*nefesh*] the murderer shall be slain" [Num. 35:30], one would have concluded that capital punishment is applied to one who kills a fetus.

H. Maimonides, M. T. Hilkhot Roẓeiaḥ 1:9
This too is a negative commandment: not to have compassion on the life of the pursuer. Therefore the sages ruled that when a woman has difficulty in labor one may dismember the embryo within her, either with drugs or surgery, because he is like a pursuer seeking to kill her. But once the head has emerged, he may not be harmed, for we do not set aside one life for another. This is the natural course of the world.

I. Arakhin 7a
Mishnah: The execution of a pregnant woman who is condemned to death is not postponed until after she gives birth. But once she is on the birthstool, the execution is postponed until after she gives birth.
Gemara: Said R. Judah in the name of Samuel: "Before such a woman is executed she is struck across her abdomen, so that the fetus will die prior to the execution, to prevent her dishonor at the time of execution." . . . Said R. Naḥman in the name of Samuel: "When a woman dies on the Sabbath while she is on the birthstool, one brings a knife to cut open her abdomen and remove the fetus . . . even if one must carry the knife by way of the public domain."

J. Naḥmanides, Torat ha-Adam, p. 29
According to the *Baal Halakhot Gedolot* the reason for bringing the knife is that according to the Torah one desecrates one Sabbath so that one will be able to fulfill many Sabbaths. Therefore the opinion of the *Halakhot Gedolot* is that the Sabbath is desecrated even to save a fetus that is less than forty days in the womb, and which has no life at all. But there are those who assert that one should not desecrate the Sabbath to save a fetus . . . but when she dies on the birthstool the fetus is considered to be born already, no longer her limb and not dependent on her, but alive and prevented from emerging, as the door is closed before him.

Thus, because it lacks only prior status as living, and we are lenient when it comes to saving lives [we can desecrate the Sabbath to save it].

K. Yevamot 69b

Mishnah: The daughter of a priest who has relations with an Israelite continues to eat *terumah;* if she becomes pregnant she does not eat *terumah.*

Gemara: Rav Ḥisda said: "She should immerse herself and then eat *terumah* until the fortieth day after conception . . . for if she is pregnant, it is considered to be mere water until the fortieth day."

L. Tosafot, Sanhedrin 59a

A Gentile is culpable for the death of a fetus, while a Jew is forbidden to cause its death but is not culpable. What of their statement that when a woman in labor is having difficulty one dismembers the embryo within her to save her life, even though this is forbidden to a Gentile? The answer is that in this case a Jew is commanded to save her; and it is possible that a Gentile is permitted to save her in this case.

M. Tosafot, Ḥullin 33a

Even though a Gentile is liable to capital punishment for aborting a fetus, as it is stated in *Sanhedrin* 58b, while a Jew is not liable, nonetheless it is still not permissible for a Jew, even though he is not liable to capital punishment.

Discussion

1. THE NATURE OF THE PROHIBITION

The earliest explicit statement of the prohibition of abortion is found in Tosafot, commenting on *Ḥullin* 33a and *Sanhedrin* 59a (L, M).[1] An earlier source, the Mishnah in *Ohalot* 7:6 (D), implies that there is a prohibition when it specifically permits an abortion where the mother is in danger of losing her life in labor. In neither instance is the nature of the prohibition explained. Such clarification is found only among later authorities.

One approach views abortion as a form of murder, or homicide. This view, identified with Rabbi I. Y. Unterman, the late Ashkenazi Chief Rabbi of Israel, points to the statement in *Arakhin* 7b (I), which permits the violation of the Sabbath to save the fetus of a woman who has died in childbirth.[2] A dispensation of this kind must imply that the fetus represents human life, for it is only to save human life that the Sabbath can be violated in this way. Rabbi Unterman refers in this connection to the opinion of the *Baal Halakhot Gedolot*, which would permit violation of the Sabbath to save the fetus even if it is less than forty days after conception.[3] The view that abortion is homicide accounts for the fact that abortion is not punishable by death by referring to the talmudic passage in *Sanhedrin* 84a (G), which limits the death penalty to the murder of a human by explicitly excluding a fetus. This limitation is based on Exodus 21:12, which states, "he that smiteth a *man* so that he dieth shall surely be put to death."

Yet if this verse excludes a fetus from the category of the human, why should the abortion of a fetus constitute homicide? Rabbi Unterman answers that the Halakhah considers not only present life but future and potential life as well. Without the abortion the fetus would become a human, since most pregnancies produce viable and healthy babies. Accordingly the fetus has a claim to life that cannot be compromised just because it is as yet unborn.

Precedent for this definition may be found in Maimonides' formulation of the law regarding the situation described in *Ohalot* (H). In that passage, *Hilkhot Roẓeiaḥ* 1:9, he explains that the fetus can be aborted if it endangers the mother's life during labor because it is considered to be a "pursuer" (*rodef*), which means that like any person who is seeking to cause the death of another, it may be killed in order to prevent its homicidal act. Several halakhists, including Rabbi Ezekiel Landau (known as the *Noda bi-Yehudah*, d. 1793) and Rabbi Ḥayyim Soloveitchik (d. 1918), understand Maimonides to be saying that a fetus has a claim to life that makes abortion an act of murder, as it is human in potential;[4] it is only because the mother's life is directly threatened by the birth process that the fetus's claim to life can be overruled so as to save the mother. Consequently, where there is no life-threatening situation, Maimonides would forbid abortion.

There is, however, another approach in defining the prohibition of abortion. This view, as expounded by such modern halakhists as Rabbi Yeḥiel Weinberg[5] and Rabbi Eliezer Waldenberg,[6] denies that abortion involves homicide. To buttress this denial they point to Exodus 21:22–23 (A), which does not require any punishment for causing an abortion other than a monetary fine (as understood by the *Mekhilta* [B]). Had homicide been a factor, they argue, there would certainly not be any monetary considerations.

They further point to the Mishnah in *Ohalot* (D), where it is only *after* its greater part has been born that the fetus attains the status of human life (*nefesh*), for while the fetus is still *in utero* the Mishnah does not invoke considerations of *nefesh* in order to save it. Rashi, in his comments to *Sanhedrin* 72b (F), seems to understand the Mishnah in a similar fashion when he says that the warrant for that abortion derives from the fact that the fetus is not human (*nefesh*). Rashi apparently rejects the Maimonidean approach.[7]

An earlier authority who also denied any equation of abortion and homicide was Rabbi Yair Bachrach (author of the *Ḥavvot Yair*, d. 1702). In his responsum no. 31 he states that as long as labor has not yet begun the fetus does not have the status of a human. The major source that he quotes is the talmudic passage in *Arakhin* 7a (I), stating that a condemned woman found to be pregnant should be executed without delay, so as to prevent any undue suffering on her part in anticipation of the execution. According to that passage one is even to induce an abortion prior to the execution so as to prevent a miscarriage or bleeding during the execution. Apparently abortion is to be preferred in that instance over her possible *nivul* (added shame). Rabbi Bachrach concludes that the Talmud does not consider the fetus human until such time as the mother goes into labor, for it is only during labor that the Talmud allows the postponement of the execution. This follows from the fact that the abortion is permitted for so minor a reason as the *nivul* of a condemned woman.

At the same time Rabbi Bachrach is aware of the dispensation given by the Talmud on the very next page (*Arakhin* 7b) permitting the violation of the Sabbath to save the life of the fetus (as quoted by Rabbi Unterman). Rabbi Bachrach answers this by saying that the Talmud itself limits this dispensation to the case where labor has already begun. From this he concludes that prior to labor, the Sabbath is *not* violated on behalf of the fetus. He also recognizes other instances where the Talmud suspends the law to prevent a miscarriage (such as the permission for a pregnant woman to eat if necessary on Yom Kippur), but he argues that this is not so much for the benefit of the fetus as for that of the mother, for whom a miscarriage represents a real danger.

Does such reasoning contradict Maimonides, who seems to view abortion as homicide? Rabbi Bachrach answers this in the negative, saying that even Maimonides agrees that the fetus is not a human being. It is just that Maimonides must justify the taking of its life, such as it might be, for there is nonetheless a prohibition to terminate its existence. Maimonides finds the justification in the notion of the pursuer (*rodef*). According to this interpretation, Maimonides might well agree with Rashi's assertion that the fetus is "not human."

But if homicide does not define the prohibition, then what does? Rabbi Bachrach answers that what is involved is the prohibition of destroying the male seed, a prohibition which forbids any frustration of the completion of a new life once there has been an emission of semen (as discussed in *Niddah* 13b, and derived, according to some opinions, from the verse "Thou shalt not commit adultery [*lo tinaf*]" [Exod. 20:13]).[8] In so doing he accepts the ruling of Tosafot *Yevamot* 12b that women are also bound by this prohibition. Rabbi Bachrach can therefore account easily for the suspension of this relatively unimportant (relative, that is, to homicide) prohibition when faced with the prospect of *nivul*, as is the case in *Arakhin*.

This definition too is not without its difficulties. As Rabbi Weinberg points out, the basis of the ban against destroying the male seed is the commandment to be fruitful, which need not apply to the well-being of seed other than one's own. Consequently the definition of Rabbi Bachrach leads to the conclusion that it is permissible to perform an abortion on a woman other than one's own wife; this Rabbi Weinberg finds, of course, unacceptable. A further difficulty is found in the writings of Rabbi Meir Dan Plocki (author of the *Ḥemdat Yisrael*), who says that ever since the revelation at Sinai, non-Jews have not been bound by the prohibition against destroying male seed or the commandment to be fruitful. From this one would have to conclude that a Noahide may in fact commit an abortion according to Rabbi Bachrach. This too is unacceptable.[9]

Rabbi Weinberg nonetheless agrees with Rabbi Bachrach that Maimonides cannot be understood as classifying abortion as homicide. Rabbi Weinberg explains that the clear import of the Mishnah in *Ohalot* is to deny the capital nature of abortion, for homicide is one of the three cardinal sins which may never be committed, even at the risk of one's life, and if so the Mishnah would never permit the killing of the fetus, no matter what the circumstance. (Rabbi Unterman counters this by saying that the law of the three cardinal sins which can never be transgressed only applies to those aspects of the three sins that are specifically prohibited by the Torah—and abortion obviously is not specifically addressed in the Torah.) As for Maimonides, Rabbi Weinberg introduces a new element: One might have thought that the one inducing the abortion would have to pay compensation to the father (in accordance with Maimonides' ruling in *Hilkhot Ḥovel u'Mazzik* 8:4 that damage inflicted under duress requires indemnity). For this reason Maimonides introduces the *rodef* (pursuer) as a factor eliminating all indemnity.

Yet another view of the prohibition is formulated by Rabbi Joseph Trani (known as Maharit, d. 1639). Denying any dimension of homicide, he asserts that what is involved is the prohibition of *ḥabbalah*, the wounding of one's body.[10] This prohibition, discussed in *Bava Kamma* 90b, is based on the verse "surely your blood of your lives will I require" (Gen. 9:5), and according to Maimonides (*Hil. Roẓeiaḥ* 1:4) derives from the fact that Halakhah considers the body to belong to God, and not to any person. Maharit is able to explain the talmudic dispensation to abort when the mother is about to be executed by saying that obviously in such a case *ḥabbalah* is not a significant factor—she is about to die anyway. As for the prohibition on aborting once labor has begun, he explains that at that point the fetus acquires independent status as a human with its own claim to life, as noted by the Talmud in *Arakhin* 7b. Maharit himself realizes that this is not conclusive proof of his definition, for one could well differentiate between a normal pregnancy and this one where the fetus is destined to die shortly anyway. Abortion here might be justified on the extraneous grounds that the time of death of the fetus is being advanced so as to spare the mother the added agony of anticipation and public dishonor.

In further buttressing his contention that there is no dimension of homicide, Maharit points out that the talmudic dispensation to violate the Sabbath on behalf of the fetus only applies after the mother has died while in labor. He argues that it is only at that point that the fetus has sufficient status as a human, no longer dependent on maternal sustenance, for the Sabbath to be violated on its behalf. Prior to that point it is not human, and the Sabbath must not be violated to save it.[11] A later authority, Rabbi Joseph Rosen (author of the *Ẓofnat Pa'aneaḥ*, b. 1858), likewise accepts *ḥabbalah* as the defining characteristic of abortion.[12]

Before leaving the question of the nature of the prohibition, there is one other aspect of the issue that should be mentioned. *Sanhedrin* 67b (C) records the opinion of R. Ishmael that a Noahide receives capital punishment for inducing an abortion. This opinion is accepted as authoritative by subsequent halakhists, such as Maimonides. It would appear, then, that in the case of a Noahide, abortion does entail homicide. If this is the case, then the same would certainly be true of a Jew inducing abortion, especially as Tosafot in *Sanhedrin* 59a and *Ḥullin* 33a (L, M) explicitly state the principle that "there is nothing forbidden to a Noahide that is permitted to the Jew" in the context of abortion. Can one therefore conclude from this source that all abortions entail homicide? The question in this form was posed to Rabbi Ezekiel Landau by his contemporary Rabbi Isaiah Pick.

Rabbi Unterman, as would be expected, answers this in the affirmative, arguing that the principle "there is nothing" makes the application of Genesis 9:6 ("he who sheds the blood of man, by man shall his blood be shed") mandatory for Jews as well. He also finds this to be consistent with his view of Maimonides that it is only because the fetus can be viewed as a threat to the life of the mother that it can be destroyed without involving the issue of homicide.

Maharit, however, takes the opposite view. He argues that even Noahide abortions do not entail homicide; they are simply under a special ban rendering them a capital crime. As articulated by R. Isaac Shor (author of *Koaḥ Shor*, 18th cent.): "It is not to be supposed that the Torah would consider the embryo as a human for Noahides but not as a human for us. The fetus is not a human for them either; the Torah is merely more severe in its practical ruling in their regard . . . for it cannot be said that the matter depends on whether it is called a human or not. It depends rather on the responsibilities which the Torah has assigned in connection therewith."[13] Tosafot in *Sanhedrin* 59a considers it quite possible that a Noahide may perform an abortion in order to save the mother's life, so that it is not altogether clear whether the death penalty in the case of Noahides derives from an equation to homicide, for if it did, abortion would not be permitted to the Noahide under any circumstances.

Consequently the status of abortion with regard to Noahides cannot throw any conclusive light on the question of abortion as pertaining to Jews.

2. ABORTION AND THE STAGES OF FETAL DEVELOPMENT

The variety of definitions encountered in the preceding section lead to a similar diversity when considering the onset of the prohibition.

The Mishnah in *Ohalot* (D) informs us that during labor itself abortion is permitted only if it is to save the life of the mother, and forbidden altogether once the major part of the fetus has emerged. (E)[14] Similarly we find that the Talmud in *Arakhin 7a* (I) does not permit the execution of a woman in labor so as to save the fetus; and furthermore once labor has begun the Sabbath may be violated for the sake of the fetus. Apparently during labor the fetus attains a special status. While not necessarily as fully human as the mother, it nonetheless has substantial claim to life, for it is no longer totally dependent on the mother for its continued well-being, being considered a body apart from hers. Prior to the onset of labor it is still totally dependent on the mother and is not at all human, at least not as viewed in its present state.

An earlier stage recognized by Halakhah is the end of the third month. The Gemara in *Niddaḥ* 17b mentions that it is at the end of the third month that the pregnancy and fetal movement become noticeable. While Rabbi Bachrach also mentions this time, he adds that one cannot make any practical distinctions between the periods preceding and following the end of the third month.

A more significant stage is the one that begins at the end of the fortieth day after conception. As Rabbi I. Jakobovits points out, this may correspond to the lapse of just under two months, according to the currently accepted calculation of gestation.[15] The Mishnah in *Niddah* 30a is of the opinion that a miscarriage that occurs prior to the fetus attaining the forty-day period does not engender *tumah*, the impurity associated with childbirth and miscarriage. *Yevamot* 69b (K) records the opinion of Rav Ḥisda that a priest's daughter who is widowed shortly after marriage may eat *terumah* (the priestly tithe, not permitted to such a daughter with children) upon returning to her father's care, until the fortieth day after conception. The reason he offers is that until that time the fetus is "mere water." These two sources could be taken to signify that until the fortieth day the fetus has no life and can therefore be aborted.

Rabbi Unterman denies this possibility. He avers that even prior to forty days the fetus represents life *in potentia*, and therefore its abortion involves homicide. He adduces proof from the *Baal Halakhot Gedolot* (J), who would suspend the Sabbath even to save the life of an embryo that has developed for less than forty days.[16]

Rabbi Bachrach also mentions the distinction of forty days, but he does not endorse it. Because he views the prohibition as deriving from that forbidding the destruction of the male seed, it is consistent to view such destruction as forbidden at any time after the emission of the seed.

Rabbi Jacob Emden (known as Ya'aveẓ, d. 1776) also accepts the definition of the prohibition against abortion as deriving from that against destruction of the male seed.[17] But he makes a further distinction by saying that the primary sense of the prohibition is the act of *coitus interruptus*, i.e., when the semen never reaches the womb in the first place. Once the semen has been properly deposited, he avers, any subsequent frustration of the birth process can only be seen as prohibited in a secondary degree. Emden nonetheless accepts the idea that this secondary prohibition applies even prior to the fortieth day of gestation.

While Maharit does not mention the forty-day period directly, there is room to understand him as accepting this distinction. The same position is taken by Rabbi Weinberg, who argues that once abortion is viewed as the wounding of a limb (in this case of the mother,) then prior to the formation of the fetus, which takes place at forty days, there cannot be any organ to be wounded. This is true, according to Rabbi Weinberg, even according to those opinions in the Talmud that do not view the fetus as a limb of the mother.[18] From this Rabbi Weinberg concludes that Maharit would permit abortion prior to the fortieth day of pregnancy. He also refers to the view of R. Shabbetai ha-Kohen (known as Shakh, d. 1662) that prior to forty days the fetus has no standing in matters affecting civil law, as it is considered nonexistent. Consequently Rabbi Weinberg himself concludes that abortion at this early stage is permitted. In subsequent writings on the subject, however, he withholds final judgment on the matter, in the light of Rabbi Unterman's strictures.[19]

An outright endorsement of abortion prior to the fortieth day was offered by Rabbi Solomon Drimer (author of the *Bet Shelomoh*) in the nineteenth century, and this in turn forms the basis for a more permissive ruling by Rabbi Eliezer Waldenberg—of which more will be seen later.

Clearly there is a significant spectrum of opinion regarding the onset of the prohibition of abortion, particularly regarding the first forty days of pregnancy.

3. THE SUSPENSION OF THE PROHIBITION

We are now in a position to examine the conditions under which abortion may be countenanced once the prohibition has come into effect.

Least problematic is the situation where there is danger to maternal life. According to the Mishnah in *Ohalot* (D), we have seen that in the event of such a hazard, abortion is permitted even after the onset of labor—just as long as the fetus has not emerged into the world. All are agreed that this would apply *a fortiori* to the stages preceding labor as well.

Yet even here there is a caveat. It is necessary to determine whether it is the pregnancy *per se* that is causing the threat to her life, or whether the pregnancy is merely complicating an already existing health problem in the mother. According to certain of Maimonides' interpreters, namely Rabbi Ezekiel Landau and Rabbi Ḥayyim Soloveitchik, Maimonides would classify the fetus as a pursuer only if it alone is responsible for the hazard to the mother. Where there is a combination of factors, the fetus alone cannot be held responsible, and Maimonides would not permit it to be sacrificed. Other interpreters, notably Rabbi Ḥayyim Ozer Grodzinsky (author of the *Aḥiezer*, 20th cent.), object to such an interpretation of Maimonides by pointing out that Maimonides speaks of the fetus as pursuer only after labor has begun, and that it is entirely possible that Maimonides would not require "pursuit" for abortion during the preceding months.[20] The same line of reasoning provides Rabbi Grodzinsky with a solution to the question why Maimonides introduces the element of pursuit altogether, for he explains that Maimonides agrees that the fetus is only a limb of the mother and can therefore be removed so as to save her whole body. This reasoning does not require the use of the "pursuer" argument. Maimonides only introduces the factor of pursuit once labor has begun, for it is at that point that the fetus ceases to be a mere limb of the mother and becomes an independent agent.

What if there is no threat to the mother's life? If it is only a question of her continued good health, can therapeutic abortion be permitted? Here too we find a variety of opinions.

Rabbi Unterman, consistent with his view of abortion as homicide, rejects abortion unless there is threat to the life of the mother. He applies this, as we have seen, even prior to the forty-day period. Rabbi Unterman is confronted by a report (recorded by Maharit) that Naḥmanides (Ramban), in the thirteenth century, performed an abortion for a Gentile woman, and there is no mention of hazard to her life. Rabbi Unterman answers that the reported event must have taken place prior to the fortieth day of pregnancy, for in contradistinction to the halakhic position regarding the Jew, Rabbi Unterman explains that the laws of Noahide abortion only recognize what is present and actual, not what is mere potential and projected for the future. Therefore, whereas abortion is forbidden for the Jew at any time after conception, it is permitted for the Noahide prior to forty days. It is only in accordance with the non-Noahide laws revealed at Sinai that one is required to give consideration to future life.

Rabbi Unterman also considers the question of mental health. If a continued pregnancy may result in insanity in the mother, can she be permitted to abort? His answer is that abortion is permitted only where there are overt suicidal tendencies or hysteria leading to a threat to her life or that of others. According to Rabbi Unterman, insanity *per se* is not sufficient threat to her life to justify an abortion.[21]

Rabbi Moses Jonah Zweig holds a view on abortion that is only slightly less stringent. As outlined in an article in *Noam* 7:36–56, Rabbi Zweig seems to permit an abortion after forty days only where maternal life is threatened, either now or in the future. His reasoning is based on his reading of Rashi's comments in *Sanhedrin* 72b (F) stating "therefore it can be killed in order to save its mother," i.e., *only* in order to save its mother. He also refers to Maimonides' requirement that the fetus be a pursuer threatening the life of the mother. Rabbi Zweig does, however, permit abortion prior to the fortieth day "if there is some need for it," for he feels that among later authorities, such as Rabbi Rosen, there is not as great a prohibition at that stage.[22]

The conclusion of Maharit's responsum on abortion[23] states that "for an Israelite woman, where there is maternal need it is permitted to assist in an abortion, on account of maternal health." While there is considerable discussion among the later authorities regarding the view of the Maharit as expounded in this responsum,[24] the implication of these words is that abortion is permitted when the mother's health is imperiled. This also would follow logically from his definition of abortion, i.e., *ḥabbalah* (wounding of the mother), which likewise has as its main concern the physical well-being of the mother's body.

A similar ambiguity is found in the responsum of Rabbi Bachrach. If the determinant in abortion is (as he states) the needless destruction of male seed, then there is room to consider abortion permitted when there is indeed some "need." Such a need might be the preservation of the mother's health. Rabbi Bachrach does say that because the prohibition of abortion is rabbinic in origin, and not biblical, one can consider it to be a prohibition in effect only *ab initio* (*lekhatḥilah*). Great need might then render the situation to be in the category of *post factum* (*bedi'eved*). But the ambiguity of Rabbi Bachrach is demonstrated by the fact that there are those who understand him as permitting abortion only where there is actual danger to maternal life—for he appears to quote Rashi's position ("to save its mother") with approval.[25]

A more explicit statement is made by Ya'aveẓ (responsum 43). Accepting the definition of Rabbi Bachrach, he goes on to say that abortion is permissible provided "there is great need, and as labor has not yet begun, even if it is not to save the mother's life but only to save her from evil caused by great pain." The openness of the idea of "great need" to a variety of lenient applications is apparent; for this reason Ya'aveẓ's position became subject to considerable controversy.[26]

In this lenient tradition we find Rabbi Ben Zion Uziel (author of the *Mishpetei Uziel*, 20th cent.).[27] He permits abortion where the mother is threatened with deafness resulting from a continued pregnancy, as long as labor has not yet begun. He states: "It is clear that abortion is not permitted without reason . . . but for a reason, even if a weak reason [*ta'am kalush*], such as to prevent her public shame, we have precedent and authority to permit it." Rabbi Uziel clearly relies on the passage in *Arakhin* 7a, a passage which is open to varying interpretations.

Somewhat more restrictive than these views is the position taken by the past Chief Rabbi of the Sephardic community in Israel, Rabbi Ovadyah Yosef (author of the *Yabia Omer*). He permits abortion for the sake of maternal health, but restricts this to the first three months of pregnancy.[28]

Rabbi Yeḥiel Weinberg is of the opinion that prior to forty days of pregnancy there is no prohibition; after forty days he permits, with much hesitation, an abortion for the sake of the mother's health. In discussing the various definitions of the prohibition, he appears to object least to that of *ḥabbalah*, and therefore can conclude that considerations of maternal health suffice to permit the act. At the same time he recognizes the minority interpretations of Maimonides, according to which only hazard to maternal life suffices for abortion. Yet he feels that because Maimonides is alone in his view, "it is possible that one can permit it by relying on Ya'avez̩."

We have seen above that Rabbi Unterman regards the threat of insanity to be insufficient warrant for abortion, unless there are also homicidal tendencies. Others disagree. Thus Rabbi Moshe Feinstein, author of the *Iggerot Moshe*, and Rabbi Eliezer Waldenberg, author of the *Z̩iz̩ Eliezer*, among others, permit abortion when confronted with the mere fact of insanity.[29] Their view is based on a responsum of Rabbi Israel Meir Mizraḥi (author of the *Pri ha-Arez̩*, 18th cent.) which rules that insanity is sufficient grounds for abortion. This in turn was based on an earlier report that Naḥmanides agreed with a judgment permitting the suspension of kashrut in the interests of curing an epileptic.[30] In this view any form of insanity represents a distinct hazard to the patient's life.

The above authorities, in permitting abortion for the sake of maternal health, agree that abortion would not be permitted to prevent the birth of a defective, retarded, or deformed infant. The general view is that there is no distinction between normal and abnormal persons in their claim to be born or to continue living after birth. A major source for this view is a responsum of Rabbi Eliezer Fleckeles (author of the *Teshuvah me-Ahavah*, 19th cent.) which rules that no matter how deformed a baby might be, the fact that it is born of a human mother gives it human status, and therefore absolute equality with other humans in its claim to life.[31]

The only recent authority to differ with this majority view is Rabbi Waldenberg. Not only does he permit abortion where there is a threat to maternal health (in the tradition of Maharit, Rabbi Bachrach, and Ya'avez as he understands them), he also finds room for abortion where medical evidence indicates that the fetus will be born deformed. He says: "If there is good reason to suspect that the baby that will be born will be deformed and experiencing pain, one can incline to permit an abortion prior to forty days of pregnancy, and even to permit this as long as three months of pregnancy have not yet passed and there is no fetal movement."[32] In a later responsum Rabbi Waldenberg goes further, permitting the abortion of a Tay-Sachs fetus at any time until the end of the sixth month of pregnancy.[33] After the sixth month he forbids it on the grounds that the fetus might well be viable. His major consideration appears to be "grave need" as he perceives it to be intended by Ya'aveẓ and Maharit.

A recent attempt by Rabbi David Feldman to formulate "the Jewish attitude" to such cases states that where there is a possibility of a deformed fetus, abortion would be granted on the grounds that "the possibility is causing severe anguish to the mother." [34] It is difficult to maintain this generalization as representative of the Jewish view, for at most it represents the view of a small minority of halakhists, such as Rabbi Waldenberg, and perhaps Ya'aveẓ and Maharit.[35]

To return to the case with which this chapter began: Where maternal health is threatened by a continued pregnancy, it is possible to say that a considerable body of opinion would permit abortion. Such a position would appear to represent a middle ground in the undulating terrain encountered in the field of abortion.

Notes

1. Whereas these two Tosafot are quite explicit in stating the prohibition, a third (*Niddah* 44b) lends itself to a number of interpretations. A minority view, identified with Rabbi Ẓ. H. Ḥayes (known as Mahariẓ Ḥayes), understands this Tosafot to permit abortion. The majority view insists that even this Tosafot, despite its misleading and ambiguous language, prohibits abortion. Cf. Yair Ḥayyim Bachrach, *Ḥavvot Yair*, no. 31, and the pertinent comments of J. David Bleich, *Contemporary Halakhic Problems* (New York, 1977), pp. 328–330.

2. Rabbi Unterman's views are expounded in *Noam* 6 (1963): 1–11, and in his earlier *Responsa Shevet mi-Yehudah* (Jerusalem, 1955), vol. 1, pp. 29 ff.

3. The view of the *Baal Halakhot Gedolot* is recorded in Naḥmanides' *Torat ha-Adam*, as found in *Kitvei ha-Ramban*, ed. C. D. Chavel (Jerusalem: Mosad Harav Kook, 1964), vol. 2, p. 29.

4. These views are found respectively in the *Noda bi-Yehudah Mahadura Tinyana, Ḥoshen Mishpat* 59; and the *Novellae of Reb Ḥayyim ha-Levi* to *M.T. Hil. Roẓeiaḥ* 1:9. For a comprehensive listing of the various attempts to solve the problems raised by this passage in Maimonides, see David M. Feldman, *Birth Control in Jewish Law* (New York, 1968), pp. 276–284. Some of these are included in the discussion that follows below.

5. *Responsa Seridei Esh* (Jerusalem, 1966), vol. 3, no. 127. This responsum appeared originally in *Noam* 9 (1966): 193–215, having been written some fifteen years earlier but not published. Its subsequent publication was in response to the widespread interest generated by the thalidomide controversy of the mid-1960s, which together with several outbreaks of German measles, led to a high incidence of deformed births.

6. Rabbi Waldenberg's writings on abortion are recorded in his *Ẓiẓ Eliezer*, vol. 7 (Jerusalem, 1963), p. 190; vol. 8 (Jerusalem, 1965), pp. 218–219; and vol. 9 (Jerusalem, 1967), pp. 225–240. See also below, n. 32.

7. The term "apparently" is used here, for later interpreters of Rashi consider him to subscribe to a view not too distant from that of Maimonides. Thus Rabbi

Moses Jonah Zweig, writing in *Noam* 7 (1964): 38, explains that Rashi also insists on hazard to maternal life as a prerequisite for abortion. See below, p. 40.

8. Responsa *Ḥavvot Yair* (Lemberg, 1896), #31. This view in defining abortion is also the view of the author of the *Zakhuta de'Avraham*, as quoted in Meir Dan Plocki, *Ḥemdat Yisrael* (Piotrkow, 1927), p. 175. Rabbi Jacob Emden also accepts this view (see below, p. 38).

9. *Ḥemdat Yisrael*, p. 75. For further elaboration of this critique, see Bleich, *Contemporary Halakhic Problems*, pp. 334–336.

10. *Responsa Maharit* (Lemberg, 1861), nos. 97, 99. These two responsa should be read together. Problems raised by this text are discussed in *Ẓiẓ Eliezer* 9:234, and Rabbi Ovadyah Yosef, *Responsa Yabia Omer*, 4:1, 7.

11. Once the mother has died the fetus cannot be regarded as a "man within a man" (as in Gen. 9:6), but rather as an independent life whose path is being blocked; it is therefore considered as if it were already born.

12. *Responsa Ẓofnat Pa'aneaḥ* (Dvinsk, 1931), no. 59.

13. *Responsa Koaḥ Shor* (Kolomea, 1888), vol. 1, no. 20. This work is quoted in Feldman, *Birth Control*, p. 261.

14. It should be noted here that in Halakhah, unlike the Catholic tradition, the question of ensoulment is quite irrelevant to abortion. This view of J. Preuss, *Biblisch-Talmudisch Medizin* (Berlin, 1911), p. 450, is accepted by I. Jakobovits, *Jewish Medical Ethics* (New York, 1975), p. 376. For a dissenting view see V. Aptowitzer, "The Status of the Embryo in Jewish Criminal Law," *Jewish Quarterly Review* 15 (1924): 115 ff. See also Feldman, *Birth Control*, pp. 271–275.

15. Jakobovits, *Jewish Medical Ethics*, p. 275.

16. Rabbi Unterman does, however, accept the permissibility of non-Jewish abortion prior to forty days. Cf. below.

17. *Responsa She'elat Ya'aveẓ* (Altona, 1739), no. 43.

18. Bleich, *Contemporary Halakhic Problems*, p. 341, understands Rabbi Weinberg to interpret Rabbi Bachrach as saying that the wounding refers to the wounding of the fetus. But this is really not what Rabbi Weinberg intends, as he refers explicitly to wounding of the mother, saying (p. 213), "by killing the fetus he is wounding the woman." This effectively answers the issues raised by Rabbi Bleich in this context.

19. See his *Seridei Esh* (Jerusalem, 1966), vol. 3:350, n. 7.

20. *Responsa Aḥiezer* (New York, 1946). vol. 3, no. 72.

21. This issue is addressed by Rabbi Unterman in *ha-Torah ve'ha-Medinah* 4 (1952): 22–29.

22. *Noam* 7 (1964): 47, 53. Bleich's view that Rabbi Zweig permits abortion during the first forty days only if "the state of maternal health is very precarious, or if necessary in order to secure relief from severe pain" (Bleich, *Contemporary Halakhic Problems*, p. 356), is not substantiated by a careful reading of this responsum. I. Jakobovits, *Jewish Law Faces Modern Problems* (New York, 1965), p. 78, points out the ambiguity of Rabbi Zweig's responsum on this issue, in that the responsum "does not make it clear whether the sanction is contingent on a threat to the mother's life, or merely to her health." A close reading of the responsum leads to the conclusion that it is the threat to her life that is intended. Such a reading would also disagree with the diametrically opposed interpretation of Rabbi Zweig that is found in Feldman, *Birth Control*, p. 291.

23. See above, p. 35.

24. Cf. David Meislish, *Binyan David* (Ohel, 1935), no. 47, and Zweig, p. 47. Also see Ḥayyim Ḥizkiyahu Medini, *Sedei Ḥemed* (Warsaw, 1903), s.v. "Pe'at ha-Sadeh," 1:52.

25. Thus Bleich, *Contemporary Halakhic Problems*, p. 355, points out that

"Ḥavvot Yair himself quotes Rashi's commentary *Sanhedrin* 72b 'a woman who is in hard labor and whose life is in danger,' from which *Ḥavvot Yair* deduces that other than in cases of actual danger to maternal life abortion cannot be sanctioned."

26. For a discussion and clarification of Emden's view, see Waldenberg, *Ẓiẓ Eliezer* 9:234–236. The responsum of Emden was the basis of a lenient ruling of the *Rav Pealim* (Jerusalem, 1905), no. 60, authored by Rabbi Yosef Ḥayyim b. Eliyahu, in which a remorseful adulteress was permitted to abort the fetus thus conceived.

27. *Responsa Mishpetei Uziel* (Tel Aviv, 1935), *Ḥoshen Mishpat* 3:46.

28. *Responsa Yabia Omer* 4, *Even ha-Ezer* 1:10.

29. See *Iggerot Moshe* (New York, 1961), *Even ha-Ezer* 1:65; *Ẓiẓ Eliezer* 9:327.

30. This report is found in the *Issur ve'Heter he-Arukh* 59:35, a work attributed to Rabbeinu Yonah of Gerondi.

31. *Responsa Teshuvah me-Ahavah* (Prague, 1909), 1:53.

32. *Responsa Ẓiẓ Eliezer* 9:237.

33. This responsum was published in *Assia*, Adar 1976. The question was occasioned by the fact that amniocentesis to detect a Tay-Sachs fetus cannot be performed prior to the fourth or fifth month of pregnancy.

34. Feldman, *Birth Control*, p. 292.

35. Of the authorities whom Feldman quotes (pp. 291–294), several can be discounted. Thus in quoting Jakobovits, he omits the crucial words "as to present a hazard to her life" (Jakobovits, *Jewish Law Faces Modern Problems*, p. 76), which puts Jakobovits on record as denying the propriety of abortion when there is mere "anguish" to the mother. Feldman also mistranslates Weinberg by taking the word *ḥoli* (which means "sickness" in Hebrew) to mean "pain," and is led thereby to the ambiguous notion of "anguish," a notion that was clearly not intended by Weinberg. It is also doubtful whether Feldman's quotation from the *Ḥatam Sofer* has any bearing on abortion, as it deals specifically with a case of sterilization. Of all Feldman's proofs, therefore, we are left only with the *Afrekasta de'Anya*. This can hardly be construed as "the Jewish view."

2

Medical Practice, Research, and Self-Endangerment

Introduction

The ongoing success of modern medicine in combating disease and suffering has in large measure been the result of research and experimentation using human subjects. At present, hundreds of thousands of patients in the United States volunteer to be treated each year with experimental therapies in a wide range of clinical studies dealing with numerous serious illnesses. In recent years there has been increasing recognition of the need to formulate objective guidelines to establish what are, and are not, ethically acceptable practices in carrying out such investigations in the search for new cures, and dealing with the potentially negative consequences to the individuals involved.

On the one hand, there have come to light certain practices by the research community that appear to be highly questionable. On occasion even reputable investigators, with or without the informed consent of their subjects, have performed unnecessary surgery, injected cancer cells, or transplanted tumors, all to evaluate the effects of such procedures. Sometimes the subjects agreed to such practices under varying degrees of stress—as prison inmates, or soldiers, or patients and their families clutching at final straws. At other times such procedures were performed with the tacit agreement of leading research institutions—and governmental agencies. As a result of increased publicity, media attention, peer-review boards (themselves subject to criticism for often being ineffectual), and the rise of the field of medical ethics, many have called for critical scrutiny of the research process itself so as to prevent excesses and abuses such as these from taking place.

On the other hand, it is possible to stifle and inhibit researchers to the point where needed breakthroughs are put beyond reach. Experimentation, once considered a good thing, might well come to be viewed as a pejorative term. As Jonas Salk, developer of the first polio vaccine, has said, "It is much more difficult to do clinical investigations now than it was 30 years ago . . . we can reach the point where we regulate ourselves to the point of paralysis." Progress requires that risks be taken, risks that necessarily involve human subjects, for there are enough differences between animal and human physiology that there is no sure way to predict on the basis of animal studies alone what effects some drugs will have in man. And while it is also true that only thirty-six percent of published scientific articles are cited two or more times in subsequent research reports—indicating that almost two-thirds of such research is of negligible value to the scientific endeavor—who is to judge which will be the one to make a significant and lasting contribution to save the lives of thousands?

In addition, there are numerous specific ethical questions that medical research generates; e.g., what are morally acceptable criteria in choosing amongst volunteers? What are permissible parameters for eliciting informed consent? When must studies be discontinued? What are acceptable policies on media disclosure while safeguarding confidentiality?

More recently, the incidence and spread (through the exchange of body fluids) of the disease known as AIDS has posed a particularly difficult dilemma for physicians and other personnel who come into direct contact with such infectious patients, and thereby expose themselves in some small degree to the risk of acquiring this invariably fatal affliction. May a physician or caregiver refuse to treat such a patient, or withhold medical treatment, because of risk posed to the practitioner? Here too, what degree of risk is permissible, required, or forbidden?

Jewish law has been utilized in dealing with a number of these issues, applying analogous biblical, talmudic, and post-talmudic precedent wherever possible. Not surprisingly, within the corpus of halakhic works there is a substantial body of writings, both modern and premodern, that can be usefully brought to bear on some of the vexing issues at hand.

This chapter attempts to understand how Jewish law has balanced the conflicting claims of the needs of the individual versus the interests of others or the community at large: what is the nature of the obligation to bring healing or lessen suffering? what human costs are acceptable and what are not? When may one life be endangered to save another? What kind of risks and odds can be properly assumed? These are difficult questions, and the answers are far from straightforward or unanimous, but as we shall see, they are all addressed by the Halakhah, in one form or another.

The Question

A man is diagnosed as suffering from AIDS, a fatal disease that is spread through the exchange of body fluids. His doctors feel that he will not live more than six months at most, were he to rely upon conventional treatment. At the same time several of his physicians are deeply concerned for their own health and their own exposure to AIDS in the course of treating him, and others with the same diagnosis, through contact with specimens of infected blood and other fluids. They are considering the option of withdrawing from active participation in the further treatment of the patient.

The patient himself has his own dilemma. He is told that there is a new, experimental, and extremely toxic drug that is believed by some researchers to show promise in the treatment of AIDS. Indeed the drug has been effective in preliminary trials, but needs to be tested in humans. If the substance turns out to be safe and effective, it might not only lead to long-term survival for this subject himself, it will also save many other lives and ameliorate much human suffering. But if the clinical trial fails, the patient faces the possibility that his condition will deteriorate rapidly, leading to immediate death. He is asked to consent to be a volunteer in this research project.

The following questions are raised by this case:

1. What is the nature of the responsibility, whether upon laymen or medical personnel, to intervene to save the life of a person who is threatened by natural or unnatural causes?
2. What if there are risks to one's own health as a result of acting to save another's life, may one—must one—endanger one's health, or life, to that end?
3. To effect a cure or extended life-expectancy for himself, may a

dangerously ill patient agree to undergo treatment that might alleviate his condition and extend his life, but which, if unsuccessful, might also hasten his death significantly?

Sources

A. Leviticus 19:16

Thou shalt not go up and down as a talebearer among thy people; neither shalt thou stand idly by the blood of thy neighbor; I am the Lord.

B. Deuteronomy 22:1–2

Thou shalt not see thy brother's ox or his sheep driven away, and hide thyself from them; thou shalt surely bring them back to thy brother . . . and thou shalt restore it to him.

C. Leviticus 25:36

Take thou no interest of him or increase; but fear thy God, that thy brother may live with thee.

D. Kings 7:3 ff.

[Ben-hadad, king of Aram, laid siege to Samaria, causing great famine. Elisha the prophet foretold impending salvation, wherein food would be plentiful. But the king of Israel and his noblemen did not believe Elisha.] Now there were four leprous men at the entrance of the gate; and they said one to another: "Why sit we here until we die? If we say: We will enter into the city, then the famine is in the city, and we shall die there; and if we sit still here, we die also. Now therefore come, and let us fall unto the host of the Arameans; if they save us alive, we shall live, and if they kill us, we shall but die."

E. Sifra, Kedoshim 2:4

Whence do you know that if you see a man drowning in a river, or thugs or a wild animal attacking him, you are obligated to save him? Because it says, "neither shalt thou stand idly by the blood of thy neighbor" (A).

F. Bava Kamma 81b (as well as Sifri, Ki Teẓe 223)

Whence do we know that we are required to save the life of another? Because it says, "and thou shalt restore it unto him" (B).

G. Sanhedrin 73a

Whence do we know that a man who sees his fellow drowning in a river is obliged to save him? From the verse "neither shalt thou stand idly by the blood of thy neighbor" (A). But do we not derive this from "and thou shalt restore it unto him" (B), which teaches the obligation to save him? The answer is that from that verse one might think that one is merely obliged to save him with one's own body, but not to hire help, while this verse teaches that if necessary one must hire others as well.

H. Bava Meẓia 62a (as well as Torat Kohanim, Behar 5)

It is stated in the Beraita: If two men are traveling in a desert, and one of them has a container of water such that if he keeps it all for himself he will survive, but if he shares it with his fellow they will both die—Ben Petura says it is better for them both to drink rather than allow his fellow to die; but R. Akiva says "that thy brother may live with thee" (C) teaches that your life takes precedence over the life of your fellow.

I. Niddah 61a

Certain inhabitants of the Galil were rumored to have committed murder. They sought refuge [from the Roman authorities] with R. Tarfon. Said he to them: "What shall I do? If I do not hide you, you might be killed; but how can I hide you when I must be mindful of the statement of the Sages that even though a person should not believe rumor, one should take every precaution lest it be true! Go therefore, and hide somewhere else."

J. Jerusalem Talmud, Terumot 8:4

R. Imi was abducted and taken to certain death. When R. Yonatan was informed he said: "Let him prepare his death shroud [as we should not endanger ourselves to save him]." Said R. Simon b. Lakish: "I will go and save him, even if I have to kill or be killed." He went and placated the abductors, thus freeing R. Imi. He then said to the abductors: "Come with me to our Elder that he may pray for you." When they came before R. Yoḥanan he said: "May you suffer the same fate you intended for R. Imi." They left his presence, and prior to reaching Afifsirus they were all killed.

K. Avodah Zarah 27b

R. Yoḥanan: If a man is so sick that it is in doubt whether he will live or die [and the only physician available is a heathen], he should not turn to him for treatment (Rashi: . . . for such a doctor will certainly kill him, hence let him leave things be, as that way he might recover on his own). But if without medical help he will surely die, then he may avail himself of such a doctor (Rashi: . . . in any case he will die, whereas there is a possibility that the physician will cure him). But what of the limited time [*ḥayyei sha'ah*] that would have been his that he stands to lose if the physician kills him right away? The answer is that such limited duration of life can be disregarded. And whence do we know this? It is learnt from the story of the four lepers (D).

L. Maimonides, Commentary to the Mishnah, Nedarim 4:4

According to the law a physician is obliged to heal a sick Jew, as indicated by the Sages' interpretation of the verse "and thou shalt restore it unto him" (B). For they interpreted it to include restoring his body. Thus if a person is in danger and can be saved, one is obliged to save him, whether it is with one's body, one's possessions, or one's expertise.

M. Maimonides, M.T. Hilkhot Roẓeiaḥ 1:14

Whoever can save another but does not transgresses "neither shalt thou stand idly by the blood of thy neighbor" (A). Thus if you see your fellow drowning, or being attacked by ruffians or a wild animal, and you can save him by yourself or by paying someone else to do so, but you do not thus save him; or if you overhear idolaters or traitors conspiring to harm him or entrap him, but you do not alert him; or if you know of an idolater or aggressor about to attack him and you are in a position to placate them or prevent their act, but you do not do so—in all of these and similar cases you transgress the verse "neither shalt thou stand idly by the blood of thy neighbor" (A).

N. Maimonides, M.T. Hilkhot Roẓeiaḥ 7:8

A man who is exiled to a city of refuge for accidental homicide is not to leave there ever, even for the sake of a miẓvah, or to give evidence in monetary or capital cases, even to save the life of an accused by his evidence, or to save someone from an idolater, or from a river, a fire, or a collapsed structure. And even if all of Israel is in need of him, such as was the case with Joab ben Zeruiah, still he never leaves the refuge, until the Ḥigh Priest dies. And if he leaves, he exposes himself to being killed.

O. Sefer Ḥasidim 674 (Bologna); 162 (Parma)

It is written "Neither shalt thou stand idly by the blood of thy neighbor." But if many are attacking him, one should not endanger oneself [in coming to his help]. . . . Thus if a man is drowning in a river, and he is heavy, one should not help him lest one be drowned with him.

Discussion

1. THE RESPONSIBILITY TO SAVE LIFE

The halakhic Midrash to Leviticus known as the *Sifra* (E) locates the responsibility to save an endangered life in the verse "neither shalt thou stand idly by the blood of thy neighbor" (A). The *Sifri* on Deuteronomy, reflected in a passage in *Bava Kamma* (E), finds a similar obligation in Deuteronomy 22:2 (B), which requires a person to "restore" the endangered goods of his fellow. As explained by Rashi, in his commentary to *Sanhedrin* 73a (G), the redundant *vav* at the end of the word *ve'hashevoto* gives the phrase the meaning "return his body to him," i.e., restore not only his possessions, but his life too.

Why require two such separate commandments, one positive and one negative? The Gemara in *Sanhedrin* (G) answers that Leviticus teaches specifically that if help is needed to save that life, the onlooker is obligated to make every effort to hire such assistance. One reason that has been offered is that the verse in Deuteronomy occurs in the context of the restoration of physical property, where no monetary outlay is required of an onlooker.[1] Hence the need for the verse in Leviticus requiring such expenditure.

Once such expenses have been incurred, who is responsible for payment? Can it be argued that once a person is obligated by the

1. *Shulḥan Arukh ha-Rav, Hil. Nizkei ha-Guf*, chap. 8. See, however, the questions raised by Rabbi Y. Liebes, *Beit Avi* (New York, 5736), p. 207, including the fact that even a commandment such as the one in Deuteronomy requires certain expenditures to be made. See also the *Minḥat Ḥinukh* 237, who takes the position, based on Deuteronomy (B), that one is not obligated to intervene and save the life of an attempted suicide, just as there is no obligation to save articles belonging to one's fellow that were deliberately discarded by him. Most authorities, however, do not agree with this argument; see N. Rakover, "Haẓalat Nefashot—Hebetim Mishpatiyim," *ha-Darom* 50 (Nissan 5740): 242, n. 5.

Torah to save his fellow's life, such obligation requires one to sacrifice of one's means in fulfilling God's command? *Bava Kamma* 81a lists as one of the decrees from the time of Joshua, that he who damages a farmer's crops while saving a life does not pay damages to the farmer. Likewise, the passage in *Sanhedrin* quoted earlier continues to state that if damages are incurred in saving a man from a pursuer (*rodef*), the intercessor is not liable, for "otherwise no man would save his fellow from a pursuer."[2] But does the victim himself, once saved, have to reimburse for expenses incurred? The thirteenth-century R. Meir Abulafia answers in the positive, arguing that the Gemara in *Sanhedrin* (G) pointedly requires the intercessor to expend the effort to hire help, but does not speak of him having to absorb such expense himself.[3] In similar vein, the Rosh requires the victim to repay all costs, assuming that he has the means to pay.[4] And while Maimonides and the *Shulḥan Arukh* do not codify this as law, Rema (R. Moses Isserles) in the sixteenth century specifically mandates reimbursement in cases where ransom was paid to save the life of an incarcerated Jew.[5]

What if the endangered party cannot reimburse the expenses, is there any limit to what the intercessor is required to expend of his own, or is he expected to spend everything he has? Several authorities in the twentieth century addressed this question. R. Abraham Isaac ha-Kohen Kook discussed the issue, but did not

2. Rakover, "Haẓalat Nefashot," n. 14. R. Ḥayyim Pelaggi (*Nishmat Kol Ḥai, H.M.* 48) is of the opinion that where the victim cannot reimburse for such damages, then the intercessor is indeed liable to pay. On the entire question of the pursuer, see below, chap. 4. Regarding the question of individual responsibility vs. communal responsibility to underwrite the cure for an individual, see Rabbi M. Hershler, *Halakhah u-Refuah* 3:45–50.

3. *Yad Ramah* to *Sanhedrin* 73a. A similar reading of this Gemara is found in *Responsa Mabit* 1:237.

4. *Piskei ha-Rosh, Sanhedrin* 8:2, as well as the *Responsa of the Rosh* 5:2, where the question involves payment of medical costs incurred without the express permission of the patient. The Rosh rules that the patient (for his estate) is nonetheless required to pay for such efforts where they were intended to save his life. A detailed discussion of this responsum is found in Rabbi Efraim Weinberger, "Shmirah al ha-Ḥayyim ve'ha-Beriyut be'Halakhah," *ha-Torah ve'ha-Medinah* 11–13 (5720–5722): 118 ff.

5. *Sh.A. Y.D.* 252:12. Likewise see *Responsa Beit Ya'akov* 148, as quoted in Rakover, "Haẓalat Nefashot," p. 246, n. 27. On this issue, see the article by Rabbi D. B. Wein, "be'Inyan Lo Ta'amod al Dam Re'ekha," *ha-Darom* 33:61–80, especially p. 69. See additional sources brought in the *Encyclopedia Talmudit*, s.v. "Hazalat Nefashot," n. 31.

give a definitive answer.[6] Not so Rabbi Yeḥiel Weinberg: he has no doubt whatsoever that this talmudic passage requires total expenditure to save such a life—and in support of this position he quotes Rashi's formulation: "search out every possibility so that your fellow's blood not be spilled."[7]

What kind of situations are included in these obligations? *Sanhedrin* (G) mentions one who is in danger of drowning, and attacks by wild animals or by thugs. Others, as seen above, speak of perils related to being pursued or lost or imprisoned for ransom (on the assumption that noncompliance with the demand might well lead to the death of the prisoner). Maimonides, in codifying this passage into law (M), mentions these and adds several required instances of intercession by a third party even prior to an actual attack by homicidal conspirators. Furthermore, it would appear, it is not even necessary that death appear certain. Even where the fatal outcome is not certain, but only possible, then according to Rabbeinu Nissim,[8] an onlooker cannot remain passive, relying on good fortune to save that life, but is required to intervene actively.

In the context of medical intervention to save life, similar sentiments are encountered. Maimonides, in his *Commentary on the Mishnah* (L), applies the talmudic passage in *Sanhedrin* (G) to obligate a physician to save a patient if he is in a position to do so. Likewise the tosafist R. Jacob of Orleans derives the

---

6. *Mishpat Kohen* 144, pp. 342 ff.

7. *Yad Sha'ul, in Memory of R. Sha'ul Weingart* (Tel Aviv, 5713), pp. 371–395 (reprinted in *Responsa Seridei Esh*, vol. 1, *Ḥiddushim u-Biurim*, pp. 303 ff., esp. p. 313, no. 9). The opposite view was apparently espoused by R. Weinberg's interlocutor, R. Moshe Shternbuch. For a view similar to that of R. Weinberg, see R. Menaḥem ha-Meiri, *Beit ha-Beḥirah* to *Sanhedrin* 73a (G).

8. *Ḥiddushei ha-Ran* to *Sanhedrin* 73a. See the very comprehensive treatment of this topic in the *Encyclopedia Talmudit*, s.v. "Hazalat Nefashot," n. 21. On the related issue of saving an individual who wishes to die, or has intentionally endangered himself, there is an extensive literature, involving two opposing opinions. On the one hand are those who do not require any intervention to save such a person. This includes *Minḥat Ḥinukh* 327, Rabbeinu Nissim, the *Yam shel Shelomoh*, and the *Responsa Shevut Ya'akov*. On the other hand is the view associated with Maharam Rothenburg that requires intervention irrespective of the wishes of the endangered party, a view accepted by R. Barukh ha-Levi Epstein, R. Eliezer Waldenberg, and Rabbi S. Y. Zevin. See the latter's discussion in his volume *le'Or ha-Halakhah* entitled "Mishpat Shylock," pp. 318–328, as well as his response to the contrary views expressed by Rabbi Yehudah Gershuni, "Ḥayyalei Yisrael ha-Mistaknim," *Or ha-Mizraḥ* 21:3–8. Also see Wein, "Lo Ta'amod," pp. 72–73.

physician's obligation to heal from the respective verses in Leviticus (A) and Deuteronomy (B).[9] Naḥmanides sees such an obligation in Leviticus 25:36 (C), as well as in the familiar exhortation to love one's fellow (Leviticus 19:18), which stipulate brotherly coexistence and responsibility.[10]

Yet it is in the context of such medical intervention that a more fundamental question is raised in the halakhic sources. Put simply, it is this: if we accept the notion that by Divine Providence our individual or collective destiny is foreordained through natural processes, what gives the physician the right to interfere with what could be considered "God's will"? Unlike the earlier cases of accidental peril or deliberate injury, should we not view disease as nature, with God's blessing, taking its proper course?

The Gemara in *Bava Kamma*, cognizant of this question, refers to the passage in Exodus regarding a fight in which a man is unjustly injured by his fellow. In this instance the Torah holds the aggressor responsible for all financial losses incurred, and in addition requires that he "shall cause him to be thoroughly healed" (Exod. 21:19). The Gemara quotes a Beraita that explains that "from here we derive that the physician is granted permission to cure," and the *Shulḥan Arukh* codifies this dispensation together with the obligation to save life[11]. Yet in spite of this specific passage in the Gemara, Maimonides in (L) and (M) does not refer to this verse at all as providing a warrant for medical intervention. An explanation of this glaring omission is offered in the twentieth century by R. Barukh ha-Levi Epstein, who explains that once Leviticus and Deuteronomy *obligate* medical intervention, as seen above, Maimonides sees no reason to quote a verse that would simply *allow* such intervention.[12]

---

9. *Sefer Berakhah Meshuleshet* (Jerusalem, 5728) to *Berakhot* 60a, in the name of *Tosafot ha-Rosh*, p. 40.

10. *Commentary of Naḥmanides to the Torah*, Lev. 25:36, as well as his *Torat ha-Adam*, *Kitvei ha-Ramban*, ed. C. B. Chavel, vol. 2, p. 48.

11. *Bava Kamma* 85a and *Berakhot* 60a, with the comments of Rashi, Tosafot, and the *Novellae of the Rashba* ad loc. See *Sh.A. Y.D.* 336:1.

12. *Torah Temimah* to Exod. 21:19, as well as the extended discussion by the same author in his *Tosefet Berakhah* ad loc. See J. David Bleich, "The Obligation to Heal in the Judaic Tradition: A Comparative Analysis," in *Jewish Bioethics*, ed. Fred Rosner and J. David Bleich (New York, 1983), pp. 1–44, especially n. 87. See also by the same author, *Judaism and Healing: Halakhic Perspectives* (New York, 1981), pp. 3 ff. A somewhat different interpretation of Maimonides is adopted by Rabbi I. Jakobovits, *Jewish Medical Ethics* (New York, 1975), p. 304, n. 8.

Those who accept this preponderant view point to the fact that talmudic literature is replete with positive references to the practice of medicine: e.g., a scholar should not live where there is no physician;[13] R. Yoḥanan b. Zakkai requested medical treatment for a colleague;[14] and R. Judah the Prince had a personal physician (being notably wealthy, he could apparently afford such exclusive attentions).[15] And in later periods Jewish history includes a long line of halakhists who practiced medicine, perhaps the most notable being Maimonides himself, who was a practitioner and the author of a number of medical treatises.[16]

At the same time, however, there was a minority that frowned on those who looked to the medical profession for cures from illness. Some, such as Ibn Ezra, noted that in Scripture King Asa was criticized for turning to a physician, instead of relying on God.[17] Naḥmanides likewise derives from that incident that "one who seeks God through a prophet does not seek physicians,"[18] for in his opinion, in a spiritually perfected world there is no need for physicians or their skills, as we would rely on God's healing, as it says "for I am the Lord your healer" (Lev. 26:11). Even so, Naḥmanides elsewhere condones, and even requires, recourse to the healing professions, until such time as the spiritual utopia will come to be, and "God will remove illness from their midst to the point that they will have no need of a physician and no need to safeguard themselves by any medical means whatsoever."[19]

Such minority opinions notwithstanding, the solid consensus of halakhic opinion enthusiastically supported medical healing wherever possible, even to the point of suspension of certain cardinal laws of Judaism in order to facilitate such ministrations. This included the desecration of the Sabbath as well as Yom

13. *Sanhedrin* 17b.
14. *Gittin* 56b.
15. *Bava Meẓia* 85b.
16. For an excellent historical and literary review of Jewish medical personalities, writings, attitudes, and practices, see Salo Wittmayer Baron, *A Religious and Cultural History of the Jews* (New York, 1971), 8:221–226 and notes thereon. See also the *Encyclopaedia Judaica*, s.v. "Maimonides," in the special section "As Physician," as well as the appended bibliography.
17. Abraham Ibn Ezra, *Commentary to the Torah*, Exod. 21:19, with reference to II Chronicles 16:12. See also the comments of Rabbeinu Baḥya ad loc.
18. See Naḥmanides' comments to Lev. 26:11.
19. See Bleich in *Jewish Bioethics*, pp. 24–28, and in *Judaism and Healing*, pp. 5 ff.

Kippur where there was any life-threatening sickness at hand.[20] So sensitive were these halakhists that they insisted that such desecration be performed neither by minors, nor by non-Jews, nor even through some change or subterfuge—but openly, deliberately, and by a sage, if at all possible.[21] All of this was intended to take every possible medical precaution to remove present or future danger to life.[22]

Illustrative of this attitude are the actions of the nineteenth-century rabbinic leader R. Ḥayyim Soloveichik. On more than one occasion he publicly suspended the laws of the Sabbath and Yom Kippur by reason of medical need. Once he forbade the synagogues in his town to recite the Kol Nidre prayer until cash was collected by his emissaries from each of the congregants on Yom Kippur itself, in order to effect the immediate release of five Jews who had been accused of a crime which might have led to their endangerment. As he explained his actions at the time, "It is not that I am lenient in suspending prohibitions of the Torah; on the contrary, I am strict in upholding the mandate to save life [*pikuaḥ nefesh*]."[23] On another occasion he insisted that his congregants eat and drink on Yom Kippur so as not to enfeeble themselves during a typhus outbreak that was raging in the city.

It is also significant in this context that the obligation to heal the sick is not limited to situations where the person's life is endangered. The term *ḥoleh* ("sick person"), on whose behalf one is bidden to act, is generally defined as any person who is weakened by sickness to the point that he is bedridden or cannot walk unaided.[24] Likewise, a person who is afflicted in even one limb or organ, but suffers to the point that his whole body is affected, is considered a *ḥoleh* whom one is obligated to heal.[25]

20. *Sh.A. O. H.* 328:3.

21. Maimonides, *M.T. Hil. Shabbat* 2:1; *Encyclopedia Talmudit*, s.v. "Ḥoleh," pp. 250–251.

22. Needless to say, the laws of healing regarding permissible and impermissible practices are complex and detailed. This is particularly true of such practice on the Sabbath and Yom Tov. It is beyond the scope of this study to examine those laws in detail.

23. Rabbi S. Y. Zevin, *Ishim ve'Shitot* (Tel Aviv, n.d.), pp. 64–65.

24. Maimonides, *M.T. Hil. Zekhiyah u-Matanah* 8–2; Naḥmanides, *Torat ha-Adam*, *Sh'ar ha-Meḥush; Sh.A. O.H.* 328:17. Such a definition is consistent with the biblical description of recovery as occurring when "he shall rise again and walk upon his staff" (Exod. 21:19).

25. Rema, *Sh.A. O.H.* 328:3, as well as the *Magen Avraham* ad loc. See *Encyclopedia Talmudit*, s.v. "Ḥoleh," n. 18.

Before leaving the question of the nature of the obligation to heal, there is one more issue that is of more than passing interest for the issue of medical malpractice and unsuccessful therapy. The question is this: does a physician who prescribes a course of therapy and treats a patient fulfill thereby his proper obligation whether or not the treatment is successful? Put somewhat differently: is the obligation to *cure* a patient, or to *treat* a patient? Does the fulfillment of obligation require a successful outcome of the therapy or procedure? The question in this form is asked by Rabbi Norman Lamm, and he answers by way of a historical analysis that demonstrates that indeed historically the Halakhah has been divided on this very point since the time of the early tannaim.[26]

Thus there are two divergent interpretations of the Beraita seen earlier that says "the physician is granted permission to cure." As we have seen, the preponderant view is that by this statement the physician need not be concerned that he is interfering with the Divine order; hence he is entitled to offer treatment. This is how Maimonides understands this particular verse (see above). But Naḥmanides goes further to perceive in this verse not merely permission but an actual obligation to intercede, irrespective of the eventual outcome, in that he should not hold back out of self-doubt or uncertainty. According to Naḥmanides the verse does not address the question of Providence at all, but rather self-doubt and the obligation to extend treatment.[27]

Rabbi Lamm traces this discussion, as reflected in subtle ways in opposing views found in the Mishnah and the Tosefta, in the context of medical manslaughter that should or should not require exile to a city of refuge. This is also true of one view among the tosafists which opposes Rashi's interpretation of (A), as to standing idly by the blood of one's neighbor. And in more recent times, the same dichotomy of views appears, in that the *Yad Avraham* agrees with Maimonides, whereas the *Arukh ha-Shulḥan* sides with Naḥmanides.

In short, there is certainly ample precedent for the view that

26. Rabbi N. Lamm, "Is it a Mitzvah to Administer Medical Therapy?" *Journal of Halakhah and Contemporary Society* 8 (Fall 1984): 5–13. A Hebrew version appeared in *Torah she'be'al Peh* 25 (5744): 140–143.

27. See Naḥmanides, *Torat ha-Adam, Sha'ar ha-Sakanah*, in *Kitvei ha-Ramban*, p. 41.

medical treatment per se, irrespective of outcome, is an act fulfilling a command of the Torah. Of course this is not to absolve the medical practitioner of all responsibility for the consequences of the treatment that he provides. But it does mean that, according to these sources at least, conscientious and reasonable medical care is in and of itself a positive and redeeming act in accordance with the Torah and Jewish law, even when the end result of the treatment is not successful.

We can conclude the discussion of the obligation to heal by referring to a responsum of the Rosh, in which he states that "every person should try to make available a cure for the sick, and whoever goes to great lengths for this purpose is to be praised."[28] He then adds that such effort and expense are proper in that "it is a known custom that when a man falls sick and cannot help himself, his relatives make every effort to find him a cure." Jewish law, apparently, considers us all "related," and hence under a similar obligation toward our fellow.

2. *RISKING ONE'S LIFE OR HEALTH*

We have seen that by most accounts there is a duty to make every effort to save the endangered life of a fellow human being. This includes making financial sacrifices if they are necessary at the time. But what if, in order to save a life, a person has to endanger his own?

Here it is helpful to distinguish between two situations. The first involves the certain or likely sacrifice of one's life that would result from helping one's fellow. The second involves the mere possibility of death to oneself—but not a probability.

Certain or Likely Self-Sacrifice

In the first situation, a pivotal text is found in *Bava Meẓia* (H), where two people are walking in a waterless desert, and only one has water. Were he alone to drink it he would survive and his fellow would die, but were he to share it with his fellow, both would perish. Ben Petura requires him to share; R. Akiva, quoting

28. *Responsa of the Rosh* 85:2. This is consistent with what we have already seen in the Rosh; see above n. 4.

Leviticus (C), does not, saying, "Your life comes before the life of your brother." It is the view of R. Akiva that is accepted by most subsequent authorities.[29]

This discussion bears further examination. Would Ben Petura insist on sharing the precious life-support irrespective of how much time they would both have to live? What if by sharing they would both die right away? Such a case would involve shipwrecked passengers where there is only one life-preserver, which, if shared, would lead to their almost immediate drowning. What of R. Akiva: is he saying that he *need* not share the water, or that he *must* not share it?

Rabbi I. Y. Unterman is certain that even Ben Petura would not counsel any sharing that would lead to immediate death.[30] The Ḥazon Ish agrees on this point.[31] Their reason is that Ben Petura is essentially concerned not to sacrifice the significant, if limited, time span (*ḥayyei sha'ah*) of the fellow-traveler in the interests of the long-term survival of the first party. But where there is no significant life-span, even as a result of their sharing (as in the case of the life-preserver), Ben Petura would agree with R. Akiva not to share. Accordingly, Ben Petura's statement that a person should not allow his fellow to die is not precise, for under certain circumstances he would in fact allow such a course of action.

But while Ben Petura would have them share the water, R. Akiva would disagree, as he sees no need for literal self-sacrifice to save another. But if the person wishes to share, may he do so? Here there are two interpretations. Rabbi Unterman says that a person is indeed obligated to save his own life, where the danger of death is certain or highly likely. And even where it is simply a matter of adding extra time to his own life, without any likelihood of long-term survival, still a person must preserve his life as long as possible; as R. Akiva says, "Your life takes precedence over the life of your fellow." The same view is held by Rabbi Moshe Feinstein, saying that no one can calculate the relative importance of

29. For certain historical and philosophical observations on this text, see Rabbi S. Lieberman, "How Much Greek in Jewish Palestine," *Biblical and Other Studies* (Cambridge, 1963), pp. 124 ff. See also S. Pines, "Shnayim She-hayu Holkhim Ba-midbar," *Tarbiz̧* 16:238 ff. Those who explicitly accept the view of R. Akiva include the Meiri to *Bava Mez̧ia* 62a, as well as the *Ḥazon Ish, H. M. Likkutim* 20.

30. I. Y. Unterman, *Shevet mi-Yehudah* (Jerusalem, 1983), 1:8 (pp. 15–16).

31. Rabbi A. I. Karelitz, *Ḥazon Ish* (*Sanhedrin, Likkutim* 26).

different lives. Just as the Talmud forbids a man to kill another to save himself, saying, "Whence do you know that your blood is redder than his?" (*Pesaḥim* 25b), so in reverse might we say, "How do you know that his blood is redder than yours?" In such a case, a person should defer to providential design, so that whoever has the resource to survive should ensure his own life first.[32]

Others, however, disagree. Rabbi Yeḥiel Weinberg refers approvingly to R. Eliyahu of Prozin, who states than even R. Akiva does not forbid self-sacrifice to save another.[33] He argues that theoretically a Jew would be required to sacrifice his life for any of the commandments; but the verse "he shall live by them" (Lev. 18:5) teaches that it is permissible to preserve one's life, instead of sacrificing it. But permission is not an obligation. Hence someone who wishes to disregard the dispensation in order to fulfill another commandment (in this case "thou shalt not stand idly by"), may do so, and is considered praiseworthy.

The Mere Possibility of Self-Sacrifice

The second category involves the "mere" possibility, but not certainty or even probability, of the death of a person trying to save another from likely death. May a person undertake any mortal risk whatsoever? Here too there is a significant spectrum of opinion.

On the one hand is the view associated with the thirteenth-century *Hagahot Maimoniyyot*. This refers to the Jerusalem Talmud (J), wherein it is recorded that R. Simon b. Lakish endangered himself to rescue a colleague who had been abducted by well-known murderers. R. Joseph Karo, author of the *Shulḥan Arukh*, interpreted this action as follows: According to the Talmud, whoever saves one life is considered to have saved the entire world. The hostage was in certain danger, whereas his rescuer

32. Rabbi M. Feinstein, *Iggerot Moshe*, *Y.D.* 2:174 (4), p. 293. This raises the major topic concerning martyrdom in the face of forced transgression *(yehareg ve'al ya-avor)*—particularly when forced to commit murder. See in this connection Maimonides' *M.T. Hil. Yesodei ha-Torah*, chap. 5, and *Ḥiddushei R. Ḥayyim ha-Levi* ad loc. See also the detailed analysis by Hershler, in *ha-Darom* 46:42–47.

33. Rabbi Y. Weinberg, *Responsa Seridei Esh* (Jerusalem, 1977), 1:314–315, and a number of sources quoted there.

would be only in doubtful danger; under such circumstances, the obligation "do not stand idly by the blood of thy fellow" requires personal intervention.[34] This, as pointed out by R. Joel Sirkes (the Baḥ), was true even though he was not at all certain that his mission would be successful, and they might both be killed.[35]

Opposed to this view, stood a solid majority of early codifiers of Halakhah, including Alfasi, Maimonides, and the Rosh, all of whom pointedly omitted any reference to self-endangerment under such circumstances. Indeed, as the Baḥ noted, when Maimonides states (M) that you must act "when you can save him," it would seem that he requires foreknowledge of a successful outcome, i.e., where there is no self-endangerment. Similar sentiment is encountered in the *Sefer Ḥasidim* (O), which states that a person should not endanger himself to save someone who is attacked by many people, or for that matter to save a heavy drowning man whose weight might drag them both down.[36]

What of the contrary position espoused by the Jerusalem Talmud? The answer, according to the Maharam Zev (author of the *Agudat Ezov*) is that the Babylonian Talmud (the "Bavli") disagrees with the Talmud of Jerusalem (the "Yerushalmi").[37] There are three passages in the Bavli which he and others quote in support of this contention. The first involves R. Tarfon in *Niddah*

34. Bet Yosef to *Tur H.M.* 426:2, based on *Bava Batra* 11a and *Sanhedrin* 37a; also by the same author, the *Kesef Mishnah* to Maimonides, *M.T. Hil. Roẓeiaḥ* 1:14. As pointed out to me by Rabbi Norman Lamm, there are two versions of this oft-quoted rabbinic maxim ("whoever saves . . ."). While the Babylonian Talmud records the dictum in more restrictive fashion as referring to the saving of a single "Israelite" soul, the Jerusalem Talmud omits the specific reference to Jewish souls, and thereby leaves intact the more universalistic implication that saving *any* human life, whether Jew or Gentile, is the moral equivalent of saving the whole world.

35. *Hagahot ha-Baḥ* to *H.M.* there. The printed editions of the *Hagahot Maimoniyyot*, as found in the *Mishneh Torah*, lacks this passage, but it is found in the Constantinople editions. Later writers who accepted the view of the *Hagahot Maimoniyyot* as normative include the *Responsa Ḥavvot Yair* (no. 146), R. Ḥayyim David Abulafia in *Responsa Nishmat Ḥayyim* 11a, as well as the Moharaf, as mentioned in the *Sdei Ḥemed, Ma'arekhet Lamed* 144. See also the *Torah Temimah* to Lev. 19:16.

36. *Sefer Ḥasidim* 674. See also R. Joseph Babad, *Minḥat Ḥinukh* 296. Others who forbid self-endangerment to save another include the *Responsa Radbaz* 627 (see, however, below n. 57), and the Me'iri to *Sanhedrin* 73a (G), as well as Rabbeinu Yonah in the *Sefer Issur ve'Heter* 59:38. A comprehensive listing of such sources is found in Rabbi Ovadiah Yosef, *Yeḥaveh Da'at*, 3:84.

37. The *Agudat Ezov* is mentioned in the *Pitḥei Teshuvah* to *Sh.A. H.M.* 426.

(I), who refused to grant refuge to fellow Jews suspected by the Roman authorities of committing murder. He explained that given the rumors of their guilt, he had to take every precaution. Apparently he refused to endanger his own life at the hands of the authorities, even though their lives were at stake. The second passage is the one we have seen in *Sanhedrin* (G). There the Gemara explains the need for the verse in Leviticus ("neither shalt thou stand idly by") as necessary to teach the obligation to hire help in saving another. But if the Bavli agrees with the Yerushalmi, it should have given a much stronger justification for this verse; i.e., that it teaches self-endangerment rather than standing idly by while another is in peril! Why settle for the "mere" obligation to hire help? It must therefore be concluded that according to the Bavli there is no such obligation at all.

The third passage in the Bavli is a Beraita found in *Nedarim* 81a, recording the proper disposition of water from a well located in one town that flows to a second town. If in time of drought the inhabitants of the first town wish to retain all of the precious resource for themselves, may they do so? The Beraita answers that if their lives depend on keeping all the water, then they may indeed deprive the second town (this would be consistent with the view of R. Akiva in [H]); if however there is more than enough for drinking, but they wish to keep the balance nonetheless for washing their clothes, then there are two views: the majority of tannaim forbid such washing, while R. Yossi permits it, on the grounds that the long-term use of unsanitary clothing could lead to mental, if not physical, perils. In considering this debate, R. Naftali Ẓvi Yehudah Berlin (the Neẓiv) says that at issue is the question of possible self-endangerment when faced with the likely death of another. The majority are in favor of such self-endangerment, whereas R. Yossi (whose view is accepted by the She'iltot) is opposed to any exposure whatsoever.[38] Indeed, according to the nineteenth-century R. Israel Lipschutz, the very reason that Alfasi, Maimonides, and the Rosh omit the ruling of the Yerushalmi is that they accept the view of R. Yossi here, i.e., one need not risk one's life at all for another.[39]

In examining these passages in the Bavli, subsequent authori-

38. *Responsa Ha'amek She'elah* 147:4.
39. Rabbi I. Lipschutz, *Tiferet Yisrael* to *Yoma* 8:7 (Boaz).

ties raised a number of questions. Starting with the narrative of R. Tarfon, several objections against the use of this text were made.

1. Rabbi Eliezer Waldenberg points out that while the She'iltot interprets the episode as explained by the *Agudat Ezov*, Rashi does not do so, but rather understands R. Tarfon to have acted on the grounds that the Torah itself forbids providing haven to a suspected murderer. According to this, R. Tarfon was not motivated by a concern for his safety at the hands of the Romans, but rather for a prohibition of the Torah.[40]

2. Even according to the She'iltot, however, the text clearly implies that R. Tarfon believed that they had other refuge available to them. Such a case, as noted by R. Unterman cannot be instructive for normal cases of endangerment where there are no similar alternatives.[41] In addition, says Rabbi Waldenberg, R. Tarfon's answer implied that had he known for sure that they were in fact not murderers, he would have been duty-bound to save them.

3. Rabbi Ḥayyim Heller, in his commentary to Maimonides' *Sefer ha-Miẓvot*, makes a salient argument against the use of this text, saying that R. Tarfon was motivated entirely by another consideration—the prohibition against thwarting the proper punishment due a murderer. As the thirteenth-century *Sefer Ḥasidim* put it, "if a murderer flees unto you do not shelter him, whether he be Jew or Gentile, as was the case with R. Tarfon in Niddah."[42] Thus again this text is disqualified in the case of pure self-endangerment.

The second proof of the *Agudat Ezov* (G) is generally accepted by subsequent authorities.[43] Indeed for Rabbi Waldenberg this passage is sufficient proof that the Bavli does differ with the Yerushalmi on this issue.[44] But two authorities remain unconvinced of such a dichotomy between the two Talmudim. One is R.

40. Rabbi E. Waldenberg, *Responsa Ẓiẓ Eliezer* 9:45 (p. 180) referring to the interpretation of Rashi found in the *Ḥavvot Yair* and the *She'elat Yaveẓ*.

41. *Shevet mi-Yehudah* 1:9 (p. 17). See also *Responsa Ẓiẓ Eliezer* p. 181. There is even a question as to the correct reading in the *She'iltot* itself; see *Ha'amek She'elah, Parshat Shelaḥ* 129.

42. Rabbi Ḥayyim Heller, Commentary to Maimonides' *Sefer ha-Miẓvot*, negative commandment 297, p. 175, with reference to *Sefer Ḥasidim* 683.

43. See *Responsa Ẓiẓ Eliezer* and Heller, with reference to the *Arukh la-Ner* and *Yad Eliyahu*.

44. Rabbi Heller does, however, reject this proof too.

Yair Ḥayyim Bachrach, known as the Ḥavvot Yair, who is of the opinion that R. Akiva in (H) requires a man to save himself exclusively only if it is certain that by sharing his water they will both die. But even R. Akiva admits that if there is a significant possibility that by sharing they might both survive, then he should indeed share with his fellow.[45] If this be the case, R. Akiva requires self-endangerment to save the life of another—in full agreement with the Yerushalmi.

The second halakhist who doubts that the Bavli disagrees is Rabbi Unterman. He too discounts the story of R. Tarfon as having any bearing on our case—and for the reasons outlined above. As to *Nedarim*, Rabbi Unterman says that it is inconceivable that R. Yossi would advocate or countenance one town using water for laundry that could be used to save the lives of the inhabitants of another town. Such profligacy is not the issue at all. He adopts instead an interpretation of this Beraita first found in the *Sefer Yiḥusei Tannaim ve'Amoraim Ben Peturin*,[46] that there is indeed other water available to the hapless second town, but only at a great distance and accessible only with great effort. Weighing the effort involved in procurement against the long-term effects of unsanitary clothing, R. Yossi permits the withholding of the water in question. Accordingly, this constitutes no evidence on the issue of self-endangerment when faced with the imminent death of another.[47] Thus, Rabbi Unterman concludes, an individual is required to undertake a modicum of dangerous exposure to save the life of another who is in immediate danger—as the Yerushalmi indicates.

Yet the predominant view among later authorities is to reject the position of the Yerushalmi. A good example of a contemporary formulation of this position is that of the eminent halakhist Rabbi Moshe Feinstein. At first he considers an outright ban on self-endangerment, arguing that if it is permissible (as it surely is) to desecrate the Sabbath, a cardinal principle of the Halakhah, in order to avoid any potential danger to life, how can we permit an individual to enter into a similar danger for the sake of upholding a conventional commandment, such as the one "not

45. *Responsa Ḥavvot Yair* 146.
46. This source is mentioned in the generally excellent entry in the *Encyclopedia Talmudit*, s.v. "Hazalat Nefashot," at n. 80.
47. *Shevet mi-Yehudah*, pp. 17–18.

to stand idly by"? But then R. Moshe formulates a distinction between this commandment and others, saying that "after all a Jewish soul will be saved thereby." This he does on the strength of Rashi's explanation (in *Sanhedrin* 74a) of why one person may not kill another to save his own life: by killing the other there is both loss of life as well as the transgression of killing, whereas by submitting to be killed at least the transgression is avoided. Apparently such a calculus can be used to substitute one life for another. With this in mind he can countenance one Jew's facing his own possible death in order to prevent a fellow Jew's certain death. But this reasoning only goes so far as to permit self-endangerment; it certainly does not require it.[48]

Authorities such as these rely in addition on certain objections to the position associated with the Yerushalmi. In the first place the Yerushalmi itself records the fact that R. Yonatan pointedly would not endanger himself as did R. Simon b. Lakish. That being the case, how can we be certain that the Yerushalmi itself accepts the actions of R. Simon b. Lakish as normative? Secondly it is quite possible that even R. Simon b. Lakish did not intend his selflessness to be taken as an act required by law, but merely as done as a measure of special, voluntary, piety (*midat ḥasidut*). How can we legislate such activity as a normative requirement?[49]

In addition there is some question as to the literal meaning of the passage itself. Rabbi Heller provides an entirely different translation that reads as follows: "Said R. Simon b. Lakish: 'If I will do battle with them, they might kill me before I can kill them. Such an eventuality I am not obligated to face at all. It would be better for me to go and attempt to ransom him, and pay money for his freedom.'" Accordingly, says Rabbi Heller, this particular passage of the Yerushalmi has no bearing on the issue of self-endangerment at all; if anything it proves the opposite of what is purported. The *Hagahot Maimoniyyot* must, he says, have been

48. *Responsa Iggerot Moshe* ad loc. Rabbi I. Jakobovits, "Medical Experimentation on Humans in Jewish Law," in *Jewish Bioethics*, p. 382, states without substantiation that "hazardous experiments may be performed on humans only if they may be potentially helpful to the subject himself." It is difficult to justify this statement on the basis of the sources we have seen (except possibly R. Meir Simḥah of Dvinsk). See Bleich's critique of this point in "Experimentation on Human Subjects," *Jewish Bioethics*, pp. 384–385.

49. Both objections are found in the *Responsa Ẓiẓ Eliezer*, p. 181. See also *Responsa Yad Eliyahu* 43.

referring to another passage in the Yerushalmi, one which is presently missing from our printed editions, a not unusual state of affairs given the condition of the Yerushalmi.[50]

Thus there is a consensus of sorts that a person need not endanger himself to save another life. But there is one passage in which Maimonides (N) goes even further. Discussing the law in the Mishnah that a man who commits accidental homicide may find safety from vengeful relatives in one of the six cities of refuge mandated in the Torah, Maimonides says that such a man does not leave the city even to save the life of another person, even if "all of Israel is in need of him . . . and if he leaves he exposes himself to being killed." In commenting on this sweeping ruling of Maimonides, R. Meir Simḥah of Dvinsk interprets the final phrase as the rationale for the entire statement, i.e., the man is exempted from leaving the city as he might be killed by the still vengeful relatives of the man he killed. R. Meir Simḥah, in his commentary of the Torah, likewise points to God's charge to Moses to return to Egypt to save the Israelites, when God said, "for all the people are dead that sought thy life" (Exod. 4:19). Clearly, he explains, Moses was not expected to return prior to that time as long as his own life was being sought, even though all of Israel needed him, for he could not be expected to endanger his own life on their account.[51]

Others, again, disagree. Rabbi Unterman for one argues that the accidental killer is in a unique category: once he enters a city of refuge he ceases to have any responsibility toward the outside world; like a first-degree murderer who is put to death, he is "dead to the world," even exempt from commandments that would require him to travel outside his circumscribed existence. Accordingly R. Meir Simḥah is in error in extrapolating from the accidental murderer to issues of self-endangerment.[52] Rabbi Simḥah Elberg also disagrees with R. Meir Simḥah, saying that this law in Maimonides reflects the special requirement that there be no *kofer*, or substitution, that might in any way mitigate the punishment of such a person. Thus even allowing him to leave temporarily would contravene the express biblical prohibition against tak-

50. Heller, p. 175.

51. See *Or Sameaḥ* to *M.T. Hil. Roẓeiaḥ* 7:8; *Meshekh Ḥokhmah* to Exodus 4:19.

52. *Shevet mi-Yehudah*, pp. 19–21.

ing "ransom for he that is fled to the city of refuge" (Num. 35:32).[53] What of Maimonides' final statement that if he does leave he exposes himself to being killed—would that not indicate that his concern is indeed for his physical safety? Rabbi Elberg answers that Maimonides does not say "for if he leaves," but rather "and if he leaves"; i.e., this is not the reason for staying in the city, but an additional law that if he disregards the prohibition against leaving he can be killed with impunity by a vengeful blood-relative.

A third view is that of Rabbi Yeḥiel Weinberg. He finds no basis for Rabbi Unterman's distinction. As to Rabbi Elberg, Rabbi Weinberg finds it inconceivable, "something which neither the mind nor the heart can accept," that the Halakhah would insist on keeping a man incarcerated when to do so would prevent him from saving the lives of others, let alone all Israel.[54] The prohibition against ransom is rather to ensure that no man avoids his sentence completely through the payment of money (as would be the case with punishment for lesser bodily injuries). Where the intent is merely a temporary dispensation designed to save another life, surely that prohibition is irrelevant. Elsewhere Rabbi Weinberg takes issue with R. Meir Simḥah, saying that if the entire concern is safety, why not simply provide an armed escort, just as is done in case of accidental exit from the city?[55] In light of this, Rabbi Weinberg gives an entirely different twist to Maimonides' ruling. Quoting the *Ḥeshek Shelomoh*, he reads Maimonides to say that it is prohibited for the man to leave the city permanently, i.e., he may leave temporarily, but must return immediately after performing his life-saving task. Accordingly Maimonides' use of the term *le'olam* in this case does not mean "ever" but rather "forever."

That a Jew is free to endanger himself for the sake of corporate Israel is abundantly clear from others quarters too, says Rabbi Weinberg. They include the story of Queen Esther presenting herself to the king without being bidden, and numerous talmudic references to martyrs in differing places and times, often in doing battle to protect the lives of fellow Jews. A similar conclusion is

---

53. Rabbi Simḥah Elberg, *ha-Pardes* 33 (2): 22–27.
54. Rabbi Y. Weinberg, *ha-Pardes* 33 (4): 8–9.
55. *Responsa Seridei Esh*, ad loc.

encountered in the writings of Rabbi Abraham Isaac ha-Kohen Kook, as well as the above-quoted responsum of Rabbi Feinstein.[56]

The discussion thus far has dealt with a danger to life. But what if to save the life of another, a person contemplates endangering a limb, or a partial disfigurement? Is such a gesture required, permitted, or forbidden? This question can be deferred to the chapter on organ transplants, where one of the key issues relates to the donor of such an organ; i.e., may a person donate an organ, even where there is no immediate danger to life.?

There is one further question that should be addressed, and that relates to percentages. What kind of odds of success or failure, life or death, are assumed by these discussions? An important source on this question is found in the sixteenth century, in the writings of R. David b. Abu Zimra, known as the Radbaz. In one place he writes that a person should not enter possible danger to save his fellow, for one who does so is a proverbial "foolish saint" (*ḥasid shoteh*). But elsewhere he says that "if the risk is less than even, i.e., less than a *safek mukhra*, and the likelihood is that he can save him without losing his own life, then if he does not save him he has transgressed against the commandment 'do not stand idly by the blood of your neighbor.' " Thus if there is a fifty percent probability that a person will lose his life by attempting to save another, then such action should not be undertaken. Where the odds are anything less than this, and survival is probable, then a person may undertake to act, and put his faith in Providence.[57] As a matter of fact, the nineteenth-century R. Moses Schick understands the Yerushalmi itself to accept this distinction, whereby it is only if the peril is unlikely to lead to death that it is mandatory to act.[58] Likewise Rabbi Yeḥiel Epstein (author of the *Arukh ha-Shulḥan*), while accepting the view that a person should not endanger himself, adds that "it all depends on the circumstance, and a person should evaluate the situation in balanced fashion so as not to guard oneself

56. *Mishpat Kohen* 143; *Responsa Iggerot Moshe*, ad loc.

57. See the *Responsa Radbaz* 627, 218. The *Encyclopedia Talmudit* (s.v. "Haẓalat Nefashot," n. 74) also identifies this view with Tosafot, but the reference appears erroneous, and I am unable to locate such a view. Compare also the article by A. S. Avraham, "Nisyonot Refu'iyim be'Va'alei Ḥayyim u-Bivnei Adam," *Assia* 10:3, pp. 24–25.

58. See his glosses to *Miẓvot Hashem* 238, as well as his views in *Responsa Maharam Schick, Y.D.* 155.

overmuch . . . for whoever saves a Jewish soul is considered to have saved the whole world."[59] Implicit in this view is a requirement to act where the danger to oneself is highly unlikely.

Rabbi Unterman adopts a somewhat different measure, saying that it depends on the individual: where an individual would act to save his own possessions in spite of personal danger, that would likewise be considered a sufficient margin of safety for him to act on behalf of another. But where he would refuse to act even at the cost of losing his possessions, he is not expected to act on behalf of another either.[60]

3. HAZARDOUS PROCEDURES TO SAVE ONE'S OWN LIFE

Thus far we have dealt with self-endangerment to save another. But what if a person is himself endangered, and facing the imminent prospect of death, may he choose a course of action that might save his life, but might also shorten his life even further? A second question relates to self-endangerment, not to save one's life, but rather to secure relief from intense pain or suffering. May one volunteer to undergo risk for the sake of such improvement?

Risking Limited Life-span for Long Term Survival

As to the first question there is scriptural precedent for precisely such a dilemma. The Book of Kings (D) records the story of the four lepers, who were facing death by starvation as a result of a famine which precluded them from acquiring food in their isolated state. Reasoning that their life-expectancy was practically nil anyway, they chose to hand themselves over to the besieging Aramean enemy, who might execute them immediately—or take them captive and feed them. This incident took on decided significance for subsequent halakhists, in that tradition identified these lepers as halakhically knowledgeable in their own right (*giborim ba-torah*, "heroes in Torah"), namely, Gehazi, servant of the prophet Elisha, and his three sons.[61]

59. *Arukh ha-Shulḥan* to *Sh.A. H.M.* 426.
60. Unterman, op. cit., p. 21.
61. See Rashi's comments to II Kings 7, based on the Jerusalem Talmud, *Sanhedrin* 10:2.

Using this as source and precedent, R. Yoḥanan in *Avodah Zarah* (K) derives the fundamental principle that where life-expectancy is extremely limited anyway (the lepers' death by starvation was imminent), risky alternatives may be undertaken. And although the Halakhah in general values every moment of life as of infinite value, especially in the last moments of life,[62] here we invoke the principle that "such limited duration of life can be disregarded (*le'ḥayyei sha'ah lo ḥayshinan*). Apparently where the purpose is to save life, and not to end or shorten it, we may legitimately take a gamble, even where the currency is life itself. Based on this precedent, the Gemara extrapolates to the case of a Jew, mortally ill, whose only available medical assistance is a pagan physician, of the kind known on occasion to kill his Jewish patients. Here too, says the Gemara, the Jew should avoid such "help," for he might unexpectedly recover on his own anyway; but where death is imminent and practically certain, the Jew has nothing to lose, for what time he has left can be discounted, in the manner of the four lepers; hence he may consult that physician on the off-chance that he might just cure him, or extend his life indefinitely. As Tosafot explains, just as we desecrate the Sabbath itself when a wall of stones has fallen and buried a man under the debris, as long as there is a possibility that such action will extend his life even momentarily, so too here, since the patient will die for sure if he does not consult the physician, therefore we should take the chance, for "in both cases we choose doubtful life over certain death."[63]

The *Shulḥan Arukh* accepts this conclusion of the Gemara,[64] and a number of later authorities accordingly permit hazardous medical treatment for mortally ill patients, including R. Jacob Reischer, R. Solomon Eiger, R. Meir Posner, R. Jacob Ettlinger, and more recently, Rabbis Unterman and Waldenberg—and a number of others.[65] But at this point several other questions

---

62. For a detailed discussion of this matter, as it relates to the issue of euthanasia, see *Jewish Ethics and Halakhah for Our Time*, vol. 1, chap 3.

63. Tosafot to *Avodah Zarah* 27b, s.v. *leḥayyei*. Such disregard of a limited life-span is to be contrasted with Ben Peturah's view (see above) that the saving of even limited life of one's fellow indeed requires self-endangerment.

64. *Sh.A. Y.D.* 155:1.

65. *Responsa Shevut Ya'akov* 3:75; *Gilyon Maharsha* to *Sh.A. Y.D.* 155:1; *Responsa Beit Meir* to Sh.A. *Y.D.* 339; *Responsa Binyan Ẓion* 1:111; Unterman in *Noam* 13:5; Waldenberg, *Responsa Ẓiẓ Eliezer* 4:13. See also Rabbi S. Goren in

arise: Are there any minimum chances of success required? How long is "limited duration of life"? Who establishes these facts—physicians or rabbis?

On the first question, regarding the likelihood of success required, there are essentially two views. Rabbi Joseph Hochgelehrter, author of the *Mishnat Ḥakhamim*, requires at least a fifty percent chance of success, whereas R. Ḥayyim Ozer Grodzinski, known as Aḥi'ezer, accepts any significant chance of success as sufficient.[66] These two views are reflected in instructive fashion in two responsa by Rabbi Moshe Feinstein, in which this eminent contemporary rabbi first embraces the view of the Aḥi'ezer and then reverses himself to adopt the opposite position. In the first responsum, written in 1961, Rabbi Feinstein, with the concurrence of his colleague Rabbi Yosef Eliyahu Henkin, permits an individual facing certain death to undergo surgery that stands even a remote chance of success.[67] This is premised on a reading of the passage in *Avodah Zarah* that R. Yoḥanan would countenance any possible alternative to certain death, including an unlikely chance from a pagan physician, or (as in the case of Gehazi) the unlikely mercies of the Arameans. This reading of the Gemara follows the comments of Rashi, regarding which R. Feinstein says, "I have seen none who differ with him."

But in 1972 Rabbi Feinstein appears to have reversed himself. For in that year he penned a responsum regarding open-heart surgery that agreed substantially with the view of the *Mishnat Ḥakhamim*, and moreover attributed this view to Rashi and the above-mentioned Tosafot as well.[68] He argues that R. Yoḥanan in

---

Shanah be'Shanah, 5736, pp. 149–155. Some of these are mentioned by F. Rosner, "Jewish Ethical Issues in Hazardous Medical Therapy," *Tradition* 19 (1): 55–58. See also, from a religious scientist's perspective, the comments of K. Stern, "Experimentation on Human Subjects: A Search for Halakhic Guidelines," *Tradition* 17 (4): 41–52, as well as Dr. Jacob Levy in *Noam* 13:77–82.

66. *Responsa Aḥi'ezer* 2:16 (6). The *Responsa Beit David* permits odds of even one in a thousand. Conversely the *Tiferet Yisrael* (to *Yoma* 8:3) permits smallpox inoculation even where there is a one in a thousand chance of contracting the disease itself as a result of the inoculation. Rabbi Jakobovits (*Medical Experimentation*, pp. 380, 382) agrees with the *Aḥi'ezer* that even the remotest chance of success should be attempted, but he then goes on to say that "it is obligatory to apply to terminal patients even untried or uncertain cures." Some years later, however, he retreated from this problematic position. See his *Jewish Medical Ethics* (2nd edition, 1975, p. 292). In this regard see Bleich, *Healing*, p. 116.

67. *Responsa Iggerot Moshe, Y.D.* 2:58.

68. *Responsa Iggerot Moshe, Y.D.* 3:36. Both the *Ḥatam Sofer* (*Y.D.* 36) and the *Ẓiẓ Eliezer* (10:25 and 5:5) adopt similar views.

this passage permits recourse to hazardous practice only where there is a fifty-fifty chance of success. (As a matter of fact, he says, where the chances of success are more than fifty-fifty, a person is *obliged* to take the chance to achieve long-term, normal living.) In the case of the pagan physician recourse is permitted because we may assume that there are enough reliable physicians who will act with every intention of curing the patient. But this assumption only holds true where the physician is himself confident of the effectiveness of his therapy. Where the physician admits that the proposed therapy is unreliable to the extent that a majority of patients will die, then we cannot permit such recourse, and we cannot discount the momentary life at hand. Rabbi Feinstein accordingly reads the Gehazi narrative as a case of even risks; they could have been killed or they could equally have been taken captive. Thus where the outcome can go either way, a person can choose to wager all or nothing. It depends on the individual; he is not obligated one way or the other. Ultimately, says R. Feinstein, this case depends on the will of people at large (*da'at inshi*). For Gehazi was indeed not a halakhic authority, but a simple, in many ways errant man, and like him, most common people would choose normal life at the risk of immediate death—where the odds of success are even. But it depends on the individual—not everyone would agree with Gehazi.

As for his previously held view, R. Moshe appreciates that it too has its proponents—notably the Aḥi'ezer—and he therefore notes that one who relies on that view to accept a long-shot chance on complete recovery is not to be faulted.

These two responsa of Rabbi Feinstein, taken together, constitute a remarkable instance of halakhic openness and flexibility. On the one hand, far from dogmatic assertion of personal infallibility, we are witness to a readiness to reconsider a firmly held and widely shared opinion. On the other hand, we can recognize an openness to the possibility of personal predilection and choice, given R. Moshe's position that would allow individual discretion, irrespective of a majority, where the mathematical odds of survival are inconclusive.

There is a somewhat different formulation of acceptable and unacceptable risk under such circumstances, whereby a distinction can be drawn between a procedure or drug that has a proven therapeutic effect, albeit with a significant possibility of death resulting under certain circumstances, and a drug that is experimental in nature, its potential benefit unsubstantiated. This distinction was first made by R. Jacob Emden, using the terms *refuah bedukah* (the former case, a "proven therapy") and *she'einah bedukah* (the latter case, being unproven).[69] As explained by Rabbi J. David Bleich,[70] this means that while a patient is obliged to seek medical cure for his condition, he need accept therapy only where the proffered treatment is of the former kind, i.e., of proven benefit. But where the treatment is entirely experimental, its effectiveness not medically established, there exists no obligation, although one is free to try it, nonetheless. Where such experimental drugs or procedures are not merely unproven, but are actually dangerous, then according to R. Moshe Dov Welner such therapy is forbidden. It is only a proven efficacy that can counterbalance a downside risk to the life of the patient.[71] Thus, he argues, the *Sefer Ḥasidim* forbids the folk usage of certain herbs which either cured or killed their user, for their benefits were not medically proven, while their hazards were known to all.[72]

How long is the "momentary duration of life" which can be discounted or disregarded? The Aḥi'ezer, saying that it makes no difference whether it be a matter of hours or months, accepts a case wherein a six-month prognosis is offered by the physician, every day of which may be the patient's last. Rabbi Feinstein, as does R. Solomon Kluger,[73] sets the limit at twelve months of expected life. But he also adds that if the contemplated therapy or surgery merely promises to extend the life-span without eliminating the likelihood of death at any time, it should not be undertaken. In an additional comment, he notes that it would not be permissible to undergo such therapy if long-term survival can be achieved instead by remaining restricted to bed continuously. Such inconvenience is to be preferred over the dire risks otherwise posed.

Finally, as to the establishment of these facts, the accepted

69. *Mor u-Kezia* to *Sh.A. O.H.* 328.
70. Bleich, *Bioethics*, p. 31.
71. Rabbi M. D. Welner, in *ha-Torah ve'ha-Medinah* 7–8 (1956–57): 314.
72. *Sefer Ḥasidim* 467.
73. *Darkhei Teshuvah* to *Sh.A. Y.D.* 155:6.

view seems to be that of the *Shevut Ya'akov*, who requires that each case be individually adjudicated, with the concurrence of the best medical opinion (by a majority of two to one) and the preeminent rabbinical authority of the city.[74]

Risking life to Avoid Unbearable Pain

Regarding this question, there are a number of relevant texts. Both Naḥmanides and Rabbeinu Nissim note that in every medical treatment there is an element of danger, whether through human error or unforeseen complications.[75] Nonetheless they accept that in the normal course of things one may have recourse to medical treatment, such potential dangers notwithstanding. Such a position is entirely consistent with the generalized mandate granted a physician to cure sickness, as discussed earlier. But where there is a heightened risk factor, such recourse needs justification. Indeed, it is the view of R. Jacob Emden that such heightened risk for the "mere" sake of alleviation of intense pain is not justifiable.[76] The case before him involved surgery to remove gallstones, a procedure which in his time occasionally led to early death. Yet others, notably the Meiri and R. Moses Isserles, implicitly permit hazardous procedures where the only purpose is the relief from great pain.[77] The comments of the latter occur in the context of the special prohibition against wounding one's parent. Isserles (the Rema) rules that it is permissible for a physician to perform surgery (that involves necessary cutting) "where there is no one else available who can do this, and the parent is in pain, the son can perform blood-letting and amputation, following parental consent." Amputation to relieve pain can certainly be classified as major surgery where there is no intent to save life (at the very least this would be true of the sixteenth century, when R. Isserles lived). Armed with such precedent, recent authorities have tended to adopt the lenient view, with permissive rulings

74. *Responsa Shevut Ya'akov* 3:75.

75. Naḥmanides, *Torat ha-Adam*, in *Kitvei ha-Ramban* 2:43; *Ḥiddushei ha-Ran*, *Sanhedrin* 84b. See Bleich, *Halakhic Problems*, 1:122. See also the *Responsa Ẓiẓ Eliezer* 10:15 (17,1).

76. *Mor u-Keẓia* to *Sh.A. O.H.* 328.

77. Meiri to *Sanhedrin* 84b; Rema to *Sh.A. Y.D.* 241:3. Both are quoted by R. Yeḥiel Ya'akov Breish, *Ḥelkat Ya'akov* 3:11.

offered by Rabbi Shelomoh Zalman Auerbach and Rabbi Shelomoh Zalman Braun.[78] What is the basis of such leniency in the face of possible death?

Both of the latter authors offer as a key rationale the fact that the therapy thus undertaken is done "for the sake of healing." Yet this should not lead one to conclude that armed with such a rationale they would permit any medical procedure or therapy. The cases which the pivotal passage of Isserles permitted involved well-established procedures, not experimental ones. Thus it is safe to say that the relief of pain justifies only medical treatment that is established, albeit with a due measure of risk to life. Put another way, we might say that a therapy or procedure which is proven and widely accepted, in spite of attendant risks, can indeed be administered. This approach is entirely consistent with the principle, seen elsewhere,[79] and articulated here by Rabbi Bleich, that Halakhah condones exposure to dangerous sources, if such exposure is commonly accepted in society at large. A person may rely on a measure of Divine Providence to protect him no less than the many who are safely delivered from such danger. As the Gemara *Shabbat* 129b puts it, "since the multitude are accustomed to doing this . . . it may be considered permissible, since 'the Lord preserveth the simple' [Ps. 116:6]." Once such an explanation is adopted, it becomes entirely possible that even Emden would not disagree, for in rejecting gallstone surgery he stated explicitly that "even though many have undergone this procedure and survived, many have also hastened their death as a result of this surgery"; i.e., the procedure in his time was indeed fraught with danger, with perhaps an equal number of patients succumbing as surviving the experience. Well might he agree to permit a more established procedure, with fewer, albeit real, attendant risks.[80]

---

78. See A. S. Avraham, "Nisyonot Refu'iyim," p. 24, reporting on correspondence with Rabbi Auerbach. See Rabbi Braun, *She'arim ha-Meẓuyyanim be'Halakhah* 190:4.

79. For a detailed discussion of this principle, as related to the hazards of cigarettes, alcohol, and nonmedical drugs, see *Jewish Ethics and Halakhah for Our Time*, vol. 1, pp. 221–243.

80. There is a connected—although separate—issue dealing with the permissibility of cosmetic plastic surgery, intended to deal with purely psychological pain or anguish related to physical deformities that are a source of social discomfort. May a person undergo such a procedure in spite of the risks inhering in every surgical situation? For a detailed review of sources, see Bleich, *Halakhic Problems*, 1:119–123.

SUMMARY AND CONCLUSIONS

We are now in a position to summarize our findings on the halakhic stance toward several issues involved in scientific research and hazardous practices involving human subjects and patients.

There is clearly an obligation to take direct action to save an endangered life—based on the prohibition against standing idle while another is imperiled. The duty extends to hiring others and undertaking the financial costs requisite to do the job (according to R. Meir Abulafia, Rosh, and Rema), but where the victim can afford it he is required to reimburse for all expenses incurred. According to R. Yeḥiel Weinberg there is no limit to monies properly spent in this cause.

Such intervention extends to every life-threatening situation, whether actual or only contemplated. Maimonides, as well as others, explicitly includes medical treatment in this obligation. There is, however, some debate of a philosophical nature as to the propriety of interfering with nature. While a minority (Ibn Ezra and Naḥmanides in particular) consider medical intervention a compromise of faith in Providence, the majority (based on numerous talmudic sources) consider the practice of and recourse to medicine to be in the best traditions of social and religious responsibility. Indeed under the rubric of *pikuaḥ nefesh*—the saving of life—cardinal principles of Judaism were set aside temporarily, including the Sabbath, major festivals, and kashrut. Such action extended even to situations of doubtful danger, where there was a less than certain threat to life.

But in the context of medical research, a more direct issue is that of self-endangerment. May a person allow him or herself to be exposed to hazardous conditions for the sake of saving another's life? Where a person wishes to volunteer for certain or probable death, most agree with the view of R. Akiva that there is no such obligation. Whether a person may volunteer if he so wishes is a matter of debate: Rabbi Unterman forbids such self-sacrifice, Rabbi Weinberg permits and even praises it. The minority view is that of Ben Petura, requiring self-sacrifice—but even there it is only where there is significant extension of life to be gained for the endangered party.

Where the contemplated action involves only a possible, but not probable prospect of death to the intercessor, there is further debate. Based on a passage in the Yerushalmi, a minority view (associated with the *Hagahot Maimoniyyot*) requires intervention. The majority sees no such obligation of self-endangerment, even where the victim faces certain death and the onlooker only possible death. This majority view, including Maimonides and the *Shulḥan Arukh*, argues that the Bavli differs with the Yerushalmi. This generated a debate over the interpretation of three key passages in the Bavli—as well as the Yerushalmi.

Consequently one could say that while all the talmudic passages are controversial, on balance the position of the Bavli, in its majority interpretation, won out. Thus one would not be obligated to face any peril whatsoever—but neither is one prohibited (where one's own death is unlikely to happen). There is one statement of Maimonides that is debated among modern halakhists, relating to the issue of saving many lives. One interpretation—put forward by R. Meir Simḥah of Dvinsk—would have Maimonides forbid self-endangerment even then, while others (notably Rabbis Unterman and Weinberg) reject such an interpretation.

This last issue has particular relevance for medical research, where a healthy person volunteers for some risk in order to save many endangered people. The majority view, it would appear, would permit such self-endangerment, even according to Maimonides. On the question of odds and degree of risk, a major source is the Radbaz, who writes that a person may entertain danger under such circumstances where the likelihood of his death is less than fifty–fifty. But where it could go either way (i.e., fifty–fifty), and certainly where death is likely or probable, such imperilment would be foolish and prohibited. The *Arukh ha-Shulḥan* counsels common sense and calculated risk, weighing the odds so as to act prudently without, however, being guilty of "just standing there doing nothing."

But what if the party facing imminent death is oneself? May one elect to risk even that limited life-span in the hope of finding long-term survival? Medically speaking, may a patient facing imminent death be treated in a manner that might cure him or kill him? Here there is ample scriptural precedent in the story of the four lepers who undertook precisely such a risk—and were saved. The Gemara quotes this instance to permit recourse to dangerous treatment where the only alternative is imminent death, saying that we may well disregard the limited life that remains. Apparently long-term survival, even if doubtful, is preferable to short-term life, even if certain. This position was accepted by all authorities.

But there was some debate over the odds involved. Some (including the Aḥi'ezer) would accept even the remotest of odds, as long as there was some chance of long-term survival. But most would stand by the requirement of at least even odds of survival with the contemplated treatment. Anything less than this is considered unacceptable. Rabbi Moshe Feinstein requires better than even odds of success; where it is fifty–fifty, he leaves room for some choice, for whereas most people would take such a risk, some might not—they may choose what they will. Anything less than even odds, however, R. Moshe forbids.

Another approach is that of R. Jacob Emden, who says that whatever the odds, there should be at least some proven therapeutic benefit associated with the contemplated treatment. A treatment which is entirely experimental and unproven to date need not be taken; but a patient nonetheless can, if so desired, choose such treatment, as long as it is not known to be dangerous.

One further question, the duration of "limited life," is also raised. Here the consensus (notably the Aḥi'ezer, R. Solomon Kluger, and R. Feinstein) appears to set the limit at twelve months of life where every day might be the patient's last. Anything beyond this is considered a normal life. In all such matters, says the Shevut Ya'akov, there should be a two to one majority of physicians in agreement over the efficacy of the steps to be taken—and also consultation with rabbinic authority in each case.

Finally, where the self-endangerment is not to save one's life, but rather to secure relief from enduring pain, the Meiri and the Rema both appear to permit hazardous therapy or surgery. And while R. Emden appears to forbid this, upon further examination it would appear that even he would permit such a course where the contemplated treatment is commonly practiced and the dangers widely assumed. In such cases, even though there is a possibility of immediate death, one may fall back on a measure of Providence to assume that one will be part of the clear majority who survive. This approach accords with the doctrine that "the Lord preserveth the simple."

To return to the case with which we began this excursus, several conclusions are indicated:

1. There is certainly an obligation to save the endangered life of another person, especially when one is in a position to act as a result of one's knowledge, training, or circumstance. This extends to the thwarting of "nature," or what some might call "God's will." Thus a physician is obliged to heal wherever he or she can.

2. Where fulfilling this obligation puts one at risk, several caveats apply: no one, not even a physician, is required to expose him or herself to certain or even probable death to save another person. Where the risk factor to the physician is only possible but not likely to cause death or disease, the majority and normative view would not require the physician to expose himself to such risk. The choice in this instance can be left to the individual. At the same time if the risk factor is as high as 50 percent, it would appear that the Halakhah would forbid such exposure. In the present case, where the likelihood of contamination is small, the choice can be left to the individual physicians, and their decisions are to be respected.

3. As to the question of experimental treatment that might shorten life: the patient may take the chance—but only if the physician feels that there is a good likelihood of a successful outcome. In the present case the odds are not sufficiently encouraging—it would seem that further testing not involving human subjects is called for. The patient, following the majority view, should not agree to the trial.

3

Organ Transplantation

Introduction

Few areas in modern medicine or science have generated as much debate and discussion as the field of human organ transplantation. The prospect of mass replacement of ailing human organs with healthy human parts procured in morally legitimate fashion has excited the public imagination. Organs that are currently viewed as able to be transplanted include kidneys, livers, corneas, bones, bone marrow, hearts, lungs, skin, and cartilage. Many of these procedures are viewed as life-saving for the recipient patients.

Organ transplantation currently occurs on a widespread basis: as of 1987, in the United States, on an average day, one heart, twenty kidneys, and sixty-five corneas were being implanted. It seems that all that prevents an even greater level of this surgery is the shortage of suitable donor organs. According to one estimate, as many as twenty-two thousand potential donors each year do not give their organs, leaving many who hope for such organs to die before medically matched donors are found.

Yet organ transplantation surgery raises many questions for professionals, ethicists, religious leaders, and laymen alike. These questions came to the fore in the late 1960s with the first heart transplants, but many of them apply to other organs as well. The initial issue involved high-risk procedures that promised little chance for long-term survival. Then the problem of organ procurement arose: were donors really dead at the time their organs were removed; if alive, was the surgeon committing homicide by shortening that life? Where the donor continued to live, what risk factors could be considered acceptable? What of the use of organ banks to store organs indefinitely, not just for implantation, but for purposes of research and teaching?

The questions were made the more pressing with the widespread medical use of so-called brain-death criteria to establish that the donor has in fact died. In a number of states laws were passed to facilitate and encourage the donation of organs immediately following death, either through prior consent (such as driver's-license consent forms) or state laws requiring hospitals to approach next of kin to consider organ donation from the deceased. As of the end of 1987, federal law has required all hospitals to identify all such potential donors, so that their families might be approached to consider such organ donation.

Yet many are troubled by these developments: are all brain-dead patients truly dead and without hope of resuscitation? What of ever more sophisticated means of resuscitation? How are scarce organs allocated—by what criteria are recipients chosen when choices have to be made? Furthermore such transplants can be extremely costly—taking away resources from other more conventional medical treatments and priorities—is this justifiable?

More recently attention has been focused on the use of babies born without most of their brains, but with the brain stem intact, as donors, and the morality of keeping such infants (known as anencephalics, practically all of whom die within days of birth) alive on respirators, so as to remove their organs for transplantation into other infants at the appropriate moment. The question, inter alia, is whether it is permissible to prolong human life for the sole purpose of providing organs to another?

For the Halakhah these questions are magnified by several other considerations. On the one hand there is the clear awareness of the imperative to save lives at almost any cost, human life being of infinite value. But on the other hand there are concerns for the rights of the donor—both in life (not to shorten life by one iota) and in death (so as to avoid the desecration of the cadaver, and to carry out proper burial). Many halakhically sensitive individuals are confronted with a dilemma over the permissibility of signing cards that would permit postmortem use of their organs to save the lives of others; is such permission forbidden, obligatory, or merely permitted? Thus it becomes a question of achieving a delicate balance: how to fulfill one commandment, without at the same time violating another—always a problematic situation. These concerns are heightened by traditional texts and customs that have served over the centuries to define life and death, procedures and practices hallowed since time immemorial.

The issue for Jewish law is how to respond to these issues, which are on the cutting edge of modern science, in a balanced yet forthright fashion. It is to the halakhic response to this challenge that this chapter is devoted.

The Question

A fifty-year-old man suffers from severe degenerative heart disease. His physicians inform him that unless he undergoes heart transplant surgery, he cannot expect to live more than three months at most, during which time he will be bedridden and in pain. If a compatible heart can be found for him, and if transplant surgery is undertaken, he has a good chance of extending his life for three years or more, while enjoying a relatively normal existence. On the other hand, given his weakened condition, he might not survive the surgery at all, and there is the possibility that the transplanted heart might fail or be rejected by his body. Should he agree to become a candidate for a heart transplant?

This case raises the following questions:

1. When may a seriously ill patient risk whatever life remains to him in order to gain long-term life-expectancy?
2. A donor heart will need to come from an accident victim, and be removed at the earliest possible moment to preserve the viability of the organ. What is the earliest time that the heart, or other organs, can be removed from the donor's body?
3. Where there is no question that death has already occurred, are there any prohibitions regarding the removal of the cadaver organs for transplantation, given the concerns of Jewish law that the cadaver be treated with utmost respect?
4. Is it permissible to transplant organs other than the heart that come from living donors who wish to sacrifice an organ, thereby possibly endangering their own lives in order to save another?
5. In the matter of the artificial heart, we can ask whether there can be life without any natural heart, or is life synonymous

with the heart? Is there any difference in this regard between the temporary use of a heart-lung machine during surgery and the use of an artificial heart?

The Sources

A. Deuteronomy 21:23
His body shall not remain all night upon the tree, but thou shalt surely bury him the same day.

B. Exodus 21:12
He that smiteth a man so that he dieth, shall surely be put to death.

C. Mekhilta, Exodus 21:12
From here we learn that one is not put to death, unless the victim was a viable person [*ben kayyama*].

D. Mishnah, Avodah Zarah 29b
The following objects, owned by idolaters, are forbidden for benefit to the Jew: . . . the heart of an animal . . . (*Rashi* to 32a: idolaters would remove the heart of an ox while it was still alive, through a round hole they made in the chest of the animal.)

E. Avodah Zarah 29b
How do we know that a cadaver is one of the things that may not be utilized for some other benefit? It is learnt by analogy to the sacrificial calf, where the word *sham* appears, just as it does at the death of Miriam, teaching that just as the calf is known to be forbidden, so is the human cadaver. And how do we know that the calf is forbidden? The school of Yannai prove it by analogy to Kodashim.

F. Sanhedrin 78a
All agree that one who kills a *treifah* (Rashi: such as one whose windpipe or brain membrane are perforated) is not liable to punishment (*Rashi:* the unanimity implies that as a result of the evident damage to his vital organs, he is considered as a dead person, a *gavra katila*.)

G. Nedarim 22a

Ulla was on his way to Israel when he was joined by two men from Ḥozai. All of a sudden one arose, killing his fellow. He turned to Ulla and said, "Was I right?" Ulla answered, "Yes, and go ahead and cut his throat all the way." When he came before R. Yoḥanan, he said, "Perhaps I encouraged the criminal improperly?" R. Yoḥanan, answered, "You [correctly] saved your life."

H. Sanhedrin 46a–47a

Whoever delays the burial of the dead transgresses a negative commandment, but if he delays it to honor the dead, or to bring a casket and shrouds, there is no transgression. . . . We have learned that for the sake of honor it may be delayed. Is this for the honor of the deceased? No, it is for the honor of the survivors. Do we really delay burial for the honor of the survivors? Yes, for the verse says that you may not leave him unburied on the tree (A), i.e., delay that involves shame, similar to being left on the tree. Thus where there is no such shame, it is not forbidden (Rashi: thus where the honor of the survivors is increased, there is no shame, and delay is permitted).

I. Ḥullin 11b

Said Rav Kahana: we derive the principle of majority (*rov*) from the murderer. For the Torah mandates the death penalty, yet how can we ever be sure that the victim was not a *treifah* (about to die anyway), and the crime is not punishable? Apparently from here we learn that we follow the majority of cases. And if you say that this is not true, in that we always examine the victim, and therefore do not rely on *rov*, how is that possible, for such an examination will certainly violate the cadaver? And if you say that we should indeed violate the cadaver in order to save the life of the accused, we can answer that such an examination is never conclusive, in that it is always possible that the evidence of dire sickness in the victim could have been obliterated by the sword of the killer at the time of the killing. Thus it must be that we rely on *rov*.

J. Bava Meẓia 84b

When R. Elazar b. Simon was about to die he said to his daughter: "I know that the sages are angry with me. (*Rashi:* because I was responsible for the arrest of many thieves, some of them related to the sages.) Consequently they will not take care of my remains in the proper manner. When I die place my body in the attic and have no fear." [Many years later] the daughter reported that the body had been left there no less than eighteen years, and possibly even twenty-two years.

K. Arakhin 7a–7b

Mishnah: We may use the hair from the cadaver of a dead woman. *Gemara*: Why is this permitted, is it not one of the things that are prohibited for use? Said Rav: "It speaks of a case wherein she had left instructions to give her hair to her daughter." And if she were to say, "Give my daughter my arm," would we do that? Said Rav: "We are speaking of a false wig of hair."

L. Maimonides, M.T. Hil. Roẓeiaḥ 2:8

One who kills a *treifah*, if the *treifah* can eat, drink, or walk in the street, is not punished in a human court. Every person is presumed to be fully viable [*shalem*], hence a killer is to be executed unless it is known for certain that the victim was a *treifah*, in that physicians attest that the victim had suffered from an incurable and terminal condition that would have killed him had nothing else intervened.

Discussion

1. HAZARDOUS TRANSPLANT SURGERY: FACING THE ODDS

We have seen in chapter 1 that there is a rabbinic consensus that would permit patients with a limited life-expectancy to undergo hazardous treatment or surgery in the hope of acquiring long term survival, even where that treatment poses a threat of immediate death. "Limited" in this context is generally assumed to refer to a period up to twelve months' duration.

A critical question is the degree of likely success or failure involved, i.e., what is the risk from that procedure? From our examination it would be appear that there is significant disagreement on this matter. The view of the Aḥi'ezer and *Shevut Ya'akov* is that even low odds of full recovery suffiçe to endorse hazardous surgery where death is imminent without that procedure. Rabbi Moshe Feinstein at first (in 1961) concurred with this view, but by 1972 had revised his position to agree with the *Mishnat Ḥakhamim* to say that a patient may elect to undergo hazardous surgery only if there is a fifty-fifty chance of success. He then adds that where the odds favor a successful outcome of the proposed procedure (i.e., more than a fifty percent chance of success), such surgery should be considered mandatory.

In addressing the risks involved in heart-transplant surgery, these considerations obviously are important. Thus in a responsum of 1968, Rabbi Feinstein bases his clear opposition on the overwhelming failure of the procedure to extend the life-expectancy of the recipients, which in his view falls far short of what is required by the Halakhah for such hazardous undertakings. He also pointed out that in many cases there is a significant possibility that the recipient would live in any case for a number of years without the transplant. For such patients, he says, such a transplant makes no sense whatsoever, given the comparative survival rates. Indeed Rabbi Feinstein expresses surprise that the civil authorities permit such transplants, and in his view those who carry out the surgery should be prosecuted for double homicide, insofar as patient consent is based on misleading counsel and information.[1]

At about the same time, Rabbi Eliezer Waldenberg came to very similar conclusions: he too requires fifty-fifty odds of a successful outcome, as opposed to the then current mortality rates of two out of three. In addition he questioned whether such radically new and experimental procedures are included in the Torah's mandate to the physician to heal.[2]

Rabbi Isser Yehudah Unterman also addressed this issue in an article written in 1969. Taking note of the poor success rate of heart transplants, he issues an unequivocal prohibition against the procedure. He then goes on to consider the minimal survival rates necessary to permit this surgery, and in so doing goes one step beyond Rabbi Feinstein's position. He argues that those authorities who permit hazardous procedures or therapy where there is only a small chance of success do so because, to start with, the patient possesses a legal presumption of life (*ḥezkat ḥayyim*). But where that presumption is inoperative or absent, even they would admit that one cannot rely on an unlikely possibility of recovery. Rabbi Unterman then postulates that it is the very act of removing the diseased heart of the recipient that compromises his *ḥezkat ḥayyim*, in that the heart is synonymous with, and represents, life itself. Consequently one may not rely on minimum odds of success to recover from the surgery. One would need to have a strong likelihood of success (i.e., much better than fifty-fifty odds) before undergoing such a procedure.[3]

Others, however, disagree with Rabbi Unterman's thesis. Thus Rabbi Menaḥem Kasher argues that while it is true (as we saw in chapter 2) that the Ḥakham Ẓvi is of the opinion that the moment the heart is removed life ceases,[4] other authorities differ with this position. Notably Rabbi Joseph Saul Nathanson, in the *Responsa*

---

1. *Responsa Iggerot Moshe, Y.D.* 2:174 (1).
2. *Responsa Ẓiẓ Eliezer* 10:25 (5). The responsum is undated.
3. Rabbi I. Y. Unterman, *Torah she-be'Al Peh* 11 (5729):15–18. This was reprinted and enlarged in the author's collected essays entitled *Shevet mi-Yehudah*, pp. 367 ff. See also *Noam* 13:1–9 and 16:13 ff.
4. See above, Chapter 2.

Sho'el u-Meshiv, points to several talmudic passages that describe how an animal may live for some time after its heart has been removed (D). Accordingly, Rabbi Kasher concludes, a transplant recipient does not lose his *ḥezkat ḥayyim*, his presumption of life, upon removal of his heart—he remains fully alive for some time, at least until the new heart is implanted.[5] He adds that this is certainly true where the functions of the heart are assumed by a heart-lung machine, so that the blood continues to circulate throughout the body. Rabbi Feinstein too, in a responsum of 1970, makes it clear that in his view life can continue for some time after removal of the heart; and the recipient who lives for some months thereafter has the full status of a living human being.[6]

Even so, Rabbi Kasher forbids heart transplants, given the poor success rate as of the writing of the article (in 1970). He does anticipate improvements in this regard (even mentioning the artificial heart as a possibility), but stipulates that even so every case would have to be adjudicated separately and on its own merits and circumstances. Rabbi Moshe Shternbuch also issued a strong rejection of heart transplants, given the track record as of 1969,[7] as did Dr. Ya'akov Levy, an Israeli physician and author.[8]

In a subsequent responsum, written in 1978, Rabbi Feinstein returned to the subject once more, only to reiterate his opposition on the grounds of the poor prognosis facing the recipient. While he recognizes that a few patients might have their lives extended by a few months, such a benefit is severely vitiated by the great pain and suffering that they must experience.[9] He notes that as of his writing the transplant procedure had been largely suspended, with the exception of certain "expert" surgeons by way of research. This he attributes to the fact that "the nations of the world are not sensitive to murder." Thus he remained completely opposed to the resumption of such surgery, as of that date.[10]

---

5. Rabbi M. Kasher, *Noam* 13 (5730): 10–20. Rabbi Kasher notes that this article was written in response to a request by Rabbi Unterman, in the latter's capacity as Ashkenazi Chief Rabbi of Israel.

6. *Responsa Iggerot Moshe, Y.D.* 2:146 (at end).

7. Rabbi Moshe Shternbuch, *Ba'ayot ha-Zeman le'Or ha-Halakhah* (Jerusalem, 1969).

8. Y. Levy, *Noam* 12 (5729): 306 ff.

9. It should be noted that this concern is consistent with his position, seen in chapter 2, that is opposed to the need to resuscitate where great suffering will be the result.

10. *Responsa Iggerot Moshe, H.M.* 2:72.

As a result of these and other rabbinic pronouncements, whether or not they were in agreement with Rabbi Unterman's approach, an early consensus emerged in opposition to the procedure. Indeed the medical community itself came to share these conclusions, faced with the overwhelming negative survival rates of heart-transplant patients (about two hundred of whom died within a short time). As Rabbi Immanuel Jakobovits pointed out in prohibiting the surgery in 1975, the rabbinic rejection of the procedure represented "an impressive example of religiously motivated suspicions and hesitations anticipating, and eventually being vindicated by, the subsequent conclusions of scientific evidence."[11]

In spite of these negative views, however, more recent data have shown encouraging developments that would eliminate this halakhic concern. Since 1978 there has been significant improvement in the long-term survival of heart recipients, when compared to those candidates for transplant surgery who do not undergo the procedure for lack of a donor organ. While there are several reasons for these improvements, the major factor has been the use of the immunosuppressive drug Cyclosporine. As described in the 1984 report of the International Heart Transplantation Registry,[12] the four-year survival rate of patients undergoing a heart transplant since 1978, when treated with Cyclosporine, is seventy-one percent. Without benefit of this drug, the rate drops to thirty-five percent. The one-year survival rate with Cyclosporine is close to ninety percent. These figures become all the more significant when it is recognized that among those candidates accepted into heart-transplant programs, but for whom an appropriate donor heart could not be found, more than ninety percent died within three months of being admitted to the program for transplantation.[13] Given such success rates, there is room to argue that at least for those patients who can benefit from Cyclosporine, heart transplants should no longer be classified as experimental, but as therapeutic in nature.[14]

11. Rabbi Immanuel Jakobovits, *Jewish Medical Ethics* (New York, 1975), pp. 286–290.

12. Michael P. Kaye et al., *Journal of Heart Transplantation* 4, no. 3 (May 1985): 290–292.

13. See also Rabbi R. Fink, *Journal of Halakhah and Contemporary Society* 5 (Spring 1983): 63–64.

14. Such too is the conclusion of Rabbi Tendler, as recorded in *Mount Sinai Journal of Medicine* 51, no. 1 (January/February 1984): 55.

Such a conclusion would seem to follow from our earlier discussion wherein authorities such as Rabbis Feinstein and Waldenberg permit hazardous procedures as long as there is a fifty percent chance of success. With the rising rate of long-term survival, most objections based on medical prognoses would be answered. It will be recalled that one of the views discussed in the chapter on hazardous therapy was the view of R. Jacob Emden, who insisted that such therapy pass the test of being proven, i.e., beyond the experimental stage. This would appear to be the case with these latest statistics, at least for certain patients and in certain institutions. As well there has been a more careful screening procedure, in that candidates must have end-stage cardiac disease (i.e., without the transplant their prognosis is less than twelve months' life). This eliminates the concern that patients might live indefinitely anyway without the hazards of surgery. In any case the entire question of *ḥezkat ḥayyim* was raised only by way of requiring more favorable odds of success, a requirement which would appear to be satisfied by these ongoing improvements in mortality rates.

We should also address the related, although somewhat different, question raised by kidney transplants. Patients with chronic kidney failure have access to either dialysis or a kidney transplant, using either a live donor or a cadaver organ. The question may be formulated thus: where a patient can continue to receive dialysis treatment indefinitely, thereby prolonging his life, under what circumstances may he choose to receive a kidney transplant, thereby freeing himself of the constraints associated with dialysis, but at the same time exposing himself to the higher risks associated with such surgery?

Again some recent statistics are in order, based on Canadian results. In 1984 thirty percent of all dialysis patients were on waiting lists for transplantation. Only eight percent did not want such surgery, the rest were simply medically unsuitable. Of those on the waiting list about seventy-five percent were actually transplanted. Of the total transplants performed, eighty-four percent were successful—and the rest returned to dialysis. As to survival rates, those receiving kidneys from live donors boasted an eighty-seven percent three-year survival rate, whereas cadaver organs enjoyed a fifty-nine percent three-year survival. For patients under sixty-five years of age, the rates were eighty-nine percent and eighty-five percent respectively.[15]

Rabbi Moshe Meiselman contends that the decision to have a kidney transplant should depend entirely on respective survival rates, not considerations of convenience or pain. He quotes the Magen Avraham that a Jew is required to undergo a measure of pain and discomfort if that will prevent the loss of his fellow's life,[16] and he argues that this should be even more true of saving one's own life. Thus he feels that the inconveniences associated with dialysis should not figure in the decision to undergo the surgery, which should be based entirely on the likelihood of survival.[17] Rabbi Meiselman, it would appear, does not consider the fact that even in the eventuality of failure of the transplanted kidney, conventional dialysis can be resumed as before, thus eliminating the threat of failure of the transplanted organ.

Of course one could argue that the actual transplantation surgery itself is dangerous, as with all surgery that carries a statistical possibility of death. The question is similar to the one raised in the context of elective cosmetic surgery, i.e., may one choose to undergo surgery that is not medically required? The consensus on that issue has clearly been to permit such surgery where the goal is to eliminate psychological stress, whether it be in finding employment or a marriage partner. As Tosafot to *Shabbat* 50b puts it, a state of mind which prevents a person from commingling with people constitutes pain as the Halakhah would understand the term.[18] In the case of dialysis, few would disagree with the premise that ongoing dialysis is fraught with discomfort, pain, and a significantly restricted lifestyle that hampers normal social interaction. Accordingly, the issue of statistical danger of surgery might well be disregarded.

What if kidney transplantation offers a better chance of survival, as is often the case? Here Rabbi Meiselman agrees that surgery becomes permissible, by reason of safeguarding and extending life, i.e., one may choose a risky procedure if it bears the best hope of long-term survival.

---

15. *Canadian Renal Failure Register*, December 1985, pp. 97–119.
16. *Magen Avraham* to *Y.D. O.H.* 156.
17. Rabbi M. Meiselman, *Halakhah u-Refuah*, 2:114–121.
18. A useful summary of the literature on this topic is found in Rabbi J. David Bleich, *Judaism and Healing* (New York, 1981), pp. 126–128.

Of course here, too, the earlier described minimum odds would be required. In addition, as we shall see, there is the question of risk to the kidney donor.[19] Interestingly, in 1984 there was actually a decrease in the number of kidney transplants using the organ of a living related donor (from fifteen to eleven percent). This may represent concern about the future prospects of the donor with respect to overall health and the risks of life with only one kidney.[20]

It is clear, then, that kidney transplantation has gone beyond the realm of the experimental. It is an accepted medical procedure, and organ recipients enjoy a high success rate, with dialysis available as a backup option. Thus it would appear that in evaluating the permissibility of kidney transplantation, the success rates and likelihood of failure should not currently pose a halakhic problem.

2. *REMOVING ORGANS FROM THE BRAIN-DEAD BODY*

In chapter 2, we discussed the halakhic definition and determination of the time of death. That question is central to the issue of heart transplantation, in that donor hearts are necessarily taken from patients who are no longer living. At the same time, a successful transplantation requires that the donor heart be removed immediately following death, while it is viable, fresh, and capable of resuming all its cardiac functions. Thus in practice most donor hearts are taken from brain-dead patients, whose hearts continue to beat until they are removed. Consequently heart transplants are predicated for the most part on the acceptance of brain death as sufficient proof that death has occurred. It is of utmost importance, therefore, that the criteria of death be established and agreed upon, especially vis-à-vis brain death.

As we saw in the earlier chapter, the classic halakhic criteria of death as formulated by the Ḥatam Sofer (at least as he was understood by most commentators) require the total absence of independent breathing, heartbeat, and movement. The presence of any one of these, therefore, indicates that death has not yet

19. This is especially true where the kidney malfunction can be traced to some hereditary factor which may turn up at a latter stage in the donor, who is directly related to the recipient.

20. See *Canadian Renal Failure Register*, p. 99.

occurred. Later authorities require in addition that even where these vital signs are absent, death may not be declared until some time has elapsed, indicating that the lack of vital signs is irreversible. But what if a patient depends on artificial life-support systems that "maintain" his vital signs? Here we encounter a difference of opinion.

On the one hand is the view that as long as the heart continues to beat unaided, life persists, even though breathing can only be maintained with the help of a respirator. This argues that life is identified with the heart—and brain death must be accompanied by heart failure before a patient may be certified as dead. According to this view, if the heart or organs are removed from such a patient, it would be tantamount to murder, and be clearly forbidden.

Yet others disagree, and feel that brain death, properly defined, is the functional equivalent of death by decapitation in the Halakhah. This, they argue, is true whether or not the heart continues to beat, for it is not the heart that is the seat of life, but the brain (including the brain stem), in its coordinating and integrative capacity. This view, identified primarily with the revised opinion of Rabbi Moshe Feinstein, would permit the removal of the heart from such a "patient," in that the patient is, correctly speaking, deceased already.[21] As we saw in that chapter, by the end of 1986 this position was endorsed by the Israeli Chief Rabbinate, which permitted removal of the heart from brain-dead patients, under carefully controlled guidelines.

Yet it is still possible that even the restrictive view might contemplate permission on other grounds. Specifically, is it possible that even if the so-called brain-dead patient is still alive, the Halakhah would consider him either a *treifah* (because of his condition he has less than twelve months to live) or a *goses biyedei adam* (about to die as a result of human malfeasance)? According to the Talmud (F), there is no statutory punishment

---

21. In a symposium dedicated to this issue, and published in the Israeli journal *Assia*, 5739, pp. 183–201, several views are put forth, including one by Rabbi Barukh Rabinowitz. In his article he permits removal of life support to facilitate organ transplantation, yet makes this dependent on a certainty that, once disconnected, both heart and lungs of the donor will cease to function. Putting aside the question as to how such certainty can be ascertained, his position is basically similar to that of Rabbi Feinstein.

for killing a *treifah* (which is also true, according to the majority view, of the *goses biyedei adam*).[22] Maimonides accepts this principle and codifies it into law (L). Does it follow, then, that such a patient might be sacrificed if that will allow another to live indefinitely?

This very question was debated in the nineteenth century by Rabbi Ezekiel Landau (the *Noda bi-Yehudah*) and his contemporary Rabbi Isaiah Pick. The former states categorically that it is forbidden to sacrifice the life of a *treifah* to save the life of a *shalem* (one who enjoys a normal life expectancy).[23] He invokes the rhetorical question of the Talmud, "Why do you think your blood is redder than his?" Yet Rabbi Pick disagrees. So too does R. Joseph Babad (the *Minḥat Ḥinukh*), when he permits a group of Jews facing a murderous enemy to sacrifice one of them who is a *treifah*, if that will indeed save the rest of the group, because "such a person is not considered a *nefesh* [a viable human being]."[24]

Rabbi Yehudah Gershuni, discussing these various views,[25] notes that the position of the *Noda bi-Yehudah* is quite consistent with the *Mekhilta* (C) to the passage in Exodus (B), which does not apply capital punishment to the killer of a *treifah*, yet does imply that the act itself is forbidden as homicide. And even Maimonides (L), in removing the death penalty from the killer of a *treifah*, implies that the act is illicit, and punishable at the hands of God. As a matter of fact, R. Meir Simḥah of Dvinsk notes that Maimonides' formulation leads to the conclusion that while a court does not punish this homicide, the Israelite King can carry out the death penalty for this crime, in his capacity as administrator of extrajudicial law.[26]

On the other hand, those agreeing with Rabbi Pick, to permit the sacrifice of the *treifah*, consider homicide to refer only to where the victim is a *ben kayyama*, i.e., has long-term viability. As the Talmud puts it, *gavra ketila katal*, "he is killing a dead man," in the interests of saving a live one. This reasoning is taken

22. See *Encyclopedia Talmudit* 5:396, 1:160.
23. *Responsa Noda bi-Yehudah, Mahadura Tinyana H.M.* 59.
24. *Minḥat Ḥinukh*, positive commandment 296.
25. Rabbi Y. Gershuni, *Kol Ẓofayikh*, pp. 375 ff. This is an expanded version of his article in *Or ha-Mizraḥ* 18, no. 1 (Tishri 5729): 133–137.
26. On this subject, see *Jewish Ethics and Halakhah*, vol. 1, pp. 155 ff.

one step further by R. Israel Lipschutz, to permit the sacrifice of a person whose death is certain and imminent, even where there is only a doubtful chance that it will save a second life.[27] He brings support for this contention from the Gemara in *Nedarim* 22a (G), where it is recounted that Ulla found himself alone with two violent men. One arose and struck the other, fatally. As the victim lay dying, the attacker turned to Ulla and, with a threatening demeanor, inquired whether he approved of the act. Fearing for his life, Ulla agreed with the man, urging him to finish the job and decapitate the victim completely. The only justification that R. Lipschutz can find for Ulla's response is to say that while Ulla could have remonstrated with the murderer, such overt disagreement might have raised the killer's ire and cost Ulla his own life. Thus he decided to encourage the killer to hasten the victim's death, in a desperate attempt to save his own life, even though his own survival remained in jeopardy anyway. From this he concludes that "even though we must safeguard momentary life, that is only where there is no counterbalancing life. Where there is viable life on the other side, certainly that life is to be preferred to the momentary life at hand, even where the latter is certain and the former is doubtful."

Given these two views, which is the correct one? Rabbi Eliezer Waldenberg considers the question in the context of heart transplants and emphatically rejects the lenient view.[28] (Parenthetically he considers an accidental victim facing death to be, not a *treifah*, but a *goses be-yedei adam*, similar to one who was attacked by his fellow.) He further quotes Maimonides' view that the courts themselves can carry out the death penalty on an emergency basis, even in those cases where the death penalty cannot be implemented by conventional means.[29] He also invokes Maimonides' view that prohibits the killing of one to save another, an act which Rabbi Waldenberg finds analogous to removal of a beating heart for transplantation. It should be noted, though, that Maimonides does not explicitly include killing a *treifah* in this prohibition.

But what of the permissive view of the *Minḥat Ḥinukh?* As a

27. *Tiferet Yisrael, Boaz*, to *Yoma* 8:3.
28. *Responsa Ẓiẓ Eliezer* 10:25 (5).
29. Maimonides, *M.T. Hil. Roẓeiaḥ* 2:5.

matter of fact, Rabbi Waldenberg quotes an even earlier authority, the late-thirteenth-to-early-fourteenth-century Meiri, who states clearly that when confronted with a threat to their lives, a group of Jews may properly sacrifice one of them who is a *treifah* rather than all be killed.[30] To these views, Rabbi Waldenberg answers as follows:

1. The *Noda bi-Yehudah* is supported in his view by several other important authorities, including the *Tiferet Ẓvi* and the Maharam Lublin, who came to their conclusions even though the view of the Meiri was known to them through secondary sources. Accordingly, one can presume that they discounted the view of the Meiri.

2. Even though the Meiri merely permits the group to hand over the *treifah* to the enemy, this does mean that he would also allow them to kill the *treifah* with their own hands, as does the surgeon who removes a beating heart.

3. In referring to the case of Jews confronted with a murderous enemy, the request is for an unspecified member of the group, all of whose members are equally at risk. Accordingly each Jew can argue that the *treifah* should be the one selected, given his limited life-expectancy anyway. But in the heart transplant, the *treifah* is not threatened with immediate death to start with, he is simply being selected to save another. And it makes no difference that the *treifah* is in agreement, for such a decision would be considered invalid on the grounds that it is made under duress or despair. And even if this were not true, his life is not his to give away.[31]

Yet Rabbi Gershuni disagrees, and inclines to permit the removal of the heart of a *treifah*, or *goses*, in order to save the life of another. He furthermore understands Maimonides to be saying (L) that whereas the *treifah* status of an animal is completely determined by the signs of disease as defined by tradition, this is not the case with human *treifot*, whose status and prognosis are to be ascertained by the attending physician.

In yet another responsum, Rabbi Yiẓḥak Ya'akov Weiss strenu-

---

30. Meiri to *Sanhedrin* 72a, quoted too in *Shiurei Knesset ha-Gedolah, Y.D.* 157, and by Rabbi Jacob Emden, *Even Boḥen* 1:79. On this passage in Meiri, see below, p. 000.

31. See *Jewish Ethics and Halakhah*, vol. 1, chap. 3, for a discussion of suicide and voluntary euthanasia.

ously opposes the removal of the heart for transplantation.[32] In the first place he points out that it is forbidden to shorten the life of the *goses* by any active means. Furthermore, he argues, most authorities agree that we even suspend the laws of the Sabbath in order to save the momentary life of a *goses*. And as the *Shevut Ya'akov* states, the only time that we may properly handle and move a *goses* is where the intention is to attempt a treatment that offers some hope of his recovery or stabilization.[33] Failing that intent, we dare not do anything that might speed up his death (although we can remove anything which impedes the natural course of events leading to death).[34] In addition one cannot argue from the view of the Jerusalem Talmud that a person is obligated to endanger himself to save the life of his fellow.[35] For that obligation is suggested only where the danger to oneself is uncertain, and one might well survive the peril. It certainly does not apply where the contemplated course of action involves the certain death of the intercessor. Thus Rabbi Weiss concludes that it is forbidden to shorten the life of a *goses* in order to lengthen the life of another person, especially where the results of the transplant are in doubt anyway.

In another article, Rabbi Ḥayyim Dubber Gulevsky takes up many of these issues.[36] First he establishes that it is forbidden for an individual to give up his own life to save that of another. What is permissible, even according to the *Noda bi-Yehudah*, is self-sacrifice to save many lives, as found in several places in the Talmud. Rabbi Gulevsky quotes the Radbaz[37] to the effect that there is no obligation to donate one's organs to save another. But while the Radbaz indicates that one who puts himself in danger by sacrificing such an organ is a *ḥasid shoteh*, an overzealous fool, there is no prohibition per se against doing precisely that, for after all "he does save an Israelite soul." Going one step beyond this, Rabbi Gulevsky then refers to the *Yad Eliyahu*, who states that an individual may choose to endanger himself to save the life

32. Rabbi Yiẓḥak Ya'akov Weiss, *ha-Ma'or* 20, no. 7 (Ellul 5728): 3–7.
33. *Responsa Shevut Ya'akov* 3:75.
34. See *Jewish Ethics and Halakhah*, vol. 1, chap. 3, for a discussion of this distinction as it emerges from the halakhic sources.
35. See above in chap. 1.
36. *Ha-Ma'or* 21:1, pp. 3–16; 21:2, pp. 22–28; 21:3, pp. 11–12.
37. *Responsa Radbaz* 1052.

of one wiser than he. Thus he concludes that such self-exposure to danger is not forbidden, even though a third party may not shorten one life to save another.

As to the *treifah* and *goses*, Rabbi Gulevsky is of the view that an accident victim is in the category of a *goses biyedei adam*, his condition being the result of a specific act or event; thus one who hastens his death is not subject to judicial punishment. Nonetheless the act itself is prohibited, as demonstrated by the *Noda bi-Yehudah*. Rabbi Gulevsky adds that this is especially true in light of the fact that some time must pass after death has occurred before death can be certified, by which time the organs will have deteriorated beyond the point of viability.

Thus it is that those halakhists who consider the brain-dead patient to be alive, for the most part (with the exception of Rabbi Gershuni) oppose removal of his heart even if he is categorized as a *goses* or *treifah*. It is only those who accept brain death who would favor the removal of vital organs, once it has been established that true brain death has occurred, giving rise to a situation of functional decapitation.

3. THE USE OF CADAVER ORGANS

The human body possesses a special aura even after life has departed, hence it must be treated with dignity and respect. More specifically there are several prohibitions that must be observed in dealing with the final remains, prohibitions that are relevant to the use of the cadaver organs for transplantation. There are three major issues: dishonor of the body (*nivul ha-met*), utilizing the body (*hana'ah min ha-met*), and timely burial (*halanat ha-met*).

Nivul ha-Met

The Torah in Deuteronomy (A) demands that the body of an executed criminal not be left unburied overnight, but is rather to be accorded a speedy and dignified burial. The *Sifri* extrapolates from this that any maltreatment bringing dishonor to the body is forbidden. And the Gemara in *Sanhedrin* (H) takes this as the basis of a general principle that extreme care must be exercised to ensure that the body not be exposed to indignity (*bizayon*).

This consideration would apply to any defacement or mutilation of the cadaver. Does this then forbid incisions such as those necessary to remove the cadaver organs for transplantation? The question is essentially whether there are any legitimate circumstances in which the integrity of the cadaver may be violated. What if there is no intentional *bizayon* or indignity, but rather the fulfillment of the wishes of the deceased?

The Gemara *Ḥullin* 11b (I) provides the basis of a solution to this question. In establishing the biblical sanction of *rov*, by which we rely on statistical majorities, it refers to the death penalty mandated for homicide. The question is this: how can the death penalty ever be carried out, given the possibility that the victim was a *treifah*, which as we have seen voids the death penalty of his killer? It must be, says the Gemara, that majority rule applies, and we can assume that he was not a member of the tiny minority of *treifot*. But is it not possible that the cadaver is thoroughly examined, and we do not rely on such presumptions alone? The answer of the Gemara is that such an examination is not done, for it would violate the cadaver. But why not do so anyway, after all a man's life is at stake (i.e., that of the accused)? The answer: such an examination would not be conclusive, for the killer's sword might have obliterated all the evidence of mortal illness, hence there is no justification for postmortem violation of the cadaver.

It is quite clear from this passage that the prohibition of *nivul ha-met*, mistreatment of the cadaver, is biblical in origin (although others debate this question). Furthermore, in theory at least, the prohibition would be set aside if in so doing the life of another human being could be effectively saved. These considerations lie at the basis of the major halakhic discussion of the propriety of autopsies, given the integral role of dissection of the dead in the cause of the advancement of medical knowledge, and the ineluctable fact that all autopsies involve the mutilation of the body in one degree or another. With the establishment of the State of Israel, and its medical requirements, the issue became a cause célèbre, generating an extensive corpus of halakhic literature. From that debate certain principles do emerge, impacting directly on the issue of cadaver organ transplantation.

The key halakhic exchange occurred in the nineteenth century, occasioned by a responsum written by the same R. Ezekiel Landau, the *Noda bi-Yehudah*. It was his view that a cadaver may be violated when the intent is to bring direct benefit to a living patient who is "before us" (*be'faneinu*).[38] In his view such an act cannot be considered a gratuitous or unjustifiable assault on the human body; to the contrary it may be taken as an honorable gesture redounding to the credit of the deceased. But the key caveat to emerge from this responsum is that such a procedure may not be done in the context of a general intent to advance the cause of science of medicine. Such a nonspecific framework is too vague, its concrete and direct effects are too unreliable, to justify the very specific and immediate violation of the corpse at hand. Thus it is only where the autopsy will provide immediate knowledge to benefit another known sufferer from the same disease that we can permit that particular autopsy to be performed. Other contemporary authorities concurred with this ruling of the *Noda bi-Yehudah*, most notably the Maharam Schick.[39]

Opposed to this relatively lenient ruling stood R. Jacob Ettlinger, author of the *Responsa Binyan Ẓion*.[40] He argued that it is unfair to compromise the prior rights of the deceased even if it is in order to save the life of an endangered human being. To buttress his view, he quotes Rashi's comments to *Bava Kamma* 60a, that it is forbidden to save oneself at the cost of the assets of one's fellow. He likewise points to several talmudic passages that forbid self-preservation involving the exploitation or compromise of the rights of others, whether it involves their bodies, their possessions, or their reputations.

But what if the deceased had indicated prior to death his willingness to have his body violated for a particular purpose? Can *nivul ha-met* be set aside by prior agreement, or where it is clear that the deceased would have wanted or favored such a step? R. Malkiel Tannenbaum of Lomza answered the question in 1901, by saying yes.[41] He argued that to honor the wishes of the dead is quite consistent with the honor due them. Thus even where there is no express agreement, if it can be reliably established that such would be his wishes, or that such a step would be to his honor (*likhvodo*), his body may be disinterred and an autopsy

38. *Responsa Noda bi-Yehudah, Mahadura Tinyana, Y.D.* 210.
39. *Responsa Ḥatam Sofer, Y.D.* 336.
40. *Responsa Binyan Ẓion* 170–171.
41. *Responsa Divrei Malkiel* 5:60.

performed. This would be the case where the intent would be to identify his killer for the sake of justice, or to prevent the death of others.

A similar view was articulated in the nineteenth century by Rabbi Joseph Saul Nathanson,[42] to permit the suspension of the prohibition against *nivul ha-met* for the sake of identifying the remains to facilitate the remarriage of an *agunah*, i.e., a woman whose husband had disappeared. In so doing, Rabbi Nathanson lays down the general principle that what is prohibited is unnecessary violation of the dead, but where there is legitimate need (*ẓorekh gadol*), the corpse may be violated. In other words, it is not just to save life that *nivul ha-met* is set aside; other situations qualify as well.

In applying this discussion to the question of transplants, contemporary authorities make a number of careful distinctions. Rabbi Isser Yehudah Unterman, in the context of corneal transplants, points out that underlying the ruling of the *Noda bi-Yehudah* is the concern for *pikuaḥ nefesh*, the saving of life, so that even if violating the cadaver is incompatible with benefiting another, still the prohibition would be set aside in the interests of saving another's life, as are other commandments of equal or greater severity.[43] Nonetheless the potential beneficiary must still be present, as required by the *Noda bi-Yehudah*.

But what does "present" mean, in an age where there is instantaneous communication over large distances, where organs can be transported thousands of miles in a matter of hours, while they are yet fresh and viable? Rabbi Unterman answers unequivocally that as long as the intended recipient of the organ, or of the pertinent information, can receive it timeously, the patient must be considered "present," even if he be across the country, "for the entire country must be considered *be'faneinu*, or as if right here." But where the harvest of information or organs is intended to be stored or banked for some future use, the prohibition of *nivul ha-met* is triggered.

It is still necessary, however, to determine what is or is not properly considered of a lifesaving nature. While the issue is

---

42. *Responsa Yosef Da'at, Y.D.* 363, as well as his *Responsa Shoel u-Meshiv* 1:231.

43. *Shevet mi-Yehudah*, p. 368.

relatively simple in the context of vital organs, there is some debate regarding other organs, most notably corneal transplants. While all would agree that a person who is completely blind is in heightened danger of a fatal accident, and therefore a transplant for such a person would be permitted by most authorities, some are opposed to *nivul ha-met* where the intended recipient does have one functioning eye. Thus Rabbis Yekutiel Greenwald and Yeḥiel Weinberg are opposed in this case, while Rabbis Unterman and Yiẓḥak Liebes permit it.[44] In addition Rabbi Greenwald insists that where the entire eye is removed from the cadaver, once the cornea has been implanted, the rest of the eye tissue must be properly buried. One authority, Rabbi S. Hubner, is opposed to corneal transplants altogether, on the grounds that even a totally blind person cannot be considered in any special danger of his life.[45]

Rabbi Ovadiah Yosef likewise finds grounds to permit the removal of the eye for a corneal transplant, but he adds several caveats. Firstly this should, if at all possible, not be done to a Jewish cadaver when there is a Gentile cadaver available; secondly, permission should be secured from the potential donor while he is yet alive; thirdly, once the cornea itself has been utilized, the rest of the eye should be returned for burial. In any case, even in the absence of these conditions, Ovadiah Yosef permits the use of cadaver organs "after the fact" (*be'di'eved*), where the potential recipient wishes to avail himself of organs improperly harvested.[46]

The area of non-Jewish cadavers presents a separate area of discussion, i.e., does the prohibition of *nivul ha-met* apply equally to Jewish and Gentile cadavers? Here too there is a significant difference of opinion. On the one hand there are those who believe that the prohibition is aimed at Jews alone. This is the view of Rashi, Tosafot Yomtov (R. Yomtov Lipman Heller), and the Ḥatam Sofer, as well as the *Responsa Or ha-Meir*.[47] On the other hand, Naḥmanides and, in our own time, Rabbi Joseph Dov Soloveitchik consider the prohibition to apply equally to non-

44. See respectively *Kolbo al Aveilut* 1:45, *Responsa Seridei Esh* 2:20, and *Noam* 14:28 ff.
45. *ha-Darom* (Nissan 5721): 54–64.
46. *Responsa Yabia Omer* 3, *Y.D.* 23.
47. See Rashi to Deut. 21:33, and *Responsa Or ha-Meir* 34.

Jews.[48] As to the rationale of the former view, the words of Rabbi Abraham Isaac ha-Kohen Kook are relevant: the prohibition of *nivul ha-met* is uniquely applicable to the Jew, an extension of the commandments that require the Jew in his lifetime to sanctify himself with special foods and other behavioral patterns. Just as the Gentile does not observe those commandments intended to preserve the sanctity of the Jewish body and the singular spirituality of the Jewish people during life, so too there should be a clear appreciation of the unique halakhic concerns affecting the Jewish body after death.[49]

Hana'ah min ha-Met

The Gemara in *Avodah Zarah* 29b (E) substantiates the prohibition against the benefit or use of a cadaver by analogy to the ritual of the *eglah arufah*, or slaughtered calf, as encountered in Deuteronomy 21. Maimonides too codifies this law that it is forbidden to use a cadaver for some other purpose or extraneous benefit.[50] Furthermore, according to most authorities, including Rashi, Rabbeinu Tam, Naḥmanides, the Shakh, and the Ḥatam Sofer, the prohibition is based on the Torah itself.[51] How then can we permit the use of cadaver organs to benefit another party?

One approach is based on the view of R. Jacob Emden. He is of the opinion that the prohibition is not biblical in origin but merely rabbinic, and thus, like all rabbinically prohibited substances, it may be permitted for medical treatment.[52] Another approach is found in the writings of R. Solomon Kluger, who writes that the reason for the prohibition in the first place is to ensure a timely burial that will prevent the dishonor of the cadaver, but once the bulk of the remains have been buried, the law allows that individual organs may be utilized without going against the original prohibition. As pointed out by Ovadiah Yosef

48. See Naḥmanides' comments to Deut. 21:23; *Torah she-be'Al Peh* 6:64. For a review of this question, see Rabbi J. David Bleich, *Contemporary Halakhic Problems* 2:56–60.

49. *Responsa Da'at Kohen* 199.

50. Maimonides, *M.T. Hil. Avel* 14:1.

51. Respectively, in Rashi to *Sanhedrin* 47b; Rabbeinu Tam as recorded in *Sanhedrin* 48a; Naḥmanides as mentioned in the *Kesef Mishnah*, *M.T. Hil. Ma'akhalot Asurot* 4:4; *Sh.A. Y.D.* 79:3; and *Responsa Ḥatam Sofer*, Y.D. 336.

52. *Responsa She'elat Yaveẓ* 1:41. See also Rema to *Sh.A. Y.D.* 155.

and others, this line of reasoning could well apply to the posthumous implantation of individual organs, as long as the rest of the body is properly buried.[53]

Rabbi Unterman offers an original solution to the problem of using cadaver organs by suggesting that upon implementation the organ is no longer to be considered dead tissue. Being literally revitalized in the body of the recipient, the prohibition of *hana'ah min ha-met* is no longer applicable to it. He brings support for his view from the fact that whereas the Talmud in *Niddah* inquires whether those resurrected from death are a continuing source of impurity, it does not inquire whether such people, having been dead, may be of benefit to others. Rabbi Unterman concludes that once revivified, the body and its organs are no longer prohibited for use.[54]

There is yet another avenue of leniency. It is the view of the Radbaz that even if the prohibition is biblical in origin, what is forbidden is only conventional uses of the cadaver, but not non-conventional ones, such as medical treatment.[55] Others, such as Rabbi Akiva Eiger, disagreed.[56] In considering these views, Rabbi Moshe Feinstein concluded in a responsum of 1958 that even for medicinal purposes, cadavers are forbidden; but he does permit the beneficial use of non-Jewish bodies.[57] Such a position is based on the Jerusalem Talmud, the Shakh, and R. Elijah of Vilna—all of whom are of the opinion that a Gentile cadaver is not subject to this prohibition.

Other contemporary authorities also prohibit the use of a Jewish cadaver. Such is the view of R. Yiẓḥak Ya'akov Weiss, who argues that it is unreasonable to assume that the deceased has any obligations toward the living, for the dead are free of any and all commandments.[58] Rabbi Waldenberg also prohibits the removal of organs from a Jewish cadaver for purposes of implantation. He agrees with R. Shalom Gagin (the Yismaḥ Lev,) that under no circumstances may an organ be removed from the dead,

---

53. *Responsa Yabia Omer* 3 (*Y.D.*): 178; *Responsa Tuv Ta'am ve'Daat* 285. See Rabbi Gershuni, *Kol Ẓofayikh*, pp. 384 ff.
54. *Shevet mi-Yehudah*, pp. 54–57.
55. *Responsa Radbaz* 3:548. See also *Responsa Shivat Ẓion* 62.
56. See his comments to *Sh.A. Y.D.* 349.
57. *Responsa Iggerot Moshe, Y.D.* 1:229.
58. *Ha-Ma'or* 20:7; *Responsa Minḥat Yiẓḥak* 5:7–8.

in light of the credo of the future resurrection of the dead in both body and soul. Rabbi Waldenberg does, however, allow the use of a Gentile cadaver.[59] He also permits, after the fact, the implantation of organs improperly taken from a Jewish cadaver, i.e., where the organs had been removed and stored—and are now available to a particular recipient in some danger of his life. In other words, while the organ may have been improperly removed, once done, it may be utilized.[60]

Yet there are others who take a more lenient stance. Ovadiah Yosef does side with the Radbaz and a long list of subsequent authorities, including R. Solomon Kluger and the Ḥida, who are of the opinion that nonconventional benefit from a cadaver is not prohibited. Thus, for medical purposes, and certainly in the context of organ transplantation, Ovadiah Yosef permits the use of cadaver organs, even those of a Jew.[61]

Halanat ha-Met

In an earlier chapter we saw that the Torah requires that the deceased be accorded a speedy burial.[62] Thus there is a question that arises when an organ is removed and permanently implanted in another—is the burial of that organ improperly delayed?

The Mishnah itself (H) indicates that the obligation to carry out immediate burial is set aside in order to accord honor to the dead, i.e., where more time is required to complete proper funeral arrangements.[63] The Gemara (H) explains that the original concern is for *bizayon*, or shameful treatment, or as Rashi puts it, that any delay might demonstrate a lack of concern for the dignity of the body.[64] This being the case, it follows that where the delay is intended to add dignity or honor to the deceased, even a delay of several days can be allowed.[65] Indeed there is a story, recounted in *Bava Meẓia* (J), that R. Eleazar b. Simon instructed his family not to his bury his body for many years, out of fear that the burial

59. *Responsa Ẓiẓ Eliezer* 13:91.
60. Ibid. 14:84. For this and several other sources, see A. Abraham, *Nishmat Avraham, Y.D.* pp. 261 ff.
61. *Responsa Yabia Omer* 3 (*Y.D.*) 21.
62. See chap. 2, sec.3.
63. *Sanhedrin* 46a.
64. Rashi ad loc.
65. *Piskei Tosafot, Sanhedrin* 105.

would not be accorded due respect by his colleagues, and as a result it was left unburied for at least eighteen years.[66] While such a case was surely unusual, it did nonetheless establish a precedent for legitimate delayed burial. Yet it is not clear that even this precedent can apply to transplanted organs, for the intent in that and other talmudic cases was always to preserve and enhance the honor of the deceased himself, whereas in transplants there is no tangible benefit to the donor; it is rather for the benefit of the recipient.

Yet there is room for a different approach to the problem of organ burial. Is it possible that once the major part of the body has been buried, the requirement of burial has been satisfied? In other words, is there an obligation to bury individual organs, even after the rest of the body has been interred? The Jerusalem Talmud implies that burial necessarily refers to the entire body (the expression is *kulo ve'lo mikẓato*),[67] and Naḥmanides appears to accept this principle.[68] In addition, the Tosafot Yomtov rules that as long as a single organ remains unburied, the obligation of burial has not been fulfilled.[69] Yet others disagree. Thus the *Mishneh le'Melekh* points out that the Jerusalem Talmud itself no longer considers a cadaver to be a *meit miẓvah*, or body in need of burial, once the head and major portion of the remains have been buried.[70]

Among contemporary halakhists, there is a significant difference of opinion. Rabbi Yekutiel Greenwald, in agreeing with the Tosafot Yomtov, is of the opinion that individual organs do indeed require burial. He points out that the Jerusalem Talmud permits a priest to defile himself in the process of burial of such organs, even after the rest of the body has been properly buried. Indeed, as he points out, the *Shulḥan Arukh* accepts this as law. And he argues that even the saving of the life of the recipient is not sufficient cause to suspend the requirements of burial, in that unlike the case of the living, there is no obligation on the deceased to compromise its dignity to save the life of another.[71]

---

66. See *Bava Meẓia* 84b, and the Maharsha ad loc. On this passage see Rabbi Ben Ẓion Firer, *Noam* 4 (1961): 202.

67. J. T. *Nazir* 7:1.

68. Naḥmanides, *Torat ha-Adam* 43a.

69. Tosafot Yomtov to the Mishnah, *Shabbat* 10:5.

70. *Mishneh le'Melekh, M.T. Hil. Avel* 14 (end).

71. *Kolbo al Aveilut*, pp. 46–47, with reference to *Sh.A. Y.D.* 374, and Shakh, ad loc. See also in the same volume, p. 183.

Similarly, Rabbi Waldenberg stands opposed to deferred organ burial, arguing that it will interfere with the eventual resurrection of the dead, which requires that the body be buried intact—or at least to be so intended by the deceased, before death.[72]

Yet others disagree, on the grounds that the early sources are referring to cases where there is no subsequent burial at all of the organs in question. Thus, Rabbi Meir Steinberg points out that when the Gemara in *Arakhin* (K) forbids a woman to bequeath her arm to her daughter, it assumes that the arm will never be buried. This, he argues, is not the case with organ transplantation, insofar as upon the eventual death of the recipient, the organ will surely be accorded full burial rights.[73] And along similar lines, Rabbi Unterman, invoking the principle of revivified organs (see above), sees no need to insist on burial of an organ that has come back to life, and is no longer in need of burial, at least until the death of the recipient.

In an extended examination of this question, Rabbi Yiẓḥak Liebes reviews the discussion in the Jerusalem Talmud, and concludes that while the latter is of the opinion that the entire body must be buried, all of the major codifiers disagree, once the major part of the cadaver is properly interred. The reason is the familiar principle of majority (*rov*) (I), which in this instance considers the major part of the body to account for the entirety (*rubo ke'kulo*).[74]

There is another consideration in favor of delayed organ burial. As we have seen, delay is permitted for the honor of the deceased. Thus if it be true that the donation of his organs after death accrues to the credit of the deceased, and brings general approbation to his memory, then it could fairly be argued that organ donation is sufficient reason to allow indefinite deferral of the burial of that organ until the eventual death of the recipient. This would certainly be the case where prior to death, the deceased indicated his desire to donate the organ, on the basis of the principle that "it is to a man's credit to have his wishes fulfilled"

---

72. *Responsa Ziẓ Eliezer* 13:91.

73. Rabbi M. Steinberg, *Noam*, 3:94, 4:202. See Rabbi R. Fink, "Halakhic Aspects of Organ Transplantation," *Journal of Halakhah and Contemporary Society* 5 (Spring 1983): 48–49.

74. Rabbi Yiẓḥak Liebes, "be'Inyan Hashtalat Evarim," *Noam* 14 (1971): 51–59.

(*reẓono shel adam zehu kevodo*).[75] Even Rabbi Ettlinger, in forbidding autopsies where a beneficiary is present, does allow an autopsy where the deceased had given express permission prior to death.[76]

Such is the variety of views engendered by the juxtaposition of two simultaneous obligations—the one requiring proper treatment of human remains, and the other that calls for the saving of one's fellow's life. Faced with their conflicting demands, the various halakhists resolve the issue in a variety of ways, but always faithful to the dictates of rabbinic sources and reasoning.

4. TRANSPLANTING ORGANS FROM A LIVING DONOR

While the issue of living donors does not arise in heart transplants, for obvious reasons,[77] other procedures, such as kidney or bone marrow transplants, do pose the risk of acceptable risk to the donor. Thus we may well ask if it be permissible to sacrifice one kidney to a sibling with kidney failure, leaving the donor with only one remaining kidney.

In chapter 1 we examined the issues of self-endangerment in general. We saw that while according to most authorities a person may not expose himself to certain death in order to save another, the situation is different where death is unlikely to follow from such risk. There are two major schools of thought, one being the Jerusalem Talmud (which requires self-endangerment to save another), and the other the Babylonian Talmud (which does not, at least according to the majority of codifiers). It was the Babylonian view which became normative.[78]

Granted, however, that one is not obliged to endanger oneself to help another, does that mean that one is forbidden from such self-exposure even if one wishes to take the chance? Clearly the minority view that accepts the Jerusalem Talmud (including the Ḥavvot Yair and Rabbi Unterman) would see no prohibition here. But what of the majority? And more specifically, what if it is not simply some possible danger from which one might emerge com-

75. *Sefer Ḥasidim* 152; J.T. *Peah* 1:1.

76. *Responsa Binyan Ẓion* 170; Steinberg, p. 93.

77. One reported exception occurs where a donor himself receives a transplanted heart/lung combination, as a result of deterioration of his own lungs.

78. See above, chap. 1, sec. 2.

pletely unscathed, but the certain and permanent loss of an organ of one's body?

The key text on this issue is a responsum of the Radbaz. The question, as put to him, was whether a Jew could agree to the demand of a tyrant to remove his ear, by way of saving the life of an imprisoned fellow Jew. The questioner reasoned thus: surely if the Sabbath, a cardinal principle of Jewish law, may be desecrated in order to save life, an organ may be sacrificed for the same purpose. The Radbaz answered as follows: if we do set aside the Sabbath to save life, that is only where the danger originated in heaven, and was not of human making. But it is unheard of to expect a man to have to sacrifice an organ, when to do so might conceivably endanger his life. For this reason, he argues, the sages refused to take an eye for an eye—lest it somehow lead to death. More generally, he states,

> The laws of the Torah should be understood as fostering a harmony that is in full agreement with rational thought. Hence it is inconceivable that a person should agree to be blinded in one eye, or have a hand or foot amputated, so that others not kill his fellow. Therefore I see no basis for such a law, other than when undertaken as a voluntary act of piety, and blessed is the man who can reach such a level. But if there is the possibility of danger to his life [*safek sakanat nefashot*] then he who does this is a pious fool [*ḥasid shoteh*], for his life [when exposed to even doubtful danger] takes precedence over that of his fellow [even though it be certain danger].[79]

This responsum gave rise to a number of varying interpretations in the context of organ donors. On the one hand it has been understood to prevent any action that could pose risk to the life of the donor. Thus, in an undated responsum, Rabbi Waldenberg refers to the Radbaz as the primary source for his view that opposes any risk whatsoever on the part of a donor. He furthermore takes the position that even the Jerusalem Talmud and the *Hagahot Maimoniyyot* would agree. For they allow self-endangerment only because one can rely on a measure of Providence to emerge unscathed from the danger—which is not the case where

79. *Responsa Radbaz* 627.

the organ will certainly be removed, and permanently so. Thus he forbids the removal of an organ unless there is clear medical evidence that there is no danger to the donor whatsoever.[80] Likewise the *Minḥat Yiẓḥak* quotes the Radbaz in support of his contention that because the loss of an organ represents significant, albeit statistical, danger to the donor, whether at the time of the surgery or subsequently when he might have need of that organ, it is forbidden to donate such an organ.[81] Rabbi Pinḥas Barukh Toledano, reviewing the sources, comes to the same conclusion.[82]

But others rely on the Radbaz to come to a more permissive position. Thus Ovadiah Yosef understands Radbaz to be speaking only of real danger, i.e., a fifty percent possibility of death.[83] He quotes the Radbaz elsewhere as saying that even Maimonides allows a small risk in saving a drowning fellow, and that therefore it is only a fifty-fifty risk (*safek shakul*) that must be avoided by a donor. Where the risk is of far lesser order, one is required to act, or else to risk being in violation of the prohibition against standing idly by at the impending death of one's fellow. Accordingly, says Ovadiah Yosef, because kidney donors have but a one percent or two percent risk of death, the procedure is certainly permissible. In a similar vein Rabbi Shaul Yisraeli comments that the Radbaz refers only to the loss of organs that impede the full functioning of the donor and would render him a *ba'al moom*, physically defective. But where the body can function fully without that organ, and the medical risk factor is very small, as in the case of a kidney donor, there is no convincing reason to forbid the procedure.[84]

So too Rabbi Moshe Meiselman extrapolates from the Radbaz that as long as the kidney recipient stands a better chance of survival than he does with dialysis, anyone who wishes to donate a kidney for that recipient may certainly do so. He furthermore avers that this is true even where the likelihood of success is only

80. *Responsa Ẓiẓ Eliezer* 9:45.
81. *Responsa Minḥat Yiẓḥak* 6:103.
82. *Barkai* 3 (Fall 1985): 23–36.
83. *Responsa Yeḥaveh Da'at* 3:84; *Halakhah u-Refuah* 3:61.
84. *Barkai* 3 (Fall 1985): 35–36, in his editorial comments.

slightly more than fifty percent.[85] One case where a donor should not sacrifice a kidney, as pointed out by Rabbi Moshe Hershler, is where the donor may be susceptible to the same hereditary kidney disease as the recipient, especially where donor and recipient are related to each other. In this case the donor's own remaining kidney is at risk, obviously a direct threat to life.[86] Rabbi Hershler adds that while we permit kidney donation, this is not the case where the intent is merely to avoid the inconvenience of dialysis as an alternative to transplantation. For while we are prepared to condone some risk in order to save an endangered life, where dialysis provides an equally effective safeguard of life for the intended recipient, even the Radbaz would forbid the removal of the donor kidney. This leads to the conclusion that such a patient should rather receive a cadaver organ if he wishes to avoid the difficulties involved in protracted dialysis. Of course this assumes that the issues raised earlier in the context of cadaver organs are properly addressed.

Rabbi Waldenberg, it would appear, has since changed his position. In a later volume of his responsa,[87] while repeating his concerns and reservations, he recognizes that the Radbaz in fact differentiates between danger to life and danger posed to a specific organ. Thus, in spite of his reservations, Rabbi Waldenberg accepts the principle of organ donation as long as the overwhelming odds are favorable to the donor. In so doing, he quotes Rabbi Jacob Emden, who permits the removal of an organ in order to save the life of a fellow human being.[88] This is as long as medical opinion is confident that both donor and recipient will in all likelihood survive.

In addition there are some authorities who do not merely permit organ donation, but actually require it, if in so doing one will save a life. This seems to be the opinion of Rabbi Yeḥiel Mikhel Epstein, author of the *Arukh ha-Shulḥan*, who says that it is improper to miss an opportunity to save another life.[89]

---

85. *Halakhah u-Refuah* 2:118. While Rabbi Meiselman speaks of identical twins whose success rate is relatively high, current success rates would allow for matching of donors and recipients beyond such limiting circumstances or immediate family connections.

86. Ibid. 2:125.

87. *Responsa Ẓiẓ Eliezer* 10:25, pp. 5–12.

88. *Migdal Oz be'Even Boḥen* 1:83.

89. *Arukh ha-Shulḥan H.M.* 426:4. This is consistent with the writings of R. Menaḥem Recanati, in the fourteenth century.

Finally, we can mention a lengthy responsum by Rabbi Moshe Feinstein, who also understands the Radbaz as permitting a person to expose himself to merely possible danger (*safek nefesh shelo*) in order to avert certain danger to one's fellow.[90] Again Rabbi Feinstein stresses that while such selflessness is praiseworthy, it is no way to be considered obligatory. And even though it is normally forbidden to expose oneself to danger in the process of avoiding a Torah prohibition, nonetheless here a life is to be saved—thus a possible risk may be permitted. A similar view is attributed to Rabbi Shelomoh Zalman Auerbach,[91] and is also articulated by Rabbi Liebes.[92]

5. THE ARTIFICIAL HEART: LIFE WITHOUT A HEART

In an earlier chapter, in discussing the determination of death, we encountered the question of the possibility of life without a heart.[93] Likewise, earlier in this chapter, in section 1, we examined in brief the question of the presumption of life in the absence of a fully functioning heart. This issue is central to the matter of the artificial heart and its effect on the continuity of life. Thus it would be helpful to take another, more detailed look at the issues raised there.

There were two diametrically opposed positions: the Ḥakham Ẓvi was of the opinion that without a natural, functioning heart, life ceases immediately (even though some nerve and muscle activity might continue temporarily). R. Jonathan Eibeschutz, on the other hand, accepted the remote possibility that other organs might assume the function of the heart, thus allowing for life without a heart present.

The Ḥakham Ẓvi makes it quite clear, in the course of his responsum, that his view is that the tradition viewed the soul as residing in the heart, and that the other organs depend completely on a fully functioning heart. In this, he says, there is no difference between humans and animals.[94] And even according to

90. *Responsa Iggerot Moshe, Y.D.* 2:174 (4).
91. *Nishmat Avraham, Y.D.*, p. 66.
92. *Noam* 14 (1971): 28–35. See also R. Yehudah Gershuni, *Kol Ẓofayikh*, pp. 391–397.
93. See above, chap. 2, sec. 1.
94. *Responsa Ḥakham Ẓvi* 77.

R. Eibeschutz, life may continue without a heart only because there is some other natural organ that takes its place and provides its function. If so, one may legitimately ask whether by removing the diseased heart from a patient, and replacing it with an artificial pump, is one not removing the basis of his life, effectively rendering him a nonviable human being?

Sure enough, on the basis of the Ḥakham Ẓvi, certain contemporary halakhists forbid heart transplants and artificial heart implants. Thus Rabbi Unterman writes that even Rabbi Eibeschutz assumed life to persist without a heart only because he believed some other natural organ took its place. Where there is no such natural transfer, but merely the surgical removal of the heart, the basis for life too is negated. Thus Rabbi Unterman introduced the notion of *ḥezkat ḥayyim*, the presumption of life, which in his opinion is irreparably destroyed by the very act of the removal of the recipient's own heart.[95] Accordingly, he concludes, the surgery must be forbidden, as it constitutes homicide. Rabbi A. L. Grossnass agrees with this conclusion, and adds that were such a person to be killed at a later time, his murderer would technically not be guilty of homicide. Such considerations would obviously extend to the implantation of a permanent artificial heart. Rabbi Waldenberg apparently also agrees with Rabbi Unterman that upon removal of the heart, the patient is no longer to be considered living—until such time as he is literally brought back to life with a transplanted natural heart.[96]

Yet it is precisely this point which is a matter of debate. Rabbi Joseph Saul Nathanson quotes the Gemara in *Avodah Zarah* (D) which refers to the pagan rite that removed the heart from a living ox, apparently intending the unfortunate beast to live for a short while thereafter.[97] And the author of the *Da'at Torah* endorses this conclusion by quoting the analogous passage in the Jerusalem Talmud that compares the removal of the heart to the severance of the windpipe without severing the gullet of an animal—an act which certainly does not cause instantaneous death.[98] In line with this, the *Knesset ha-Gedolah* ruled, in

95. *Shevet mi-Yehudah*, pp. 371 ff.
96. *Responsa Ẓiẓ Eliezer* 10:25 (5).
97. *Responsa Sho'el u-Meshiv* 108.
98. *Da'at Torah*, *Y.D.* 40, with reference to J.T. *Avodah Zarah* 2:3.

opposition to the Ḥakham Ẓvi, that a chicken found to be without a heart is to be considered nonkosher and defective.[99]

On the basis of these sources, Rabbi Menaḥem Kasher comes to the conclusion that death is not the automatic consequence of the removal of a functioning heart, for life can continue for some time thereafter. And if physicians can extend that time period until a replacement heart can become functional, death can be said to have been averted altogether.[100] He reinforces this view by referring to several other passages: *Ḥullin* 32b assumes that a cow's life can continue for some time even after the heart has been effectively stopped (in this case by the severance of the windpipe); the Rashba considers an animal to remain alive as long as there is residual movement (*pirkhus*) even after severance of both windpipe and gullet;[101] and Jonathan b. David ha-Kohen of Lunel explicitly extends this assumption to humans, saying that a man who gives a writ of divorce subsequent to the severance of his windpipe and gullet, is considered to have acted while alive.[102] In other words, says Rabbi Kasher, such a person can be said, in the talmudic phrase, "to have passed from life, but not to have reached death." This state of suspended animation prevails until the situation is resolved with finality either way. And if an artificial heart is implanted, it too prevents the onset of death. Where the life-expectancy is extended indefinitely, the person with the artificial heart is to be considered fully alive.[103]

Very similar conclusions are reached by Rabbi Ḥayyim Dubber Gulevsky. He argues that the Ḥakham Ẓvi was referring only to the overt absence of a natural heart without any obvious substitute. Where substitute means provide the functions of the heart, even the Ḥakham Ẓvi would admit that life has not ceased. This, says Rabbi Gulevsky, is surely the case in all instances of open-heart surgery where the heart is temporarily immobilized and its functions taken over by artificial pumps. Why should the physical

99. *Knesset ha-Gedolah, Y.D.* 40.

100. Rabbi Menaḥem Kasher, *Noam* 13 (1970): 10–20.

101. Rashba, *Torat ha-Bayit he-Arokh, Hil. Treifot* 2:3.

102. *Avodat ha-Leviyyim* to *Ḥullin* 29b, in Kasher, pp. 14–15.

103. It should be noted that as of 1987, such permanent implantation of the artificial heart is no longer performed; instead the artificial heart is used exclusively as a bridge until a suitable donor heart can be found and transplanted. This in turn raises other ethical questions, most particularly that of triage, i.e., who gets the donor hearts that are in such demand?

removal of the diseased heart, while its functions are assumed by the same machines, be any different? Thus it is his view that life would continue without interruption even in the case of the permanent artificial heart.[104]

Rabbi Moshe Hershler makes the point that the Halakhah does not recognize any nonmiraculous revival of the dead. Where a patient is resuscitated by medical means, after a complete absence of vital signs, it must be said that death did not occur in the interim—whereas life persisted in some residual undetected form, until the vital signs were restored. The result of this thesis is that the removal of a diseased heart that is followed by implantation of a donor heart, is to be viewed as uninterrupted life.[105] Furthermore, he asserts, the heart does not possess any inherent spiritual status as separate from the brain, in that it is an organ that can be replaced without violating the spiritual integrity of the person. Thus the principle of the artificial heart does not in his view present any unique halakhic problems.

One other contemporary halakhist who takes issue with Rabbi Unterman is Rabbi Ḥayyim David Regensburg. He argues that if the presumption of life is vitiated upon removal of the diseased heart (as Rabbi Unterman argues), the same would have to be true of all open-heart surgery that involves the temporary immobilization of the heart. This, he says, is demonstrably not the case, in that patients subject to such surgery continue all other functions in normal, uninterrupted fashion. Furthermore he questions the very issue of "presumption of life" in this context, saying that in halakhic literature this principle is invoked only where there is genuine ignorance as to the whereabouts or condition of a person known previously to have been living. But in this instance, the person is present, and the facts of his condition are known. Thus there can be no question whatsoever that he is to be presumed, and pronounced, a living human being.[106]

Finally we can refer to the responsum of Rabbi Moshe Feinstein, written in 1970 in response to Rabbi Gulevsky. Although he says that the function of the heart goes beyond merely pumping blood, and that it maintains life even after it has stopped beating,

104. Rabbi Ḥayyim Dubber Gulevsky, *ha-Maor* 29; no. 1 (1969): 27–28.
105. Rabbi M. Hershler, *Halakhah u-Refuah* 4:87–89.
106. Rabbi H. D. Regensburg, *Halakhah u-Refuah* 2:3–8.

nonetheless it is his considered view that life does continue even after the heart has been physically removed. As he explains, life is a function of both heart and brain, but if their role can be effectively taken over by other means, life will persist. And he specifically affirms the continuity of life through the process of a heart transplant, even though he stood opposed, as of that time, to the implementation of the heart transplant on other grounds, i.e., the poor record of success.[107] While Rabbi Feinstein does not refer to the artificial heart, it is a short step from this reasoning to an endorsement of the principle of the artificial heart as a means to extending life, all other concerns being satisfied.

Thus it would appear that for the majority of authorities, life can be said to continue uninterrupted in the absence of a heart—as long as some alternative means of blood circulation is adopted. If the use of an artificial heart does that, it can be utilized without compromising the spiritual integrity of the recipient. In addition the artificial heart would eliminate certain other doubts relative to the natural heart transplant, i.e., determination of death, the use of cadaver organs, and the shortage of donors, as seen earlier.

SUMMARY AND CONCLUSIONS

It is evident that there is no shortage of questions, answers, and opinions generated by the availability of organ transplants, especially heart transplants. We may summarize our major findings as follows:

The first question relates to the likelihood of successful surgery. While some authorities allow hazardous procedures or treatment with even a small likelihood of success (notably the Aḥi'ezer and the *Shevut Ya'akov*), most modern authorities require that at the very least there be even odds of success (i.e., a fifty percent chance of surviving twelve months with the new organ). This group includes Rabbis Feinstein, Waldenberg, Unterman, and Kasher. Given the dismal success rates in the first years of heart-transplant surgery, this meant an effective consensus opposed to the procedure.

Since 1978, however, the statistics have improved the average life expectancy of such recipients well above the fifty percent

107. *Responsa Iggerot Moshe, Y.D.* 2:147 (end).

mark, even approaching ninety percent in many cases. These are patients who would without the surgery be expected to live no longer than a few months. Given such results, the halakhic concerns on the issue of effectiveness are largely disposed of. Indeed, according to Rabbi Feinstein at least, the surgery might be considered requisite, being an effective lifesaving step.

This is equally true of renal (kidney) transplants, in that the results are, if anything, even better than for cardiac transplants, with the added bonus that in the unlikely eventuality of transplant failure, dialysis can be resumed indefinitely. While Rabbi Meiselman feels that kidney transplants should not be attempted where dialysis offers better chances of long-term survival, there would appear to be no major problem in performing such a transplant where the success rates are high and the discomforts of dialysis are keenly felt.

The second question, in heart transplants especially, is raised by the problem of organ procurement from the deceased. This requires a precise definition of the moment of death. Two views, or trends, are discernible in the halakhic literature. The first cannot countenance or allow any assumption that death has occurred as long as the heart continues to beat unaided. This is the position of Rabbis Waldenberg, Weiss, and Bleich, amongst others. This view, then, would forbid a determination of death based exclusively on brain-death criteria, and thereby effectively eliminate heart donation.

The other view takes brain death as the functional equivalent of decapitation, which in Jewish law is the equivalent of death, irrespective of heart function. Once it is clinically determined that the brain and brain stem are irreversibly out of commission, and all autonomous breathing is absent, then death can be certified, and the organs can be removed, under certain circumstances. This is the view of Rabbis Feinstein, Goren, and Tendler—and most recently of the Israeli Chief Rabbinate.

We have also examined the question whether the restrictive view might consider other grounds to permit removal of organs for transplantation from brain-dead patients. Specifically, the issue is whether a *treifah*, with extremely limited life-expectancy, can be sacrificed with permission, to enable another person to enjoy long-term survival. To the *Noda bi-Yehudah*, the answer is in the negative, but R. Isaiah Pick and the *Minḥat Ḥinukh* answer positively. Subsequent authorities split over the issue, so that while Rabbis Waldenberg and Weiss stood opposed, Rabbis Gershuni, Gulevsky, and Rabinowitz were more favorably disposed to a permissive ruling.

The third question relates to the issue of the appropriate treatment afforded the cadaver, when its organs are needed for transplantation. We have seen that there are three prohibitions. The first was *nivul ha-met*, or dishonoring the body, by physical disfigurement. While every effort at respectful treatment must be made so as to avoid dishonor, the *Noda bi-Yehudah* does permit such disfigurement where the beneficiary of that action is both known and present. This is based on a talmudic dispensation to set aside the prohibition in order to save life. While the *Responsa Binyan Ẓion* opposed this lenient ruling (except where express permission had been granted prior to death), most subsequent authorities accepted it, including the Ḥatam Sofer, Maharam Schick, and R. Saul Jonathan Nathanson. It was left to Rabbi Unterman to make the point that under current conditions, given instantaneous worldwide communication and rapid transport facilities, the range of "immediate" beneficiaries is greatly extended. Nonetheless, even the lenient view would prefer where possible to utilize a Gentile cadaver, and to obtain prior consent from the donor.

The second prohibition involves the utilization of the cadaver for others. R. Solomon Kluger permitted such benefit once the bulk of the body had been buried; R. Emden allowed medical utilization; and Rabbi Unterman found room for leniency on the assumption that the transferred organs are no longer dead, strictly speaking. The Radbaz and, following him, Ovadiah Yosef permit nonconventional use of organs, although others disagree. In this area too, Rabbis Waldenberg and Weiss are opposed to the utilization of such organs, and disagree with these various mitigating considerations.

Delayed burial of the transplanted organs poses another problem. Here too, however, other factors enter: delay can be contemplated in order to bring honor to the deceased; some (*Mishneh le-Melekh*, Rabbis Steinberg, Unterman, and Liebes) permit such deferment, as long as the bulk of the body is buried right away; but others (Naḥmanides, Tosafot Yomtov, Rabbis Greenwald and Waldenberg) disagree and insist on burial of the entire remains.

There is a fourth question: the risk to the living donor. Here there is a significant movement toward some kind of consensus. Whereas the Jerusalem Talmud requires possible self-endangerment to save another from certain death, the more authoritative Babylonian Talmud disagreed. A pivotal text is a responsum by the Radbaz, variously interpreted. Some, such as Rabbis Weiss, Toledano, and initially Waldenberg, understand the responsum to forbid any exposure to risk whatsoever, especially when the certain result will be the permanent loss of a vital organ. But others, notably Rabbis Ovadiah Yosef, Meiselman, Hershler, Yisraeli, and eventually Waldenberg, understand his view to be that while the Babylonian Talmud does not require any exposure to risk, it does allow for personal predilection, whereby one can take a chance to save another, as long as the chances of successful outcome are at least fifty percent. Indeed according to this view, such selflessness is praiseworthy. Rabbi Feinstein also agrees with this latter group, while disagreeing with those who, like the Jerusalem Talmud, would require self-exposure.

The final question that this chapter has dealt with relates to the artificial heart. Does the Halakhah accept the possibility of viable life without the heart? On the one hand the Ḥakham Ẓvi says no, arguing that at most he can be considered a *treifah*. His view is reflected in the writings of Rabbis Unterman, Grossnass, and Waldenberg. The other view, however, is that where there is a reliable substitute for the heart, life may indeed continue. This would encompass the opinions of Rabbis Feinstein, Kasher, Gulevsky, Hershler, and Regensburg. They argue that the artificial heart is no different than the heart-lung machine in use during conventional open-heart surgery while the heart is incapacitated.

On November 2, 1986, the Israeli Chief Rabbinate issued its ruling to permit physicians at selected Israeli hospitals to perform heart transplants under careful rabbinic scrutiny and supervision. As explained at the time, the ruling was based on a number of considerations.[108] In the first place, there was the recognition of the high odds favoring successful implantation and survival of the recipient. Secondly, it was understood that donors are indeed

108. The full text of the ruling, together with various addenda, letters, and explanatory articles by Ashkenazi Chief Rabbi Mordecai Eliyahu, and Rabbi S. Israeli, is found in *Barkai* 4 (Spring 5747): 7–41.

demonstrably brain-dead, completely devoid of any independent breathing function, and irreversibly comatose, hence classifiable as deceased. Thirdly, the rabbis satisfied themselves that every precaution against error or premature judgment was to be taken, by way of various clinical tests and procedures. Fourthly, they required written consent from the donor or the family, and finally the rabbis were assured of periodic review of the procedures involved at every stage. Besides these explicit grounds, it is evident that these rabbis were able to satisfy themselves on the various additional questions and potential problems raised in this chapter, by relying on the permissive views that we encountered in each instance.

This ruling was a remarkable illustration of halakhic process and dynamics, involving change and responsiveness to evolving realities in modern life. Whereas but twenty years previously the rabbinic consensus had been to condemn the heart-transplant procedure for a variety of reasons, during the intervening years a significant proportion of rabbinic authorities arrived at radically new conclusions, based both on medical changes and improvements, as well as a careful reconsideration of traditional halakhic texts. Of course other halakhists remained opposed to the procedure, preferring to stay with their original approaches and perceptions. One such recent view is that of Rabbi Immanuel Jakobovits, Chief Rabbi of the British Commonwealth, who argues that the brain-death criteria are themselves far from scientifically proven, being subject to ongoing debate in the medical world. He also has difficulty in dispensing with the traditional role of heart function and blood circulation as part and parcel of the halakhic definition of death.[109]

This variety of opinions, too, has served to highlight the pluralistic nature of post-Sanhedrin halakhic conclusions, which has always, within reasonable bounds, allowed for a measure of dissent, variety, and internal debate.

In examining the many and complex halakhic issues involved in organ transplantation, it becomes clear that there can be no simple answers to the questions we posed at the beginning of our

---

109. See his article in *Jewish Chronicle*, May 29, 1987, p. 29. Likewise see his unequivocal statements, leaving no room for dissent, in "Ethical Problems Regarding the Termination of Life," *Jewish Values in Bioethics*, ed. Rabbi L. Meir (New York, 1986), p. 92.

investigation, especially not where heart transplants are involved. The entire area is an admirable specimen illustrating how halakhic positions emerge and evolve in a living process subject to many factors: scientific progress, changing social realities, and then textual interpretation and reinterpretation in the light of preexisting attitudes toward sacrosanct principles of faith, tradition, change, and reverence for life, in the face of death.

In conclusion then, should our fifty-year-old patient have the surgery? It depends on whom you ask. But a number of rabbinic authorities would tend to permit, and indeed encourage, a heart transplant, if in so doing there is a good likelihood of a successful outcome. It would also appear that many authorities would permit donation of one's vital organs, where intended to save the life of the recipient, with the proviso that the organ removal at the time of death follows carefully prescribed directions, i.e., brain death as halakhically defined and rabbinically supervised. Yet on this question, too, others would dissent.

As for the rest, we can be sure that the issue will continue to be debated and argued for a long time to come, as further medical developments occur, and new rabbinic insights into the talmudic and responsa literature evolve. Here, as elsewhere, we should be mindful of the rabbinic prescription that says, in the words of the Talmud, *zil gemor*, "go and study for yourself."

4

Euthanasia

Introduction

Recent advances in medical technology and practice have enabled practitioners to sustain the lives of patients significantly beyond what was heretofore possible. Intravenous feeding, new drugs, respirators, artificial kidneys and even hearts, have combined to make it possible to extend the lives of seriously ill patients by artificial means, even after the patient's own body has lost the capacity to function independently. Sometimes the patient is reduced to a vegetative state, being only partially or not all conscious. At other times, the patient may be conscious but in great physical pain or mental anguish. Prolonging life artificially, or even continuing to treat such patients, becomes problematic when either the patient or the family (when the patient is incompetent) requests termination of life-sustaining procedures or treatments. Euthanasia (from the Greek meaning "a good death") therefore becomes one option that confronts such patients, their loved ones, and professionals charged with their care.

There are three kinds of responses to the issue of mercy-killing, as it has come to be known. One argues for the right of a person to choose whether to live or die. There are several groups in a variety of countries that subscribe to this view, arguing that a person has a right to "death with dignity," to escape artificially prolonged pain where there is no realistic hope for remission. They furthermore argue that such a person should be able to actively terminate his life when and how he sees fit.

A second view, directly opposed to the first, argues against any withholding of treatment that might sustain life. This view maintains that it is not for man to choose death over life, especially when it is always possible that a cure or remission might intervene at some point. The finality of choosing to die means that one rules out the possibility of a mistaken diagnosis or unexpected turn of events. Furthermore, euthanasia is dangerous for society, in that once it is permitted in whatever form, there is a "slippery slope" that might lead to permissive attitudes toward terminating the lives of defective infants, the old or senile, the hopelessly insane—and even the racially or politically undesirable.

The third view, or group of views, embraces the broad middle ground of the issue, arguing that there are critical distinctions to be made between various kinds of euthanasia. Thus some distinguish between active euthanasia (where an act is committed that deliberately brings about the death of the patient, such as by injection of a lethal drug) and passive euthanasia (where treatment or support is simply withheld, leading to natural death in the course of time), viewing the latter with more leniency than the former. Others distinguish between voluntary euthanasia (where it is the patient himself who requests such steps) and involuntary euthanasia (where it is someone other than the patient doing so). Most often, the medical profession has supported this third view in one or another of its forms.

Generally speaking, Judaism affirms the sanctity of life without any qualification. Yet sometimes questions do arise where there is a possible conflict with other principles and considerations of Jewish law. It is with the resolution of such tensions that the halakhic discussion of the issues raised by euthanasia is concerned, leading to a variety of views and decisions.

The Question

A seventy-year-old man with terminal cancer is suffering unbearable pain. He wishes to hasten his death so as to be free of pain. He asks his physician to do one of four things:

1. Enable him to commit suicide by taking an overdose of medication.
2. Administer a lethal dose of medication causing immediate death at the hands of the physician.
3. Eliminate all treatment to prevent any unnatural prolonging of suffering.
4. Prescribe any medication or surgery that might alleviate the pain, even though it may hasten death.
5. May the physician agree to any of them?

Sources

A. 1 Samuel 31:3–4

And the battle went sore against Saul, and the archers overtook him; and he was in great anguish by reason of the archers. Then said Saul to his armor-bearer: "Draw thy sword and thrust me through therewith; lest these uncircumcised come and thrust me through, and make a mock of me." But his armor-bearer would not, for he was sore afraid. Therefore Saul took his sword and fell upon it.

B. Beraita, Semaḥot 1:4

One may not close the eyes of a dying person [*goses*]; one who touches him so as to move him is a murderer. R. Meir would say: "It is to be compared to a sputtering candle which is extinguished as soon as a person touches it—so too, whoever closes the eyes of a dying person is considered to have taken his soul."

C. Mishnah, Shabbat 151b

One who closes the eyes of the dying when death is about to occur is considered to have spilled blood.
Rashi ad loc.: For the slightest travail hastens his death.

D. Avodah Zarah 18a

They took R. Ḥaninah b. Tradyon and wrapped a Torah scroll around him, and encompassed him with faggots of vine branches, to which they set fire. They brought woolen tufts, soaked them with water, and laid them on his heart, so that his soul should not depart quickly. . . . His disciples said to him: "Open your mouth that the fire may penetrate." He replied: "Better is it that He who gave the soul should take it, and that a man should do himself no injury." Then the executioner said to him: "Master, if I increase the flame and remove the woolen tufts from off thy heart, will you bring me to the life of the world-to-come?" "Yes," said Ḥaninah. "Swear it," demanded the executioner. Ḥaninah took the oath. Forthwith the officer increased the flame and removed the woolen tufts from over Ḥaninah's heart, and his soul departed quickly.

E. Sanhedrin 45a

Said R. Naḥman in the name of Rabbah b. Abuha: " 'Love thy neighbor as thyself'—choose for him a good death [*mitah yafah*]."

F. Sanhedrin 73a

How do we know that if one sees his fellow drowning in a river, or a wild animal mauling him, or robbers attacking him, one must save him? Therefore it is said, "neither shalt thou stand idly by the blood of thy neighbor" (Lev. 19:16).

G. Yoma 85a

Mishnah: If a person is found alive under a fallen house [on the Sabbath] the debris may be removed.

Gemara: Isn't this obvious? The answer is that this teaches us that this may be done even if only to permit him to live for a short while.

H. Meiri ad loc.

If, when they remove the debris, they examine his breath and find him still alive, they can complete the removal even though he cannot live more than an hour; for in that hour he may repent and utter the confession.

I. Gittin 47b

It once happened that four hundred boys and girls were abducted to be abused (*Rashi:* the boys for sodomy and the girls for harems). When they realized why they were taken they said: "If we drown in the sea we will attain the life to come." . . . they all jumped and fell into the sea.

J. Tosafot ad loc.

As for the statement in *Avodah Zarah* 18a, "better is it that He who gave the soul should take it, and that a man should do himself no injury," in this case they were afraid of torture. . . . Furthermore, they would have been forced to submit without being killed.

K. Maimonides, M.T. Hilkhot Avel 4:5

A dying person [*goses*] is considered to be alive in every respect. . . . Whoever touches him is a murderer. . . . whoever closes his eyes as he dies is a murderer—one should wait a short while, as perhaps he is in a swoon.

L. Sefer Ḥasidim, chapter 723, followed by chapter 234

If a person is suffering terrible pain, and he tells someone: "You can see that I am not going to live; kill me, as I cannot suffer any more"; one may not touch him. . . . whereas Saul was permitted [to shorten his life] to prevent a desecration of the divine name before Israel.

If a person suffers great pain, and he knows he cannot live, he may not commit suicide. This we learn from R. Ḥaninah b. Tradyon, who did not want to open his mouth. But if there are factors preventing a speedy demise—such as a man chopping wood in the vicinity of a dying man's home, and the noise of the chopping prevents the soul from escaping—we remove the chopper from there. Likewise we do not place salt on his tongue to prevent his death. But if he is dying and he says, "I cannot die until you put me in a different place," they may not move him from there.

M. Rema (R. Moses Isserles) on Yoreh Deiah 339:1

It is forbidden to cause the dying to die quickly, such as one who is moribund over a long time and who cannot die, it is forbidden to remove the pillow from under him on the assumption that certain birdfeathers prevent his death. So too one should not place the keys of the synagogue under his head, or move him so that he may die. But if there is something that delays his death, such as a nearby woodchopper making a noise, or there is salt on his tongue, and these prevent his speedy death, one can remove them, for this does not involve any action at all, but rather the removal of the preventive agent.

N. Mishnah, Bava Kamma 90b

It once happened that a man uncovered a woman's head in public. She came before R. Akiva, and he required the man to give her four hundred zuz fine. Said the man to him, "Rabbi, allow me some time," and R. Akiva concurred. The man observed the woman standing at the door of her house, then broke a jug containing about an issar of oil before her. She uncovered her head, bent down so as to put the oil on her head with her hand. The man brought witnesses of this before R. Akiva, saying, "To one such as this should I give four hundred zuz?" Said R. Akiva to him, "What you say is nothing, for even though one is not permitted to do damage to oneself, if one does so there is no penalty, whereas if another does damage to him, that other is culpable."

O. Bava Kamma 91b

Rabbi Eleazar ha-Kappar said: "Why does the Torah say, 'and the priest shall make atonement for the Nazirite for having sinned against the soul' [Num. 6:11]? Against which soul did the Nazirite sin? He sinned by depriving himself of wine. Accordingly, if one is called a sinner even though he only deprived himself of wine, then how much more so should one who deprives himself of everything (*Rashi:* deprives himself by fasting) be considered a sinner."

Discussion

1. SUICIDE

The Mishnah in *Bava Kamma* 90b records the opinion of R. Akiva that one is not permitted to wound one's body (N). The biblical origin of this prohibition is generally taken to be the verse "surely your blood of your lives will I require" (Gen. 9:5).[1] Maimonides (Rambam) summarizes the reasons put forward for such a prohibition when he says that one's person belongs to no one but God Himself.[2] This applies whether it is suicide or merely wounding that is involved; both are forbidden (O). Maimonides classifies one who commits suicide as a murderer, punishable at the hands of heaven.[3]

A further reason is adduced for the prohibition of suicide: Every sinner is normally afforded a measure of forgiveness by the very act of death, for death itself is a punishment or deprivation that is taken into account in the heavenly tribunal (hence the appropriate means of carrying out a death penalty is of great importance (E).) But the suicide must be denied even this, for his very death is criminal beyond any atonement by a subsequent act. This, according to R. Moses Schreiber (Ḥatam Sofer, 1762–1839), is the reason that burial practices for suicides are significantly downgraded.[4]

Yet can there be exceptions to this rule, such as a situation where terrible pain and suffering are the only alternative? The story of R. Ḥaninah b. Tradyon (D) in *Avodah Zarah* 18b provides an authoritative precedent to deny permission to hasten one's death by an overt act (such as opening one's mouth to swallow the flames surrounding one), even when confronted with the prospect of great pain preceding death.

There are, however, two sources that appear to permit an act of suicide when faced with great suffering. The first is biblical, referring to the suicide of King Saul (A) in 1 Samuel 31:1–10.

Saul, confronted with the certainty of an ignominious death at the hands of the enemies of Israel, falls upon his own sword so as to die at his own hand—an act that did not result in any condemnation by King David. The second source (I) is the talmudic discussion in *Gittin* 57b and the comments of Tosafot thereon. In that place the Talmud mentions the unhappy fate of some four hundred youngsters who committed suicide rather than face the calumnies of their abductors. Tosafot (J) elucidates two possible justifications for that suicide in spite of the contrary example of R. Ḥaninah b. Tradyon (D): (1) they were afraid of torture; (2) they would be forced to sin without even the option of choosing death instead. The first of these answers apparently finds sufficient grounds for suicide in the prospect of pain and suffering.

The earliest source discussing the death of Saul is found in *Midrash Rabbah* to Genesis, chapter 34. Quoting the standard verse "surely your blood of your lives will I require" (Gen. 9:5), the Midrash makes an explicit exception in the case of Saul, based on the word *akh* ("surely"). Thus Saul's death is viewed as different, and consequently not to be confused with ordinary suicides.

But even this Midrash is not clear or unambiguous, for it is not certain whether it is the instance of Saul's death itself that is excepted or whether Saul's death is the archetype of a certain category of suicides that can be performed. According to the latter interpretation of the Midrash, suicides that share characteristics with Saul's situation can be permitted.[5]

What these characteristics may be is discussed in later literature. Thus Ritva (R. Yomtov b. Abraham Ashbili, 1250–1330) explains that Saul's concern was that his enemies would attempt to convert him to their faith; accordingly his suicide was permitted.[6] The *Shulḥan Arukh, Yoreh Deiah 345:3*, states that all cases similar to that of Saul, who was an *anus* (one subject to unavoidable circumstances), are condoned. Thus a Jew should sacrifice his life rather than be forced to worship other gods in the presence of ten other Jews.[7]

Recent authorities point to the special nature of Saul's suicide. Rabbi N. Z. Friedmann (author of *Neẓer Matta'ai*) takes the position that the case of Saul was *sui generis*, in that he acted for the greater glory of the Israelite kingship, so that that institution would not be cheapened by the Philistines. Accordingly it was for the sake of the entire people of Israel that Saul's action was undertaken.[8] A slightly more inclusive criterion is formulated by Rabbi N. Telushkin, who includes Saul's action in that class of actions performed by singular individuals for the sake of heaven.[9] In the case of Saul, he avers, the intention was to prevent the enemies of Israel from actually killing the anointed one of God.

The result of these various qualifications is to deny any suggestion that it was the prospect of pain *per se* that permitted King Saul's suicide.

The second source mentioned above, the Tosafot which apparently permits suicide in the face of suffering, has likewise been discussed in subsequent literature. Rabbi I. Unterman (author of *Shevet mi-Yehudah* b. 1886) pointed out that the discrepancy between the two answers of Tosafot (whereby according to the first answer suicide is permitted when faced with suffering, while according to the second, suffering alone is not sufficient warrant) really reflects a larger debate within the medieval sources. That debate concerned the propriety of suicide by a Jew in a time of religious persecution. According to one view, held most prominently by R. Solomon Luria (known as Maharshal, 1510–1575), there can be no permission to commit suicide even when confronted with the prospect of torture and forced conversion. The only justification for suicide under these circumstances would be the anticipated possibility of endangering the lives of others if tortured.[10] The other view, as ascribed to Ritva and Rabbeinu Tam (R. Jacob b. Meir, 1100–1171), permits suicide rather than the alternative of forced conversion. In fact, Rabbeinu Tam considers such a suicide to be a miẓvah, and interprets the case of the four hundred who jumped into the sea as motivated by a similar desire to avoid the desecration in store for them.[11] The many instances of martyrdom recorded in the *piyyut* (liturgical poetry) for Tisha Be'Av were apparently permitted in accordance with the second and more permissive view.[12]

As pointed out by Rabbi I. Jakobovits (b. 1921), even the permissive view insists that there be an element of religious persecution, so that the action of the sufferer can be viewed as ultimately motivated by pietistic concerns.[13] Physical suffering alone cannot be reason enough to permit suicide by the patient. Maimonides himself makes this distinction by stating that a person can be punished by a court of law for transgressing one of the cardinal sins (i.e., idolatry, incest, and murder) when the goal is to recover from an otherwise incurable disease, for such an act is considered to be voluntary; whereas if the goal is to avoid religious coercion by Gentiles, there is no statutory punishment.[14] Apparently Maimonides considers actions undertaken to avoid sickness or pain insufficient reason to be classified as *ones* (unavoidable circumstance).

A similar conclusion is to be drawn from a responsum of R. David b. Solomon Ibn Abi Zimra (known as Ridbaz, 1479–1573).[15] The case under discussion is that of a man whose physician insisted that the Sabbath be violated so that his life could be saved. The patient himself refused to break the laws of the Sabbath, even though death would result. In such a case the patient is to be coerced into breaking the Sabbath, as the saving of his life is paramount. Now if the significant weight of the Sabbath laws is not sufficient to overturn the prohibition of suicide, it would certainly be the case that the mere avoidance of pain would not suffice to overturn the laws against suicide.[16]

An interesting exception to this general rejection of suicide as an alternative to suffering is found in a volume of responsa entitled *Besamim Rosh.* This work, attributed to the authoritative Rabbeinu Asher (1250–1327), has stirred considerable controversy regarding its authorship, for many authorities consider it to be of later vintage, and consequently of lesser authority. In the responsum under discussion, we are told of a man who committed suicide because he could no longer suffer the dire poverty and degradation of his life. The author of the *Besamim Rosh* permitted full burial rights to be accorded the man, for "in any case of suicide for a multiplicity of troubles, worries, pain, or utter poverty, there is not the slightest reason to deny mourning rites." The major source for this view is apparently the suicide of Saul, committed to prevent his suffering at the hands of the Gentiles. As we have seen, this is, of course, a point debated among other authorities. R. Moses Schreiber (Ḥatam Sofer) takes issue with this responsum and finds its conclusion in direct contradiction to the talmudic account of R. Ḥaninah b. Tradyon, who refused to hasten his own death.[17]

While most authorities likewise disagree with the *Besamim Rosh,*[18] there is one poignant responsum that makes it a pivotal part of the argument permitting a lenient ruling regarding suicide. Rabbi Ephraim Oshry, author of *mi-Ma'amakim* and rabbi of the Kovno ghetto during the World War II German occupation, permitted a Jew to commit suicide rather than witness the certain killing of his wife, children, and grandchildren before his very eyes. The man did not believe that he would be able to withstand such torture; his heart would fail and he would die. Rabbi Oshry accepted the major conclusions of the *Besamim Rosh*, adding that the prospect facing this man was certainly as painful as any confronting King Saul.[19]

It should be added that the conditions surrounding the dispensation granted by Rabbi Oshry make it most difficult to place this responsum in the perspective of the others treated thus far. This kind of treatment accorded the problem at hand is therefore a prime example of the possibility of individual consideration in the halakhic process.

2. ACTIVE EUTHANASIA AS ADMINISTERED BY A PHYSICIAN

Are there any circumstances in which someone else may mercifully shorten the life of the one desiring to die?

The Beraita in *Semaḥot* 1:4 (B) states unequivocally that one who so much as moves the limb of a dying man in such a way as to shorten his life by a few moments is a murderer. So too the Mishnah in *Shabbat* 151b (C) brands such an act as homicide. The reason is clearly as the opening words of *Semaḥot* indicate: Until the precise moment of death the dying person has every claim on life and the living. This principle is codified verbatim by Maimonides in *Hilkhot Avel* 4:5 (K).

Not only is such direct contact with the dying proscribed, but also indirect causation as well. Thus R. Moses Isserles (known as Rema, d. 1572) in his authoritative gloss to the *Shulḥan Arukh, Yoreh Deiah* (M), states that it is even forbidden to remove the pillow from beneath a patient in order to make him more comfortable in his protracted death-throes.[20] And lest one think that this is forbidden only because it involves the lowering of the entire upper torso, Rema adds that even the placing of synagogal artifacts that have some occult power to shorten life is forbidden as an overt act to shorten the natural process of death.[21] Thus it is not only the physical contact with the dying which is to be eschewed, but any attempt, no matter how indirect, to anticipate the destined moment of death.

But perhaps this does not apply to an attending physician, who after all might be considered the one who has thus far lengthened and extended the life processes of the patient? Does he possess any special status or dispensation to choose the time and manner of death? The answer in Jewish law is a resounding no, and the reason is as follows: The authority of the physician to attend and care for a patient does not derive from the patient, for the patient himself does not "own" his body (as we have seen above). The activities of the physician are permitted only because there is a derived dispensation in the Torah. The words "he shall cause him to be thoroughly healed" (Exod. 21:19) are understood by the Gemara in *Bava Kamma* 85a as teaching, "with these words the Torah gives permission to the physician to heal." Thus defined, the physician's authority only extends to the art of healing and no further. Once he can no longer heal the patient, his dispensation to treat the patient cannot be extended to include any active determination of the time of death.[22] Having made the patient as comfortable as possible, he must recognize the limitation of his calling.[23]

3. PASSIVE EUTHANASIA: THE WITHDRAWAL OF TREATMENT

We have seen that there can be no possibility of actively hastening the patient's death. But is it permitted simply to withdraw all life-prolonging treatment and allow the natural process culminating in death to take its course without medical attempts to keep him alive?

Unlike the earlier alternatives discussed above, there is a significant difference of opinion in this case. Rema, in the same gloss discussed above (M), goes on to make a distinction between removing the pillow from beneath the patient's head, which is forbidden, and the removal of an extraneous factor interfering with the natural deterioration of bodily functions that results in death. The instance that he cites is that of the noise of a nearby woodchopper that disturbs the equanimity of the patient so that a speedy death is made more difficult.[24] The reason Rema offers is that "this is merely the removal of the preventive agent."

Rema's words in this passage are taken directly from an earlier source, R. Joshua Boaz b. Simon Barukh, the sixteenth-century author of the *Shiltei Gibborim*.[25] The latter in turn based his comments, and the distinction between causing a speedy death and the removal of an impediment to natural demise, on several explicit passages in the thirteenth-century *Sefer Ḥasidim* (attributed to R. Judah ha-Ḥasid), which had invoked the precise examples mentioned in the writings of Rema (L).[26] In affirming the same distinction in his commentary to the *Tur* (written by R. Jacob b. Asher, d. 1343), Rema goes one step further: Not only is one permitted to remove any source disturbing the natural demise, one is even *required* to remove it.[27]

A possible source in the Talmud for this distinction is the passage describing the death of R. Ḥaninah b. Tradyon (D). According to that narrative, while the martyr refused to open his mouth so that the flames could enter his body the sooner, he did agree to permit the woolen tufts wrapped round his body to be removed, even though by so doing his death would occur the sooner. Apparently he considered the tufts to be artificially impeding the natural course of death, and therefore needlessly prolonging his suffering, at a time when his death was certain and imminent.

At the same time there are other sources that are crucial to this issue. The Gemara in *Yoma* 85a (G) explains that the dispensation in the Mishnah to violate the Sabbath to uncover the victim of a collapsed house extends even to include one who can live but for a short while as a result of his injuries. The fact that there is no prospect whatsoever for recovery, and that the pain or suffering of the victim has no bearing on the issue, is a strong indication that the preservation of life—irrespective of its length or quality—cannot be compromised, even if it means the violation of the cardinal principle of the Sabbath. The Tosafot in *Niddah* 44b likewise affirms that the Sabbath is to be violated for the sake of the dying (*goses*). R. Menaḥem ha-Meiri (d. 1306) provides the succinct rationale in this case: "for in that hour he may repent and utter the confession" (H).

This last assertion itself is a matter of differing opinions. For as opposed to the opinion of Tosafot, R. Nissim Gerondi (d. 1380), known as Ran, pointedly omits mention of the dispensation to violate the Sabbath for the dying.[28] Based on this omission, the sixteenth-century R. Jacob b. Samuel (author of the *Bet Ya'akov*) comes to the conclusion that the Sabbath should *not* be violated for the dying, for he assumes that the general principle that we follow the majority applies here too; i.e., most moribund patients do in fact die within a short period.[29] According to this, the Gemara in *Yoma* is to be restricted to a case where the victim is crushed (*meruẓaẓ*); in all other cases, there is the possibility that any attempt to help or attend the patient in any way will merely result in the prolonging of the death process, and is therefore forbidden.

This conclusion of R. Jacob b. Samuel is vehemently opposed by several authorities. R. Jacob Reischer, the author of the *Shevut Ya'akov*, insists that the plain meaning of the Gemara in *Yoma* requires every attempt to prolong the life of the dying. It is to be understood, of course, that such help should be given only by an expert who is trained in the treatment of that condition, thereby minimizing any undesired results.[30] Rabbi Reischer also accepts the position of Tosafot permitting the violation of the Sabbath, as well as the principle that in matters of life or death one should not follow the majority, but rather pursue every possibility to save every moment of life.

These sources and the differences among them are reflected in several responsa and writings on the subject in the twentieth century. With regard to passive euthanasia we can group these writings into two convenient categories: those that oppose any form of euthanasia, and those that permit passive euthanasia under certain conditions.

Primary among the former is Rabbi Israel Meir ha-Kohen (author of the *Mishnah Berurah*), who died in 1933. In his *Be'ur Halakhah*, he agrees completely with the position of Rabbi Reischer, arguing that even if we accept that the Gemara in *Yoma* is speaking only of a crushed victim, nonetheless its conclusions that the Sabbath may be violated on his behalf would apply *a fortiori* to the general class of moribund persons, for in the latter instance there is at least a small minority that does survive.[31]

There are two questions, however, that arise in connection with the pivotal discussion in *Yoma*. The first concerns the explanation of R. Menaḥem ha-Me'iri (H) regarding the possibility of a last-minute repentance: If the victim is incapable of such repentance or confession (e.g., is comatose, unconscious, or mentally deranged), could one then, in the absence of any possibility of cure, leave him to die peacefully?[32] And secondly, what is the difference whether or not there is a minority of such cases that can be cured; even if there are none who can survive this, should we not do whatever is in our power to add even a moment of life to the victim? In other words, is the Gemara implying that in another situation, where there is no possibility at all of recovery (i.e., where there is no significant minority who survive), we can leave the victim or patient to die quietly?

Rabbi Israel Meir ha-Kohen answers both these objections. Regarding the first he asserts that Meiri was merely attempting to provide a reason for the discussion in the Gemara, but that in reality the operative principle is that we suspend a particular miẓvah (in this case the Sabbath) not merely for the sake of other miẓvot, but more significantly for the sake of saving a life (F). Thus it is not necessary for the victim, or patient, to be able to carry out any acts of religious significance. As for the second question, he answers that the issue of a minority who do survive is only raised by Tosafot in *Niddah*, and for a specific reason at that: In case the physician indicates his belief that his dying patient can survive if a particular course of medication is adhered to, we can accept his prognosis to the extent that it requires the violation of certain laws, and this for the reason that "a minority of moribund patients do in fact survive." But this in no way means that the victim or patient can be left to die if in his case there is no such minority.

A similar position regarding passive euthanasia is found in the *Ẓiẓ Eliezer* of Rabbi Eliezer Waldenberg.[33] This authority finds support for the view that life is to be sustained, no matter what its quality or brevity, in a talmudic passage regarding the unfaithful wife (*sotah*).[34] In that passage Rabbi (R. Judah ha-Nasi, 2d–3d cent. C.E.) opines that if she is guilty of infidelity she will die immediately following her taking of the "bitter waters," as outlined in Numbers 5:11–31, unless she has the special merit of having observed certain commandments, in which case her death will be postponed while she suffers from a debilitating sickness and severe pain.[35] Apparently, says Rabbi Waldenberg, the sickness, pain, and suffering are to be preferred to death, even though death is assured in both cases.

Another source adduced by those opposed to passive euthanasia is the scriptural account of the sickness of King Hezekiah (Isaiah 38). In that chapter Isaiah informs Hezekiah that he is about to die from his sickness, whereupon the king prays to God and is granted an extension of some fifteen years of his life. The Gemara in *Berakhot* 10a reconstructs the precise exchange that took place between the prophet and the king, and teaches that at one point Hezekiah put forth a suggestion that might change the decree. Upon the demurral of Isaiah at the thought of challenging the divine decree, he is excoriated by Hezekiah with the words "Ben Amoẓ, finish your business and leave; for I have a family tradition that says, 'though the sword be laid against his throat, let a man never despair of divine mercy,' as it is said, 'Though He slay me yet will I trust in Him' [Job 13:15]." As expressed by Rabbi Nathan Friedmann (author of the *Neẓer Matta'ai*), this exchange has direct significance for our problem. For if even a divine decree of death can be altered by some means, then certainly a medical prognosis that is ignorant of God's will cannot be relied upon as certain and unquestionably terminal.[36] And whereas the Halakhah recognizes the expertise of the informed physician to the point of permitting the violation of the Sabbath on the basis of a medical diagnosis, that is only the case where the purpose is the saving of life, not where the intended goal is to facilitate death. The charge of Job's "Though He slay me yet will I trust in Him" is to maintain a constant hope and faith in the face of the most dire predictions of death. As Rabbi Friedmann reminds his reader, even the medical profession recognizes that there are factors, presently unknown, that may cause a small percentage of terminal cases to reverse themselves over a long period of time.

How does the school of thought opposed to passive euthanasia explain the two instances that would seem to favor such action, i.e., Rabbi Ḥaninah b. Tradyon's agreeing to have the woolen tufts removed, and Rema's permitting the removal of the woodchopper? Rabbi Nissan Telushkin answers that what differentiates both these sources from a situation involving euthanasia is the fact that there is an obligation to preserve life by any medical means available, whereas there is no such necessity when the continuation of the status quo serves merely to perpetuate pain and suffering inflicted in order to torture (as in the case of R. Ḥaninah b. Tradyon) or caused by inadvertence (as in the case of the woodchopper).[37] In addition, as pointed out by Rabbi J. David Bleich, Rema himself limits his comments to apply to a *goses*, which Rema elsewhere defines as a patient whose death is imminent,[38] and certainly not more than three days away.[39]

At the same time, we do encounter several modern authorities who take a more lenient view of passive euthanasia. Prominent among these is Rabbi Moshe Feinstein, author of the *Iggerot Moshe*. In that work he states that it is forbidden to maintain the life of a person "who is not fit to live" by artificial means.[40] Discussing a situation wherein doctors wish to maintain such a patient on machines so as to use his organs in a transplant, he states that because the intention of such a course of action is not to heal the patient but merely to prolong his life for a time, then if the time thus gained by artificial means is characterized by pain and suffering for the patient, it would be forbidden. While it is clear that this line of reasoning follows the position of R. Jacob b. Samuel in the *Bet Ya'akov*, Rabbi Feinstein suggests that even R. Jacob Reischer, in the *Shevut Ya'akov*, would agree with his view.

In explaining his reasoning, Rabbi Feinstein says that the case is quite analogous to the woodchopper who can be removed from the vicinity of a *goses* according to Rema. He further argues that were it permissible to prolong life artificially in spite of the suffering, then Rema would have required bringing additional "disturbances" to supplement and augment the effect of the woodchopper. Nonetheless, Rabbi Feinstein categorically prohibits any semblance of active euthanasia by means of an overt act to hasten death, even if the patient is in pain or suffering.

A significant definition of "pain and suffering" (*yissurim*) is likewise introduced by Rabbi Feinstein when he says that even if the patient is comatose, and the doctors are of the opinion that he has no further pain, we must still consider it possible that he experiences pain. For it is possible that there remains some subliminal sensitivity to physical discomfort even when there is no overt consciousness and the patient is *in extremis*.

Rabbi I. Jakobovits, in several articles on the subject of euthanasia, finds room to permit passive euthanasia.[41] On the basis of the lenient tradition personified by the *Sefer Ḥasidim*, R. Joshua Boaz b. Simon Barukh, Rema, R. Jacob b. Samuel, and others, he concludes that there is no obligation to extend the life of a terminally ill patient, and thereby to perpetuate his pain artificially.[42] He thus permits the removal of medication and treatment—but not of the natural means of subsistence, such as food and water. He even goes so far as to permit the suspension of life-saving insulin in a patient suffering from diabetes who subsequently contracts cancer causing him excruciating pain.

Rabbi Jakobovits explains his position by describing the dialectical tension of the Halakhah on this question. On the one hand, there is the inestimable value and priority attached to life itself. This is seen in the suspension of the Sabbath to preserve but one moment of precious life. But on the other hand, there is the concern to avoid needless pain even in the case of the worst criminal, for whom the Halakhah is concerned to find the least painful form of execution. This is likewise seen in the intense desire to provide a speedy execution for the condemned prisoner, so as to avoid the agonizing anticipation of death to the greatest extent possible.[43]

Faced with this conflict, argues Rabbi Jakobovits, the Halakhah would countenance inaction (*shev ve'al ta'aseh*) and the readiness to let nature (i.e., God's will) take its course.[44]

Rabbi Moshe Dov Wollner arrives at the same conclusion, and he does so by defining the forbidden act as one which contributes to the weakening of the natural life forces of the body. Hence, any act which does not interfere with the natural forces, but merely serves to remove an unnatural factor prolonging the patient's life, can be permitted.[45] His primary source for this definition is the death of R. Ḥaninah b. Tradyon.

Rabbi Barukh Rabinowitz, discussing the propriety of maintaining the donor of an organ for a transplant by hooking him up to a respirator, states that one is not permitted to artificially prolong the natural demise of the patient once all natural signs of life (i.e., breathing and pulse) have ceased to function spontaneously.[46] Accordingly, one would be required to disconnect life-support systems once that point has been reached. This position seems to be in complete agreement with the conclusions of Rabbi Feinstein, both based on the authority of Rema.

An even more permissive ruling is found in an article authored by Rabbi G. A. Rabinowitz and Dr. M. Koenigsberg.[47] They conclude that there is no requirement whatsoever to maintain a comatose patient with no hope for recovery. They go so far as to permit the withholding of food and nutrition, as they consider these to be included in Rema's "something that delays his death." As for the talmudic dispensation to violate the Sabbath and uncover the dying, even if only for the sake of a brief period of life, they argue that the Gemara is speaking of a case where there is some reasonable chance of reviving the victim, unlike the case of the terminal patient in an extended coma.

As can be seen, there is a considerable spectrum of opinion regarding passive euthanasia. The variety of sources and the possibility of varying interpretations by later authorities lead to a Halakhah that is responsive and dynamic, yet also critical and conservative in maintaining traditional values.

4. *TREATMENT THAT MAY SHORTEN LIFE*

Where the contemplated treatment has but one purpose, and that is to alleviate great pain, Rabbi Wollner quotes R. Abraham Gombiner (d. 1683), author of the *Magen Avraham*. That rabbi explains in his commentary to the *Shulḥan Arukh* that in a case where a very sick patient insists that he must have a certain food on the Sabbath, and it can only be obtained by violating the Sabbath, then one may violate the Sabbath, even though the physician is of the opinion that the food will harm his health.[48] The reason offered is that the patient himself can recognize his weakness better than the physician, and therefore knows that he requires a specific food to overcome his malaise. We can overlook future harm in the light of present needs as determined by the patient. Accordingly, argues Rabbi Wollner, in a case where both patient and physician agree that the medication will be of help in overcoming pain and discomfort, one can disregard possible future ramifications of the course of treatment.

In a situation where the contemplated treatment is intended to lengthen the life of the patient, and there is a significant possibility that the treatment may in fact shorten his life, there appears to be general agreement to permit such a course. R. Jacob

Reischer, reiterating his concern for every moment of life, including the violation of the Sabbath, permits such a step, but only after a clear majority of physicians and competent rabbinic scholars concur that there is a good chance of success.[49] Rabbi Ḥayyim Ozer Grodzinsky, author of the *Aḥiezer* , was confronted with the case of a patient who was not expected to live longer than six months unless major surgery was performed, which itself was hazardous.[50] He too permits the surgery, reasoning that momentary life may be sacrificed in order to save a life, irrespective of how "momentary" the sacrificed life may be. He too insists that the most expert physicians must agree on the positive chances of successful surgery. This is understood by Rabbi I. Y. Unterman as permitting such medication or surgery even where the majority of such cases are not successful and death is hastened.[51] Rabbi Unterman agrees with this decision.

Of the four options available to the physician described at the outset of this chapter, we can see that the first two (assisting with suicide; actively causing an early death) are overwhelmingly rejected by Halakhah. Regarding the third (withdrawal of all treatment to permit natural demise), we have seen that there is a significant difference of opinion, ranging from those who forbid such a step under any circumstances to those who would even countenance the withdrawal of food and vital sustenance. In the middle are those who permit withdrawal of medication if such treatment artificially prolongs life at the cost of great pain and suffering to the patient. As to the fourth option, there seems to be general agreement that one can undergo a course of treatment that endangers life if there is a good possibility that one can extend one's life beyond what would otherwise be the case.

It should be noted that all authorities do permit recourse to prayer, i.e., praying to God to shorten the life of the patient so as to escape the pain and suffering that is being endured. The Talmud itself records instances of such prayer, notably the prayer of R. Judah ha-Nasi's maidservant, whose request to God to put her master out of his misery was speedily fulfilled.[52] This precedent is quoted approvingly by Ran in his commentary on *Nedarim* 40a, and is likewise accepted by all later authorities, who even view such prayer as a miẓvah.[53] The difference is clear: while every practical measure possible should be invoked to prolong life in the best way possible, there would be no contradiction in praying to God to act speedily in His own ineffable way to end the suffering of the patient.

The dilemma of euthanasia is a particularly painful one for all concerned, not merely for the patient. Jewish law recognizes the benevolent motives that impel the physician to consider euthanasia as an answer to the request, spoken or unspoken, of the patient. This can be seen from the statement in the Mishnah that says, "among physicians, the good are consigned to hell" (*Kiddushin* 82a), which is explained by *Tosafot Ri ha-Zaken* (R. Isaac the Elder, d. 1185) as referring to "those who kill the sick."[54] This, as understood by Rabbi Friedmann, must be referring to the physician who practices euthanasia out of the goodness of his heart. In spite of his good intentions and kind thoughts, his end must be perdition.[55]

Clearly much care and precision are absolutely necessary in these questions; there are no easy answers or general prescriptions that provide blanket prescriptions. Sensitivity to the patient's suffering must be accompanied by an ear that is attuned to the nuances of tradition and text, and a concern for the larger issues of law and human destiny from a Jewish perspective.

Notes

1. This is the majority view. There are those who assert that one is permitted to wound oneself (cf. the opinion of Rema as quoted in *Shittah Mekubbeẓet* to *Bava Kamma* 90b), and those who affirm that there is no biblical prohibition involved (cf. *Leḥem Mishnah* to *M.T. Hil. Deot* 3:1). Further discussion of this issue can be found in the *Encyclopedia Talmudit*, s.v. "Ḥovel."

2. Maimonides, *M.T. Hil. Roẓeiaḥ* 1:4. Cf. also *M.T. Hil. Ḥovel u-Mazzik* 5:5 and the comments of Ridbaz to *M.T. Hil. Sanhedrin* 18:6.

3. Maimonides, *M.T. Hil. Roẓeiaḥ* 2:2.

4. *Responsa Ḥatam Sofer, Yoreh Deiah* 326:23. Cf. also his commentary to the Torah, Gen. 15:6. With regard to burial practices for suicides, see *Semakhot*, chap. 1, and *Sh.A. Yoreh Deiah* 345.

5. For such an interpretation see N. Friedmann, *Neẓer Matta'ai* (Bnai Berak, 1957), p. 125.

6. See Moshe Dov Wollner, "The Physician's Rights and Qualifications," *ḥa-Torah Ve'-ha-Medinah* 8 (1957): 316.

7. On the nature of these cardinal precepts, as they have come to be known, see *Sanhedrin* 74a, *M.T. Yesodei ha-Torah* 5:2, and *Sh.A. Yoreh Deiah* 157:1.

8. *Neẓer Matta'ai*, p. 125.

9. N. Telushkin, "The Extent of Man's Ownership of His Body," *Or ha-Mizraḥ*, 1962, p. 22.

10. *Yam shel Shelomoh* to *Bava Kamma* 8:59. This view considers Saul to have violated Jewish law by commiting suicide as he did.

11. See the comments of Tosafot to *Avodah Zarah* 18a. Rabbeinu Tam himself was miraculously saved from death at the hands of the Crusaders. Ritva, in his

comments to *Avodah Zarah*, chap. 1, writes in the name of Rabbeinu Tam: "An Israelite who is afraid that he will be forced to abandon Judaism and violate its commandments, and kills himself, is not denied any burial or mourning rites. This was the reason that during the persecutions [of the Crusades] fathers slaughtered their children with their own hands."

12. Isser Yehudah Unterman, *Shevet mi'-Yehudah* (Jerusalem, 1955), pp. 42–47.

13. I. Jakobovits, "Regarding the Law Whether It Is Permitted to Hasten the End of a Terminal Patient in Great Pain," *ha-Pardes* 31, no. 1 (1956): 29. Rabbi Wollner, in *ha-Torah ve'ha-Medinah*, p. 317, has a similar understanding of Tosafot, i.e., when both death and sin are unavoidable, then only is suicide permitted.

14. Maimonides, *M.T. Hil. Yesodei ha-Torah* 5:4, 6.

15. This is recorded in the *Darkei Teshuvah* to *Sh.A. Yoreh Deiah* 157:12.

16. Jakobovits, *ha-Pardes*, p. 29; Telushkin, *Or ha-Mizraḥ*, p. 22.

17. *Responsa Ḥatam Sofer* to *Yoreh Deiah* 326. Cf. also to *Yoreh Deiah* 328 and *Even ha-Ezer* 1:69.

18. Cf. *Neẓer Matta'ai*, p. 126, who points out that the alleged "real" author of the work, the sixteenth-century Isaac Molina, is purported to have committed suicide subsequently.

19. *Responsa mi-Ma'amakim* (New York, 1959), vol. 1, pp. 45 ff. In the course of this responsum Rabbi Oshry provides a comprehensive discussion of the status of the suicide in general. While he was well aware of the disputed status of the *Besamim Rosh*, Rabbi Oshry quotes several sources who do accept its authenticity as emanating from Rosh. This responsum is described in Irving J. Rosenblum, *The Holocaust and Halakhah* (New York, 1976), pp. 35–40.

20. This is in accordance with the reading of Rema offered by R. Joshua Falk (d. 1614) in his *Derishah* to that paragraph of the *Shulḥan Arukh*.

An interesting sidelight to this comment of the rabbis is found in a British medical journal (*Lancet*, April 22, 1978, pp. 632–634), regarding the care of "very ill patients." It was found that in such patients, "routine nursing care, involving movement of the patient, caused pronounced falls of blood oxygen concentration . . . and they raise the question about the importance of such measures in the very ill." I am indebted to Rabbi M. D. Tendler for this reference.

21. This follows the interpretation of Yeḥiel Michael Epstein (d. 1908), in his *Arukh ha-Shulḥan* ad loc.

22. Telushkin, *Or ha-Mizraḥ*, p. 23; and Friedmann, *Neẓer Matta'ai*, p. 128, based on *Sh.A. Yoreh Deiah* 336.

23. Jakobovits, *ha-Pardes*, p. 31. Rabbi Jakobovits proves conclusively that any action on the part of the physician to hasten the death renders the physician in the category of a murderer.

24. This is mentioned by Rema in his gloss to the *Shulḥan Arukh* as well as to the *Tur* (in his glosses known as *Darkei Moshe*).

25. See the *Shiltei Gibborim* to Alfasi's notes on *Moed Katan* 3:1237.

26. *Sefer Ḥasidim*, ed. J. Wistinetzky (Frankfurt, 1924), pars. 315–318. This is according to the Parma MS, whereas according to the Bologna MS the paragraphs are 723, 234.

27. *Darkei Moshe* to *Tur Yoreh Deiah* 339.

28. This comment of Ran is recorded in R. Shabbetai ha-Kohen's *Shakh* (d. 1662), in the comments on *Sh.A. Yoreh Deiah* 339:1.

29. *Responsa Bet Ya'akov* 59.

30. *Responsa Shevut Ya'akov* 1:13.

31. *Mishnah Berurah* (Jerusalem, 1963), vol. 2, p. 338, in the commentary *Beur Halakhah* to *Sh.A. Oraḥ Ḥayyim* 329:2.

32. The question is raised in this form in *Neẓer Matta'ai*, p. 126.

33. Eliezer Waldenberg, *Ẓiẓ Eliezer*, vol. 5, "Ramat Raḥel," pp. 38–40; vol. 10, pp. 122–124.

34. *Sotah* 22b.

35. Maimonides accepts this view as decisive—cf. *M.T. Hil. Sotah* 3:20.

36. *Neẓer Matta'ai*, pp. 123–124.

37. Telushkin, *Or ha-Mizraḥ*, pp. 22, 24.

38. Cf. his glosses to *Sh.A. Even ha-Ezer* 121:7 and to *Sh.A. Ḥoshen Mishpat* 211:2, where he defines this state to be one wherein the patient "regurgitates a liquid in his throat on account of a constriction in the chest."

39. See Bleich's note to his "Karen Ann Quinlan: A Torah Perspective," in *Contemporary Jewish Ethics*, ed. M. Kellner (New York, 1978), p. 306.

40. *Iggerot Moshe* (New York, 1973), *Yoreh Deiah*, 2, pp. 289 ff.

41. Rabbi I. Jakobovits, *ha-Pardes* 31 (1956): 1:28–31; 3:16–19; idem, Noam 6:272–273; *Jewish Medical Ethics* (New York, 1975), pp. 121–125, 275–276, and notes thereon.

42. Jakobovits, *ha-Pardes* 31, no. 3, p. 18.

43. *Arakhin* 7a.

44. While this is the formulation found in the article in *ha-Pardes*, there appears to be some uncertainty in Jakobovits's words in *Jewish Medical Ethics*, p. 124, where he writes that "our sources advert only to cases in which death is expected to be imminent; it is, therefore, not altogether clear whether they would tolerate this moderate form of euthanasia, though that thought cannot be ruled out."

45. Wollner, *ha-Torah ve'ha-Medinah*, p. 318. He likewise prohibits the administration of an injection intended to postpone death for a few hours.

46. B. Rabinowitz, in *Assia*, Sivan 1971, pp. 27–28.

47. G. A. Rabinowitz and M. Koenigsberg, "The Definition of Death and the Determination of Its Occurrence," *ha-Darom*, 1971, p. 75.

48. Cf. the comments of *Magen Avraham* to *Sh.A Oraḥ Ḥayyim* 328:1.

49. *Responsa Shevut Ya'akov* 3:75.

50. *Responsa Aḥiezer, Yoreh Deiah* 16. Rabbi Grodzinsky quotes in support of his position the precedents set by the *Gilyon Maharsha*, the *Binyan Ẓion*, and the *Tiferet Yisrael*.

51. I. Y. Unterman, "The Problem of Heart-Transplants from the Point of View of the Halakhah," *Noam* 13:5–6.

52. *Ketuvot* 104a. Cf. also *Bava Meẓia* 84 and *Ta'anit* 23.

53. See especially *Neẓer Matta'ai*, p. 127; Telushkin, *Or ha-Mizraḥ*, p. 24; and Bleich, "Quinlan," p. 302. Other issues are raised by Wollner, p. 321, but he too arrives at the same permissive conclusion.

54. This comment is recorded in the *Gilyon ha-Shas* ad loc. See *Neẓer Matta'ai* p. 127.

55. *Neẓer Matta'ai*, p. 127.

Law and Public Policy

5

Legal Counsel and the Truth

Introduction

When in February 1983 the American Bar Association's House of Delegates voted to prohibit lawyers from disclosing their clients' illegal or fraudulent plans, even where such activity is ongoing and results in harm to innocent victims, the debate on the proper role and standards for lawyers became a matter of public concern. That policy proposal came on top of a general agreement that when a client comes to a lawyer and confesses a completed crime or fraud, the lawyer should keep the confession in confidence, while helping the client avoid or minimize any punishment or liability.

At issue in this ongoing debate is the place of the lawyer in the judicial system. On the one hand there is the view, evidently supported by a majority of lawyers, that a lawyer has the principal function of protecting his client and the rights of the accused, rights which are fundamental to Western concepts of justice. They argue that lawyer-client confidentiality is essential, for if a client feels his lawyer will "blow the whistle," he will not disclose fully the facts of the case and consequently will not receive effective assistance of counsel. This in turn would undermine the whole adversary system, by which every defendant is entitled to a lawyer who is obliged to do everything he legally can to keep his client out of jail, whether the client is guilty or not. Thus, even if most criminal defendants are in fact guilty, the defense lawyer who uses a technicality to get an obviously guilty criminal off the hook is, in this view, doing exactly what he is supposed to do. Of course certain exceptions are allowed, as when there is imminent danger to human life or bodily harm, or for cases of perjury in the lawyer's presence.

On the other hand, there are those who argue that a lawyer should not permit himself to be used as a shield for crime and fraud. In this view, the lawyer is charged with the protection of the truth and the interests not only of his client but of the public too. By not disclosing ongoing malfeasance, the lawyer can become an accessory to a crime or fraud, either by providing a legal cover or by preventing others from stopping the crime. By defending the guilty and covering up a succession of lies or frauds, the lawyer effectively becomes a "hired gun," no more than the client's mouthpiece, with no larger responsibility as a caretaker of the law that would further obedience to the law for the well-being of society. Yet even this view agrees that in the case of a completed crime or fraud, a lawyer who is apprised by his client that he did in fact commit the crime should keep the confession in confidence and help the client avoid or minimize any punishment or liability.

At issue here is not merely the place of the lawyer in the judicial system, but the very nature of that system itself. If the system is oriented primarily in the direction of the human and civil rights of parties before the court, and is meant to assure "due process" regardless of the outcome, then it would tolerate a significant measure of dishonesty or at least cover-up in protecting the rights of the defendant. But if one takes the view that justice cannot be divorced from truth, and that the primary task of the judicial system is to ascertain the truth even while protecting the interests of the respective litigants, then no liberties with the truth can be tolerated, whether such practices emanate from lawyers, prosecutors, law-enforcement officials, or judges themselves.

As far as the Halakhah is concerned, it is fair to say that it is not "rights-oriented" as a rule, but rather "duty-oriented," i.e., it is not so much concerned with what any given party may demand of the system as it is with mutual obligations and contractual agreements. At the same time, it is also true that the Halakhah is sensitive to the need to respect the integrity of the individual in areas such as privacy, self-incrimination, and civil disobedience.

It is in balancing these sometimes conflicting considerations that the halakhic discussion of the issues raised by legal practice develops its response. Just how different the halakhic response is from the prevalent practice will soon become clear.

The Question

The financial secretary of a large corporation is sued for $10,000, an amount allegedly stolen over a period of time from the firm. He confides in his attorney that he did take $1,000—but that the rest of the money was cash received by the company and pocketed by his superiors, who now wish to use him as a scapegoat to account for the missing monies. What should the attorney do if the client wishes to deny all charges?

From a halakhic point of view, there are several issues here:

1. Is it permissible to give legal advice to a defendant, thereby enabling the defendant to present a more effective case?
2. May a lawyer represent a client, arguing on his behalf, with or without the presence of his client?
3. If the attorney knows that the client is lying, may he counsel or defend him in court? Is there a presumption of innocence in Halakhah?

Sources

A. Exodus 23:7

Keep thee far from a false matter; and the innocent and the righteous slay thou not; for I will not justify the wicked.

B. Proverbs 31:8–9

Open thy mouth for the dumb, in the cause of all such as are appointed to destruction. Open thy mouth, judge righteously, and plead the cause of the poor and needy.

C. Mishnah Avot 1:7

Judah ben Tabbai says: "Do not play the part of a counselor [in court]."

D. Jerusalem Talmud, Bava Batra 9:4

A woman who was related to R. Simon bar Va contracted an eye disease. She came [for advice] to R. Yoḥanan, and he said to her: "It depends on the duration of the problem, for if it requires only temporary treatment, then you must pay for its care. But if the care is indefinitely extended, your husband is obligated to pay for the care." How could he advise her thus? Does not the Mishnah say, "Do not play the part of a counselor," which, as R. Haggai in the name of R. Joshua b. Levi said, means that it is forbidden to reveal to a litigant the criteria by which a case is decided? The answer is that R. Yoḥanan knew that she was an honest woman, and for that reason he told her the criterion. But still, why did he reveal this to her, and give her unfair advantage, for where there is a dispute over the duration of care needed, the husband is to be believed as a rule if he says that the treatment is of limited duration? Now generally, the husband would not know this if no one tells him, so by R. Yoḥanan telling her the criteria, is he not giving her an unfair advantage? The answer, according to R. Matnei, is that such advantage is only improper if the claim of the litigant is unjustified, but where the claim is justified, it is permissible to reveal these criteria.

E. Ketuvot 52b

Relatives of R. Yoḥanan whose deceased father's second wife required daily medical care came to him for help in disputing any obligation to pay for the care. Said he to them, "Arrange with a physician to provide perpetual treatment, to be paid for all at once." Later, R. Yoḥanan regretted having said this, and exclaimed, "I have played the part of a counselor." Why did R. Yoḥanan advise them in the first place, and why did he subsequently change his mind? Initially he acted out of consideration of the prohibition "hide not thyself from thine own flesh" [Isa. 58:7]; subsequently he came to feel that a man of renown such as himself should not act in this way.

F. Jerusalem Talmud, Sanhedrin 3:8

Rav Huna rebuked a judge for saying to a defendant, "Do you admit the evidence of this witness against you, even though two witnesses are required for such evidence to be acceptable in court?" Rav Huna preferred that the defendant himself be given the opportunity to confess or to deny the validity of one witness. If Rav Huna perceived some argument favoring one or the other litigant before him, whereas the litigant was ignorant thereof, he would prompt the defendant in the articulation of that argument.

G. Jerusalem Talmud, Sanhedrin 2:1

Halakhah: The high priest judges and is subjected to judgment. *Gemara:* That the high priest judges is understandable; but that he be subject to judgment—how can that be? It is done by appointing a proxy [*antler*] on his behalf to appear in his place in court. But what if an oath has to be taken—how can his proxy take an oath?

H. Shevuot 30b, 31a

We have learned: Whence do we know that a judge may not play the part of defense counsel [*sanigron*, cf. Rif, Rabbeinu Ḥananel]? Because it says, "Keep thee far from a false matter" [Exod. 23:7]. . . . Whence do we know that if a scholar is present when a case is brought to his teacher for judgment, and the scholar can adduce an argument favoring the disadvantaged, the scholar should not remain silent but should speak up? Because it says, "Keep thee far from a false matter."

I. Responsa Yehudai Gaon (in Oẓar ha-Geonim, Ketuvot 52b)

You furthermore ask the meaning of "do not play the part of a counselor." It refers to a case in which a litigant comes to you, saying that his case is to be judged elsewhere, but that he wishes to review his arguments with your help. You should not accede to his request, so as not to play the part of the counselor.

J. Maimonides' Commentary on the Mishnah, Avot 1:7

"Counselors" are those who study laws and arguments till they become specialists in their legalities, anticipating questions and answers. Thus they advise their clients, "If the judge says this, then you say that; if your adversary argues this way, then you may answer him in the following manner." It is as if the counselor orchestrates the law and the litigant, and hence he is called *orekh din* [arranger of the law]. It is this which the Mishnah forbids, opposing the teaching of arguments or denials which might benefit one litigant. And even if you know that this litigant has been wronged, and that his opponent is lying in order to deprive him of what is rightfully his—nonetheless it is not permissible to teach this litigant any arguments that might acquit or help him at all.

K. Maimonides, Responsa nos. 37, 411

Is it proper for a defendant to appoint a proxy [*mursheh*] who will respond on his behalf to the accusations of a plaintiff claiming certain monies owed? Or can a proxy be appointed only by one who assigns court-awarded monies to his proxy, making that proxy in effect a litigant in his own right, collecting from the award to the plaintiff? If the latter case be true, then a defendant cannot appoint a proxy, for he does not know what is being claimed, and even if he did, how could he assign monies so as render the proxy a co-defendant? . . . The answer is that indeed under no circumstances may a defendant appoint such a proxy [unlike a plaintiff, who may]. Such a thing is inconceivable, and no one ever made such an error . . . for the defendant has no claim on the plaintiff by which his proxy can become a litigant. Such is the law in all Jewish courts.

L. Rabbeinu Ḥananel to Sanhedrin 18a

From the Jerusalem Talmud (G) it is apparent that a defendant may appoint a proxy [*antler*], for the high priest must appear only when an oath is required. Otherwise why does the Talmud not ask instead, "How can a defendant appoint a proxy?" By asking instead regarding the possibility of an oath, the Talmud implies that normally a proxy is permissible.

M. Naḥmanides, Novellae to Shevuot 30a

We see that there is a difference of opinion on court procedure. There are those who say that if a man wishes not to appear in court, he may appoint a proxy [*shaliaḥ*] in the presence of witnesses, to argue on his behalf in court. And there are those who differ and say that he may not do this, their reason being "that a court should not take evidence from the mouth of an interpreter [*meturgeman*] speaking falsely." This latter view explains the discussion in the Jerusalem Talmud (G) that permits such a proxy to be an exception respecting the honor due a high priest, of whom it is written, "and you shall sanctify him."

Discussion

1. *GIVING LEGAL ADVICE TO A LITIGANT*

In civil proceedings, the halakhic judicial process has two fundamental objectives: to uncover the truth, and to assist the disadvantaged wherever possible. These objectives find their ultimate sanction in the Bible, as symbolized by two verses. "Keep thee far from a false matter" (A) requires upholding the truth, while "Open thy mouth for the dumb . . . plead the cause of the poor and needy" (B) enshrines the protection of the unfairly disadvantaged. Yet these objectives are not always congruent; sometimes a tension arises, creating the need to resolve their conflicting claims, and to steer a course that will ensure justice for all involved.

The earliest halakhic sources say very little regarding legal counsel or lawyers as we know these terms. While there is no precise talmudic term corresponding to what we would call a lawyer, halakhic literature does utilize several terms to discuss different forms of legal counsel, such as *orkhei ha-dayyanim, antler, mursheh*, and *meliẓ*. The truth is that in ancient Israel there was no such thing as a professional class of lawyers or legal counsel. Litigants simply presented their own cases before the judges as best they could, while it was left to the judges to examine their evidence, clarify their arguments, and hear any witnesses that might come forward.

A pivotal Mishnah in the subsequent discussion of this issue occurs in the *Ethics of the Fathers*, which says: "Judah ben Tabbai said, 'Do not play the part of a counselor' " (C). Here the term for "counselor" is *orekh din*, literally "one who arranges the judicial procedure." While the *Avot de R. Natan*, a parallel formulation of many statements found in *Avot* (the *Ethics of the Fathers*), understands this statement to be advice for a judge to observe the minutiae of the law in the adjudication of a case before him,[1] certain later commentators, and indeed talmudic sources too, understood Judah b. Tabbai to be referring to a third party who intervenes improperly in the business of the court.[2]

Now it is this somewhat ambiguous formulation of Judah b. Tabbai that appears in several talmudic passages that are central to the issue of legal counsel. The Jerusalem Talmud (D) records an incident in which R. Yoḥanan proffered advice to a relative who was suing her husband to pay for her medical care. While his counsel consisted merely in informing her of the law in her case, the Talmud invokes Judah b. Tabbai's dictum against R. Yoḥanan's behavior. It does so by quoting a view attributed to R. Joshua b. Levi, who interprets the Mishnah in *Avot* as prohibiting even telling a litigant the law according to which his case will be decided. The Talmud then absolves R. Yoḥanan on two grounds: In the first place he knew that the woman was honest; secondly, he knew that her claim was justified.

What emerges from this passage is that the objection to a third party's offering counsel is motivated by a concern that the litigant will lie and tailor his case to suit the requirements of the law. This concern holds true even if the counselor himself scrupulously observes the truth and merely informs the litigant of the law at hand. What apparently does make a difference in permitting such counsel is (1) whether the counselor knows for certain that the litigant is completely honest and will not exploit this legal knowledge, and (2) whether the litigant is justified in his claims or his defense.[3]

A very similar concern is found in the post-talmudic period in a responsum of Yehudai Gaon (I), who lived in eighth-century Babylonia. This responsum, also quoted by Rashi,[4] forbids any scholar to listen to an argument presented for evaluation prior to its use in court, for that would in turn lead to the litigant using such knowledge to tailor his arguments in court. Yehudai Gaon refers to such practices as being widespread among Gentile counselors in his time. Implied in this responsum, as noted by Rabbi Binyamin Lipkin, is that if the scholar is certain that the facts and arguments presented to him by the litigant are true, then he may indicate his agreement with them, and his belief that they will be effective in court.[5]

In the fourteenth century this view was echoed in a responsum of R. Isaac bar Sheshet (Rivash, d. 1408) in which he explained that had he known that the man requesting his view was a litigant, he would never have provided a halakhic opinion, out of concern that the litigant "would learn with this help to argue his case, thereby rendering the scholar to be a counselor."[6] Further sanction for this view was added in a gloss of R. Moses Isserles (Rema, d. 1572), forbidding a scholar to indicate his opinion in any way that might assist a litigant in the presentation of his case before the courts.[7]

The above cases involved scholars who were simply asked to give an opinion of an argument proffered by a litigant. But what if a scholar is asked by one party to assist by providing arguments that will help that party in court? Such a case occurs in *Ketuvot* 52b (E), where R. Yoḥanan counseled his relatives to reach an understanding regarding payment of a physician, in such a way that a court would not find them liable to make the payment.[8] By so doing R. Yoḥanan was in effect informing them of a technical evasion that was legally defensible but morally questionable. The Talmud explains that R. Yoḥanan initially permitted himself such a role in consideration of the halakhic imperative to assist a blood-relative in need (based on the verse in Isaiah "hide not thyself from thine own flesh"), but that subsequently he regretted his advice as unbecoming a scholar of his renown, whose reputation demanded that he be above such personal considerations.

Implicit in this discussion is that where the scholar is unrelated to the litigant, he may not use his expert knowledge of the law to provide the litigant with a course of action that will enable him to avoid his moral obligations. The same is true if he suggests an argument that exploits a loophole in the law that is not completely applicable to the case at hand, as in the present case, where payment of the physician would normally have had to be undertaken by R. Yoḥanan's relatives. Furthermore, as pointed out by Rabbi Lipkin, it makes no difference in this case whether or not the litigant is known to be honest or scrupulous in wanting to follow a righteous path.[9]

Now it might be argued that the closing words of the talmudic discussion ("a man of renown such as himself should not act in this way") imply that this standard of behavior is not to be applied except to men of great halakhic standing and piety, such as R. Yoḥanan, whereas under "normal" circumstances we cannot insist that a third party desist from giving advice that is, strictly speaking, legally effective. Yet a close reading of the passage reveals that the fact of his being a "man of renown" is introduced as a consideration in order to neutralize the special consideration of his being a relative of the litigant; i.e., a man of renown should not invoke his relatedness in order to intercede in such a dispute. Having thus neutralized this consideration, the Talmud is left with the original prohibition, applicable to all third parties, namely, "do not play the part of the counselor," i.e., do not provide a litigant with morally questionable ammunition.

But what if it is obvious that the claim of the litigant is justified, both legally and morally? If the third party sees quite clearly that the litigant is justified in his claim against the other, but that he might have difficulty in proving his case before the court, may the third party suggest some arguments that themselves are not completely proper, simply so as to see "justice" done? Is such behavior condoned by the Jerusalem Talmud (D) when it permits outside counsel where the litigant is "justified in his claim"? The answer here is likewise to forbid such counsel, for, as Rabbi Lipkin points out, improper means are not permitted any litigant in presenting his case. This is clear from the Gemara in *Shevuot* 31a, which expressly enjoins a litigant from resorting to false strategies in order to establish a just claim. Likewise, the Jerusalem Talmud permits only truthful argumentation to substantiate a claim that is justified. To construe the Jerusalem Talmud any other way would be a distortion, for as we saw earlier, it forbade any counsel that might lead to falsehood, and therefore would certainly oppose counsel which is itself false, albeit well-intentioned. All that the Jerusalem Talmud permits is counsel that provides a truthful argument in support of a justified claim, or at the very least where the counselor is convinced that the litigant is perfectly scrupulous and will avoid any argument or claim that is improper.

But even such "honest counsel" is a matter of opinion. In a rather forthright statement, Maimonides (J) interprets Judah b. Tabbai to be saying that it is not permissible to teach a litigant *any* argument that might acquit or help him at all. Maimonides refers to people who specialize in such counsel as literally "arrangers of the law," rehearsing questions and answers prior to the deliberations of the court, and he finds such procedures unacceptable "even if you know that this litigant has been wronged." This statement by Maimonides can be interpreted in two ways.

On the one hand, he is saying that no counsel, no matter how truthful, can be proffered by a third party. This is the interpretation of Maimonides offered by Rabbeinu Yonah in his commentary on *Avot*.[10] But on the other hand, such a reading of Maimonides is faced with a problem: There is also a legal obligation, based on scriptural admonitions to "keep far from a false matter" (A) and to "open thy mouth for the dumb" (B), to speak up in defense of one who is or might be wronged. This obligation is found, for instance, in *Shevuot* 31a (H), where anyone who recognizes an argument favoring the disadvantaged is told not to remain silent, but should speak up and assist in the presentation of their case. Given such an obligation, how can anyone in a position to help refuse to offer counsel that will establish the justice of a particular claim?

For this reason, the above passage in Maimonides is interpreted by Rabbi Lipkin as forbidding only counsel that suggests the use of improper arguments to establish a legitimate claim. He argues against the interpretation of Rabbeinu Yonah, saying that Maimonides himself, in his *Mishneh Torah*,[11] accepts the view of Rav Huna in the Jerusalem Talmud (F) that even a judge may help a litigant before him in articulating an argument if the judge sees that the litigant is having trouble presenting his arguments. If so, surely a counselor may assist, according to Maimonides, in the formulation of truthful argumentation by a litigant. Hence, argues Rabbi Lipkin, Maimonides in his commentary on this Mishnah is only forbidding improper arguments—and not those that are entirely truthful.[12]

This view of Maimonides, however, is somewhat problematic, and for two reasons: (1) The literal meaning of the passage in Maimonides' commentary (J) appears to forbid all outside counsel, for Maimonides does not seem to make a distinction between truthful and untruthful arguments. (2) What Maimonides permits in the *Mishneh Torah* is assistance to a litigant who already knows his arguments but for some reason is having trouble articulating his thoughts in coherent verbal form. In such a case he can be prompted and "helped a little to clarify how to go about the matter, so as to 'open thy mouth for the dumb.' " And even this, says Maimonides, must be done with great care so as not to play the role of a counselor.[13]

According to the interpretation of Rabbeinu Yonah,

Maimonides limits the obligation to "open thy mouth for the dumb" to cases where the "dumb" knows *what* he wants to say in his self-defense but cannot verbalize it properly. In such a case, the counselor performs a function that is largely organizational. In thus restricting the obligation to speak up for the "dumb" (*ilem*), Maimonides is quite consistent with the talmudic definition of the *ilem* as one who is intelligent in all respects, quite knowledgeable, but simply lacking in verbal powers.[14] Hence the counselor may only play a role that makes up for the litigant's verbal deficiencies but not for his lack of knowledge *per se*.

May a "counselor" adopt a "client," not out of his conviction that the client is justified, but simply so as to find every feasible legal argument that might convince a judge to rule in his favor? In other words, can counsel provide all the possible arguments for one side of the case, on the grounds that irrespective of its truth, every litigant's claim should have the benefit of access to any legal argument in its favor? This question directs itself particularly at the "professional" who makes it his business to defend the "rights" of a client, including every possible legal argument on his behalf.

The answer to the question appears to be in the negative. In explaining the term *orkhei ha-dayyanim* ("arrangers of the law") as it appears in *Ketuvot* 52b (E), and as used by R. Yoḥanan, Rashi says that such a one is "he who is partial to one litigant, providing him with suitable arguments to acquit him before the judges . . . by convincing them to act to benefit this litigant." In other words, it is not so much the truth that is being defended as the client at hand. This is unlike the case where a counselor is convinced of the truth of a litigant (D), or where a third party might step in to assist a litigant under unusual circumstances, in a nonprofessional context (H).[15] It is also to be distinguished from the case of a blood-relative to a litigant, who may assist with counsel and advice even if he is not convinced of the justice of his relative's claim.[16] Of course, if he knows that the relative is not telling the truth, he may not assist him, for the relative himself is acting in a forbidden manner.

Accordingly, a professional counselor may assist an unrelated client only when he is convinced of the truthfulness of his case, and then only through the use of arguments whose truth is unimpeachable. According to one interpretation of Maimonides, even this is not permissible.

There is one more point that emerges from the sources: A litigant may even be deliberately kept uninformed of a favorable legal point, in order to ascertain "the truth." The Jerusalem Talmud (F) records Rav Huna's view that if a plaintiff were to produce only one witness, instead of the required two, to buttress his claim, then a judge should give the defendant time to admit the truth if he is under the mistaken impression that one witness is accepted as evidence in court. In other words, the defendant in this case, because he is ignorant of the law, is denied even such counsel that might acquit him, because of the concern of the court to get at the truth. Maimonides goes even further and adds that the judge should actually confront the defendant with this "evidence," and in that way force the defendant to admit or deny the validity of the witness or his evidence.[17]

With these views, it would appear that the pendulum of halakhic opinion has swung decidedly in favor of Exodus ("keep thee far from a false matter"), and away from Proverbs ("open thy mouth for the dumb"). There were, however, those who took a more supportive view, favoring a more activist defense of a litigant, particularly where the litigant was genuinely ignorant and thus helpless.

Hence, R. Jacob b. Asher (known as the *Baal ha-Turim* and also as the *Tur*, d. 1340) differed with Maimonides in his interpretation of the Jerusalem Talmud (F). According to R. Jacob, Rav Huna in this passage favors the judge who prompts one of the litigants before him if it is clear to the judge that the litigant is entirely ignorant of the existence of such an argument in his favor. This is true even where it is not clear to the judge that the claims of the litigant are justified. The problem with this view, however, is that Rav Huna seems to contradict himself earlier in the same passage when he opposes any judge intervening to inform a litigant of an argument in his favor, as we saw earlier in the case of one witness. Later halakhists attempted to reconcile the conflict,[18] but it remains true that in the view of R. Jacob b. Asher, and apparently of his father, Rabbeinu Asher (Rosh), as well,[19] a judge may indeed help a litigant to articulate a supporting argument if he was previously ignorant thereof. And if this be the case with a judge, it is certainly true of a third party or counselor, who may provide such an argument for one or the other litigant who may be unaware of it. At the very least he may prompt or suggest the beginnings of such an argument, just as a judge might do in court in consideration of "open thy mouth for the dumb." That permission to provide such assistance can be extended to a third party is proven by Rabbi Lipkin with reference to a responsum of R. Solomon b. Adret (Rashba, d. 1310), for the latter writes that "on occasion *even* a court of law may argue on behalf of a litigant, because of 'open thy mouth for the dumb,' whenever the court sees that the litigant is ignorant of a supporting argument. . . . On this basis, the court should judge according to its perception of the truth, for the Torah, which is perfect and truthful, chooses only ways that are ways of truth."[20] By writing that "even" the court may argue in this fashion, Rashba clearly implies the permissibility of such argument by a third party.

2. *REPRESENTING A LITIGANT IN COURT*

May a third party argue on behalf of a litigant before the court, with or without the presence of the litigant? Normally third-party representations are permitted under the operative principle that "a man's *shaliaḥ* [representative] is like himself." But when a litigant appoints a *shaliaḥ*, or proxy, the Halakhah recognizes that the opposing litigant can refuse to deal with the proxy, saying, "You are not a party to this conflict, therefore you may not dispute this matter with me."[21] Such a refusal is valid because the proxy's authorization (*sheliḥut*) might have been rescinded in the interim without the proxy knowing it (as explained by Rosh),[22] or else because there might be counterclaims which the proxy cannot deal with, or because of similar considerations (as explained by Shakh).[23] To overcome such objections, therefore, the Halakhah recognizes the principle of *harsha'ah* (literally "empowerment"), by which a litigant may appoint a third party as a co-litigant who will share in any court-awarded proceeds. This third party, known as a *mursheh* (from the term *harsha'ah*), is in effect arguing on his own behalf, and only coincidentally on behalf of the original claimant.[24] Because he has a personal stake in the outcome of the case, he is in fact a "party to the conflict" and thus cannot be excluded by the opposing litigant.

Yet the question may properly be asked whether a strategy of this kind is consistent with what we saw earlier regarding the intervention of an outside counsel, i.e., is such intervention conducive to ascertaining the truth in a given dispute? Indeed, in the opinion of Rav in the Gemara to *Shevuot* 31a, the verse "he did that which is not good among his people" (Ezek. 18:18) refers to a co-opted third party who acts as a litigant and thereby enters into a dispute to which he is not a party. As explained by Rashi, such an arrangement is disparaged because it reduces the possibility of a compromise being struck—in that the co-opted agent would have greater difficulty in compromising assets belonging to another.

In light of this question, certain medieval authorities, such as Rema, favored co-option of a third party only where the litigant so represented was (at least to the co-opted agent) clearly justified in his claim. In that case it was not only permissible but obligatory to act in his stead, if that would assist his case.[25] This position would be quite consistent with our earlier findings regarding counsel to a litigant with a completely justifiable claim. Other authorities, notably R. Abraham b. David (Ravad, d. 1198), favored co-option only where the two litigants were in separate cities, and therefore as a practical matter a third party was required to pursue the legitimate claims of the injured party.[26] As R. Jacob b. Asher put it, were such an arrangement not permitted, "anyone could abscond with his fellow's possessions [and not be subject to prosecution]!" In any case, where a person was capable of assisting the cause of justice, and could help by articulating a truthful argument that would assist a legitimate claim, he was morally obliged even to be co-opted in this fashion.[27]

Now, all the above discussion relates to a litiga. t who can co-opt a third party by agreeing to share all or part of w. at the court might award, thereby making the co-opted individual a direct party to the litigation. Some authorities even insist that the remuneration be on a percentage basis, for in their view, it is only when his remuneration is a function of the total amount awarded by the court that the co-opted agent can insist on his personal stake in the total amount of the claim. Were the agent simply to accept a set fee for his services, the opposing litigant could well argue against the agent's presence, saying, "You are not a party to the rest of the disputed claim."[28] But what if it is not the plaintiff but the defendant who wishes to co-opt an agent? Since there are no court-awarded proceeds to a defendant that could be shared with the agent, how can *harsha'ah* be implemented, so as to permit a third party to argue on behalf of a defendant?

The Babylonian Talmud does not discuss this question, but the Jerusalem Talmud does, in the context of a high priest who may be represented by an *antler*, or agent (G). During the geonic period, the assumption was that a defendant could *not* be represented, for the very reasons outlined above.[29] But Rabbeinu Ḥananel (Kairouan, d. 1055), a pioneer in the frequent use of the Jerusalem Talmud, broke with the geonim in rare fashion to permit a third-party defense of a defendant, based on his reading of the Jerusalem Talmud. Thus, Rabbeinu Ḥananel argues (L) that the talmudic passage, by raising only the question of the *antler* taking an oath, implicitly accepts the idea of a co-opted agent under more normal circumstances.

Yet among Sephardic authorities the geonic view held sway. Most emphatic among these was Maimonides, who, while not mentioning the issue in the *Mishneh Torah*, in several responsa (K) did discuss and strongly oppose such appointments. Maimonides saw no possibility of this whatsoever, saying, "For the defendant has no claim on the plaintiff by which his proxy can become a litigant. Such is the law in all Jewish courts." But in spite of the last phrase, certain Ashkenazic authorities did countenance the representation of a defendant under limited conditions. Among them was R. Eliezer b. Nathan (Ravan, d. 1170), a scholar who was much influenced by Rabbeinu Ḥananel.[30] He too quotes the Jerusalem Talmud, and concludes that "an adult may indeed appoint an *apotropos* [agent]."[31]

How, according to these authorities, can such an agent be co-opted in the absence of an award to a defendant? One suggestion is found in the *Sefer ha-Ittur* of Isaac b. Abba Mari of Marseilles (d. 1190): The agent should deposit a security with the court, out of his own monies, so that in the event the defendant is found culpable, the agent himself will pay the debt.[32] In this fashion, the agent becomes a party to the dispute and can thus represent the defendant even in the absence of the latter.

A significant development in the thinking of those opposed to the appointment of an agent to represent a defendant was introduced by Naḥmanides (Ramban) in the thirteenth century (M). While he mentions the views of both sides regarding the issue, he seems to agree with those who were opposed to such an appointment,[33] and provides two reasons for their view: (1) the treatment accorded a high priest (G) is *sui generis*, and cannot be quoted to permit such appointments for other less important persons; and (2) "the court should not take evidence from the mouth of an interpreter speaking falsely." Now whereas the latter formulation utilizes a well-known principle found in the Mishnah in the context of the translation of evidence before the court,[34] Naḥmanides' final words ("speaking falsely") introduce a whole new element—whether a third party will be beholden to the truth. Naḥmanides apparently felt that an outside agent, who might be functioning in an impersonal, somewhat "professional" capacity, might feel able to take liberties with the truth. Naḥmanides' student, R. Solomon b. Adret (Rashba, d. 1310), echoed this concern when he wrote that "it may happen that a defendant who knows he is wrong will not dare to deny the truth in the presence of the claimant, who also knows the truth, whereas an agent will deny the truth, not knowing the facts independently."[35] Rashba does, however, permit such representation on condition that the agent says only what the defendant himself tells him.[36] Clearly though, this condition hardly satisfies the concern that the defendant might take advantage of not having to face the claimant with a false denial, and Rashba himself elsewhere expresses his discomfort with this loophole, which might lead to a distortion of the truth.[37] Perhaps as a result of this reservation, the accepted custom among his Spanish contemporaries was not to permit such representation as a rule, except under special circumstances.[38]

In any case, Rashba's view on this question is quite consistent with his view, discussed earlier, that in the interests of the truth, the court as well as a third party should indeed intervene to assist either of the litigants if it is clear that his claim is justified.[39] Under such circumstances Rashba's reservations would be more than satisfied if such a representative before the court was permitted.

During the next period of Jewish history, the fourteenth century appears to have been a time of transition and flux, with some Sephardic authorities permitting third-party representation (such as Ritva, d. 1330, who argued that "we do not suspect an agent of lying when it is not his own gain that is at stake"),[40] while others remained opposed (including Rosh, d. 1327, and his son,

R. Jacob b. Asher).[41] At the same time, certain Ashkenazi authorities limited the manner in which a defendant could appoint an agent. For example, Rabbeinu Pereẓ of Corbeil (Raf, d. 1295) insisted that an agent could appear before the court only if his commission had been given before two witnesses who subsequently attested to that commission.[42]

A little later the view of those who were opposed to agency was given added impetus by Rabbeinu Nissim Gerondi (Ran, d. 1375). He explained that Maimonides too opposed third-party appointments, because of the general prohibition (encountered earlier in the words of Naḥmanides) against taking evidence via an interpreter, a prohibition which Maimonides extended to cover a representative of the defendant.[43]

For the next several centuries, the predominant view was that which opposed such representation. R. Samuel Kallai (Greece, d. 1582),[44] R. Moses of Trani (known as Mabit, lived in Israel, d. 1580),[45] and R. Samuel di Modena (Rashdam, d. 1589)[46] all opposed the co-option of a third party to represent a defendant. It was this view which received the imprimatur of the *Shulḥan Arukh*, forbidding such representation in the absence of the defendant himself.[47] A concurring opinion was offered by R. Moses Isserles (Rema, d. 1572) in his commentary to the *Tur*.[48] In his view, when the defendant is absent, he cannot be represented by another, whereas the claimant does not have to be there; however, when the parties are present in court, they must both speak for themselves, and neither can be represented by another. A further justification for this negative attitude toward an agency in general, and that of a defendant in particular, is found in the writings of R. Joshua Falk Katz (Sema, d. 1614), a pupil of Rema, when he says that the talmudic presumption that "a man as a rule does not dare [to deny the truth] to the face of his creditor" cannot be said to apply when he appoints an agent to act on his behalf.[49]

But there was another reason for this attitude, and it was the result of the questionable tactics and ethical standards practiced by certain individuals in representing defendants. A contemporary source describes such people as "searching in texts for arguments and laws that they favor, and in most cases what they adopt is the refuse, while the real food they throw out, for they know that the law does not accord with their argumentation."[50] Similarly, R. Yair Ḥayyim Bachrach (author of the *Ḥavvot Yair*, d.

1702) speaks of those who study the laws for ulterior motives, "leading to argumentation and strife, deception and the adoption of false argumentation to justify the wicked and defame the righteous."[51] R. Ḥayyim Benveniste (d. 1673) refers to Venice as a place where "advocates" have recourse to lies to the extent that "the greater the lies, the deceptions, and the trickeries, the more the litigants pursue their services with financial reward."[52] These things and more are described as current practice in Livorno, Italy, by R. Abraham Ḥayyim Rodriguez, in the late seventeenth century.[53]

Yet in spite of these observations, and the long history of determined opposition, it was during this period that a change in communal practice began to be effected. Here and there, the sources reveal local decrees and rabbinic enactments that permitted outside representation of either litigant under controlled conditions. Such was the case in the communities of Altona, Hamburg, and Ansbach, where in 1726 permission was granted for such representation, as long as the agent thus appointed was approved of by the local authorities and invested with the title *ḥaver*.[54] In this way, apparently, it was hoped to avoid some of the excesses practiced in other communities. In Kushta, Turkey, as early as 1575, a rabbinic enactment permitted the use of representation by either litigant, as long as the litigants themselves stayed out of court.[55] This was likewise permitted in Venice, as the above responsum of R. Ḥayyim Benveniste indicates, as well as in the Italian community of Mantua.[56] In the nineteenth century, the Turkish community of Smyrna enacted a decree that permitted the defendant to appoint a proxy whenever the plaintiff had taken a similar step.[57] And in Sofia, there developed a rather surprising custom whereby the court itself urged both litigants to appoint representatives to argue their respective cases. This procedure was justified on the grounds that the litigants themselves might become emotionally overwhelmed in court, whereas third-party representatives would be more amenable to compromise and reason.[58] In such cases, however, there was a significant proviso: The representatives could not be "professionals" but were required to be either relatives of the litigants or recognized rabbinical scholars whose credentials were unimpeachable. In this way it was hoped to avoid any improprieties or excesses.

Even in Jerusalem, in the nineteenth century, the prevailing custom permitted a defendant to appoint an agent on his behalf.[59] According to these customs, the *Shulḥan Arukh*, in forbidding such agents, was understood to be speaking only of cases wherein the plaintiff himself appeared; but where the plaintiff appointed an agent, even the *Shulḥan Arukh* would permit the defendant to do likewise. Ultimately, even in Poland itself, where Rema and his students had been so opposed to an agency of this kind, the nineteenth century saw the acceptance of that institution as part of proper legal procedure, even if it entailed an agent representing a defendant in the presence of the plaintiff. This view was codified by Rabbi Yeḥiel Michael Epstein in his *Arukh ha-Shulḥan*, with the proviso that in case of difficulties, the litigants themselves would be called upon to clarify the facts more directly.[60]

The practice of permitting bilateral representation has since been confirmed by later authorities, in spite of reservations and doubts. Thus the head of the rabbinical court of Lomza, Poland, Rabbi Malkiel Ẓevi Tenenbaum, permitted a salaried employee to argue the merits of his employer's case, where the employer is too busy or otherwise occupied to appear himself.[61] He reasoned that the employee would be at least as conversant with the business affairs of the employer as the latter himself, and hence could be considered a party to the conflict, not liable to argue falsely. More recently, the reknowned Rabbi Abraham Isaiah Karelitz (known as Ḥazon Ish, d. 1953), while affirming a strong preference for the personal presence and evidence of the litigants themselves, nonetheless accepted the widespread practice whereby legal counsel represents both clients, adding that the practice is justifiable only if both litigants agree to the presence of representatives.[62] An important source supporting these lenient rulings is found in the writings of the Sema, who permits the appearance in court of outside counsel on two conditions: (1) the representation is not instead of, but in addition to, the words of the litigant himself; (2) the counsel must be expressly empowered by the litigant to act fully on behalf of the litigant, as if a party to the case.[63] Ḥazon Ish adds that the arrangement can be further justified because it safeguards the litigants' honor, dignity, or money, for "we may not cause any loss of equity to a fellow Israelite."

In 1960, the Israeli rabbinate formally accepted these practices permitting legal counsel to argue on behalf of either litigant, on condition that such counsel be legally or halakhically licensed and competent to appear in court, and furthermore that the litigants themselves be present in court, except under extreme circumstances.[64]

In this fashion, halakhists have come to accept the practice of legal counsel before the court, in spite of earliest opposition to such practices. By incorporating certain safeguards and verbal warnings, they hoped to utilize the offices of the legal profession to further the goal of the attainment of the truth in court.

3. *LEGAL COUNSEL AND A PRESUMPTION OF INNOCENCE*

In the preceding discussion we have seen how the Halakhah moves within the tension created by the need to establish the truth and the need to protect the individual. One point that emerged with some clarity was the third party's permission to assist a litigant if it is clear to him that the litigant is innocent or justified in his claim.[65] But the question that immediately arises is when a litigant is to be considered innocent. Is he to be considered innocent until proven guilty? If there is a presumption of innocence until the court proves otherwise, may a third party come to his defense or assistance even if there is reason to believe that he is guilty or lying?

There appears to be general agreement among post-talmudic authorities that there is a presumption of innocence (*ḥezkat kashrut*) until proven otherwise. While the Talmud does not mention the matter directly, later halakhists, including Maimonides,[66] Ravad,[67] and Rosh,[68] indicate that all Israelites can be presumed to follow the dictates of the Torah unless the opposite is proven true.[69] Hence, wherever possible one should assume that an action was undertaken in a manner that was permissible, albeit unlikely; and furthermore, if it *was* done in a forbidden manner, it should be assumed to have been done in error.[70] This presumption was codified by the *Shulḥan Arukh* and ratified by Rema.[71] According to most authorities, the presumption remains true even in regard to rabbinic prohibitions, although we might think that people would not be as careful in this area as they would be with biblical prohibitions.[72]

What if the defendant admits his guilt to a third party, or

concedes that his claim is without basis or untruthful? Whereas generally speaking a litigant is not permitted to incriminate himself, the Halakhah does permit admissions of guilt or wrongdoing in purely civil disputes involving monetary restitution.[73] In such cases the principle that is adopted is that "the confession of a litigant has the weight of one hundred witnesses." Accordingly, even outside of court, an admission of guilt made to a counselor would seem to destroy any presumption of innocence. Hence no legal counsel or assistance would be permitted.

Where the litigant does not admit any wrongdoing or untruthfulness, but the legal counsel has reason to believe that the litigant is less than honest, is there still a presumption of innocence? From the sources examined in Section 1 above, it would appear that the answer is no, and that assistance may be given only if the counselor is sure in his own mind of the justice of the litigant's argument, whether it be the plaintiff or the defendant. In such a case it is the consideration of "open thy mouth for the dumb" (B) that would motivate any intervention. But where doubt exists as to the propriety of a claim, it is for the court alone to determine the innocence or guilt of the respective parties. In other words, it is the court that must presume the innocence of both parties, not a third party, unless the third party is certain of the innocence of one side.

All of this is in contrast to cases involving capital punishment. As we will see in the chapter devoted to capital cases, every means possible that might acquit such a defendant is to be adopted, including a third party who has anything positive to say that might save the defendant. As R. Isaac bar Sheshet wrote in one responsum, "in capital cases . . . the accused may appoint an advocate who will argue in his behalf and defend him, for we always pay heed to anyone who comes in defense of the accused."[74]

But in more "normal" circumstances, where the concern of the court is to get at the truth alone, the Halakhah, as we have seen, would favor minimal outside involvement, even where there is reason to believe that one party is being unjustly treated by the other. It is only where the third party is convinced of the rectitude of one or the other party that he may intercede on the side of justice.

We are now in a position to summarize the various views among the halakhic authorities on the status and function of legal counsel.

When it comes to giving legal advice without representing the litigant in court, we have seen that from the earliest times there was at best a reserved attitude toward those who gave such advice. The Jerusalem Talmud evinced the concern that such advice might result in the litigant resorting to false arguments in court, but it permits such advice where it is clear to the counsel that the litigant is either completely honest or is justified in the case at hand. Similar views were adhered to by Yehudai Gaon, Rivash, and Rema, all of whom required exceeding circumspection on the part of a counselor. Their reservations were strengthened if the advice was morally questionable or involved the use of a loophole in the law. And even where the litigant is seen to be quite justified in his claim, a counselor may not suggest the use of a "tactical lie" that will ensure that "justice" be done—as is clear from *Shevuot* 31a and from the Jerusalem Talmud, both of which permit counsel only when it involves truthful arguments in support of justified claims.

Even this, however, is disputed by Maimonides. In his view (according to one interpretation, that of Rabbeinu Yonah), no counsel whatsoever may be offered a litigant. Others, notably Rabbi Binyamin Lipkin, understand Maimonides to be opposed only to improper argumentation to establish a legitimate claim. Maimonides does explicitly permit the court to assist a litigant in articulating his arguments, as long as they are arguments which the litigant himself had suggested. Furthermore, according to the Jerusalem Talmud, and Maimonides, a litigant may be kept uninformed of a legal point that favors him if doing so will induce him to spontaneously admit the truth.

A more lenient view is adopted by R. Jacob b. Asher, the author of the *Tur*, and by Rosh, who are of the opinion that both judges and counselors may properly suggest arguments to a litigant who is ignorant of the arguments in his favor. This would also seem to be Rashba's view.

As to the question of counsel representing a litigant in court, there appears to be a historical evolution in attitudes. Initially, the sources were quite opposed to such representation, unless (as in the case of a claimant) the third party could be personally involved in the case by becoming a party to any monies awarded to the litigant. This, according to some authorities, would require the agent to receive his remuneration on a percentage basis of the award, thereby rendering him a party to the entire disputed amount.

But starting with Rabbeinu Ḥananel in the eleventh century, a more lenient view began to take root, based essentially on a permissive reading of a crucial passage in the Jerusalem Talmud. Scholars who followed in this path were Ravan, Ra'avyah, R. Isaac b. Abba Mari (author of the *Ittur*), Rashba, and Ritva. By and large, however, the Sephardic authorities remained opposed to the representation of a defendant. This was the view of Maimonides, Naḥmanides, Rosh (who moved to Spain in his later years), R. Jacob b. Asher, and Ran. The predominance of these views was reflected in the *Shulḥan Arukh* and its commentators in the sixteenth and seventeenth centuries. The opposition to legal representation seems to have been motivated by a combination of textual nuance and negative experiences with "professional" counselors whose intent was mainly pecuniary, so that they would often resort to a variety of dishonest stratagems and arguments.

Yet by the seventeenth century there were already signs that local authorities were beginning to countenance legal representation as a reflection of currents in the larger society. Turkish, German, Adriatic, Polish, and Palestinian communities gradually came to accept such practices, albeit with careful restrictions and rules governing their use, so as to minimize the possibility of abuse. In the twentieth century, Israeli rabbinical courts and authorities (notably Ḥazon Ish) have expressly permitted legal representation of claimant and defendant, in recognition of the universal practice, but here too it was with certain safeguards stipulated to prevent any excesses.

Of course, one of these stipulations was that the counsel be convinced of the justice of his "client." The question is whether there might be a presumption of innocence by his counsel until proven otherwise. Generally, the Halakhah does presume innocence; this is formulated by Maimonides, Ravad, and Rosh. This presumption was codified by the *Shulḥan Arukh* and ratified by Rema. But it is clear that in purely monetary matters, such a presumption is destroyed by an admission of guilt by either party, whether that admission takes place in court or out. Hence where a litigant confides his guilt, he cannot be presumed by his counsel to deserve a proper defense. Where the counsel has reason to believe that the litigant may be lying, or at least is not sure that he is telling the truth, the consensus of opinion would be opposed to representing the client or in any way assisting his case by prior counsel or advice.

To return to the case with which the chapter began, it is clear that once the client admits in confidence that he did in fact improperly take monies not belonging to him, the counselor should neither advise nor represent the client, other than to urge him to present the truth before the court. Where the counsel feels that there is some legally permissible strategy that might help the litigant to be believed in presenting the truth, he should certainly offer such help, out of consideration both of "keeping far from a false matter" and of "open thy mouth for the dumb."

Notes

In preparing this chapter, two outstanding articles were most helpful in scope and insight. The first was by Rabbi Binyamin Lipkin, "Arikhat Din be'Mishpat ha-Torah," *Sinai* 30 (1952): 46–61; 31 (1953): 165–183. This article was reprinted in its entirety in *Torah she-Be'Al Peh* 22 (1981): 107–142, together with an accompanying essay by She'ar Yashuv Kohen that essentially recapitulates the substance of the article and makes certain concrete proposals on the basis of its findings, *apropos* of Israeli religious courts. The second article appeared as the eighth chapter in N. Rakover, *ha-Shelihut ve'ha-Harsha'ah be'Mishpaṭ ha-Ivri* (Jerusalem, 1972), entitled "Mursheh le'Nitva: le'Ma'amado shel Orekh Din," pp. 308–353.

1. *Avot de'R. Natan*, chap. 10. Similarly see also the first explanation found in Rashi's commentary to this Mishnah in *Avot*, and the second and third explanations mentioned by R. Obadiah Bartenura in his commentary, ad loc. Cf. also the discussion in Rav Ẓa'ir, "ha-Sanegoria be'Vatei Dinin shel Yisrael," *ha-Shelaḥ* 3 (1898): 419.

2. See in particular Maimonides' *Commentary to the Mishnah* on *Avot* 1:8, the first view mentioned in Bartenura's commentary, and the talmudic passages in *Shabbat* 139a, *Sotah* 47b, and Rashi *ad loc.*

3. A similar case is described in J. T. *Ketuvot* 4:10, where only the first justification is provided, i.e., if the counselor knows the litigant to be completely honest.

4. Rashi to *Avot* 1:8.

5. Lipkin, "Arikhat Din," 30:49.

6. *Responsa Rivash* (Vilna, 1878), no. 179. Similarly, see the responsum of Rashba, quoted in the *Bet Yosef* to *Ṭur Ḥoshen Mishpat* 17, at the end.

7. *Hasagot ha-Rema, Hoshen Mishpat* 17:4. The *Pitḥei Teshuvah* ad loc. discusses the various considerations involved in offering legal opinions to one

disputant, and concludes that a scholar should not provide a responsum in such a dispute, on the grounds that if the disputant recognizes that his arguments will not be very convincing before the court, he will refuse to go through with the *din torah* (court proceeding). Others, including the *Knesset ha-Gedolah* (*Tur Ḥoshen Mishpat* 17:19), disagree, if the disputant involved is known to be honest. Cf. also L. Finkelstein, *Jewish Self-Government in the Middle Ages* (New York, 1924), pp. 72–73.

8. A similar situation is likewise recorded in *Ketuvot* 86a, this time involving a question posed to R. Naḥman.

9. Lipkin, "Arikhat Din," 30:53. Rabbi Lipkin notes the question, raised by Rav Ẓa'ir, p. 418 n., that there would appear to be some inconsistency between this incident and the case mentioned in the Jerusalem Talmud, which permits such counsel where the litigant is justified in his claim. Lipkin argues quite justifiably that there is a crucial difference between the two cases: In the Jerusalem Talmud no special action was necessary on her part, and the facts of the case alone were sufficient to favor her case. But in *Ketuvot*, R. Yoḥanan's relatives would have to make special arrangements with the physician, in accord with the requirements of Halakhah, in the absence of which their claim would be questionable at best.

10. Commentary of Rabbeinu Yonah to *Avot* 1:8.

11. *M.T. Sanhedrin* 21:11.

12. Lipkin, "Arikhat Din," 30:54–56.

13. Rabbi Lipkin understands Rabbeinu Yonah to interpret Maimonides as forbidding even such prompting by a third party. But it is not necessary to understand Rabbeinu Yonah in this fashion, for while he does mention the function of a counselor to "order the litigant's own arguments", Rabbeinu Yonah also says that Maimonides is speaking of a third party who "arranges the laws and tells the individual his case." He clearly understands Maimonides to be criticizing a counselor who does all these things.

14. *Ḥagigah* 2b, *Yevamot* 104b. Cf. Maimonides himself in *M.T. Hil. Ishut* 2:26. For a general discussion, see *Encyclopedia Talmudit* 2:13.

15. Cf. likewise Rashi to *Sotah* 47b.

16. See above, p. 101.

17. Maimonides, *M.T. Hil. Sanhedrin* 21:10, *Hil. To'en ve'Nit'an* 5:1. This raises the whole issue of the legal status of an admission of guilt. Generally speaking, the Halakhah recognizes a confession in monetary matters (except where there is a financial penalty involved), but not in the area of prohibited behavior (*issur ve'heter*). Cf. *Encyclopedia Talmudit* 1:548 for a discussion of the principle *ein adam meisim aẓmo rasha* ("a man is not believed if he incriminates himself in court"). For a detailed analysis of the whole issue of self-incrimination in Halakhah, see the excellent study by Aaron Kirschenbaum, *Self-Incrimination in Jewish Law* (New York, 1970), in particular pp. 114–115, 184.

18. Cf. Sema to *Sh.A. Ḥoshen Mishpat* 17:42, and *Birkei Yosef* to *Sh.A. Ḥoshen Mishpat* 16:21. Lipkin, "Arikhat Din," 31:273, attempts to distinguish between the two cases by saying that in the case where there was only one witness, the judge was not sure whether the defendant knew that in fact two witnesses were necessary. This is a rather difficult distinction to maintain.

19. The *Tur* refers to the *Responsa of the Rosh* 81:1.

20. *Responsa Rashba* (Leghorn, 1825), vol. 2, no. 393. Cf. Lipkin, "Arikhat Din," 31:274.

21. Naḥmanides, *Milḥamot Hashem* to *Bava Kamma* 70a; and *Shittah Mekubbeẓet* to same, in the name of the students of Rabbeinu Pereẓ.

22. Rosh, Bava Kamma 9:21. See also Ra'avan to *Bava Kamma*, chap. 79.

23. Shakh to *Sh.A. Ḥoshen Mishpat* 122:4.

24. *Bava Kamma* 70a, and Maimonides, *M.T. Hil. Sheluḥin* 3:1; *Tur Ḥoshen Mishpat* 124:4. For a general discussion of the meaning and parameters of *harsha'ah*, see *Encyclopedia Talmudit* 11:15 ff.

25. *Hasagot ha-Rema* to *Sh.A. Ḥoshen Mishpat* 123:16.

26. *Hasagot ha-Ravad to M.T. Sheluḥin* 3:5. The Vilna Gaon finds the source for this condition in *Bava Batra* 104b.

27. Tosafot to *Shevuot* 31a, as well as the comments of R. Mordecai b. Hillel ha-Kohen (the *Mordecai*) ad loc. in the name of Ri.

28. *Hasagot ha-Ravad* to *M.T. Sheluḥin* 3:2. But Naḥmanides disagrees; cf. *Encyclopedia Talmudit* 11:31, nn. 166 ff.

29. Such was the opinion of Saadya Gaon, as quoted by the *Ittur* 75a, 107a; and of Hai Gaon, in *Responsa of the Geonim*, ed. Harkavy (1887, 1849), no. 180.

30. Cf. *Encyclopaedia Judaica* 6:627.

31. *Sefer ha-Ra'avan*, chap. 115. His grandson, Ra'avyah, likewise mentions and appears to adopt this view [cf. the *Mordecai* to *Bava Meẓia*, chaps. 275–276.

32. *Sefer ha-Ittur* (Warsaw, 1801; Lemberg, 1860), s.v. *harsha'ah*, 72:4.

33. His student (once removed), Ritva, understood him in this way too. Cf. *Novellae of Ritva* to *Shevuot* 30a.

34. Mishnah *Makkot* 1:9. For analysis of the use of translators in court, see B. Zolti, in *Noam* 3 (1960): 26 ff.

35. *Novellae of Rashba* to *Shevuot* 30a.

36. *Responsa Rashba* 2:393.

37. The *Bet Yosef* to *Tur Ḥoshen Mishpat* 124 refers to such a responsum of Rashba.

38. *Responsa Rashba* 1:743. Such an exception would be a case involving "important women," where there was a tradition going back to Alfasi (see Rakover, "Mursheh le'Nitva," p. 314, for the view of Ri Ibn Migash) permitting the deposition of their claims before a special court-appointed messenger, to spare them the loss of dignity of appearing in court.

39. See above, p. 106.

40. *Novellae of Ritva* to *Shevuot* 30a, who also refers to the concurring view of his contemporary R. Aaron Halevy (known as Rah), saying, "he permitted this every day."

41. *Piskei ha-Rosh* to *Shevuot* 4:2; *Tur Ḥoshen Mishpat* 124.

42. *Tosafot Rabbeinu Pereẓ* to *Bava Kama* 70a, and *Shittah Mekubbeẓet* ad loc.

43. *Novellae of the Ran* to Alfasi, *Shevuot*, chap. 4, s.v. *gemara*. Abraham A. Neuman's *The Jews in Spain* (Philadelphia, 1942), vol. 1, pp. 118–120, provides a good cross-section of attitudes to lawyers in late-medieval Spanish-Jewish communities.

44. *Responsa Mishpetei Shmuel* 121.

45. *Responsa Mabit* 33.

46. *Responsa Maharashdam* (Lemberg, 1862) 439.

47. *Bet Yosef* to *Tur Ḥoshen Mishpat* 124; *Sh.A. Ḥoshen Mishpat* 124.

48. *Darkei Moshe* to the *Tur* ad loc.

49. Sema to *Sh.A. Ḥoshen Mishpat* 124:1, and similarly *Levush Ir Shushan, Ḥoshen Mishpat* 124. Regarding the dictum *ein adam me'iz panav bifnei ba'al ḥovo*, see *Encyclopedia Talmudit* 1:543.

50. R. Samuel b. David Halevy, author of *Naḥalat Shivah* 44:1.

51. *Responsa Ḥavvot Yair* (Lemberg, 1896) 124.

52. *Responsa Ba'i Ḥa'i, Ḥoshen Mishpat* 2:75.

53. *Responsa Or la-Ẓaddik, Ḥoshen Mishpat* 1.

54. See Rakover, "Mursheh le'Nitva," p. 336, n.188.
55. Ibid., nn. 196–197.
56. Ibid., nn. 204–205.
57. See *Responsa Masa Ḥayyim* 4:22, authored by R. Ḥayyim Pelaggi (d. 1868), rabbi of that community.
58. *Responsa Ḥoshen ha-Efod, Ḥoshen Mishpat* 43.
59. *Sefer Sha'al ha-Ish, Ḥoshen Mishpat* 12.
60. *Arukh ha-Shulḥan* (Warsaw, 1900–1912), *Ḥoshen Mishpat* 124:4, and likewise the commentary of R. Jonathan Eibeschutz, *Urim ve'Tumim to Ḥoshen Mishpat* 124.
61. *Responsa Divrei Malki'el* 3:167.
62. Ḥazon Ish, *Ḥoshen Mishpat* 4:1, 5.
63. Cf. Sema to *Sh.A. Ḥoshen Mishpat* 17:14. See likewise *Encyclopedia Talmudit* 7:324, n. 246: "This is just how we today maintain the practice of appointing a lawyer [*orekh din*]."
64. *Takkanot ha-Diyyun be'Vatei Din ha-Rabbaniyim be'Yisrael*, 1960, par. 41. For a general discussion of *harsha'ah*, see *Encyclopedia Talmudit* 4:103–104.
65. Cf. above, Section 1.
66. Maimonides, *M.T. Hil. Kiddush ha-Ḥodesh* 2:2.
67. Gloss of Ravad to *M.T. Hil. Gerushin* 10:19.
68. *Novellae of Rosh* to *Ketuvot* 1:18. See also *Responsa Rosh* 20:17.
69. Cf. *Encyclopedia Talmudit* 14:26 ff., which discusses these and other views on this issue.
70. *Responsa Rivash* 447, 310.
71. *Sh.A. Ḥoshen Mishpat* 34:12, Rema ad loc.
72. Maimonides, *M.T. Hil. Malveh ve'Loveh* 4:10, and *Maggid Mishnah* ad loc.; *Bet Yosef* to *Tur Yoreh Deiah* 166; *Responsa Maharit, Even ha-Ezer*, 1; and *Responsa Maharashdam, Ḥoshen Mishpat* 310.
73. See Kirschenbaum, *Self-Incrimination*, pp. 38–41; 100–103, based on the Mishnah *Ketuvot* 3:9; Tosefta *Bava Meẓia* 1:10. See also N. Lamm, "Self-Incrimination in Law and Psychology," *Faith and Doubt* (New York, 1971), pp. 274–275.
74. *Responsa Rivash* 234–239, and Kirschenbaum, *Self-Incrimination*, p. 89.

6

Violence in Self-Defense and the Defense of Others

Introduction

All civilized societies presume the rule of law, the purpose of which is to regulate social behavior so as to prevent any individual or group from acting in ways that are injurious to others who live in that society. Thus, by a so-called social contract, those who live in a particular society are presumed to have given up certain freedoms and prerogatives in return for receiving the protection and privileges provided by those who govern that society.

It follows from this that most systems of government are opposed to the idea that individuals or groups should be free to renege on this "contract." It is difficult, to say the least, to permit individuals to function as a law unto themselves, carrying out their own justice, living by their own standards of right and wrong, without reference to the conventions of the larger society in which they live. Yet there are circumstances in which the laws of the land or society are inadequate for the protection of its law-abiding individuals. Thus there arises the question as to when it is permissible to have recourse to actions deemed necessary to preserve life or limb—when the government or society does not, or cannot, provide for such needs.

The issue occurs most commonly in cases of violent attack. How may a person dispose of that peril to himself or others? The context may be an urban setting in which a man or woman is robbed while threatened with physical injury; it might occur in more politicized situations, in which members of a group feel physically threatened by the overt or covert actions of another group. Instances of such situations have abounded in recent years, wherein individuals or groups have taken up arms in defense of the innocent, causing injury or death to those they deem a threat. In the United States there is a widespread and popular image of the vigilante who takes the law in his own hands to bring "justice" in the face of an "inefficient" system of justice; individuals who have attempted to maim or kill their alleged "muggers" are often seen as public heroes; and the right to bear arms for self-defense is promulgated by a powerful national lobby which maintains that the right of self-defense is a basic guarantee of the American system of law. In the State of Israel the issue has taken on the additional weight of religious and nationalist sentiment and doctrine, most particularly in the angry debate over the so-called Jewish Underground, many of whose members were observant Jews, responsible for certain violent (and homicidal) actions directed against Palestinians perceived as being Arab terrorist sympathizers. On another level, the issue of preemptive war raises similar questions: i.e., may a sovereign state, or society, unleash preemptive war or battle when they perceive (as did the Israelis in 1967) that they are about to be attacked?

Responses to such cases are varied. On the one hand, there are those who consistently oppose the use of violence to stem violence. They argue that no civilized society can permit individuals, no matter how innocent or provoked, to take up arms in violation of the social contract. Violence, it is said, merely begets more violence. Some, as did Gandhi, advocate forms of pacificism or social reform to remove the "underlying causes" of violence, claiming that in the long run, this is the only hope for a just society. Others, along similar lines, argue that the state alone can be empowered to use force of arms, thus the coercive power of the state must be strengthened, even though individual lives may be forfeit in the short run. Common to these views is the fear of the anarchy that might result were any individuals to be permitted to act with violence to bring about their own vision of justice: where would we draw the line on this slippery slope?

On the other hand, there are those who see individual rights as primary. What is good for society is what is good for its individuals, especially those who are weak and without immediate recourse to justice. Thus society, it is argued, must allow an individual to protect himself or his fellows under all reasonable circumstances. In this view, laws are often impractical and faulty, and a person should not be required to sacrifice his life or limb for some long-term gain to society. To the contrary, if people are allowed to defend themselves or other innocent victims, society will benefit, in that criminals will perceive the need to act in lawful fashion. But if such preventive action is not permitted, and criminals are permitted to "get away with murder," all of society will suffer, in that such aggressors will feel free to pursue ever-wider circles of violence.

In between these opposing viewpoints stand a number of others, qualifying the terms and conditions under which recourse to arms can be endorsed. For them it becomes a question of circumstances, intent, background of the assailant, perceptions and subjective judgments, and the degree of violence that might be permitted as a response, as well as the issue of direct vs. indirect threat.

In this debate, the Halakhah treads a careful path, as always attempting a delicate balance of opposing principles: a deep respect for government, yet also a sensitivity to the primacy of the individual; the affirmation of the surpassing value of each human being, yet the need to safeguard societal structures and institutions. In discussing this issue, we will deliberately avoid politics and ideology, leaving it to the reader to draw his own conclusions in such matters.

The Question

A man is arraigned in a court of law and charged with an act of homicide. He had been sitting in a park when approached by two young males demanding his wallet. When he refused them, they proceeded to make aggressive gestures, insisting that he give them money, without, however, explicitly threatening his life. While bystanders looked away, he tried to escape, to no avail. Finally, feeling himself in danger of his life, he drew a licensed gun, firing one shot into the chest of one of the young males. While the other fled, the one so shot died a short while later of his wounds. When questioned by the police, the defendant indicated that he felt his life had been in imminent danger and had acted in self-defense, adding that the bystanders had not come to his help, nor had his attempts to dissuade his assailants yielded positive results.

This case raises a number of questions that require clarification of several halakhic principles:

1. Where a person is being, or is about to be, physically attacked, does the Halakhah mandate violent intervention by either the potential victim or by others?
2. Where the nature of the aggression is not absolutely clear, and there is some doubt as to the intent of the assailant, who determines the proper response, and how? May subjective judgments be made by the potential victim or others?
3. Is any preventive response, even homicide, permitted, or does the Halakhah require a proportionate or reasonable response, e.g., some attempt to disable or wound the attacker?
4. Where the threat is the result of indirect or involuntary action by an attacker, may the one so threatened (or others) injure or kill the assailant?

The Sources

A. Exodus 22:1–2
If a thief be found breaking in, and be smitten so that he dieth, there shall be no bloodguiltiness for him. If the sun be risen upon him, there shall be bloodguiltiness for him—he shall make restitution.

B. Numbers 25:16–18
And the Lord spoke unto Moses saying: "Attack the Midianites and smite them. For they attack you by their wiles by which they have beguiled you in the matter of Peor."

C. Deuteronomy 22:25–26
If a man find a damsel that is betrothed in a field, and the man take hold of her and lie with her, then the man only that lay with her shall die. But unto the damsel thou shalt do nothing . . . for as when a man riseth against his neighbor, and slayeth him, even so is this matter. For he found her in the field, the betrothed damsel cried, and there was none to save her.

D. II Samuel 2:12–3:39
And Abner the son of Ner . . . went out from Maḥanaim to Gibeon. And Joab the son of Ẓeruiah . . . went out, and they met together. . . . And Abner said to Joab: "Let the young men, I pray thee, arise and play before us." . . . And the battle was very sore that day; and Abner was beaten, and the men of Israel, before the servants of David. And the three sons of Ẓeruiah were there, Joab and Abishai and Asahel; and Asahel was as light of foot as one of the roes that are in the field. And Asahel pursued after Abner . . . And Abner said to him: "Turn thee aside to thy right hand or to thy left" . . . but Asahel would not turn aside from following him . . . wherefore Abner . . . smote him in the fifth rib . . . and he fell down there, and died in the same place. . . . But Joab and Abishai pursued after Abner. . . . then Abner called to Joab and said:

"Shall the sword devour forever? Knowest thou not that it shall be bitterness in the end . . ." So Joab . . . pursued after Israel no more, neither fought they anymore. . . . And when Abner was returned to Hebron Joab took him aside into the midst of the gate to speak with him quietly, and smote him there in the fifth rib that he died, for the blood of Asahel his brother. And afterward when David heard it, he said: "I and my kingdom are guiltless before the Lord for the blood of Abner the son of Ner; let it fall upon the head of Joab, and upon all his father's house . . . these men the sons of Ẓeruiah are too hard for me; the Lord reward the evildoer according to his wickedness."

E. Sanhedrin 72a

Said Rava: why is the killer of a thief found breaking in not subject to prosecution? The answer is that there is a presumption that no man will tolerate the loss of his possessions without resistance. Knowing this, the thief reckons that the homeowner will stand his ground and resist the intruder. Faced with this resistance, he intends to kill the homeowner. Accordingly, the Torah has said, "if a man comes to kill you, kill him first." (*Rashi*: the words "there shall be no bloodguiltiness for him" teach that insofar as he comes to kill you, you should kill him first.)

F. Sanhedrin 72a

The Sages have taught: " '. . . there shall be no bloodguiltiness for him. If the sun be risen upon him . . .'—surely the sun does not rise up only upon him? Rather the intent is that if it is as clear to you as the sun that his intentions toward you are not peaceful, then you may kill him, but if not, do not kill him." However, another tannaitic statement says: " 'If the sun be risen upon him, there shall be bloodguiltiness for him.' Surely the sun does not rise up only on him? Rather the intent is that if it is as clear to you as the sun that his intentions toward you are peaceful, then you may not kill him, but if not, kill him." Do these two anonymous statements not contradict each other? The answer is that the first is describing the case of an intruder who is the father of the homeowner, while the second deals with a case where the intruder is the son of the homeowner. (*Rashi*: this latter case includes by extension all other men, for they are to be killed when there is any doubt, for they can be presumed to have entered intending to kill upon meeting any resistance. The only exception is where it is as clear to you as the sun that the intruder is mercifully disposed, as in the case of a father who intrudes upon his son.) Said Rav: I will kill any man whom I discover intruding on my home, except for Rav Ḥanina bar Shila, because I know for certain that he has mercy on me as a father on a son.

G. Sanhedrin 72b.

The sages have taught: The verse refers to "breaking in" [*maḥt-eret*]; what about the case where the thief is encountered on the roof, in the courtyard, or an outdoor enclosure? When the verse says "if the thief be found," it intends them to be included. If so why does it say "breaking in"? The answer is that term teaches that once he breaks in he needs no warning before being killed. (*Rashi*: by a forced entry, he demonstrates careful forethought with a readiness to kill, whereas if the thief is encountered outdoors, or coming through an open door, he must be warned first, for in such a case we can say that it was an opportunistic crime, without homicidal intent, in that he intended to run away if discovered.) Said Rav Huna: If a pursuer is a minor he may be killed. It would appear that Rav Huna believes that a pursuer does not require forewarning [before being killed], thus it makes no difference whether he be an adult or a minor. But Rav Ḥisda disagrees, saying: where the head of a fetus has emerged from the birth canal [and the mother's life is in danger], we may not kill the fetus, for we do not take one life in order to save another, according to Rav Huna this makes no sense, for the fetus should be killed, because it pursues the mother to kill her? The answer of Rav Huna is that the fetus itself is not pursuing her, rather it is from heaven. It would appear that support for Rav Huna is found in the statement that where one person is in pursuit to kill another, he is warned as follows, "You are pursuing a fellow Jew, and for this you can be killed . . . " (*Rashi*: the pursuer may be killed, even though he does not explicitly accept the warning.)

H. Sanhedrin 73a

Mishnah: The following are saved (*Rashi*: from committing the transgression) even if they have to be killed: a person who is pursuing another either to kill him or to commit homosexual rape, or to rape a betrothed woman.

Gemara: Whence do we derive permission to kill a man in homicidal pursuit of another? From the verse "you shall not stand idly by the blood of your fellow" [Lev. 19:16]. . . . And how do we know that we may even kill him? It is derived by extension from the law of the betrothed woman: for surely if the Torah permits us to kill a man whose intent is merely to defile a betrothed woman, certainly we may do that where the intent of the pursuer is murder. But it is not proper to derive such a punishment by inferred reasoning! The school of Rebbe answers that there is in this case a legitimate analogy, in that the text of the betrothed woman itself refers to homicide, saying, "for as when a man riseth against his neighbor, and slayeth him, even so is this matter." Why does the Torah invoke the murderer? . . . we can learn therefrom that just as the rapist can be killed, so too the one intending homicide. But how do we know that the rapist himself can be killed? The school of Reb Ishmael teaches that the words "and there was none to save her" imply that if there was someone able to save her, he is obligated to do so with any means at his disposal. (Tosafot: There is an obligation to save another.)

I. Sanhedrin 74a

R. Jonathan b. Saul said: When a person (*Rashi*: either the intended victim or an onlooker) can stop a homicidal pursuer by disabling part of his body, but does not do so (*Rashi*: instead he kills the pursuer outright), he is subject to the death penalty. What is the source for this? The Torah says: "And if men strive together and hurt a woman with child, so that her fruit depart, and yet no harm follow, he shall surely be fined . . . but if any harm follow, then thou shalt give life for life" [Exod. 21:22–23]. R. Eliezer learns from this last phrase that the men had homicidal intent, otherwise why "life for life"? But even though the intent was homicidal, the Torah says that there is a monetary fine [where the fetus is lost]. This, [reasons R. Jonathan b. Saul], can only make sense if we assume that the attacker does not forfeit his right to life, for if he does indeed forfeit his right to life, then he would be automatically exempt from any monetary fine resulting from his action, so a monetary fine would be impossible. The fact that he is not exempt here, but rather "shall surely be fined," teaches that he does not automatically forfeit his life. [Thus a person may not stop him by killing him, if he can stop him by merely disabling part of his body.]

J. Sanhedrin 49a

Joab was summoned to the court. The King said to him: "Why did you kill Abner?" Joab answered: "I was the blood-avenger of Asahel." Said he, "Asahel was pursuing Abner with the intent to kill him [so Abner acted in self-defense]." Said Joab: "Abner should simply have disabled Asahel in part of his body." Said the King: "He was not able to do that." Said Joab: "If Abner was able to pierce precisely the fifth rib from the bottom, could he not have disabled another part of his body?" Said he: "Let the case of the death of Abner be dismissed." (Rashi: you are acquitted of the death of Abner.)

K. Maimonides, M.T. Hil. Roẓeiaḥ 1:6, 7, 9, 13, 15

All Israel is commanded to save a person being pursued for his life, even if it means killing the pursuer, and the pursuer is a minor.

Thus, if warning is issued, and he continues to pursue, the pursuer can be killed even without his acknowledging the warning. But if the pursuer can be stopped by disabling part of his body, by striking him with an arrow, a stone, or a sword, to cut off his hand, break his leg, or blind him, then that should be done. . . .

And this is a negative commandment, i.e., not to take mercy on the life of a pursuer. Thus the sages taught that it is permissible to take apart the fetus of a woman whose life is threatened in labor. This can be done by medication or by surgery, for the fetus is considered a pursuer threatening her life. But once his head has emerged, he may not be harmed, for we do not take one life to save another, and this occurs in the course of nature [*tiv'o shel olam*].

Whoever can save the victim by disabling part of the pursuer's body, but does not take care and instead kills the pursuer, then that person is a murderer, and is guilty of a capital crime, however a court does not execute him . . .

If a person sees another pursuing his fellow to kill him or to rape, and can save the victim but chooses not to—such a person has negated a positive commandment, which is "and thou shalt cut off her hand" [Deut. 25:12], and he has transgressed two negative commandments, which are "thine eye shall have no pity" [ibid.] and "thou shalt not stand idly by the blood of thy fellow" [Lev. 19:16].

L. Maimonides, M.T. Hil. Melakhim 9:4

If a Noahide kills another person, even an unborn fetus, he is subject to the death penalty . . . And likewise if he kills a homicidal pursuer, when he can disable him in one part of his body, he is subject to the death penalty. But this is not the case with an Israelite. (Ravad: The case of Abner poses a problem for him.)

M. Maimonides, M.T. Hil. Ḥovel U-Mazzik 8:15

If a ship is about to founder because it is overloaded, and one of those on board casts part of the cargo overboard, he is not liable for the value of the lost cargo. For it is like a pursuer intent upon killing them, so by his action he performed a great service and saved their lives.

Ravad: In this matter there is neither rhyme nor reason [in Maimonides' words]. For this case has nothing at all to do with the law of the pursuer. And it is not the same as the case of the ass that was cast off from the ferry in *Bava Kamma* 117b. Instead in such a case, where one man casts it overboard, the cost should be shared by them all.

N. Meiri, Sanhedrin 72a

Where does the Torah state that (D) "if a man comes to kill you, kill him first"? It is explained in the Midrash Tanḥuma as coming from the verse (B) "attack the Midianites . . . for they attack you," i.e., they habitually attack you, hence you may attack them in view of the fact that they are disposed toward attacking you.

O. Sefer Ha-Ḥinukh 600

We are commanded to save the victim of a homicidal pursuer, even at the cost of his life, i.e., we are commanded to kill the pursuer, if we cannot save the victim without killing the pursuer. Regarding this it says, "thou shalt cut off her hand, thine eye shall have no mercy" [Deut. 25:12]. On this the *Sifri* comments that "and she taketh him by the secrets" teaches that where the aggression poses a mortal danger, the limb of the attacker is to be cut off, but if that is not possible, then "thine eye shall have no mercy" teaches that his life is forfeit . . . and this is true of every such person.

P. Shulḥan Arukh, Ḥoshen Mishpat 425:1

A homicidal pursuer who continues to pursue after he has been warned, even though he be a minor, all Israel is commanded to stop him by injuring his limb. And if that cannot be done without killing the pursuer, then the killer can be killed, even though he has not yet killed.

Rema: A thief who is found breaking in has the status of a pursuer. But if it is known that he only came for financial reward, so that if the homeowner should offer resistance he will not kill the homeowner, it is forbidden to kill the thief. And the *Tur* says that if an individual endangers many by engaging in counterfeiting where the government is punitive, he is in the category of a pursuer, and can be denounced to the government.

Discussion

1. MEETING VIOLENCE WITH VIOLENCE

In an earlier chapter we saw that, generally speaking, the Halakhah does not favor the exchange of one life for another, i.e. it is forbidden to sacrifice one life in order to save another.[1] More particularly, where deliberate homicide is involved, and an individual must choose between killing an innocent man or being himself killed, there is a clear and unambiguous talmudic ruling that forbids the taking of such innocent life, even at the cost of one's own equally guiltless one.[2] Thus the taking of innocent life is one of the three so-called cardinal commandments (the other two are idolatry and prohibited sexual liaisons of the most severe kind, *arayot*) for which *yehareg ve'al ya-avor*, i.e., one should submit to be killed rather than transgress.

Furthermore, where an individual is known to be guilty of a capital offense, even then his life is not forfeit. Thus Maimonides enumerates as one of the 613 commandments the law that witnesses to a capital crime may not themselves execute the criminal prior to his proper appearance in a court adjudicating the case.[3] Clearly the Halakhah does not countenance either the saving of

---

1. See chap. 3, where, in the discussion of heart transplants, it is forbidden to sacrifice or shorten even momentarily the life of a donor, moribund and facing imminent death, in order to save the life of a potential recipient. See also *Jewish Ethics and Halakhah for Our Time*, vol. 1, chap. 2, where, at the other end of the lifespan, if the fetus has partially emerged from the birth canal and a crisis arises to threaten the life of the mother, we may not sacrifice the newborn to save the mother, for "we do not sacrifice one life to save another." This general principle is articulated in the Mishah *Ohalot* 7:6 and codified by Maimonides in *M. T. Hil. Yesodei ha-Torah* 5:6–7.

2. The classic formulation reads: "What makes you think that your blood is redder than his—maybe his is redder than yours!" See *Pesaḥim* 25b, *Yoma* 82b, *Sanhedrin* 74a.

3. Maimonides, *Sefer ha-Miẓvot*, prohibition 292.

one life at the expense of another or the punishment by execution of a murderer without full due process under judicial sanction.[4]

Yet were one to conclude from this that it is always forbidden to kill a person outside of full judicial proceedings, such an inference would be in error. To the contrary, in the very next commandment, Maimonides explicitly enumerates the law of the pursuer (*rodef*), a law that does not merely condone, but actually insists upon the nonjudicial attack to be carried out against a person, e.g., a homicidal man stalking another, where the assailant poses a mortal threat to his intended victim. Such extreme action is called for if necessary to save the life of another, in apparently total circumvention of all due process.

Such is the dialectical tension characteristic of the halakhic prescription for the saving of life: on the one hand, no life is more valuable than another, no exchanges or substitutions can be contemplated; but on the other hand, there is a clear acceptance of the principle of violent, and if necessary murderous, attack against any person who represents a threat to the life of his fellow, and is about to implement his purposes.

Now it is necessary to examine the parameters of this rather startling law of the *rodef*, or pursuer. For it is the key to understanding the halakhic attitude toward the use of force in self-defense, or for that matter the defense of others.

The Mishnah in *Sanhedrin* 73a (H) enunciates the law of the pursuer, saying that the pursuer himself is to be "saved" from his transgression, even at the cost of his life. Included under this rubric are pursuers who intend murder, homosexual rape, or the rape of a betrothed woman. The Gemara, discussing the issue (H), finds sanction for the principle in the biblical admonition, found in Leviticus, against doing nothing to save one's fellow who's life is in jeopardy, i.e., "you shall not stand idly by the blood of your fellow" (Lev. 19:16) But this only teaches that "something" must be done—how do we know that "something" extends to an

4. As a matter of fact, Naḥmanides goes so far as to forbid wounding of a man, even if by wounding him the life of another would be saved. For he includes wounding under the rubric of *avizraihu de'reziḥah*, i.e., a derivative of murder, equally forbidden under all circumstances. See *Torat ha-Adam* in *Kitvei ha-Ramban*, p. 14. Rabbeinu Yonah of Gerondi went so far as to prohibit the public shaming of a man (*halbanat panim*) where intended to save another's life. See his *Sha'arei Teshuvah* 3:137–139. This view did not become normative.

act of killing? To this question the Gemara invokes another biblical passage, this time in Deuteronomy (C). The passage deals with the case of a betrothed woman who is raped—a capital crime. In fact the verse itself explicitly equates such an act to the crime of murder, she being the entirely guiltless victim of aggression. The Gemara, in the name of R. Ishmael, infers from the phrase "and there was none to save her" that had a bystander been present, he would have been obligated to save her—by any means whatsoever, even the killing of the rapist. Once this principle is established, says the Gemara, it can properly be extended to murder *per se*, the Torah itself having invoked homicide in this very context. Actually the Gemara could just as well have quoted the early rabbinic Midrash known as the *Sifra* in its comments to the verse in Leviticus, for the *Sifra* derives from that verse an actual obligation to save such intended victims by killing the attacker if necessary, but perhaps the Gemara chooses to avoid this source, because the verse does not really specify this principle of *rodef* in sufficient degree. As opposed to the *Sifra*, the *Sifri* to Deuteronomy does invoke the passage of the betrothed woman, as does the Gemara here.[5]

This is not the only source of the principle of *rodef*. Deuteronomy 25:11–12 describes the case of a woman who, to protect her husband, attempts to mortally wound his antagonist—and the Torah permits an onlooker to disable her, saying "thou shalt cut off her hand, thine eye shall have no mercy" (O). The *Sifri* concludes from this formulation that if need be, the woman may be killed to prevent her from killing her intended victim. And Maimonides, in the *Sefer ha-Miẓvot*, and the *Mishneh Torah* (K), as well as the author of the *Sefer ha-Ḥinukh* (N), both quote this source as providing sanction to interdict murderous intent.[6]

But perhaps the most significant paradigm for the law of the pursuer, especially vis-à-vis action by the intended victim him-

5. See *Sifra* to *Kedoshim* 2:4–5, and the *Sifri* to *Kee Teẓe* 243. For these sources, see Rabbi E. Ben Zimrah, "Shefikhut Damim mi-Tokh Ẓorekh," *Shenaton ha-Mishpat ha-Ivri* 3–4 (1976–77): 123.

6. See Maimonides' *Sefer ha-Miẓvot*, prohibition 293, where he effectively combines this source with that of the betrothed woman discussed earlier. Yet in his *Mishneh Torah* (K), Maimonides pointedly omits any reference to the talmudic derivation of *rodef* from the rape of the betrothed woman in Deuteronomy. On this, see below. The *Sefer ha-Ḥinukh* concludes that one who does not intercede is guilty of the infraction of one positive and two negative commandments.

self, is the law of the thief found breaking in (*ha-ba be'maḥteret*). Exodus 22:1–2 (A) posits the law that if a thief is encountered while breaking and entering, and the resident kills the thief on the premises, he is not held liable for such a homicide, except if "the sun be risen upon him." The Gemara in *Sanhedrin* 72a (E) quotes Rava to explain why there is no liability for what is ostensibly a grossly disproportionate response to a mere act of theft: there is a generally valid presumption that no man on his own domain will give up his possessions without a struggle of some sort. Thieves who intrude onto private property know this, and thus if they persist anyway, it must be that they are prepared to overcome such resistance by any means necessary, not excluding the possibility of killing any person encountered. Thus one who discovers a thief in the act is in mortal danger of his life. If he kills the intruder, the act must therefore be classified as one of self-defense. Rava concludes with the words, "for the Torah says 'if a man comes [ready] to kill you, kill him first.' "

Now this passage is not without problems. In the first place it is not clear where the Torah "says" what it is reported as saying, for the words as quoted are not found in the Torah itself. Secondly, the verses in the passage in question are themselves unclear: What does "breaking in" include? And why is there a difference if the sun is up or not?

Rashi, it would seem, feels that Rava here is simply stating that this passage itself is the source of the principle, i.e., by holding the person guiltless for killing an intruder, the Torah is here teaching the principle of the legitimacy of self-defense.[7] The Meiri, however, is of a different view, for he quotes the *Midrash Tanḥuma*, which sees the source in the biblical exhortation to the Israelites to attack the Midianites (B), in the light of the ongoing Midianite practice of attacking them.[8] The same source is quoted by the Midrash in *Numbers Rabbah* 21.

But the question of the source or prototype aside, it is necessary to determine the parameters of the law of the thief found breaking in. What does "breaking in" include, what are the

7. See Rashi's comments to *Berakhot* 58a, and 62b, where he refers to this passage in the Torah as the source of the principle. Likewise see his comments to *Bava Kamma* 117b.

8. See Meiri's comments in his *Beit ha-Beḥirah* to *Sanhedrin* 72a, quoting the *Tanḥuma* to *Parshat Pinḥas*, chap. 3.

essential, defining characteristics of such an intruder that would carry over to aggression in general? In this matter there is a basic disagreement between Rashi and Maimonides. Rashi, in his comments to *Sanhedrin* 72b (G), is of the view that the manner of entry is the critical factor, in that if it is evident that the thief made a forced entry, breaking through a physical barrier, it can be concluded that the crime was planned, to the extent that violence would be used where necessary. Where there is such forced entry, no warning need be given the intruder prior to disabling or killing him. But where the entry occurred in a manner that would indicate an opportunistic crime, e.g., where the thief chanced upon an open door or window, and enters to steal without foresight or prior intent, we can assume that the intruder might well flee if accosted. In that case, he cannot be killed without prior warning, for he is not strictly speaking, "breaking in," according to Rashi. This latter case includes any situation where the thief is found in the open air (on the roof, backyard, etc.). Maimonides, on the other hand, defines the intruder as any thief who enters private property to steal where he knows it is likely he will find someone within.[9] It is this probability of encountering resistance that is the key—and it makes no difference whether it be indoors or out; he can be killed without warning, on the presumption that he knew, or should have known, that he would encounter resistance. According to Maimonides, therefore, the term *maḥteret* (which he would translate as "indoors") simply reflects the location where thieves are most commonly encountered.

Rabbi Moshe Feinstein examined several aspects of the law of the intruder, based on this passage in Maimonides.[10] He notes that Maimonides classifies this law in the Laws of Theft (*Hil. Geneivah*), and not in the Laws of Assault (*Hil. Gezeilah*). He concludes that Maimonides, paradoxically, applies the law of the intruder only where the thief enters as a *ganav*, i.e., where he does not intend to take things by physical force, but rather by avoiding detection. Apparently, such a thief, if actually confronted, is liable to react with deadly force because of his genuine

9. Maimonides, *M. T. Hil. Geneivah* 9:8, 12. See especially the comments of the Maggid Mishnah ad loc.

10. *Responsa Iggerot Moshe*, 2:54 (1), dated 1980.

fear. But where entry is made as a *gazlan*, i.e., where the thief is certain of his physical prowess and his ability to intimidate any opposition, then apparently Maimonides feels that there is a greater likelihood that the thief will flee if he encounters real and unexpected resistance. Thus in the latter case (the *gazlan*) warning needs be given, but not in the former (the *ganav*). The problem, however, is that elsewhere, Maimonides' position reflects the majority view in a Tosefta in *Bava Meẓia* that a thief (*ganav*) who enters intending to avoid detection and confrontation, is not to be considered homicidal, even if he is armed, and thus a guard who discovers him should stand his ground.[11]

Rabbi Feinstein resolves the two passages by noting that the latter speaks not of the owner of the premises, but rather of the guard. In such a case the thief feels that a guard will not endanger his life as would the proprietor, and consequently the thief will not resort to force against him, thus in turn the guard should stand his ground. But where two such thieves come together, giving reason to believe that they are indeed ready to attack a guard who might discover them, then he need not stay and confront them. By contrast, where two thieves come openly and brazenly (*gazlanim*), there is room to conclude that anyone who discovers them should stand his ground, in that their intent is to take by intimidation, not actual force—and if unexpectedly confronted, they will probably flee the scene. Accordingly Rabbi Feinstein suggests that a guard openly accosted by two thugs should theoretically offer resistance, either verbal or physical, thereby thwarting their attempt to intimidate him. For there is reason to believe that behind their bravado they are not as strong as they appear. Yet he concludes that this is not what the Gemara is saying, but rather that one should consider the real possibility that they will kill him for having the gall to stand up to their threats. Indeed Rabbi Feinstein points out that most authorities agree with the minority view of the Tosefta, i.e., an armed thief (*ganav*) is to be considered homicidal so that the guard may withdraw, and in addition if there are two thugs (*gazlanim*), then even if they are not armed, it is not necessary to offer resistance or stand one's ground.

On the basis of this, one can conclude that on one's own

11. See Maimonides, *M. T. Hil. Geneivah* 1:3; Tosefta *Bava Meẓia* 8:6.

property, if accosted in aggressive fashion by a single armed thief, or two or more who are not armed, a person should properly consider his life in danger, and act accordingly. If he cannot defend himself he should accede to their demands, but if he is capable of defending himself he may do so, even if it involves taking their lives. And this is true even where there is no explicit death threat made by the attackers. For the law of the *maḥteret* renders the intruder at the mercy of the person within. And according to the *Mekhilta*, this is true whether the intrusion be by day or night, whether the intent of the intruder be peaceful or injurious.[12]

What if a person is attacked, but it is quite clear that homicide is not a factor, in that the intent is merely to injure the innocent party? The Rosh, on the basis of the statement in the Jerusalem Talmud that "where one man injures another, and the attacker is himself injured, there is no liability," permits self-defense that causes injury to the attacker.[13] He also allows a third party to intervene, whether it be a relative coming to the defense of a family member, or even an unrelated observer who wishes to prevent the attack on an innocent man. Such action, while not required (as in the case of a life-threatening attack) is permitted, in order to safeguard the innocent victim and prevent the commission of a transgression (as Maimonides puts it, it is forbidden to raise one's hand against one's fellow, whether or not one strikes him).[14] Yet he also makes it quite clear that such a response must be proportionate; i.e., if it is not necessary to kill the assailant, then the least injurious response is called for. This is based on the Torah's uncompromising response (O) to the actions of the woman whose husband is under attack, if she acts overzealously in his defense. Similar sentiments are expressed by the thirteenth-century *Hagahot Maimoniyyot* (R. Meir ha-Kohen) and the Maharam Rothenburg.[15] So, too, R. Joshua Falk (the Sema) does not limit such preventive action to the victim or a

12. *Mekhilta de'R. Ishmael, Mishpatim* 13. The *Mekhilta de'Rashbi* is somewhat more restrictive, holding the person within responsible if circumstances would have allowed a less violent response.

13. *Piskei ha-Rosh* to *Bava Kamma* 3:13 and the comments of the *Nimmukei Yosef* ad loc. See also the *Tur H. M. Sh.A, H. M.* 421.

14. Maimonides, *M. T. Hil. Ḥovel u-Mazzik* 5:2, based on *Sanhedrin* 52a.

15. See *Responsa Or Zarua* 25, in the name of the Rosh, and *Teshuvot Maimoniyyot, Nezikin* 15. See *Encyclopedia Talmudit* 12:744.

relative but extends it to cover any fellow Jew privy to the impending act of aggression.[16]

R. Joseph of Trani, expanding on the Rosh, explains that where one man raises his hand to strike another, the intended victim may certainly strike him in anticipation—but only at that moment, not in the course of any subsequent heated argument, unless of course the attacker renews his threatening posture.[17]

From a responsum of the Radbaz, R. David b. Abu Zimrah, seen in an earlier chapter, it would appear that he would even allow the potential victim to take the life of his attacker where the attacker threatens only a limb. The responsum dealt with the question of sacrificing an ear in order to save another person, and Radbaz had answered in the negative; i.e., it is not necessary for one person to lose a limb in order to save the life of another, in that the loss of a limb could well turn out to be a threat to his own life.[18] In other words, any possible threat to one's own life takes precedence over the definite danger to the life of another person. Rabbi Israel Shepansky extrapolates from this principle that where another person is about to endanger one's limb in a manner that might subsequently turn out to be a potential threat to one's life, one need not tolerate the loss of that limb, but may instead kill the attacker.[19] He then goes one step further, to say that this principle of *rodef*, or pursuer, includes situations where the attacker intends "merely" to inflict some permanent injury on the body of his victim. He derives this from the fact that the Gemara in *Sanhedrin* (H) chooses to derive the law of the pursuer from the biblical case of the rapist. For it may be asked why such biblical sanction is necessary—can one not, by pure logic, conclude that threat to one life can be removed by killing the assailant, if necessary? It must be, says Rabbi Shepansky, that from the law of the rapist we learn the additional principle that even where the attack threatens only the physical "wholeness" of the victim by permanently disfigurement or *pegimah* (in rape, the victim is not killed but permanently scarred in body or mind), even there the assailant should properly be killed. This, of course,

16. See *Sema* to *Sh. A. H. M.* 421:25, 28.
17. *Responsa Maharit, Y. D.* 29, in the case of a messenger of the court who encounters a violent response.
18. See above pp. 116 ff.
19. See Rabbi Israel Shepansky, *Or ha-Mizraḥ*, 1970 (20), pp. 24–25.

is not the case where the injury to the innocent party is of a temporary nature, one from which the victim would in time fully recover.

Two other halakhists also took sides in this issue. Where one man attacks another, but without posing a threat to his life, and the one so attacked responds by killing his assailant, R. Solomon Luria considers him subject to the death penalty for not being more careful.[20] But as opposed to this, R. Jacob Emden tends to exonerate the intended victim, arguing that given the provocation, and the anger at being attacked, it is not proper to condemn him to death for his retaliatory action.[21]

There is one other assault that can be thwarted at the cost of the aggressor's life, and that is the situation of betrayal to alien authority (*mesirah*). Of the many crimes that a Jew might commit, the denunciation of a fellow Jew to a capricious authority was always considered of particularly heinous character. For such duplicity might lead not only to the unjust death of that one Jew, but also to the death of many of his coreligionists. For this reason, this crime was subject to the death penalty at the hands of rabbinic courts during the Middle Ages, and even later.[22] Now where it becomes known to the intended victim, or another person, that someone is about to commit an act of *mesirah*, or threatens to do so, there is a clear talmudic mandate to treat that person as a *rodef* in the fullest sense. A number of such instances are recorded in the Gemara, where several amoraim killed *mosrim* and thereby prevented their acts of betrayal.[23] And while in these instances the killing was carried out only by outstanding scholars, Maimonides' formulation of the law clearly allows the masses of the Jewish people to act in similar fashion.[24]

Before concluding this section, we can attempt to conceptualize the notion of *rodef*, at least as seen through the eyes of Maimonides. For Maimonides invokes the *rodef* principle even beyond human acts, to situations where inanimate objects qualify under the rubric of pursuer. Thus, in *Hilkhet Ḥovel u-Mazzik* (M), he postulates, based on the Gemara *Bava Kamma* 117b, that where

20. *Yam Shel Shelomoh* 3:26.
21. *Responsa Yaveẓ* 2:9.
22. See *Jewish Ethics and Halakhah*, vol. 1, chap. 6.
23. *Berakhot* 58a, *Bava Kamma* 117a.
24. Maimonides, *M. T. Hil. Ḥovel. u-Mazzik* 8:10–11.

a ship is in danger of sinking because it is overloaded, the offending cargo may be cast overboard because it is "like a pursuer," and the person who acts thus is not liable for restitution to the owner of the sacrificed goods. His classic interlocutor, the Ravad (M), differs sharply and asserts that the financial loss is to be shared by the owners of all the cargo. While subsequent commentators attempt to explain these respective views,[25] and take sides accordingly, it is clear that for Maimonides the principle of *rodef* extends to any threatening situation where the immediate cause of the threat is readily identifiable and can be removed.

However, it is necessary to make a careful distinction between two facets of the law of *rodef* according to Maimonides. The distinction, as first formulated by R. Ḥayyim ha-Levi Soloveichik,[26] is between the law of the pursuer (*din rodef*) and the obligation of the pursuer (*ḥiyyuv rodef*). The former occurs in all cases of pursuit not involving a conscious act by the source of the threat. In such cases, the threat is to be removed forthwith, and without establishing prior intent to kill or harm. Such cases include the unborn fetus or the cargo that threatens to capsize the ship and endanger human life. But where the source of the threat to life comes from a human possessed of a soul, then it is first necessary to establish prior intent to harm, before the principle of *rodef* can be acted on. Such a case includes a baby already born and a human aggressor at any subsequent point. Thus Maimonides accounts for the fact that once it is born, the baby, being fully human, cannot be killed to save the mother, for the baby does not actually intend the mother's death.

And so it is evident that the law of the pursuer was extended to embrace a significant spectrum of threatening behaviors, not all of them actual physical assault. Common to them all, however, was the principle that unless the aggressor is thwarted, there will follow the destruction of the life or limb of his victim or victims. In so doing, the assailant effectively abrogated his presumption of innocence, and relinquished his own right to life or limb, as

25. See Z. Kaplan, "Sefinah she-Ḥishvah le'Hishaver," *Sinai* 67 (5730): 38–42, who offers an insightful analysis of Maimonides' position.

26. *Ḥiddushei R Ḥayyim ha-Levi*, as quoted in R. Isser Zalman Melzer, *Even ha-Ezel* to *M. T. Hil. Ḥovel u-Mazzik* 8:15. See Shepansky, p. 23, and Kaplan, p. 42.

the case might be. The Halakhah, in not merely permitting, but actually requiring, a preemptive response, was demonstrating its awareness of the need to respond to violent aggression as and when needed, not merely after the fact. And if, in so doing, the principle of not substituting one life for another was to be vitiated or weakened, that was apparently an acceptable price to pay in the long-term interest of maintaining a law-abiding society.

2. SUBJECTIVE AND OBJECTIVE DETERMINATIONS OF AGGRESSION

Where there is doubt whether an act of pursuit is being committed, or there is a question as to the nature of the harm that is liable to occur (*safek rodef*), i.e., the intent of the attacker is unclear, there is a real question as to whether action may be taken against that attacker. May the decision properly be taken based on a subjective judgment, or must certain objective requirements be satisfied first?

As pointed out by Rabbi Eliyahu Ben Zimrah, the evaluation of the real intent of the attacker depends in the first place on his prior behavior and record.[27] Only thus can we account for the rather contradictory reports found in various talmudic passages on the subject of proper response to aggressive or threatening behavior. Thus R. Naḥman is quoted as saying that "men threaten much but do little,"[28] but on the other hand a number of instances are recorded where such threats were taken seriously.[29]

The Gemara in *Sanhedrin* (G) again constitutes an important source for the resolution of this question. Specifically, there is the question of *hatra'ah*, or forewarning, as it applies to the *rodef*. Normally such warning must be given a transgressor before punishment may be meted out by a court, in order to assure that the infraction was committed with full knowledge of the improper nature of the act, as well as its consequences. In the case of the *rodef*, is this warning necessary before the assailant is disabled or killed? If so, it would appear that the reason is that it is

27. Rabbi Eliyahu Z. Ben Zimrah, "Shefikhut Damim mi-Tokh Ẓorekh," *Shenaton ha-Mishpat ha-Ivri* 3–4 (5736–37): 117–153, esp. p. 127.
28. *Shevuot* 46a.
29. *Gittin* 14b, *Nedarim* 22a.

necessary to establish the real intent of the assailant beyond any reasonable doubt.

In fact, warning the assailant is required before he can be disabled, as codified by Maimonides (K). Clearly the intent of the *rodef* must be established. Must warning always be given? In (G), Rav Huna and Rav Ḥisda debate the question of a minor who pursues another with the apparent intent to do harm. Rav Huna feels that such a minor may indeed be killed, if necessary, for warning is not required for a minor. Rav Ḥisda disagrees, arguing that warning is always necessary, but in the case of a minor it cannot be given, and thus he may not be killed or disabled as a *rodef*. In discussing their differences, the Gemara—at least as understood by Rashi—brings proof for the view of Rav Huna from a Beraita that permits the killing of a pursuer even though he did not explicitly acknowledge the warning given him. Yet another Beraita is quoted in support of Rav Ḥisda, yet Rav Huna counters that as with the thief who breaks in, warning is not required. There is some question as to the precise position of Rav Huna. Rabbi Shepansky is of the view that while it is not necessary for the minor to acknowledge the warning, nonetheless even Rav Huna agrees that such warning must be given. Ben Zimrah, on the other hand, considers Rav Huna to dispense with the need for warning in this case. In any event, most subsequent authorities accepted the view that a pursuer must be forewarned, even though he be a minor, and whether or not he acknowledges the warning thus given. Such is the view of Maimonides (K), and the *Shulḥan Arukh* (P).

Yet there is a prominent minority view that sometimes dispenses with the need for warning. Thus the Sema, in commenting on this law in the *Shulḥan Arukh*, indicates that where it is not feasible, warning may be dispensed with, and "the proof is from the case of the minor who cannot discern warning, but nonetheless can be killed if in pursuit." Likewise the *Minḥat Ḥinukh*, in commenting on (O), quotes the Sema and allows the killing of a pursuer where warning is not given, for it is *safek nefashot*, i.e. a life is at stake.

Others too make certain pertinent distinctions. R. Isaac bar Sheshet (the Rivash), quoting R. Aaron ha-Levi, exempts the potential victim himself from the need to issue a warning to his assailant, for "he is in fear of his life, concerned to save himself, therefore he is not required to issue warning—instead, when he sees the attacker coming to kill him, he may act first to become the attacker himself."[30] Indeed as far as R. Aaron is concerned, this dispensation is universally accepted. Among other medieval authorities, it was the Meiri who formulated the mandate to the intended victim to act in cases of doubt. Thus he says that where the life of a woman in labor is threatened by a fetus that has partially emerged from the birth canal, she herself may dismember the fetus that is a *rodef*—even though others present are forbidden to do so because as far as they are concerned it is unclear who is threatening whom, she the baby, or the baby her. Nonetheless, insofar as she is the putative victim, she need have no such dilemma, and she may act with all necessary force to remove the threat.[31] As pointed out by Ben Zimrah, this view is based on the Jerusalem Talmud.[32]

As to an onlooker who intervenes, the Rivash indicates that while he must issue a warning, that is only if there is sufficient time prior to the attack. In other words, under normal circumstances a pursuer should be warned so as to clarify his real intent, prior to a third party taking action against him—unless such warning would cause such a delay that the life of the intended victim might be lost. But the intended victim himself need not issue such warning to ascertain the nature of the threat to his life; he may act without delay. Such a formulation would seem to allow for a significant measure of subjective judgment by the putative victim under most circumstances, and by a third party in certain limited situations, e.g., where time is of the essence. And as we have seen above, the Radbaz permits the taking of the life of an aggressor even where the threat is not to one's life per se, but merely to a limb of one's body; even there, it would appear, warning is not always required.

Earlier in this chapter, we saw the special status of an intruding thief (*ha-ba be'maḥteret*), whose life is forfeit if confronted on the premises. In Exodus (A), this dispensation is dependent on the sun not having "risen upon him," in that if the sun has

---

30. *Responsa Rivash* 238, in agreement with the view of Rav Huna in *Sanhedrin* that warning is not always necessary. See the note preceding.

31. Meiri to *Sanhedrin* 72b, in the name of "the sages of the generations."

32. See Ben Zimrah, p. 124, n. 34, with regard to J. T. *Sanhedrin* 8:9 and 26:3.

risen, then indeed he may not be summarily killed by his discoverer. Now the Gemara in *Sanhedrin* (F) examines these verses carefully, quoting certain contradictory tannaitic statements, and concludes that where there is any doubt about the intentions of an intruder, he may be killed. It is only where it is "as clear as day" that his intentions are peaceable (as in the case of a father intruding on the property of his son) that the intruder may not be killed. Rashi, commenting on this passage, extends the mandate to take preemptive action against all intruding strangers. Yet in a parallel passage in *Pesaḥim* 2b, the opposite conclusion seems to prevail, i.e., the intruder may be killed only where his homicidal tendencies are known, but where any doubt exists, he may not be attacked. And as explained by Rashi there, this is true of all men, not merely where the intruder is the father. Rabbi Shepansky, in discussing these passages, suggests that as a rule there is no doubt that an intruder is homicidal (as in Rava's principle, seen earlier). In such a case, no warning is necessary. But where there is genuine doubt as to the intent of the intruder, indeed warning must be given prior to taking any action.

Here again, it would appear that a distinction is to be made between the intended victim and a third party. While a third party should, by warning, clarify the intent of the assailant wherever any doubt exists, an intended victim is not under any such obligation, and may kill an intruder upon contact. And such a conclusion is supported by a careful reading of Rava's principle in *Sanhedrin*: as Rabbi Naftali Ẓvi Yehudah Berlin (the Neẓiv) notes, it should really not be necessary to introduce the principle "if a man comes to kill you, kill him first"; after all, an intruder is a *rodef*, and that by itself should suffice to take action against him. If, therefore, it is introduced, it must be to add an extra dimension to the notion of self-defense that does not exist in the conventional *rodef* dispensation, and that dimension is to kill him "first," i.e., without the delay or hesitation involved in forewarning the intruder.[33]

In summary, it would appear that an individual about to be attacked, whether in the privacy of personal property or in the public domain, is entitled to react in a preemptive manner, and moreover to do so as a result of his own subjective perception or

33. See Neẓiv, *Bimromei Sadeh*, *Yoma* 85, as quoted in Shepansky, p. 21.

judgment of the gravity of the situation. While it would certainly be preferred for some independent or objective determination to take place, the Halakhah recognizes that the intended victim cannot be held responsible or blameworthy for acting with immediate force. In the final analysis, it is his judgment which must be accepted. But this is not the case for a third-party witness to the intended attack, for such an outsider must perforce establish the intent of the assailant by some objective means, notably by warning the assailant and then seeing him persist in his path; only then may, nay must, he properly intercede even at the cost of the assailant's life.

Of course there is the further question posed by the potential self-endangerment of such a third party who "gets involved." As we have seen in an earlier chapter, it is a real question whether any individual is required or even permitted to endanger himself for the sake of another whose life is in danger. To say, as Maimonides does, that there is a positive commandment to stop an assailant does not mean that it is obligatory irrespective of the danger to oneself. For the majority view, including that of Maimonides, is that one is not required to endanger oneself for the sake of saving another's life. Thus again it is for the third party to make a subjective judgment as to the relative dangers posed to the life of the intended victim and to his own life if he chooses to confront the assailant.

3. CHOOSING A REASONABLE RESPONSE: INJURY OR DEATH?

Once it is determined that an act of aggression is about to be committed, the question then arises as to an appropriately violent preventive act. When may the aggressor be killed, and when merely disabled? A useful distinction may be drawn between a situation where it is a third party who intercedes aggressively and the situation where the intended victim is the one to respond with violence.

Third-Party Intervention

The early rabbinic Midrashim made it clear that where possible the response to aggression should use minimal violence. Thus the *Mekhilta De'R. Ishmael* derives from the Deuteronomic case of rape (C) that a violent response is appropriate only where there are no peaceable alternatives.[34] The reason: gratuitous violence is not only unnecessary, it is also subject to punishment. Likewise, the *Sifri* to Deuteronomy 25:12 (O) requires a graduated response, i.e., first only those limbs necessary to commit the act of aggression are to be removed, and only where this proves ineffectual may the aggressor be killed. This in turn served as the basis for the tannaitic statement, found in the Tosefta, that described the appropriate incremental response to a murderous attack: "first he cuts off one of his limbs, but if this does not stop him, he should kill him preemptively."[35]

This demand for an incremental response that seeks where possible to avoid the death of the aggressor was subsequently codified as law by Maimonides (K), the *Minḥat Ḥinukh* (O), and the *Shulḥan Arukh* (P). At the same time, however, there was some debate among the medieval halakhists as to whether such care was necessary in dealing with the threat of an intruder on the one hand, or the threat of denunciation of a fellow Jew to hostile authority on the other. Maimonides, for one, did not require it, whereas the Ashkenazi authorities (such as the Mordecai and Maharam Rothenburg) generally did.[36]

What if, in spite of this ruling, an assailant is summarily killed without any attempt at an incremental response? Can the person who acted thus be punished for his overzealous response? This question is addressed for the first time in *Sanhedrin*, in the name of R. Jonathan b. Saul (I). In his opinion, such gratuitous killing is indeed categorized as culpable homicide subject to the death penalty. His view is based on the passage in Exodus 21 that seems to assume that an aggressor does not automatically forfeit his life, but rather is subject to lesser penalties (whether financial or otherwise). Maimonides, in codifying this law (K), accepts the principle of culpability, but adds that in practice the sentence is not under normal circumstances carried out by a court of law.[37]

34. *Mekhilta De'R. Ishmael, Mishpatim, Nezikin* 13.

35. Tosefta *Sanhedrin* 11:10.

36. See *M. T. Hil. Geneivah* 9:7–8, *Hil. Ḥovel u-Mazzik* 8:10–11. On this point see Ben Zimrah, p. 133, n. 85.

37. Ben Zimrah is of the opinion (ibid., p. 133) that Maimonides in this passage does not differentiate between homicide committed by the intended

Such a distinction between guilt and punishment is a Maimonidean trademark: it is found as well in his insistence that while it is forbidden for a Jew to submit to idolatry, even under the pain of death, nonetheless if he does submit, he is exempted from punishment, in that he acted under duress.[38]

When It Is the Victim Who Responds

While there is no significant dissent or debate involving the appropriate and graduated response required of a third party presented with an imminent attack, there is such a controversy when it comes to self-defense by the intended victim.

The discussion revolves around two biblical incidents. The first occurs in Genesis 32, where Jacob anticipates an epochal confrontation with his estranged brother Esau, and experiences deep fear. *Genesis Rabbah* is puzzled at this fear; after all, Jacob was a man of great faith. It answers, as quoted by Rashi to Genesis 32:8, that Jacob's fear was that he might in self-defense kill Esau's cohorts in battle, an act of bloodshed which he wanted to avoid. R. Elijah Mizraḥi, in his classic commentary to Rashi, notes the fact that Jacob was not fearful of killing Esau, at least not on moral grounds. Why not? Mizraḥi answers that as for the cohorts, Jacob honestly did not know their true intent, and were he to kill them rather than injure them, he would be culpable—but as for Esau himself, his murderous intent was clear to Jacob, and on moral grounds Jacob would be within his rights to kill Esau in self-defense, without resort to inflicting a disabling injury.[39] Thus, Mizraḥi concludes, the intended victim himself may properly kill his attacker, even without any prior attempt to disable him.

The second biblical narrative occurs in the Book of Samuel (D), in the days of King David. In the internecine intrigues of the day,

---

victim and that by a third party. Yet a careful reading of the passage in question, especially halakhah 15, gives the clear impression that Maimonides in these laws has in mind only actions committed by a third party who comes to the aid of an intended victim. This would be a precise reflection of his understanding of R. Jonathan b. Saul, as opposed to Rashi's interpretation. On this see below.

38. See Maimonides, *M. T. Hil. Yesodei ha-Torah* 5:4: ". . . even so, if he transgresses against his will he is not given corporal punishment, and certainly not put to death by a court, even if he killed against his will [*be'ones*]".

39. Mizraḥi to Gen. 32:8, s.v. *va-yeẓer lo*.

David's lieutenant Joab got into a confrontation with Abner ben Ner, and on one occasion, Abner found himself pursued by Joab's brother Asahel. Abner attempted to dissuade his assailant, but to no avail, whereupon he turned on Asahel and stabbed him to death. Some time later, in spite of a promise to foreswear violence against each other, a vengeful Joab lured Abner to a secluded spot and killed him in cold blood—much to the consternation of King David.

In elaborating upon this narrative, the Gemara in *Sanhedrin* (J) recreates the scene in the courtroom wherein Joab is taken to task by the King, who accuses him of murdering an innocent man (Abner) who had acted in self-defense. Joab's answer is that, given his expertise with the sword, Abner could have simply injured his assailant (Asahel), without actually killing him, i.e., he could have used an incremental response. This defense by Joab was accepted, and the case against him dismissed. It would appear both from the narrative and this talmudic adumbration that even the intended victim (in this case Abner) should properly attempt to disable his attacker before resorting to the ultimate response, i.e., homicide. If this is indeed the conclusion yielded by this passage, it would stand diametrically opposed to the view of Mizraḥi, who, as we have seen, allows summary homicide under such circumstances. If so, it is necessary to clarify the relationship of these two biblical passages and the conclusions that follow from them.

Rabbi Ovadiah Yosef sets out to clarify this matter at some length.[40] In his view it is quite possible to reconcile the position of Mizraḥi with the acquittal of Joab, in that he might have been acquitted for other reasons, e.g., Joab acted on the spur of the moment, or out of ignorance of the correct law (i.e., that Abner was entitled to kill his pursuer). The fact that he was acquitted, therefore, does not in and of itself indicate that Abner acted improperly. And the fact that Abner did not attempt to justify his killing of Asahel might merely have been because he chose not to answer Joab's charge. In any case, Mizraḥi would argue that Abner was not required to adopt a graduated response, for being in danger of his life he was under extreme stress, and thus was permitted to kill Asahel.

40. *Responsa Yabia Omer*, vol. 4, *H.M.* 5:4.

A number of other sources tend to agree with the position of Mizraḥi. Thus the *Tur* codifies the law that a pursuer who causes damage to material goods is exempt from liability, because his life is automatically forfeit at the hands of his intended victim.[41] And others who take a similar position include the *Mishneh la-Melekh* and the Levush.[42] Among the moderns, Rabbi Samuel Alkalai goes one step further: it is entirely up to the perception of the individual who intercedes to stop the attack, whether it be the victim himself or a third party, right then and there, it being unnecessary in his view to establish what might have been the response of some hypothetical reasonable man.[43] Yet many authorities do not accept the position of Mizraḥi. What is the reason?

Rashi, in comments to the passage of R. Jonathan b. Saul in *Sanhedrin* (I), explicitly extends the principle of an incremental response to the actions of the victim himself (an extension that he repeats in *Sanhedrin* 57a). And the Tosafot, in commenting on the narrative of Jacob and Esau, indicate that Jacob's fear was that he would improperly kill his attackers, Esau included, without first disabling them as the Torah requires.[44] In other words, Tosafot too is of the opinion that the intended victim has to exercise caution in responding to his assailant. Other medieval authorities who side with Rashi include R. Meir Abulafia (the *Yad Ramah*) and Meiri.[45]

What is the basis for Rashi's position? In the first place, it is Rashi's interpretation of R. Jonathan b. Saul. But what makes him read it this way, and not as excluding the victim? There is the fact that Joab was acquitted for having killed Abner, even though the latter acted in self-defense in killing Asahel. Yet Ovadiah Yosef, as above, finds room to defend the position of Mizraḥi, further quoting the view of the *Iyyun Ya'akov* that the case is quite analogous to an intruder who may be summarily killed by the person whom he confronts within.

What is the position of Maimonides? From his formulation of these laws in the first chapter of *Hilkhot Roẓeiaḥ* (K), it would

41. *Tur H. M.* 380, 425.
42. See *Mishneh la-Melekh* to *M. T. Hil. Ḥovel u-Mazzik* 8:10.
43. Responsa Mishpetei Shmuel 93.
44. *Moshav Zekenim on the Torah* to *Vayishlaḥ*, Gen. 32:8.
45. See the *Yad Ramah* to *Sanhedrin* 49b and 57a; Meiri to *Sanhedrin* 73a.

appear that, unlike Rashi, he considers the view of R. Jonathan b. Saul to be speaking only of a third-party intervention. Thus he describes the need to limit the response to such provocation in terms of the third-person singular. And while we have seen too that Maimonides certainly favors the use of minimal force wherever possible, preferring some disabling action rather than outright homicide in the prevention of an attack, nonetheless in *Hilkhot Melakhim* (L) it would appear that he sides with Mizraḥi, when he states that an Israelite may kill an assailant and not be subject to the death penalty, even though he could have simply disabled him instead of killing him. Interestingly, Maimonides' classic contender, Ravad, takes issue with this ruling, and as prooftext quotes the case of Abner and Joab, in which Abner was ostensibly held accountable and put to death by Joab for killing Asahel without the proper effort to disable him. It would appear that Ravad identifies with the view of Rashi. Similarly in *Hilkhot Roẓeiaḥ* (K), Maimonides states that an Israelite is not executed by the court for killing an assailant when he could have injured him instead. Why does Maimonides disregard the case of Abner? One Maimonidean commentator, the *Mishneh la-Melekh*, comes to his defense, explaining that the case of Abner has nothing to do with normal cases of self-defense, in that Joab was acquitted on other grounds, i.e., he was a blood-avenger (*go'el ha-dam*) whom the Torah permits to exact retribution for the killing of his brother.[46] Thus Abner was not really subject to judicial execution, in that he acted in self-defense. Any other person who might have killed him would have been guilty of murder. Thus it is that Abner was not liable, and this would be true of all similar situations.[47] Yet Ovadiah Yosef contends that this is not quite true, in that Joab could not have been acquitted merely on the grounds that he was a blood-avenger, for Abner had not killed in error (*be'shogeg*), and thus the entire concept of blood-avenger is extraneous to this case.

Subsequently R. Jacob Reischer too examined the question, and substantially corroborated the position of Rashi, as opposed to Mizraḥi and Maimonides. A similar conclusion is arrived at by

46. For the laws of the blood-avenger, see Numbers 35 and the extensive treatment in *Encyclopedia Talmudit* 5:220–233.

47. *Mishneh la-Melekh, M. T. Hil. Ḥovel u-Mazzik* 8:10.

R. Ḥayyim Benveniste (author of the *Knesset ha-Gedolah*),[48] and R. Israel Ginzberg (author of the *Mishpatim le'Yisrael*).[49] Given this preponderance of halakhic authority, Ovadiah Yosef considers the possibility that even Mizraḥi himself does not give a blanket dispensation to all intended victims to take the life of their assailants, but instead refers only to wartime conditions. In war, death is widespread and largely uncontrolled, as was the case in the biblical narrative of the battle confrontation of Jacob and Esau. Accordingly, Mizraḥi intended merely extreme combat situations, to the exclusion of more conventional circumstances. Indeed Ovadiah Yosef finds reason to believe that such was the intent behind David's reprobation of Joab, in that it was a time of war, and Abner was entitled to act as he did, in self-defense. Malbim, in his comments to the story of Abner and Joab, appears to make the same distinction. The *Knesset ha-Gedolah* also distinguishes between peace and wartime, saying that under conditions of war, even a third party does not have to try to wound the assailant but may kill him outright, in that there are many assailants who might attack even as the present one is wounded.[50]

Rabbi Eliezer Waldenberg attempts to understand why Maimonides in (K) insists that while he is guilty of the death penalty, a man may not be executed by a court for not taking less drastic action, in apparent contradiction to R. Jonathan b. Saul.[51] R. Joseph Karo, in commenting on this passage in Maimonides, had answered that in fact this was the intent of R. Jonathan b. Saul, to say that his culpability was in theory only, i.e., death at the hands of heaven, but not judicial execution, given the defendant's circumstances at the time. Rabbi Waldenberg, however, has a different answer, namely that Maimonides understands the story of Abner to yield the conclusion that where a man acts (improperly) to kill an assailant, he can be killed with impunity by a blood-avenger of the dead man, even though a court may not kill him. A similar position is taken by the Ḥazon Ish, when he states that even though Abner killed his assailant intentionally, and was

48. See *Responsa Yabia Omer* p. 388, par. 6, who locates this view in Benveniste's *Dina de'Ḥayyei*. Ben Zimrah, on the other hand, is of the opinion that the *Knesset ha-Gedolah* agrees with Mizraḥi, but in this instance Rabbi Yosef appears the more correct.

49. Ginzberg, *Mishpatim le'Yisrael*, p. 337, no. 72.

50. *Knesset ha-Gedolah, H. M.* 388:62.

51. *Responsa Ẓiẓ Eliezer* 4:24.

therefore not really committing accidental homicide, nonetheless Joab can fairly be considered a blood-avenger, who may kill and not be held culpable, and for this reason was acquitted by the court.[52] This approach differs markedly with that of Ovadiah Yosef, in arguing that Joab was acquitted as a blood-avenger, even though Abner's original act was not punishable by a court. Hence Maimonides rules that a court may not execute for such gratuitous violence. In any case, in the view of Rabbi Waldenberg, Mizraḥi and his fellow thinkers are contradicted by the story of Abner, who was considered in error for having killed his attacker, Asahel.

Thus, according to Rabbi Waldenberg, Maimonides, far from being impugned by the story of Abner, actually finds his source in that narrative. This is indeed the same answer as given by the *Mishneh le-Melekh* in commenting on (L). But if this is the case, why does the Ravad quote the case of Abner as being in contradiction to Maimonides? Rabbi Waldenberg's novel answer is that the Ravad in this instance is not dissenting at all! By saying that the case of Abner "poses a problem for him," Ravad is merely explaining why Maimonides takes his position, i.e., Maimonides is bothered by the case of Abner and why Joab did not bring Abner before the court to face trial—thus he answers that Abner could not have been convicted or executed for his wanton homicide, and only Joab could act in a nonjudicial capacity, to carry out "justice."

Yet other halakhists for the most part do perceive Ravad as taking issue with Maimonides here. Thus R. Meir Simḥah of Dvinsk explains their differences as follows: There is a distinction between a pursuer who is acting in legitimate fashion (as was Asahel), and one who is not. The former requires of his intended victim that he act with care and attempt to merely disable him, whereas the latter permits summary execution by the intended victim.[53] Maimonides in this law is speaking of the latter instance (i.e., wanton violence), whereas the case of Abner is of the former kind, i.e., Asahel was within his rights (it was a military exercise initiated by Abner himself at which the confrontation occurred), so Abner should have taken care not to kill him, and thus was

52. *Ḥazon Ish, H. M.* 17:1.
53. *Ȯr Sameaḥ, M. T. Hil. Roẓeiaḥ* 1:13.

subject to the death penalty. Ravad, on the other hand, rejects this distinction, and thus finds the case of Abner to be in contradiction to Maimonides. Having said this, R. Meir Simḥah can then explain that Mizraḥi is speaking only of cases where the pursuer is without any legal justification (notably Esau), not where some justification exists.

Ovadiah Yosef has some difficulties with this view of R. Meir Simḥah. Specifically it appears to be contradicted by a talmudic comment regarding the scriptural narrative of Pinḥas and Zimri (Numbers 25:1–9). Zimri, it will be recalled, was in the process of an act of flagrant violation of the law of sexual idolatry. Pinḥas pursues and kills him on the spot. The Gemara *Sanhedrin* 82a posits that had Pinḥas inquired first, he would have been told not to intercede as he did, and that furthermore, "had Zimri ceased his act and turned on Pinḥas and killed him, Zimri would have been innocent of murder, in that Pinḥas was a *rodef*, i.e., a murderous assailant." This, says Ovadiah Yosef, contradicts R. Meir Simḥah, in that Pinḥas was certainly entitled to act as he did, subsequently receiving the divine endorsement for acting correctly. If so, Zimri would have no right to kill his assailant Pinḥas without first deflecting the attack by other means, either by ceasing his provocation or by wounding Pinḥas. Thus it must be, he says, that it makes no difference whether the assailant is justified or not; in neither case is the intended victim held guilty. In addition, says Ovadiah Yosef, it is difficult to maintain that Abner had acted correctly in the first place in initiating such perilous military exercises—indeed the Jerusalem Talmud (*Sotah* 1:8) takes him to task for needlessly endangering the lives of the young men involved, and as a result considers his death at the hands of Joab as divine punishment for such irresponsibility.

Yet on the first point of Ovadiah Yosef, R. Meir Simḥah himself disposes of the objection from the story of Pinḥas, explaining that while the Gemara does say that Zimri would have been acquitted had he killed Pinḥas, nonetheless it remains true that he would have been found guilty had he killed a third party who jumped to the rescue of Pinḥas, without first attempting to wound him, in that such a third party would be under an obligation to save an endangered person. Thus, he concludes, where an intended victim turns on his attacker and is about to kill him, the attacker, who is now in danger of his life, may indeed kill his pursuer, and be held blameless, in that he acted in self-defense at that point.

This last point is a matter of debate between Rashi and the Meiri. Rashi, commenting on the Gemara *Sanhedrin* 82b, explains that if the building collapses on a thief breaking in, there is no obligation to save his life, in that "the moment he breaks in he has forfeited his life." In other words, for the duration of the hostile activity, and until it is completed, he retains the status of a *rodef*, and he may be attacked with impunity—or left to die.[54] Meiri, however, differs, saying that if it is certain that the thief remains alive, there is every obligation to save him, in that at that moment he no longer poses a threat to others' lives, thus his life is no longer forfeit. According to the Meiri, therefore, we judge each stage of the episode separately, and if at one point the pursuer becomes the pursued, then he is accorded the status of an intended victim who may defend himself at all costs. This, apparently, is not the case according to Rashi. Amongst later authorities, R. Moshe Margaliyot takes the side of Rashi.[55] And R. Meir Simḥah would be fully compatible with Meiri, i.e., whosoever is threatened at any given time may act to save himself, irrespective of what may have transpired prior to that point.[56]

In reviewing these sources, it is readily apparent that on the question of the intended victim wounding, as opposed to killing, his assailant, there is a significant divide among the halakhic decisors. As to what the majority view might be, whether in support of Rashi's restrictive position or the more permissive stance of Mizraḥi, it is difficult to tell. Ovadiah Yosef feels that Rashi represents a majority, whereas Ben Zimrah ascribes the majority to the support of Mizraḥi. In any case, there is significant dissent on either side.[57]

A similar picture emerges with situations where it is quite clear that there is no intended threat to the life of a victim, i.e., but the

---

54. See similarly *Ḥiddushei R. Ḥayyim ha-Levi, M. T. Hil. Roẓeiaḥ* 1:13, and *Encyclopedia Talmudit* 12:698, listing this and the opposing views of the *Responsa Minḥat Bikkurim* and *Ḥasdei David*, which are in more in line with Meiri.

55. *Mar'eh Panim* to J. T. *Sanhedrin* 8:9. See Ben Zimrah, pp. 134–135.

56. On this issue see Rabbi Asher Levitan, *ha-Pardes* 27, no. 3 (1952): 1–3, with reference to a possible Maimonidean position as well.

57. See too Rabbi Y. D. Moseson, *ha-Pardes* 16, no. 11 (1942): 16–18; and Rabbi Eliyahu Ḥazon, *ha-Pardes* 37, no. 2 (1963): 14–16.

assailant is about to hurt his victim. What kind of response is permitted in such instances?

The Rosh, in a passage which we saw earlier,[58] refers to the Torah's prescription for the woman who injures her husband's assailant (O), and concludes that her indiscretion occurred in that she did not first attempt a less drastic response to her husband's situation. She, like her husband himself, is required to make every effort to respond to violence in an effective manner, yet with as little violence as possible.[59] This requirement is echoed by the Meiri, including possibly a requirement that one attempt to withdraw from the scene if at all possible.[60]

Yet here, too, others disagree so as to permit, or at least not to punish, disproportionate violence in response to harmful attack. Thus R. Jacob Weil (the Mahariv) permits an entirely subjective judgment on the part of the victim, given his state of intense arousal at being attacked.[61] And R. Solomon Luria similarly holds blameless anyone who uses gratuitous violence in response to an unwarranted attack on his person, given the heat of the moment and the fear of renewed attack unless completely effective action is taken.[62] This dispensation was subsequently extended by R. David ha-Levi, known as the *Taz*, to include the relatives of a person under attack, on the principle that "a relative is like oneself."[63] These authorities, it would appear, like the Rosh, do permit disproportionate violence in deflecting an attack designed to injure.

4. *WHERE THE THREAT IS UNINTENTIONAL, OR INDIRECT*

Thus far we have seen that the principle of *rodef* permits a violent preventive response, whether by the intended victim or a bystander, where there is a deliberate threat to the life or limb of a person. We can now take up the related question as to the appropriate response in cases where the threat is not consciously

58. See above p. 146.
59. *Piskei ha-Rosh, Bava Kamma* 3:13; *Sh.A. H. M.* 421:13.
60. Meiri to *Bava Kamma* 28a. See Ben Zimrah, p. 138.
61. *Responsa Mahariv* 26.
62. *Yam Shel Shelomoh, Bava Kamma* 3:26.
63. *Taz* to *Sh.A. H. M.* 421:13.

intended by the one who poses the threat—or alternatively, where the threat is indirect.

Maimonides in (K) codified the law that a fetus may be destroyed to save the life of the mother, as long as its head has not emerged. The reason he offers is that "the fetus is considered a pursuer [*rodef*] threatening her life." But once the head has emerged, the baby may not be sacrificed. We saw earlier that this dichotomy is to be accounted for with the distinction between *din rodef* and *ḥiyyuv rodef*, so that once birth has occurred, the status of *rodef* must be preceded by intent to kill or maim. From this formulation of Maimonides it would appear that where humans are involved he requires intent to harm as an integral part of the law of pursuit. In other words, if the "assailant" is impelled by circumstances beyond his control (i.e., *ones*), his life or limb is not forfeit.

What is the basis for this? For it would appear that Maimonides is contradicted by the Gemara in *Sanhedrin* (G) that in the name of Rav Huna considers a minor in pursuit to be a *rodef*; i.e., it is permitted to kill such a minor, even though he technically has no culpable intent (*deiah*). In other words, homicidal intent is not necessary to qualify as a *rodef*.

The question, it would appear, is whether the principle of *rodef* is essentially one of punishment or rather one of rescue. If the reason it is permitted to kill an assailant is because justice requires his punishment, then criminal intent is clearly needed before punishment can figure. But if it is purely rescue of a threatened person, then no such intent is needed. In this regard, Rabbi Ezekiel Landau, the *Noda bi-Yehudah*, points out that this talmudic passage seems to be divided. While Rav Huna considers a minor to be a *rodef*, Rav Ḥisda disagrees, arguing that because the minor cannot properly acknowledge the warning that must be given to him, he cannot be killed.[64] His reasoning, says the *Noda bi-Yehudah*, is that the action is indeed one of punishment. Of these two views, the majority of halakhic authorities side with the definition of rescue as the operative concept in *rodef*.[65] But

64. *Responsa Noda bi-Yehudah, Mahadura Tinyana H. M.* 60. See Shepansky, p. 28.

65. As the author of the *Simḥat ha-Ḥag* points out, the very idea that if possible a *rodef* should be injured rather than killed indicates that it is not a question of punishment, but rather of saving the intended victim, that is uppermost. See *Simḥat ha-Ḥag* 17, and Ben Zimrah, p. 131.

for Maimonides, it would follow, there is the element of punishment too.[66] This understanding of Maimonides can be said to follow from his view of the source of the principle of *rodef*; i.e. as we saw earlier, in his view it is the punishment meted out to the woman who attacks her husband's adversary, and not the rape of the betrothed woman, where the essential concern is rescue of the victim.[67]

Once this principle is established, it follows that even where the assailant acts merely to set up a chain of events intended to lead to the death of his victim, he is to be considered a *rodef*. The technical term here is *gramma*, or indirect action leading to a desired effect. Whereas one who causes a death by such indirect means cannot be executed by a court of law,[68] nonetheless it would appear that the law of *rodef* permits violent interception, if necessary by killing, if that is necessary to save the endangered life in question.[69] Such is the view of the Rivash, the *Hagahot Maimoniyyot*, and more recently, R. Meir Simḥah, the Aḥi'ezer, and Rabbi Unterman.[70]

Both these considerations come together in another set of circumstances that have engendered some interesting differences of opinion. What if a group of people finds itself at the mercy of a murderous band (or, for that matter, government), and they are threatened with death unless they hand over one of their group demanded by their enemy. Can that person be considered a threat to their lives, and if so, does the law of the pursuer apply to him, so that they can sacrifice him? In this case, he neither intends to kill them nor is he the one to kill them himself, yet is he a *rodef* in fact?

The Tosefta *Terumot* 7:23 deals with precisely such a situation, and requires that they all be killed rather than hand over a single soul, unless the demand was for a specific named individual,

66. A similar formulation of Maimonides' position is found in the extensive analysis of Rabbi Yosef Rekhes, "Birur be'din Rodef," *Noam* 13 (1970): 259–268, esp. p. 264.

67. For an analysis of this line of thinking, see Rabbi Meir Blumenfeld, *Moriah*, 2, no. 11 (1971): 21–25.

68. See Maimonides, *M. T. Hil. Rozeiaḥ* 2:1–5.

69. See Unterman, *Shevet mi-Yehudah*, pp. 355–359, who quotes the *Or Sameaḥ* and several other authorities.

70. *Responsa Rivash* 338; *Hagahot Maimoniyyot, Hil. Rozeiaḥ* 1, *Or Sameaḥ* ah loc.; *Responsa Aḥi'ezer, E. H.* 19; *Shevet mi-Yehudah*, p. 95.

such as Sheba ben Bikhri, then they may hand him over. In a similar passage in the Jerusalem Talmud, Resh Lakish and R. Yoḥanan differ over this question: regarding the individual who is requested by the adversary, is it necessary that he be guilty of a capital crime, or is that irrelevant, in order to save the lives of the rest of the group? Resh Lakish requires that he in fact be guilty, whereas R. Yoḥanan says that he may be handed over "even if he is not guilty of a capital crime."[71] Of these two views, Maimonides accepts that of Resh Lakish, whereas others, such as the Meiri and Rabbeinu Nissim, accept the view of R. Yoḥanan.[72] Maimonides, in taking this position as opposed to his usual adoption of the view of R. Yoḥanan, appears to be consistent with the notion of *ḥiyyuv rodef*, i.e., there must be an element of punishment present, not simply rescue of threatened lives. Rema, in his comments to the *Shulḥan Arukh*, favors the latter view.[73]

This question became a subject of some debate in this century too. In a rather far-reaching analysis, R. Avraham Yeshayahu Karelitz, popularly known as the Ḥazon Ish, interpreted the view of Resh Lakish to permit handing over an individual, even if according to the laws of the Torah the individual had not committed a capital crime at all.[74] In other words, even the strict view permits his sacrifice as a *rodef* just as long as the enemy has justification by its own laws for his execution. What is the reason? The Ḥazon Ish explains that "it is incumbent upon us to limit as much as possible the loss of Jewish lives." He draws an analogy to the following situation: a man sees a missile about to hit a group of people; if he is able to deflect it he should do so, even if he knows that in so doing he will kill a single individual in the new path he has caused. The reason: we do sacrifice one if that is necessary to save many, and even if the one so sacrificed was not in danger in the first place. In any case, the Ḥazon Ish concludes,

---

71. J. T. *Terumot* 8:10. For a lengthy discussion of this passage and its implicatins, see A. Enker, "Reẓaḥ mi-Tokh Hekhreḥ," *Shenaton ha-Mishpat ha-Ivri* 2 (5735): 161 ff. See also *Jewish Ethics and Halakhah*, vol. 1, chap. 5, pp. 140 ff.

72. Maimonides, *M. T. Hil. Yesodei ha-Torah* 5:5; Meiri to *Sanhedrin*, p. 271; Ran to Alfasi, *Yoma* 82a.

73. *Rema* to *Sh.A. Y. D.* 157:2.

74. *Ḥazon Ish* to *Sanhedrin* 5. See also his comments to *M. T. Yesodei ha-Torah* 5:5.

against Maimonides, that the view of R. Yoḥanan is to be accepted.

Rabbi Unterman takes sharp issue with this view.[75] In the first place he argues that the reason the group may not hand over an individual who had not been named by the besiegers is that if they do so, they themselves become *rodfim*, i.e., they now pose a threat to his life, in that they single him out for death, albeit indirectly in that they do not kill him with their own hands. It is only once he is named by the opposing camp that they can no longer be considered *rodfim*. Furthermore, he says, it is incorrect to consider the named individual a *rodef* just because he was singled out by the enemy for their own reasons; it is necessary in addition that he indeed be guilty of a capital crime according to the Torah. For it is inconceivable to him that Maimonides would, in accepting the view of Resh Lakish, permit the sacrifice of a person whose guilt is not established, other than by some capricious wish of an inhuman enemy.[76] In a postscript, Rabbi Unterman records an incident in nineteenth-century Poland wherein a group of some twenty young Jewish men, on their way to assist a neighboring community suffering a pogrom, were handed over to the authorities by their fellow Jews on the point of death, and immediately executed. For many years thereafter, the inhabitants of the village where they had been handed over were universally ostracized for their act of betrayal.

These two opposing perspectives on this issue are encountered and reflected in several heartrending responsa delivered to Jews during the Nazi Holocaust.

One responsum, adopting a position similar to that of the Ḥazon Ish, was authored by R. Shimon Efrati. The case involved a group of Jews hiding in an underground bunker from the Gestapo. During a search that required absolute silence, a baby in the group started to cry. One of the men covered the baby's face, and as a result the baby suffocated to death. The question

75. *Shevet mi-Yehudah*, pp. 98 ff.

76. In editing the second edition of Rabbi Unterman's work, Rabbi Avraham Bick comes to the defense of the Ḥazon Ish, explaining that the latter's meaning is not to allow such handing over where there is no reasonable justification whatsoever for their demands, but rather that their demand is in accordance with their accepted law or practice, albeit not in accord with the laws of the Torah. Under this circumstance, he argues, that life can be sacrificed in order to save the lives of the others. See *Shevet mi-Yehudah*, p. 100.

arose: did he act in accordance with the Halakhah?[77] Rabbi Efrati examined the question and found two grounds on which to rule that the act had been within permissible parameters. In the first place he points out that the Tosefta in *Terumot* records the view of R. Judah that where the person who poses the threat to the group is part of the endangered group anyway, and therefore will die in any case if he is not given over, then he should be given over whether or not he is guilty of a capital offense. In the case of the baby, says Rabbi Efrati, were the group to be discovered, the baby would die with the rest of the group, thus he can be "given over" to death to save the others. In this, the baby could be said to be like Sheba ben Bikhri, in that both would die in any case. The second principle leading to Rabbi Efrati's conclusion is that of *rodef*. For he considers the baby in this instance to be a *rodef*, albeit one without intent to harm. He argues that even according to the view that where there is no intent to harm the *rodef* may not be killed, nonetheless where the *rodef* himself will die in any case, he may be killed, if that will save the others. Like the Ḥazon Ish, therefore, his position was that the one posing the threat to the life of the group may be sacrificed, even if there is no prior guilt associated with that person.

On the other hand, we encounter a responsum by Rabbi Efraim Oshry, rabbi of the Kovno ghetto.[78] The Germans at one point ordered the Jewish leadership of the community to issue a limited number of life-saving identity cards to members of the ghetto. The leadership carried out the order, and thereby relegated the rest of the ghetto to almost certain death. In the process a number of workers resorted to irregular means to acquire these cards, thereby ensuring that other Jews would be killed. Were these people acting in accordance with the Halakhah? Was it permitted to effectively "hand over" some Jews to save others, or to sacrifice another to save oneself? Rabbi Oshry, in answering these questions in the negative, effectively followed a line of reasoning similar to that taken by Rabbi Unterman. Firstly, he considers Maimonides' acceptance of Resh Lakish's view to be normative and correct, i.e., we may not hand over another person to certain

77. *Responsa mi-Gei ha-Harigah*, p. 23. Also see, in detail, Irving Rosenbaum, *The Holocaust and the Halakhah*, pp. 31 ff., and Enker, "Rezaḥ mi-Tokh Hekhreḥ," p. 172.

78. *Kuntres me-Emek ha-Bakha*, no. 1.

death unless that person is guilty of a capital crime, like Sheba ben Bikhri. This is certainly the case where the enemy has not itself named the ones to be handed over to their death, but leaves that determination to the Jews themselves. Hence the Kovno leadership had no right to make such a determination at all.[79] Secondly, he disagrees with the actions of those who saved themselves and thereby condemned others to death. While the Shakh permits an individual Jew to take whatever steps he can to avoid being put to death, even though he knows that another Jew will face death as a result,[80] that is only where the death of the other Jew is not inevitable. This was not the case in the Kovno ghetto. In this sense, those who improperly took the cards for themselves were the direct cause of the deaths of others. This, he argues, is true even according to the Yad Avraham who permitted a person to save himself, but not if it would lead automatically to the endangerment of another.[81]

On another occasion, Rabbi Zvi Hirsch Meisels was confronted with a situation in Auschwitz in which the father of a boy condemned to death was able to save his son by substituting another boy in his stead. The father's question was simple: could he sacrifice one to save another?[82] In responding, Rabbi Meisels could find no clearcut precedent that would permit such substitution, given the fact that the one so substituted was certain to die, as is clear from the position of the Yad Avraham. Further complicating the situation was the fact that it was not a case of a person saving himself at the expense of another, but as a father saving his son, he was acting as a third party. As a result, the father did not attempt to save the boy.

SUMMARY AND CONCLUSIONS

In retrospect, it becomes clear that the law of self-defense in the Halakhah is a multifaceted one. While in general Jewish law

---

79. Rabbi Oshry himself quotes the view of Rabbi Avraham Shapiro, Chief Rabbi of Kovno at the time, that did in fact advocate cooperation with the Germans, and to "take upon themselves the responsibility of doing whatever needs to be done to save a part of the community." See Rosenbaum, p. 31.

80. Shakh to *Sh.A. H. M.* 163:11.

81. *Yad Avraham* to *Sh.A. Y. D.* 157.

82. *Responsa Mekaddeshei Hashem* 1:3. On this responsum, see Ben Zimrah, pp. 146–147; Rosenbaum, pp. 3–5 and 157–158.

insists on due process and judicial review, it does also permit, under the rubric of the law of *rodef*, nonjudicial violence in the prevention of physical attack on an innocent person. Maimonides enumerates this among the positive obligations incumbent on a Jew. What are the sources for the law of *rodef*? We have seen that they are several: not to stand idly by the blood of our fellow (Lev. 19:16); the Deuteronomic law of the obligation to save by any means a betrothed woman threatened with rape; the sanction to disable a woman who poses a mortal threat to a man fighting with her husband (Deut. 25:11); and most particularly the law in Exodus 22 that permits the killing of a thief found breaking in.

This last principle involves a number of disputes: what is its source (Rashi: it is its own source, vs. Meiri: from the attack on the Midianites); what is included in this law (Rashi: only instances of forced entry, vs. Maimonides: only cases where people would be expected to be encountered within); is an armed thief who enters private property assumed to be homicidal (two views in the Tosefta, as quoted by Rabbi Feinstein). Rabbi Feinstein does consider him homicidal, allowing the intended victim to act accordingly. The same, he says, is true of two or more thieves, even if they be not armed.

Where the intended victim is clearly not in danger of his life, but merely subject to grievous injury, several views are recorded. The Rosh permits, without requiring, a violent response, by either the intended victim or his relative, as long as the least injurious response necessary to stop the attack is used. And the Sema extends such a mandate to any bystander. R. Joseph of Trani likewise permits an immediate preemptive attack to provocation, and the Rivash, it would appear, goes so far as to permit a homicidal response by the intended victim so as to stop a threat to any of his limbs or organs from which he would not be able to fully recover in time. Yet most authorities avoid permitting such an extreme response, leaving the question rather as to whether a homicidal response is indeed a capital crime (as R. Solomon Luria argues) or is forgivable given the provocation (the view of R. Jacob Emden).

We also saw that Maimonides extends the principle of *rodef* to all sources that present a threat to life, animate or inanimate alike. Thus he classifies a ship's cargo as a pursuer if it poses a peril to the ship. As clarified by R. Ḥayyim Soloveichik, such a threat does not need to be intended or conscious to be disposed of in any way possible. It is only when a human, already born, poses a threat that prior intent to harm is necessary before a violent response is mandated.

How do we determine whether a grievous attack is about to occur? Must certain objective criteria be satisfied before preemptive violence is permitted? While it is important to consider the past record of an assailant (if it is available), the major clarification of this issue revolves around the issue of warning (or *hatra'ah*). Based on a dispute between Rav Huna and Rav Ḥisda in *Sanhedrin*, most authorities accept the view that even a pursuer must be forewarned, to establish his intent to harm—and it makes no difference whether the pursuer is a minor or acknowledges the warning given him. A significant minority (notably the Sema, Rivash, and Minḥat Ḥinukh) dissents, and takes the position that under extreme circumstances, where the life of a victim is at stake, warning may be dispensed with.

Certainly, it would appear, the intended victim himself may dispense with warning, and act with all necessary haste (and violence) to dispel the perceived threat. This view, formulated by the Rivash, R. Aaron ha-Kohen, and Meiri, seems to have been an accepted one. Where the attack is made by an intruder onto private property, the upshot of the talmudic discussion is to dispense with the need for warning, in that it can be assumed that such an intruder will resort to violence, if necessary. Even so, a third party who comes across such a situation should if at all possible issue a warning prior to acting with force.

Thus we can conclude that the intended victim himself can make a subjective judgment on the spur of the moment and act accordingly, without having to ascertain by some objective means (e.g., forewarning) the true intent of the attacker. But a third party cannot intervene without warning, under most circumstances, thereby to establish some objective, reasonable, standard of violent intent.

What kind of violent response is permitted? It is clear from the early rabbinic midrashim that a third party must use only the minimum level of violence available to him to thwart the attacker's intent. If he kills when he need not have, he is himself subject to the death penalty. This too is the point of a pivotal statement in

Sanhedrin by R. Jonathan b. Saul, and codified by the major authorities.

The situation is more complicated, however, when it is the intended victim himself who acts with gratuitous violence, killing the attacker when mere injury would have sufficed. A major debate on this issue seems to have divided the halakhists over the course of generations, based on their respective interpretations of two key scriptural passages, in Genesis 32 (where Jacob confronts Esau) and the Second Book of Samuel (the events surrounding the death of Abner). R. Elijah Mizraḥi derives from the former that the intended victim may indeed resort to homicide even where he can otherwise disable his attacker, and be held guiltless. Others who support his view are the *Tur, Mishneh la-Melekh*, Levush, and R. Samuel Alkalai. Yet others are opposed to this dispensation, notably Rashi (in extending the principle of R. Jonathan b. Saul to cover the actions of the intended victim as well), Tosafot, R. Meir Abulafia, and Meiri. The position of Maimonides is somewhat more complex, but (unlike the Ravad) he seems to side with Mizraḥi's viewpoint. Among later authorities, a majority agrees with Rashi, and holds an intended victim liable for gratuitous violence. And Ovadiah Yosef considers the possibility that even Mizraḥi only permits homicide under wartime conditions, where extreme responses are sometimes called for.

Maimonides' ruling that gratuitous violence by an Israelite is not actually punishable by a court leads a number of twentieth-century halakhists to consider his precise understanding of the passage in Samuel detailing the death of Abner, who had acted in self-defense and killed Asahel. Was Abner's death at the hands of Asahel's brother Joab legitimate or not? Rabbi Eliezer Waldenberg considers the latter to have acted as a blood-avenger. Ovadiah Yosef, however, disputes this. Rabbi Meir Simḥah of Dvinsk makes a pertinent distinction between a pursuer who acts with the permission of the court (such as Asahel or Pinḥas) and one who does not act properly (such as Esau). The former cannot be summarily killed, but the latter, according to Maimonides, may.

Yet another difference of opinion surfaces in the context of a pursuer turned pursued: may he defend himself by killing his intended victim who is now his attacker? Rashi seems to feel that he may not, in that once he became a pursuer he forfeited his legal rights to self-defense. Meiri, however, disagrees, and argues that whatever preceded is extraneous to his present predicament, and the fact is that he is now in danger of his life, thus he may defend himself at all costs. Again these respective views are encountered in later times (the *Mareh Panim* vs. the *Or Sameaḥ*).

Similar differences surface when we consider the appropriate response to nonmurderous assault. The Rosh joins the Meiri in requiring a minimalist reaction wherever possible, but R. Jacob Weil, R. Solomon Luria, and the Taz hold a murderous response blameless, even in the absence of a murderous assault, given the exigencies and intense emotions of the moment.

The final question is that of unintended or indirect threat to life. To qualify as a *rodef*, must a person intend the harm of the one so endangered? Maimonides, it would appear, answers in the positive, and thus codifies the law that once the fetus has emerged, it is a person who intends no harm, and thus cannot be killed. In so doing, Maimonides seems to be following the view of Rav Ḥisda in *Sanhedrin*, which disqualifies all minors from the category of *rodef*. But others, indeed a majority, follow the view of Rav Huna: intent is not required, hence a minor can be considered a *rodef*. As explained by the *Noda bi-Yehudah*, what is at stake here is whether we consider the principle of *rodef* to be intended primarily as rescue or as punishment. If it is punishment, then punishment requires intent to harm on the part of the perpetrator; if it is rescue, then intent is irrelevant, just so long as the threatened life or limb can be saved.

Similar considerations lead to the related issue of indirect cause: where a person sets up a chain of events leading to the death of his intended victim, a majority of halakhic authorities consider him a *rodef* in the fullest sense, even though a court cannot execute him on technical grounds. This principle in turn leads to the question of the surrender of one person to save a threatened group; can that person be classified as a pursuer, and be handed over to be killed, in that his life poses a threat to theirs? The Tosefta records several views, and in the Jerusalem Talmud Resh Lakish and R. Yoḥanan differ: the former requires that the named individual be guilty of a capital crime, while the latter does not. Here again, the authorities divide on the issue: Maimonides for once sides with Resh Lakish (consistently, it would appear, in requiring a measure of guilt as part of the criteria of *rodef*), whereas Meiri, the Ran, and R. Moses Isserles prefer the view of R. Yoḥanan.

In this century, two parallel views emerged. The Ḥazon Ish, agreeing with R. Yoḥanan, sees no point in requiring guilt or intent to harm; more important is the calculus of saving lives. Thus an individual is to be sacrificed under such circumstances. Rabbi Unterman dissents sharply, siding with Resh Lakish and Maimonides, against R. Yoḥanan. Similar divisions are encountered in the Holocaust responsa literature: Rabbi Efrati found reason to endorse the sacrifice of a baby posing a threat to the survival of a group of adults in hiding, absent all intent to harm on its part, while Rabbi Oshry (and on another occasion Rabbi Meisels) cannot give his assent to those who saved some Jews (themselves included) and thereby condemned others to almost certain death.

What are the conclusions of all this, in the context of the questions with which we started this chapter? In the first place, it is clear that a violent response to the threat of violence is permitted, and often required. Secondly, the intended victim is entitled to make a subjective judgment as to the intent of the assailant, especially where there is more than one such pursuer. But bystanders must be more careful in attempting to establish objective intent before they may act. Thirdly, while it is clear that a third party must without question attempt to intervene if at all possible without taking the attacker's life, there is a genuine difference of opinion as to whether that requirement is germane to the intended victim himself; i.e., while it is certainly preferable to avoid homicide, if he kills anyway there are opposing views as to any guilt he might bear.

Accordingly, if the man in question did not aim to kill he would be exonerated by most halakhic authorities. If he did aim to kill, even though he was quite capable at that moment of merely disabling his attackers, then many halakhic authorities would hold him liable on charges of manslaughter, while others would dissent.

7

Capital Punishment

Introduction

Capital punishment, or the imposition of the death penalty by the state, has been practiced since the earliest times. Since the eighteenth century the modern movement for the abolition of this penalty has gathered force, resulting in the limiting of the imposition of this form of punishment in many countries. In 1972 the Supreme Court of the United States ruled that the death penalty, because it was being arbitrarily imposed, was no longer legal. At the same time this ruling left the way open for Congress or state legislatures to enact new capital punishment laws in the future. A number of legislatures enacted such laws thereafter, and as a result the death penalty has been implemented in a number of states, using the firing squad, electrocution, gas, or lethal injection. The major issue is whether capital punishment, by its very nature, is moral under any circumstances. Is it ever a justifiable form of punishment?

Those who argue that the death penalty is a justifiable form of punishment do so for a variety of reasons. Some say that it is the most effective deterrent to certain major crimes, particularly murder, in that the very possibility of being executed will deter potential murderers from acting. Furthermore, those who are convicted of such crimes constitute a potential threat to society, and the only way that society can protect itself from the possibility that such persons will strike again is by executing them. Others argue that justice itself demands that the punishment fit the crime, insofar as those who murder forfeit their claim to life. It is also stated that imposing the death penalty leads to a net saving of lives—that is, the lives of future victims, whose potential killers may be influenced to desist by the severity of the death penalty. This, it is argued, is true even if it is granted that there is a possibility that an innocent man could be executed, for the lives of future innocent victims are also at stake.

These arguments are contested by the so-called abolitionists. The opposition to the death penalty bases itself in the first place on the fact that there are no statistics proving any relationship between the death penalty and the crime rate. It has never been proven that the prospect of execution has deterred anyone from committing murder. Other factors would seem to play a more decisive role in producing serious crime, factors such as personality defects and socioeconomic deprivation. The death penalty, it is argued, is inconsistent with the sanctity and supreme value of human life, even that of a murderer, and in any case destroying his life will not right the wrong he has done or bring the victim of his crime back to life. Furthermore, there is always the possibility of a mistaken verdict, and once the death penalty has been carried out there can be no posthumous "correction." Punishment should be designed to rehabilitate criminals and at the same time protect the interests of society; carrying out the death penalty only serves to intensify the level of violence and bloodshed.

A Jewish response to these arguments needs to reflect a variety of conflicting principles: a surpassing reverence for all life, the biblical acceptance of capital punishment, an abiding respect for public law and order that demands extreme measures to protect the innocent, and the historical opposition of many authorities to the carrying out of the death penalty. Only when all of these principles are given due consideration in a framework that preserves the integrity of the whole is it possible to understand the halakhic attempt to balance justice and compassion, law and morality over the issue of capital punishment.

The Question

A man is found guilty of murder in the first degree. He is quite sane, and takes full responsibility for his actions. The crime reflects a general breakdown of law in society. Would Halakhah sanction the death sentence?

There are several issues here:

1. Was the death penalty ever accepted in Jewish law, and carried out by legal authority as punishment for murder?
2. In contemporary times, in the absence of classic court procedures and standards, is there any halakhic sanction for the death penalty for murder?
3. Are there alternative penalties in the absence of the death penalty; and who might be qualified to pass such a sentence?

Sources

A. Exodus 21:14

And if a man come presumptuously upon his neighbor, to slay him with guile, thou shalt take him from My altar that he may die.

B. Deuteronomy 17:9

And thou shalt come unto the priests, the Levites, and unto the judge that shall be in those days; and thou shalt inquire and they shall declare unto thee the sentence of judgment.

C. Mekhilta deR. Simon bar Yoḥai, Exodus 21:14

From whence do we know that the Sanhedrin must function adjacent to the altar? From the words "from My altar thou shalt take him that he may die," i.e., if there is an altar you may execute him, but in the absence of an altar you may not execute him.

D. Midrash Tannaim, Deuteronomy 19:13

"Do not pity him": this is an admonition not to spare the killer out of mercy. One should not say that a person has already been killed, of what use is the killing of another? Rather than neglect the execution, therefore, the murderer should be executed. Abba Ḥanon says in the name of R. Eliezer, "Wherever the Torah specifies an [apparently] unjust punishment, it is written 'do not pity.' "

E. Avodah Zarah 8b

Forty years prior to the destruction of the Second Temple, the Sanhedrin moved from the Temple and met in the marketplace, so as not to judge capital cases. What was the reason? Because they recognized the proliferation of capital crimes which they were unable to judge properly, thus they relocated so as not to pass the death sentence. This is learned from "and you shall do according to that which they shall tell you from that place"; i.e., their place [within the Temple] had to be part of the judicial procedure.

F. Mishnah, Makkot 7a

The Sanhedrin functions within Israel as well as outside of Israel. A Sanhedrin that passes the death penalty once in seven years is called a violent court. R. Eleazar b. Azariah says that this is true of a court that passes such sentence even once in seventy years. R. Tarfon and R. Akiva say, "Had we been members of the Sanhedrin, no one would ever have been executed." R. Simon b. Gamaliel says, "[By avoiding all capital punishment] they too would have caused a proliferation of murderers in Israel."

G. Sanhedrin 46a

R. Eleazar b. Jacob says, "I have heard that a court may decree capital punishment without the warrant of the Torah. This would not be in violation of the Torah but to protect it. Such was the case with a man who rode a horse on the Sabbath in the days of the Hellenists, for which he was brought to court and stoned to death. It was not that such a punishment was biblically mandated for that act, but that the times required it."

H. Sanhedrin 52b

Bat Tali, the daughter of a priest, had illicit sexual relations. R. Ḥama bar Tuvia wrapped her in branches and burned her to death. Said R. Joseph, "R. Ḥama thereby erred doubly. He contradicted R. Matna [in using that particular mode of execution], and he contradicted the Beraita that says . . . that capital punishment occurs only when there is a priest [and Sanhedrin functioning in the Temple]."

I. Sanhedrin 27a

Bar Ḥama was alleged to have committed an act of murder. The exilarch ordered R. Abba bar Jacob to investigate the matter, saying, "If he indeed killed, then he is to be blinded."

J. Maimonides, M.T. Hilkhot Sanhedrin 24:4

A court may execute one not subject to the death penalty. This would not be in violation of the Torah but to protect it. Thus, if the court recognizes that the people willfully ignore the law, the court may issue special decrees to strengthen the law as it sees fit. This is by way of a temporary decree, not as a permanent statute for all generations. . . . Such was the case of the man who rode a horse on the Sabbath . . . and was stoned, and such was the case when [*Sanhedrin* 45b] Simon b. Shetaḥ hanged eighty women on one day, even though there was no proper cross-examination, forewarning, or unequivocal evidence. He acted by way of a temporary measure as he saw fit.

K. Maimonides, M.T. Hilkhot Roẓeiaḥ 2:4

If there are murderers who are not subject to the death penalty, then an Israelite king may execute them by his royal prerogative and by reason of societal need, if he so wishes. Likewise if a court wishes to execute such a person as a temporary measure, they may do so if such are the needs of the hour.

L. Maimonides, Commentary on the Mishnah, Ḥullin 1.

There is an established procedure, one which we follow in practice, whereby a person who is guilty of a crime for which the punishment is death is instead excommunicated and whipped, and never given an opportunity for pardon. The reason is that today we no longer carry out the death penalty.

M. Nimmukei Yosef, Sanhedrin 52b

According to certain commentaries, the Gemara (H) could likewise have said that R. Ḥama, in executing Bat Tali, made the mistake of passing the death penalty without a properly ordained court. For there are authorities who insist that the court must consist of ordained members. As for the execution of the man riding the horse on the Sabbath—that was a permissible penalty, for it was the Sanhedrin itself that was involved, unlike an ordinary court. Likewise, note that the exilarch did not require the execution of Bar Ḥama.

N. Rosh, Responsum 17:8

In all the lands of my acquaintance, the death penalty is not practiced, except here in Spain. When I arrived here, I was most surprised that this was done without a Sanhedrin. I was told that it was by way of a royal dispensation utilized by the Jewish court to save lives that would be lost were they to be left to Gentile courts. And while I permitted them to maintain this practice, I never agreed with their taking of life in such fashion.

Discussion

1. CAPITAL PUNISHMENT AS A SANCTIONED PRACTICE

In the Torah, it is quite clear that intentional murder is a crime punishable by death (A). Murder constitutes one of the three cardinal sins singled out for biblical anathema.[1] The Torah explicitly forbids any other punishment for this crime, saying, "moreover ye shall take no ransom for the life of the murderer that is guilty of death, but he shall surely be put to death" (Num. 35:31).

How is the death penalty passed? Under optimal conditions, such as those that prevailed during Temple times, when the judicial system of Halakhah functioned in its entirety (C), the death penalty could be implemented in one of two ways. The first, and more conventional, mechanism occurred by way of the judicial procedure that allowed for a court of twenty-three judges to pass the death sentence. The procedure involved, *inter alia*, the fullest compliance with due process, in particular *hatra'ah*, i.e., forewarning the culprit before the crime, and *edut mekhuvenet*, i.e., impeccably qualified witnesses able to withstand severe cross-examination.[2] Besides this judicial process, the death penalty could be implemented by the king. He could invoke his royal prerogative when the courts were unable or unwilling to pronounce sentence in spite of a preponderance of evidence indicating guilt (K). This royal power was justified as a necessary discretionary alternative to the courts, to ensure "the well-being of society, as dictated by the needs of the hour."[3]

The relation between these two mechanisms is described by R. Nissim b. Reuben Gerondi (d. 1375) in his *Derashot ha-Ran*.[4] He explains that when, in the days of the prophet Samuel, the people requested a king, they wanted him to replace the normal judicial process entirely.[5] What God in fact sanctioned was merely a supplemental role to be invoked in the occasional cases where the courts were unable to act decisively. But, having empowered the king to act in matters of life and death, the law then dialectically limited the powers of the crown. Thus, in Deuteronomy, the king's freedom is curtailed, his marital arrangements circumscribed, his trade with foreign lands minimized, and he is always to be accompanied by his own scroll of the law.[6]

In any case, the death penalty could be, and was, carried out in these two ways. But having legitimized the penalty in principle, the Halakhah invoked and practiced it with extreme caution. The Mishnah (F) records an anonymous view that considered a court that passed the death penalty even once in seven years to be overly zealous; in the opinion of R. Eleazar b. Azariah this could be said of even once in seventy years. Yet a third, much-quoted view, attributed to the tannaim R. Tarfon and R. Akiva, was so opposed to the death penalty that, in their words, "had we been members of the Sanhedrin, no one would ever have been executed." As explained by the Gemara, they would have exploited every legal means available to discredit and weaken the evidence leading to a conviction.

Why were R. Tarfon and R. Akiva so opposed to the death penalty? Did they negate the very possibility of a conviction? There are two interpretations here. Rashi, in commenting on this passage, takes it in its literal sense to be saying that no witnesses could ever emerge from their examination with their evidence intact, and furthermore, that R. Tarfon and R. Akiva would always have disqualified the witnesses in capital cases. Ritva (d. 1330), however, understood them to be saying that a court could always disqualify the witnesses, if it chose so to act, given certain social conditions. Such conditions prevailed in the period immediately preceding the destruction of the Temple, when homicides were on the increase and the courts were loath to practice capital punishment. But at other times, according to Ritva, and his teacher Naḥmanides (d. 1270), even R. Tarfon and R. Akiva could have approved of the death penalty and chosen not to disqualify the witnesses. Accordingly, the statement attributed to them in the Mishnah is not to be taken literally, but simply as indicating the extreme unlikelihood of the death penalty.[7]

Among later authorities the view of R. Tarfon and R. Akiva became, as might be expected, a rallying point for those opposed to the death penalty in principle. Of course, the Mishnah itself records the counter-argument in the form of the opinion of R. Simon b. Gamaliel, who accused R. Tarfon and R. Akiva of fostering an attitude that would cause the proliferation of murderers (F). Apparently, his view was that the death penalty would act as a deterrent to crime, and its absence as an incentive to murder for those predisposed to such violence.

In the twentieth century, the view of R. Tarfon and R. Akiva was explained by Rabbi Binyamin Rabinowitz-Teomim as motivated by the practical problem of the possibility of a mistaken verdict. He explains their view to be concerned with the ever-present possibility of executing an innocent man.[8] Others, however, such as Moshe Leib Lilienblum, understood them to be rejecting the death penalty in principle, and in fact to be representative of the entire body of tradition that stood opposed to any and all executions.[9]

In those cases where the Torah does mandate the death penalty, is it possible to discern a rationale? Rabbi J. M. Tykocinski, like others, recognizes that on several occasions the Torah appends the words "and all the people shall hear and fear and do no more presumptuously,"[10] a verse that implies the value of the death penalty as a deterrent to crime. Yet, he argues, such verses do not attempt to justify the execution itself, but merely the desirability of a *public* execution. A more instructive verse occurring in the context of the death penalty for murder is "thine eye shall not pity him, but thou shall put away the blood of the innocent from Israel, that it may go well with thee" (Deut. 19:13). This, argues Tykocinski, requires the removal of the murderer from the midst of the people. Ultimately, the execution is to be viewed as an act of atonement for the individual thus punished, who thereby achieves forgiveness for his crime. Hence the evil is removed not only from the people of Israel but from the sinner in addition.[11] As Rabinowitz-Teomim puts it, "Notwithstanding the high regard for man, the cherished value of every unique individual, and the great love that we have for every individual made in the image of God, even those condemned to death . . . nonetheless an evil man cannot be permitted to remain alive, for by his death he gains atonement, even as he is removed from life."[12]

2. CAPITAL PUNISHMENT IN THE ABSENCE OF THE SANHEDRIN OR KING

Ever since the Sanhedrin disqualified itself (E), there were attempts to implement the death penalty. While those who made these attempts recognized that they were going beyond the biblical warrant for the death penalty, they believed that doing so could be justified by other considerations of Jewish law.

A pivotal text in this discussion was the statement of R. Eleazar b. Jacob (G) affirming a tradition known to him whereby "when the times require it," the death penalty can be implemented even in the absence of conventional conditions and procedures, and even if deemed necessary as punishment for acts not normally punished by death. Such precipitate action can be undertaken in order to protect the larger concerns of the Torah. This statement was subjected to careful scrutiny, and there subsequently emerged two opposing viewpoints in post-talmudic literature.

Thus, starting with R. Isaac Alfasi (Rif, d. 1103), there were those who found in this statement ample warrant for the death penalty even in the absence of the Sanhedrin or the king.[13] Rif, as understood by later authorities, took R. Eleazar b. Jacob to be referring to the implementation of monetary, corporal, and capital punishments.[14] Maimonides (J) quotes R. Eleazar b. Jacob approvingly and clarifies the parameters of the "needs of the hour" by saying that "when the court recognizes that the people willfully ignore the law, the court may issue special decrees to strengthen the law as it sees fit," punishable by death. This, he hastens to add, is possible only as a temporary decree, contingent upon local conditions (B). Maimonides illustrates this principle by referring to the celebrated—and controversial—case of Simon b. Shetaḥ, who hanged eighty women in one day for practicing witchcraft, without recourse to normative judicial procedure.[15] Elsewhere (K), Maimonides records the royal prerogative to execute a criminal by way of a temporary decree by reason of "societal need."

These passages in Maimonides were subject to some controversy and interpretation. R. Jacob b. Asher, author of the *Tur* (d. 1340), understood Maimonides to be permitting the death penalty in any country and at any time where conditions required drastic action.[16] A similar view of Maimonides was offered by the *Birkei Yosef*, and by R. Joel Sirkes, known as the *Baḥ* (d. 1640).[17] This interpretation of Maimonides, and indeed of the permissive approach to capital punishment in general, drew on several distinct passages in talmudic literature. One such case involved the Babylonian exilarch who empowered a messenger of the court to blind a murderer who was proven guilty (I). In that case it was clear that even in the absence of a Sanhedrin, severe punishment could be meted out to a murderer. Of course it is true that the exilarch pointedly did not execute the criminal, preferring simply to blind him. This could be explained, however, as the result of the considered judgment of the exilarch that the blinding was sufficient punishment for that crime and that place. As R. Isaac b. Sheshet (Rivash, d. 1407) put it, the exilarch, had he so wished, could indeed have executed the culprit.[18]

Another passage quoted in support of the death penalty concerned the daughter of a priest who was condemned to death by burning for having committed an act of harlotry (H). While the Talmud disagreed with both the verdict of death and the method of execution, there were subsequent authorities who nonetheless took this as a warrant for the death penalty. Thus, for instance, R. Solomon Luria (Maharshal, d. 1573) argued that the judge in that case acted within the parameters of R. Eleazar b. Jacob's "needs of the hour," and so was justified in going beyond the conventional judicial procedure.[19]

Faced with a viewpoint favoring the death penalty, other halakhists took the opposite stance. In their opinion, R. Eleazar b. Jacob was referring exclusively to the days of the Sanhedrin, when the death penalty was practiced anyway. His statement intended merely to add certain crimes or improper acts to the list of those for which the punishment was death. Such extraordinary punishment could be given by the Sanhedrin, or court of twenty-three, for relatively minor infractions, as an emergency measure. What was critical, however, was that the judges be properly ordained (*musmakhim*). Hence, where there is no Sanhedrin even R. Eleazar b. Jacob would oppose the death penalty as an emergency measure, for without the Sanhedrin there is no ordination.

This line of reasoning was articulated by Rabbeinu Nissim b. Reuben Gerondi (author of the *Ḥiddushei ha-Ran* and *Derashot ha-Ran*, cf. above) and his pupil R. Joseph Ḥabiba (author of the *Nimmukei Yosef*, fl. early 15th cent.).[20] As the latter explained (M), R. Eleazar b. Jacob does not refer to contemporary courts lacking ordination; he is simply referring to a received tradition dating back to the days of the Sanhedrin. Besides, he argues, a careful reading of the pertinent talmudic passages would confirm opposition to the death penalty in contemporary times. Thus, for instance, the fact that the exilarch did *not* impose the death penalty, but chose instead to impose another form of corporal punishment, indicates the lapsing of the death penalty. Likewise the fact that the Talmud condemns R. Ḥama b. Tuvia for executing the priest's daughter points in the direction of the impermissibility of the death penalty since the demise of the Sanhedrin.

The exponents of these views found further support in the same passages of Maimonides as those who took the opposite view. Thus R. Malakhi b. Jacob ha-Kohen (author of the *Yad Malakhi*, d. 1785) and R. Isaac Meir Rothenberg (author of the *Ḥiddushei ha-Rim*, d. 1866) noted a significant omission by Maimonides in the critical passage (J).[21] Whereas Maimonides does say that a court may properly execute one who is not biblically subject to the death penalty, he omits the words "in all places at all times." Ordinarily, this would not be significant, except that in the immediately following statement, dealing with one who is suspected of incestuous behavior, Maimonides pointedly includes the phrase "in all places at all times." Hence, they argue, where that phrase is omitted, one can reasonably assume that Maimonides is limiting such punishment to a particular time and place, i.e., where the Sanhedrin functions. Such a reading likewise points to Maimonides' explicit statement elsewhere (L) that "today we no longer carry out the death penalty."

Such a reading of Maimonides was recognized somewhat earlier by R. Joel Sirkes but rejected by him on the grounds that when Maimonides does add that phrase in the adjacent statement, it is prefaced with the word *vekhen*, i.e., "and similarly." Hence, argues Sirkes, the two statements share this detail, and Maimonides can be said to consider the death penalty applicable even subsequent to the demise of the Sanhedrin, given the requisite conditions.[22]

There was another important figure who opposed the death penalty: R. Asher b. Yeḥiel, known as Rosh (d. 1327). When late in his life he moved from Northern Europe to Spain, he encountered the phenomenon of Jewish communities empowered by the state to carry out the death penalty, and in fact exercising that right.[23] When asked for approval, Rosh demurred, saying that while he could not forbid such punishment, nonetheless "I never agreed with them regarding the taking of life" (N). He preferred instead to administer some form of corporal punishment.[24]

Implicit in the views opposed to the implementation of capital punishment is the recognition of the fact, recorded in the Talmud (E), that when faced with an increased rate of homicide, far from further implementing the death penalty the Sanhedrin deliberately chose to suspend it as a judicial response to "the needs of the hour." Thus, the view of R. Eleazar b. Jacob could be seen to be consistent with the action of the Sanhedrin in suspending the death penalty only if we understand him to be saying that the Sanhedrin carried out this particular punishment only when in its view it would deter such a crime for one reason or another. The mere fact of widespread acts of homicide by itself was not reason enough to implement the punishment; on the contrary that would be reason to suspend it. Accordingly, "the times require it" refers to the entire complex of criteria and reasoning that the Sanhedrin would need to invoke in deciding whether or not to carry out capital punishment. According to this view, therefore, with the dissolution of the Sanhedrin two factors require consideration: (1) the technical impossibility of acting without the Sanhedrin; and (2) when the crime rate increases, indicating that the deterrent function of the death penalty is irrelevant, there is even more reason to oppose its implementation.

But in spite of such opposition, the majority of authorities, in that generation and subsequently, favored the death penalty as an emergency decree. Of Rosh's own children, two dissented from his view. One, as we have seen, was the author of the *Tur*; another was R. Judah b. Asher (known as Ri b. ha-Rosh, d. 1349), who was outspoken in support of the death penalty. He considered the measure to be important for two reasons: Catholic courts would have executed many more Jews had Jewish courts not assumed responsibility for such cases; furthermore, it was necessary "to execute those guilty of capital crimes according to our own laws, such as those who betray Jews to Gentile authorities [*mosrim*]."[25] Similar positions were espoused by the renowned R. Menaḥem ha-Meiri (d. 1306)[26] and R. Solomon b. Adret (Rashba, d. 1310).[27] The latter specifically exempted such cases from the need for *hatra'ah*, or forewarning, and properly admissible evidence.[28]

An echo of this permissive trend is found in the responsa of R. Isaac b. Sheshet Perfet (Rivash, d. 1408). By his time, as he writes, the death penalty was no longer practiced by the Jewish communities of Spain. Yet he permits such measures in lands where they are permitted by the Gentiles.[29] The case in point involved a murderer, and is therefore all the more significant than a more conventional concurrence to the execution of an informer. Rivash likewise does not insist on the usual standards of evidence, just as long as there is a "clear indication" (*amtela'ot berurot*) of guilt.[30] As to the action of the exilarch (I), he explains that the blinding was considered sufficient in that instance, even though the exilarch could well have ordered the culprit's execution.

The permissive views found their way into the *Shulḥan Arukh* of R. Joseph Karo (d. 1575). Karo codified the statement of R. Eleazar b. Jacob adding that such punishment does not require a court of ordained judges or even conclusively established evidence in the classical sense.[31] R. Moses Isserles (known as Rema, d. 1572) concurs in his gloss to the *Shulḥan Arukh*, and likewise in his commentary on the *Tur*, stating that "whatever is necessary for the needs of the hour, to erect a fence around the Torah, is permissible."[32]

One notable dissent from this view was the opposing stand of R. Mordecai b. Abraham Joffe (Levush, d. 1612). Invoking the authority of Rosh, he rejected the death penalty as a contemporary option, even in those cases where the Torah mandates capital punishment. He argued instead for a substitute punishment, in the manner of the exilarch (I), to prevent the mistaken impression that the death penalty can be operative in the absence of a properly ordained court.[33]

Perhaps the most outspoken responsum in favor of the death penalty was written in the same period by R. Meir b. Gedaliah (known as Maharam Lublin, d. 1616). In a case involving a Jew arrested by the Gentiles and found guilty of murder and then turned over to the Jewish court for punishment, he affirmed the right of the court to execute the murderer, as also its right to execute for lesser infractions, if the court saw fit to do so as an emergency measure. Such, he adds, is the authority of *any* contemporary court, especially where Gentile authorities are involved, lest the Jews be ridiculed and God's name desecrated.[34]

Thus we can see that there is a broad cross-section of halakhists who would countenance the death penalty as an extraordinary measure. But what precisely are the conditions necessary before a court may properly invoke such powers? Here too there is a difference of opinion.

On the one hand there are those who require conditions of large-scale breaches of the law on the part of a majority of Jews before a court may invoke its emergency powers. This standard is first encountered in Rashi, who says that R. Eleazar b. Jacob spoke of a time when "there was widespread crime . . . and the commandments were despised in their eyes," as a result of Hellenizing tendencies.[35] Similarly, Maimonides speaks of "the populace willfully ignoring the law," as do the *Tur* and the *Shulḥan Arukh*, as referred to earlier.

But on the other hand there is the view associated with R. Joshua b. Alexander ha-Kohen (known as Sema, d. 1614). This commentator on the *Tur* and the *Shulḥan Arukh* was of the opinion that even without mass defections from the law, a court could properly sentence an individual to death if he was shown to be an inveterate offender of incorrigible proportions.[36] Sema was supported in this by R. Shabbetai b. Meir ha-Kohen (Shakh, d. 1662)[37] and R. Jacob b. Joseph Reischer (author of the *Shevut Ya'akov*, d. 1733),[38] but explicitly opposed by R. Jonathan Eybeshutz (d. 1764).[39]

Up to this point we have concentrated in the main on the possibility of judicial proceedings in the absence of the Sanhedrin. But, as we have seen, there is also the royal route to the death penalty. Of course, the institution of Jewish monarchy has long lapsed, but there is some discussion among the authorities as to whether the royal power might have passed to some other agency or person.

In formulating the role of the king in ancient Israel, Rabbeinu Nissim, as we saw earlier, made it clear that the king had powers enabling him to carry out the death penalty. What he furthermore says is that "in the absence of an Israelite king, a judge can assume both roles," i.e., the right to punish in accord with the well-being of society. Meiri goes further when he states that when permission is granted by the Gentile authorities, and the Jewish community accepts the legitimacy of the Jewish leaders thus empowered, then those leaders may pass the death penalty "by virtue of their prior agreement, and the needs of the hour."[40] Accordingly, it would appear that the critical factor is the agreement of the people themselves, all the more so when it is not a Gentile government granting such permission, but rather an autonomous Jewish entity. This is the conclusion that Rabbi Eliezer Waldenberg draws from the statement of Meiri.[41]

However, it is precisely this point that is debatable. Can the people, by virtue of their prior agreement, transfer the royal powers to some other agency or person, or does the law require that the king's power can only be transmitted by certain fixed procedures?

On the one hand, it is a historical fact that in several medieval lands Jewish leaders carried out the death penalty by reason of permission granted by the Gentile authorities and the agreement of the Jewish masses.[42] Such permission would not apply to the emergency judicial powers accorded a Jewish court; hence one can reasonably conclude that such punishments were handed out at least partly on account of some vestige of royal power and prerogative, conferred by the will of the people. In recent times this "democratic" view has been espoused by several authorities, notably Rabbi Shaul Yisraeli, who feels that Meiri in fact represented a majority view among the earlier authorities. He argues that there is no clear biblical source for the king's extrajudicial function, and hence the parameters and procedures of that function depend entirely on the will of the people at any given time and place.[43] Accordingly, the people may indeed empower other persons with that prerogative, as for example a committee of "seven distinguished personages"[44] or, for that matter, a representative legislature such as the Israeli Knesset.

On the other hand, there is a view that insists on certain preconditions irrespective of the people's will. This view relies in the first place on Maimonides, who states explicitly that only the Sanhedrin and a prophet can confer royal powers.[45] Naḥmanides too requires at least a Sanhedrin to effect that prerogative.[46] As for Meiri's view that permission from the Gentile rulers suffices to permit a Jewish leader to pass the death penalty, other halakhists take issue with him. In the first place, Ran permits such punishment only if the condemned Jew is likewise culpable in Gentile law. This in effect would render the Jewish leader no more than the proxy of the Gentile authorities.[47] In the second place, Maimonides implies that the power wielded by the exilarch derives not from Gentile permission or the popular will but from the fact that he is a descendant of the Davidic dynasty. As Maimonides puts it, it is not his wisdom that counts but his lineage.[48] Hence, if such a lineage is doubtful, as it must be in the absence of prophecy, it would seem that the royal prerogative would lapse. This Maimonidean position was accepted by the author of the *Tur*, who formulated it to say that "a concession granted by a [Gentile] king is worthless, for such power is derived from the verse 'the scepter shall not depart from Judah' [Gen. 49:10], which refers to the Babylonian exilarchs."[49]

In addition to such arguments against the implementation of the royal prerogative, more recent scholars argue that even medievals like Meiri who favored the translation of the royal power into some contemporary embodiment would be opposed to such powers being granted a secular governing body, such as the Knesset in Israel. Thus Rabbi Rabinowitz-Teomim argues that such permission was only contemplated on the assumption that those wielding the power would demonstrate complete fealty to the Torah and its commandments. To permit a secular leader to implement his own ideas regarding capital punishment, deriving from a variety of nonhalakhic sources, would contravene the values and concerns of the Halakhah in so serious an area as life and death.[50]

In light of these considerations, and particularly the secular nature of the governments prevailing in modern times, together with the comparatively limited power of religious courts, many contemporary scholars have opposed the implementation of the death penalty. Besides Rabbi Rabinowitz-Teomim, Rabbi Kalman Kahane likewise[51] stands opposed in view of the serious doubts raised by the status of Jewish leaders who do not "go in the way of the Torah and the commandments."[52] Others have taken a similar position.[53]

There is, however, one notable halakhist who is inclined to accept even a secular Jewish authority in lieu of a king, and that is Rabbi Abraham Isaac ha-Kohen Kook (d. 1935). In a volume devoted to issues related to the reconstitution of the Jewish homeland, he states that in the absence of a king, his powers revert entirely to the people insofar as they affect the "general condition" of the nation. Hence, with the appointment of a contemporary judge or head of state, all royal powers of a public nature become his own.[54] Rav Kook makes no attempt to distinguish between religious and secular leaders, as long as the leadership has the backing of the people, and effective power over the extended community of Jews.

3. *ALTERNATIVES TO CAPITAL PUNISHMENT*

If, for one reason or another, the death penalty is not the appropriate contemporary response to murder, does Halakhah allow for alternative punishments? The Talmud, as we have seen, mentioned the blinding of a murderer at the behest of the exilarch (I). Apparently even then alternatives were available, in spite of the scriptural prohibition of taking ransom for the life of the murderer (Num. 35:31). This is the thrust of Rashi's comments to that passage of the Talmud, saying that "capital punishment had ceased, and such substitution was by way of a penalty."[55] Rabbeinu Ḥananel (d. 1056) records the opinion of "most of the geonim," who took this blinding to mean any punishment that "would take away his strength and his spirit."[56] Such punishment could vary according to the given land or age, at the discretion of the halakhic authorities of the time.

This geonic view, according to Rabbi Y. M. Ginzberg, is Maimonides' source for saying[57] that in the absence of a court's emergency powers and the royal prerogative, a court may still "whip him extensively, almost to the point of death, imprison him under severe conditions for many years, and afflict him with a variety of sufferings," by way of an example to others.[58] Precedent for such harsh treatment can be found in the Mishnah itself with reference to the *kippah*, or cell, in which a prisoner was incarcerated for extended periods of time, effectively shortening his life.[59] Such drastic measures were undertaken in those cases where guilt was certain, but the death penalty was inadmissible for technical reasons.[60]

Whether or not corporal punishment could be properly undertaken by nonordained courts became a matter of debate. Rosh, in rejecting the death penalty, had favored some alternative physical pain or disfigurement.[61] His view forms the basis for R. Joseph Karo's statement that a court may inflict corporal punishment in a case where there is no conclusive evidence, but where there is incessant indication of criminal behavior (*kala de'lo pasik*).[62]

Rivash ruled similarly, as did Maharshal, quoting an earlier Spanish responsum.[63]

But others were opposed to any form of corporal punishment by such courts. As we have seen, Rabbeinu Nissim explicitly denied a court the right to impose such punishment.[64] His reasoning is that any emergency powers that a court might invoke require, if anything, *more* expertise than even classic and conventional procedures, hence the necessity of a fully ordained court. As for the blinding ordered by the exilarch (I), that was not in his judicial capacity, but a reflection of the royal prerogative, and hence not subsequently applicable. For different reasons, Maharam Lublin was likewise opposed to corporal punishment, as he felt that the person so afflicted would subsequently turn against his religion and his people, causing significant harm to them and to himself.[65]

If such penalties are proper, who would be qualified to hand them out, in the absence of properly ordained persons? Here too there is some disagreement among the authorities, based on variant readings in Alfasi. Rosh quotes the latter to say that only the leading rabbinic figure of each generation (*gadol ha-dor*), or judges universally respected, may mete out the death penalty.[66] While our editions of Alfasi do not include a statement to this effect, such a version did exist, as recorded in the *Hagahot ha-Baḥ*, Maharik, and the *Tur*.[67]

However, Rashba quotes Alfasi to say that corporal punishment may be meted out "even by us, and in a variety of places . . . for in such cases I have not found that a special court is required."[68] Maharik likewise mentions that such a lenient view exists, without attributing it to Alfasi. This position received its most clear-cut formulation in the above-mentioned responsum of Maharam Lublin, who indicated that any duly constituted court can invoke emergency powers, as long as it acts without haste and as a result of extensive deliberations.[69]

Of these two views, the former received the imprimatur of the *Shulḥan Arukh*.[70] As the code puts it, punishment of a corporal nature requires either the leading rabbinic figure of the time or else judges approved by popular acclaim and judicial concurrence. Others followed suit.[71]

Rabbi Eliezer Waldenberg, in discussing these views, takes a moderate position, explaining that both sides agree on the desirability and fitness of a court that is specifically empowered to handle matters of public policy. In other words, even Maharam Lublin requires a court that has the authority to decide how the people will be required to act, as opposed to a conventional court that deals exclusively with ritual or matters of arbitration. Similarly, according to Rabbi Waldenberg, all are agreed that the leading rabbinic figure is not required, just as long as the court has demonstrated expertise in its rulings on community affairs.[72] Rabbi Waldenberg himself concludes that it is halakhically feasible to institute a contemporary form of the death penalty. He quotes the *Mishpetei Shmuel* as saying that in modern times every hour is such that emergency measures can be properly invoked. Waldenberg adds that this is particularly true of the situation since the rise of the modern State of Israel "as a protective measure, that the people not embrace sin," even though contemporary judges and leaders do not possess proper ordination.[73]

As a rationale for his view, he quotes R. Isaac Arama (author of the *Akeidat Yiẓḥak*, d. 1494), who explained the rabbinic dictum that one should always follow the instructions of one's contemporary halakhists, even if they declare "that the right is left and the left right," as follows: Sometimes one's general sense of fairness and justice is to be suspended in light of exceptional circumstances and exigency. Hence, while capital punishment is exceedingly harsh retribution, it might sometimes be necessary to prevent further bloodshed, or to bring atonement for a heinous crime. The determination of such circumstances is left by Scripture and tradition to the rabbinic leadership of each generation, as the final arbiters of right and wrong, justice and compassion, good and evil. It is this larger perspective that must prevail.[74] A similar statement in defense of the death penalty, is found in the Midrash Tannaim (D), urging the disavowal of one's natural abhorrence of the death penalty, in deference to the clear scriptural mandate.

In summary of the various strands that we have examined, the following picture emerges: The biblical punishment for premeditated murder is death, typically imposed by the Sanhedrin, or court of twenty-three judges. An Israelite king retains the prerogative to execute a murderer, if he perceives that such action is necessary for the good of society. Nevertheless, the death penalty was rare in the extreme, with certain tannaim (R. Tarfon and R. Akiva) seemingly opposed to it on principle.

After the cessation of the Sanhedrin and the monarchy, there were two broad trends discernable. One permitted the death penalty as an emergency measure available to contemporary courts, based on the dictum of R. Eleazar b. Jacob that such exceptional edicts are necessary for the well-being of society and the Torah. The major proponents of this view include Alfasi, most interpretations of Maimonides, the *Tur*, R. Judah b. Asher, Rivash, as well as the *Shulḥan Arukh* and Rema. The other view attracted support from notable authorities who understood R. Eleazar b. Jacob to be referring exclusively to the days of the Sanhedrin and the unbroken chain of ordained judges. Hence, in their opinion, the death penalty has ceased to be a sanctioned response to the crime of murder. Such authorities include Ran, Nimmukei Yosef, Rabbeinu Yonah, a minority interpretation of Maimonides, Rosh, and Levush. These authorities tended to play down any deterrent effect of the death penalty, even where there might be an elevated crime rate, such as prevailed toward the close of the Second Temple era, when the Sanhedrin suspended the penalty for the same reason, i.e., it had lost its deterrence.

As for the royal prerogative, while Meiri in particular would permit the leaders of the Jewish community to arrogate that privilege to themselves, with the concurrence of the Gentile authorities and the people, most halakhists follow Maimonides, who proscribes this route to the death penalty in the absence of the king or his direct biological descendants, such as the exilarchs. In the absence of a Sanhedrin or prophet, such a determination is impossible, hence the royal prerogative cannot be invoked. Besides, in all likelihood Meiri himself would agree that such discretionary powers do not accrue to a secular body such as those that prevail in modern times. A minority of halakhists dissent, and permit even such a body to issue the death penalty, including Rav Kook and Rabbi Yisraeli.

As to alternatives to the death penalty, there are those, such as Maimonides, Rosh, Rivash, and Maharshal, who maintain the geonic tradition of corporal punishment. This includes lengthy imprisonment, flogging, and a variety of deprivations. While this view received the imprimatur of the *Shulḥan Arukh*, others, notably Ran and Maharam Lublin, disagreed.

On the question of fitness to serve on such a court, there are likewise two views: those, like Rosh, suppported by the *Shulḥan Arukh*, who require outstanding rabbinic personages; and those, like Rashba and certain readings of Alfasi together with Maharam Lublin, who believe that any properly constituted court may take upon itself the responsibility to carry out corporal punishment or even, as we have seen, the death penalty. Rabbi Waldenberg would side with the latter, with certain minor caveats.

In conclusion, a halakhic response to the case with which this chapter began would need to reflect at least one of the divergent views seen above. Thus, on the one hand, an individual could be sentenced to death under the rubric of an emergency ruling necessary for the well-being of society, at the behest of a court with religiously impeccable credentials, or alternatively by a recognized representative body standing at the head of a given Jewish society. On the other hand, it could be concluded that there is no possibility of capital punishment since the dissolution of the Sanhedrin, even as an emergency decree, in the absence of a properly empowered judicial body. The third alternative discussed in the sources is some kind of substitute corporal punishment or imprisonment. This alternative is also a matter of discussion among the various authorities, some favoring it, and others opposed. While it is clear that the modern temper tends to oppose physical disfigurement, it is apparent that one view among the authorities examined here considers such punishment to be a lesser evil than the death penalty or even lengthy imprisonment. In so doing it would reflect the midrashic comment to Ecclesiastes 7:16 ("be not righteous overmuch") that says: "whoever shows compassion where he should show stern justice will in the end come to show stern justice where he should demonstrate compassion" (*Eccles. Rabbah* 7). In this view, corporal punishment is more conducive to the rehabilitation of the offender than, say, a lengthy prison term.

Which of these views will prevail in any given case is as much a factor of halakhic logic as it is one of contemporary societal and religious attitudes toward crime and punishment in general terms—at least, that is, until the rebuilding of the Temple and the reconstitution of religious laws and procedures under the aegis of the Sanhedrin.

Notes

1. The other two cardinal sins are idolatry and certain forbidden sexual liaisons. See Maimonides, *M.T. Hil. Rozeiah* 1:4.

2. For details of court procedure in cases involving capital punishment, see Maimonides, *M.T. Hil. Sanhedrin* 11–15. Maimonides enumerates thirty-six crimes, the punishment for which is death.

3. Maimonides, *M.T. Hil. Melakhim* 3:10.

4. Rabbeinu Nissim, *Derashot ha-Ran* (Jerusalem, 1974), pp. 192 ff.

5. The episode is related in 1 Sam. 8.

6. Deut. 17:17–20. The classic statement of the dialectical tensions in the halakhic attitude toward the Israelite king is found in Maimonides, *M.T. Hil. Melakhim* 2–5, which on the one hand demonstrates his enormous royal powers, but on the other hand shows the severe restrictions imposed on an Israelite king. A related question is whether the royal prerogative to execute a criminal applies other than to murder. Rabbi Meir Simhah of Dvinsk (*Or Sameah* to *M.T. Hil. Melakhim* 3:10) understands Maimonides to restrict such powers to murder cases, whereas Rabbi Y. M. Ginzberg, *Mishpatim le'Yisrael* (Jerusalem, 1956), pp. 128 f., disagrees by incorporating a wider spectrum of crimes in Maimonides' view.

7. Ritva to *Makkot* 7a. In this view he was preceded by his teacher Nahmanides. Cf. Nahmanides' comments to *Makkot* 7a. Ritva refers to the opposing view of R. Meir Halevy that, like Rashi ad loc., understands R. Tarfon and R. Akiva to be opposed to capital punishment in principle.

8. B. Rabinowitz-Teomim, "Mishpetei Nefashot be'Din ha-Sanhedrin u-ve'Din ha-Malkhut," *ha-Torah ve'ha-Medinah* 4 (1952): 50.

9. Moshe Leib Lilienblum, "Hakirot Talmudiot," *ha-Shelah* 5 (1899): 42. Lilienblum goes so far as to assert that every case of capital punishment found in the Talmud can be shown upon examination to have been improper or in error. Such a position is difficult to justify, especially for the period preceding the destruction of the Second Temple.

10. Deut. 17:3, 19:20, 21:21.

11. J. M. Tykocinski, "Mishpat ha-Mavet be'Avar u-be'Hoveh," *ha-Torah ve'ha-Medinah* 4 (1952): 40.

12. Rabinowitz-Teomim, "Mishpetei Nefashot," pp. 48–49. A similar position is adopted by H. Z. Reines, "Mishpat Mavet be'Halakhah," *Sinai* 39 (1956): 162 ff, who adds that with the destruction of the Temple, the sages became more and more restrictive and opposed to the idea of the death penalty, successively delimiting the possibility of such punishment. In effect the sages negated entirely the biblical sanction for the death penalty.

13. *Hil. ha-Rif* to *Bava Kamma* 96b.

14. See *Responsa Maharik* (Warsaw, 1884), no. 185; *Novellae Yam shel Shelomoh* to *Bava Kamma* 9:6; and *Responsa Maharam Lublin* (Venice, 1618), no. 138.

15. *Sanhedrin* 44b–45a.

16. *Tur, Hoshen Mishpat* 2.

17. See the comments of the *Birkei Yosef* to *Sh.A. Hoshen Mishpat* 3, and the *Bah* to the *Nimmukei Yosef* on *Sanhedrin* 52b.

18. *Responsa Rivash* (Vilna, 1878), no. 251.

19. See his comments in the *Ḥokhmat Shelomoh* to *Sanhedrin* 52b. It is for this reason, he explains, that the method chosen in that case was death by burning instead of the more conventional suffocation—precisely so that the execution would be recognized as extraordinary.

20. Ran's view is stated in his commentary to *Sanhedrin* 27a, and that of the *Nimmukei Yosef* on *Sanhedrin* 52b. Similar sentiments are likewise encountered in the comment of Rabbeinu Yonah (Jonah b. Abraham Gerondi, d. 1263) to *Sanhedrin* 52b. In one respect Ran differs from the *Nimmukei Yosef:* He is of the opinion that even penalties less than death require courts that are ordained, i.e., contemporaneous with the Sanhedrin.

These comments of Ran are consistent with the earlier-quoted *Derashot ha-Ran* by the same author, in that it is the Sanhedrin and the courts that retain priority of place in capital cases, because they alone possess the requisite ordination. Cf. below, n. 40.

21. *Yad Malakhi* (Leghorn, 1767), Principles, chap. 415; *Ḥiddushei ha-Rim* to *Sh.A. Ḥoshen Mishpat* 3.

22. *Baḥ* on the *Tur Ḥoshen Mishpat* 2.

23. For further instances of the practice of the death penalty in medieval times, see Assaf, *ha-Onshin Aḥar Ḥatimat ha-Talmud* (Jerusalem, 1922), notably nos. 42, 46, 48. Likewise see the *Encyclopaedia Judaica*, s.v. "Capital Punishment." Maimonides himself refers to the "everyday executions of *mosrim* [who denounce fellow Jews to Gentile authorities] in the cities of the west [i.e., Spain]," in *M.T. Hil. Ḥovel u-Mazik* 8:11. See also E. Ben Zimrah, "Din Mavet shelo Bifnei ha-Bayit," *Ḍeot* 19 (1962): 16.

24. *Responsa Rosh* (Vilna, 1881), 17:8, 18:13, 32:4. In the last-mentioned responsum, he permits the killing of a Jew of whom it is certain that he is about to denounce his fellow Jews, i.e., prior to the criminal act, as a preventive measure similar to the law of the pursuer. On this, see Kalman Kahane, *Ḥeker ve'Iyyun* (Tel Aviv, 1960), vol. 1, p. 200.

25. *Responsa R. Judah b. ha-Rosh*, nos. 58, 63, 75, as quoted in Assaf, *ha-Onshin*, nos. 73, 77, 79.

26. Menaḥem ha-Meiri, *Bet ha-Beḥirah* to *Sanhedrin*, ed. A. Sofer (Frankfurt am Main, n.d.), p. 212.

27. *Responsa Rashba* (Leghorn, 1825), vol. 5, no. 238.

28. *Responsa of Rashba Attributed to Ramban* (Warsaw, 1883), no. 279. See S. B. Werner, "Mishpatim le'Ẓorekh ha-Sha'ah," *ha-Torah ve'ha-Medinah* 3 (1951): 49.

29. *Responsa Rivash* (Vilna, 1878), no. 251. The letter is addressed to the Jewish community of Salmonica (Salonika).

30. Ibid., no. 234.

31. *Sh.A. Ḥoshen Mishpat* 2. It appears that Karo was not always of this opinion, for in his earlier commentary on the *Tur*, he quotes the view of the *Nimmukei Yosef*, as if in agreement with that view. See Werner, "Mishpatim," p. 45, and Kahane, *Ḥeker ve'Iyyun*, p. 198.

32. See Rema's gloss to *Sh.A. Ḥoshen Mishpat* 2 and his *Darkei Moshe* to the *Tur Ḥoshen Mishpat* 2.

33. See the *Levush* to *Sh.A. Ḥoshen Mishpat* 2.

34. *Responsa Maharam Lublin*, no. 138. This work is quoted, for example, in Abraham Shranchild, *Eitan ha-Ezraḥi*, 43.

35. Rashi to *Sanhedrin* 46a.

36. Sema to *Sh.A. Ḥoshen Mishpat* 2:3.

37. Shakh to *Sh.A. Ḥoshen Mishpat* 2:2.

38. *Responsa Shevut Ya'akov* (Lemberg, 1860), 1:445, 130. See also the *Pithei Teshuvah* to *Sh.A. Ḥoshen Mishpat* 2:2. For an explanation of certain technical considerations leading to this view, see Eliezer Waldenberg, *Hilkhot Medinah* (Jerusalem, 1952), vol. 1, p. 50.

39. *Urim* to *Sh.A. Ḥoshen Mishpat* 2:2.

40. This passage is quoted in the *Shittah Mekubbeẓet* to *Bava Kamma* 84b. To be consistent, Rabbeinu Nissim would have to be interpreted here as meaning that only a judge who is properly ordained can assume these royal duties. Cf. above, n. 20.

41. Eliezer Waldenberg, "Shoftim ve'Shotrim bi-Medinah Yehudit le'Or ha-Halakhah," *Sinai* 22 (1948): 164.

42. *Responsa Rosh* 17:8; *Responsa Rivash* 234.

43. Shaul Yisraeli, "Tokef Mishpetei ha-Melukhah be'Yameinu," *ha-Torah ve'ha-Medinah* 2 (1950): 85 ff.

44. Cf. *Tur Ḥoshen Mishpat* 2, and *Encyclopedia Talmudit* 3:377.

45. Maimonides, *M.T. Hil. Melakhim* 1:3, 8.

46. *Naḥmanides' Commentary on the Torah*, ed. C. D. Chavel (Jerusalem, 1962), to Deut. 17:15.

47. Rabinowitz-Teomim, "Mishpetei Nefashot," pp. 76–78.

48. Maimonides, *Commentary on the Mishnah, Bekhorot* 4, as quoted by Rema to *Sh.A. Ḥoshen Mishpat* 3.

49. *Tur Ḥoshen Mishpat* 3. This position is further elucidated by Karo in the *Bet Yosef* to the *Tur*.

50. Rabinowitz-Teomim, "Mishpetei Nefashot," pp. 79–80.

51. Kahane, *Ḥeker ve'Iyyun*, pp. 198 ff.

52. Maimonides, *M.T. Hil. Melakhim* 1:8.

53. Cf. similarly Ben Zimrah, "Din Mavet," p. 17, and Werner, "Mishpatim," p. 50.

54. Abraham Isaac ha-Kohen Kook, *Mishpat Kohen* (Jerusalem, 1966), pp. 336 ff. (no. 144, sec. 14).

55. Rashi to *Sanhedrin* 27a.

56. Rabbeinu Ḥananel ad loc.

57. Maimonides, *M.T. Hil. Roẓeiaḥ* 2:5.

58. Ginzberg, *Mishpatim le'Yisrael*, pp.137-138.

59. Mishnah, *Sanhedrin* 81b.

60. Maimonides, *M.T. Hil. Sanhedrin* 18:4, 5; *Roẓeiaḥ* 4:8.

61. *Responsa Rosh* 17:8.

62. *Bet Yosef* to *Tur Ḥoshen Mishpat* 2; *Sh.A. Ḥoshen Mishpat* 2. Cf. also the *Beur ha-Gra*, loc cit., n. 4, and the comments of Rav Kook in his *Be'er Eliyahu* thereon.

63. *Responsa Rivash* 251; *Yam shel Shelomoh* to *Bava Kamma* 8:6.

64. Cf. above, n. 20.

65. *Responsa Maharam Lublin* 138.

66. Rosh to *Bava Kamma* 9:5

67. *Hagahot ha-Baḥ* to the Rif, *Bava Kamma* 96b; *Responsa Maharik* 184; *Tur Ḥoshen Mishpat* 2.

68. *Responsa Rashba* (Piotrkow, 1883), 4:264.

69. *Responsa Maharam Lublin* 138.

70. *Sh.A. Ḥoshen Mishpat* 2.

71. *Responsa Mizraḥi* 46, and the comments of Rabbi Solomon Kluger to *Sh.A. Ḥoshen Mishpat* 2.

72. Waldenberg, *Hilkhot Medinah*, pp. 47–48.

73. Waldenberg, "Shoftim ve'Shotrim," p. 170.

74. Isaac Arama, *Akeidat Yiẓḥak* (Salonika, 1522), Exodus 43.

Psycho-Social Ethics

8

Parents and Children

Introduction

One of the more salient features of family life in recent times is the widespread incidence of value conflicts between parents and their grown children. While this is not an "issue" in the sense that the other topics in this volume are, it is nonetheless a significant problem that poses several ethical challenges to the families concerned, to psychotherapists and counselors who are increasingly confronted with such situations,[1] and to society as a whole. Intergenerational conflict is an important component of the weakening of the family unit, at least as understood in traditional terms. Resolving such tensions should be seen as desirable not merely from a social point of view but also from the point of view of the mental health of the individuals involved.

This conflict is encountered with particular force in the Jewish setting, where the family has traditionally maintained strong ties between the generations. With many younger Jews in the forefront of changes in social and familial patterns, such ties are now commonly challenged, yet in spite of the widespread nature of the problem, there has been relatively little analysis of the halakhic response to such situations, other than the usual appeal to authority and family unity.[2]

There are several conflicting principles in Halakhah involved here, to ensure that the individuals concerned are treated with fairness and sensitivity, and at the same time to safeguard the integrity of family life. Hopefully such positive resolutions, as they emerge from the halakhic literature, can serve as a model for the amelioration of this vexing social problem that is so much a by-product of modernity.

The Question

A woman seeks the help of her therapist. Her twenty-four-year-old daughter no longer shares many of the family values, as evidenced by the daughter's manner of dress, speech, attitudes to work and to leisure activities. As a result there is considerable domestic tension. The mother shows signs of hysteria: she is distraught and tearful; complains of insomnia, indigestion, and significant weight-loss; her blood-pressure has been adversely affected. In choosing a mode of treatment, to what extent may the therapist involve the daughter, assuming that her behavior is a major cause of the mother's condition? What is the daughter's responsibility toward her parents in choosing a lifestyle?

There are several issues that require clarification, within the context of Halakhah:

1. What is the nature of the obligation to "honor" one's parents once one has reached maturity?
2. What are the limits of this obligation when it conflicts with the values or other religious obligations of the daughter?
3. Where the parent displays hysteria or emotional dysfunction, are there any special responsibilities or, on the other hand, exemptions to be applied to the daughter?
4. Are there halakhic guidelines for a parent who is confronted with an actual or potential conflict regarding the values of a mature son or daughter?

Sources

A. Exodus 20:12

Honor thy father and thy mother, that thy days may be long upon the land which the Lord thy God giveth thee.

B. Leviticus 19:3

Ye shall fear every man his mother and his father, and ye shall keep My Sabbaths: I am the Lord your God.

C. Sifra Leviticus, Kedoshim 1:10

Because one might think that one is obliged to obey one's father or mother who desires that one violate a commandment, therefore the Torah says, "and ye shall keep My Sabbaths"—you are all required to honor Me.

D. Exodus 21:15, 17

He that smiteth his father or his mother shall surely be put to death. . . . And he that curseth his father or his mother shall surely be put to death.

E. Deuteronomy 27:16

Cursed be he that dishonoreth his father or his mother.

F. Kiddushin 31b

What constitutes fear and what constitutes honor? Fear is when the son does not stand in his father's place, sit in his place, contradict him, or pass judgment over his father's opinion. Honor is when he provides his father with food, drink, clothing, or shelter, and accompanies him on his way in or out.

G. Kiddushin 32a

They asked R. Eliezer what is the limit to honoring one's father and mother. Said he: "To the point where the parent takes a wallet of money and throws it into the ocean, and his son does not rebuke him."

H. Kiddushin 32a

Eleazar b. Matya said: "If one's father says, 'Bring me some water,' while one has a commandment to perform, one delays the father's honor in order to fulfill the other commandment, for both father and son are subject to the commandments." Issi b. Judah said: "If it is possible for the other commandment to be done by others, let them do it, so the son can engage in his father's honor." R. Matnah said: "The law accords with Issi b. Judah.

I. Kiddushin 31b

R. Assi had an elderly mother. She said to him, "I desire jewelry," so he made it for her. Then she said, "I want a husband," so he agreed to look for one for her. Then she said, "I want one as handsome as you," at which point he left her and went to the Land of Israel.

J. Yevamot 6a

Should we not conclude from (C) that all positive commandments should be deferred when a negative commandment contradicts them? Were one to answer this and say that the laws of the Sabbath are different because they are so important, and cannot therefore set a standard for the other commandments, one could rebut this by pointing to another statement where other commandments do, like the Sabbath, defer parental honor. Thus the Beraita says: "Because one might think to obey a parental command to 'defile yourself in order to return my possessions to me; bring me food rather than return that lost object to its owner,' therefore the Torah says, 'You shall fear every man his father and you shall keep my Sabbaths,' i.e., you are all required to honor God [therefore you may defer parental honor]." It is, however, possible to deny the general applicability of these instances by pointing out that they have one thing in common: The act that violates the prohibition is only preparatory to the act whereby the parent is honored, and because they do not coincide the prohibition remains in effect, and the parental honor is deferred.

K. Tosafot, Yevamot 6a

Ri is of the opinion that one never defers a prohibition so that one can honor parents, even if the very act of honoring coincides with the violation of the prohibition. For the Talmud concludes that because in most instances the actual honoring merely follows after the violation of the prohibition, and they do not coincide, the Torah indicates that in all cases one should not violate a prohibition.

L. Tosafot, Kiddushin 32a

Ri is of the opinion that one should defer parental honor as well as the return of a lost object to another, in order to recover one's own lost object. For when the Talmud says that parental honor has precedence, that is only in a case such as permitting one's parent full license with one's money, for that is honor *per se*. However, when it comes to recovering one's lost article, the son need not forgo its recovery on account of his father's honor, for the father does not have benefit from the loss itself. And even though the Talmud states (G) that the parent may throw the son's wallet into the ocean without being rebuked, that is only when that act causes the father some satisfaction from the strengthening of his authority over the members of his household. For if he does not act with such an intention, he is a sinner who profanes "thou shall not destroy" [Deut. 20:19]. And even if he acts unintentionally, such as acting out of anger, he nonetheless has benefit from throwing the wallet, and therefore is not to be rebuked.

M. Rashba to Yevamot 6a

. . . the essence of "honor" is only when the parent enjoys some benefit from the act of the son, as it says in *Kiddushin* (F). But if a parent tells a son to do something which does not bring some benefit to the parent, that is not included in "honor" as commanded by the Torah, and he is not required to defer any kind of biblical prohibition in order to obey the parent.

N. Maimonides, M. T. Hilkhot Mamrim 6:10

When parents become insane, one should attempt to deal with them according to their mental capacity, until they are healed. But if it is impossible to do this on account of their being totally insane, one may leave them to go elsewhere, and instruct others to take care of them according to what is proper for them.

O. Ravad, M. T. Hilkhot Mamrim 6:10

This is an incorrect teaching, for if he leaves, whom could he have take care of the parent?

Discussion

1. THE NATURE OF THE OBLIGATION TO HONOR ONE'S PARENTS

The Torah requires children to honor their parents (A), as well as to fear (or show reverence for) them (B). Yet it is not specific in defining the precise meaning of "honor" and "fear." While the Torah mandates punishment for striking, cursing (D), or dishonoring (E) a parent, it does not describe which behavior is or is not either forbidden, permitted, or required by the commandments to honor and fear parents. One exception might be the rebellious son (*ben sorer u-moreh*) who, as described by his parents, does not hearken to their voice (Deut. 21:20). But even here it is not clear that it is in fact his disobeying his parents' wishes that is his crime—most commentators understand the major infraction to be his rebelling against the laws of the Torah in general.[3] Thus he is described by the Torah as a "glutton and a drunkard."

The oral tradition provided more details. *Kiddushin* 31b (F) offers formal definitions of the biblical terms: "Fear" is the avoidance of certain activities that might lessen the public stature or dignity of parents (standing or sitting in their place, contradicting or passing judgment over their views); "honor" requires of children that they provide certain amenities for their parents (food, drink, clothing, shelter, and personal escort upon arrival or departure). While these definitions appear simple enough, later authorities differed in their interpretation. Thus the question arose whether these duties were archetypal and mere examples or actually exhaustive, i.e., whether these specific activities were intended and no other. If the former, could the emotional and spiritual needs of a parent make equal demands on filial responsibility? In addition there was the question of whether "honor" required unquestioning obedience to a parent's will and authority, irrespective of whether that will as expressed by the parent was in the parent's own best interest.[4]

In commenting on this passage, Tosafot presents the view of Ri (L), which states that a son should fulfill a parental directive if that action will benefit the parent.[5] Tosafot further defines this "benefit" as some positive outcome, such as "the assertion of the father's authority over the members of his household." This, however, does not mean that any parental directive must be honored, for as Tosafot explains, it is always possible that a parent might desire a criminal action, such as the willful destruction of property. Ri's view is, therefore, that a parental directive is to be disobeyed if the son regards it as bringing no real benefit to the parent or as injurious to the parent or another party. There is, however, a problem with this interpretation of Ri, for Tosafot concludes by saying that a parental wish should be obeyed as long as it affords some "satisfaction" to the parent. This obedience, it would appear, is required by Tosafot because of the statement of R. Eliezer (G), referred to by Tosafot, that necessitates the acceptance of provocative parental behavior. This would certainly dilute the original criterion of "benefit," for taken at face value it would require a son to accede to every conceivable wish that provides pleasure to the parent. Later commentators, such as R. Solomon Luria (1510–1574, known as Maharshal), resolved the problem by understanding the addition of "satisfaction" or "pleasure" to be speaking only in the context of a parent who is not in possession of his full emotional faculties. His reasoning is that Ri would not accede to parental demands that are deliberately and consciously perverse, even though they might afford the parent some personal satisfaction.[6] A similar view is attributed to another tosafist, Rabbeinu Tam, who according to Ritva, demands that "one accord honor to a parent only when that results in a benefit." This is understood by Ritva as permitting a son to disregard any parental directive that does not lead to some constructive purpose similar to the five activities specified in *Kiddushin*.[7]

Spanish halakhists who reached essentially the same conclusion included Naḥmanides (R. Moses b. Naḥman, known as Ramban, d. 1270). In his view, when a father tells a son to do something which does not in itself provide any benefit to the father, the son need not comply, for "this is not the honor required by the Torah."[8] Naḥmanides' student, R. Solomon b.

Adret (Rashba, d. 1310), appears to share this view (M).[9] His formulation, however, was such as to lead subsequent scholars to perceive a subtle but important shift away from the views of Tosafot and Naḥmanides. Thus R. Elijah of Vilna, (the Vilna Gaon, d. 1797)[10] and more recently Rabbi Abraham Isaiah Karelitz (known as Ḥazon Ish, d. 1953)[11] both understood Rashba to be saying that even if there is no benefit to the father, the son must obey him, as long as there is no conflict between the act desired by the parent and any law of the Torah. Thus it is only if the parent requires the child to disregard a law of the Torah that Rashba permits the son to ignore the parental directive.[12]

R. Menaḥem b. Solomon ha-Meiri (d. 1306) is likewise understood to permit the disregarding of a parent's wish only if the wish contradicts another law.[13] Meiri further implies that where there is no such contradiction, then any need articulated by the parent is to be honored, for there is a general presumption that a parent will not wickedly impose himself on his children without real need.[14]

An even more outspoken statement of this view is found in the eighteenth-century *Sefer ha-Makneh*, which says that "it appears that obedience to anything commanded by the father, even if the father derives no benefit from its fulfillment . . . is included in the obligation to 'fear,' as long as no loss is caused the son,[15] for if the son does not obey his father, it is the same as contradicting him."[16] The *Sefer ha-Makneh* here shifts the emphasis away from "honor" and toward "fear." It will be recalled that in *Kiddushin* (F) one of the applications of "fear" was the prohibition of contradicting one's parent. The *Sefer ha-Makneh* apparently equates the refusal to obey a parent with contradicting a parent. In fact the Jerusalem Talmud in *Kiddushin* 1:7 says specifically that a mother's desire "is also her honor,"[17] a phrase that equates a parent's wishes not only with fear but even with honor. Ḥazon Ish points out that Tosafot itself on the preceding page (*Kiddushin* 31b) quotes and approves of this formulation of the Jerusalem Talmud, and thereby appears to contradict its own formulation made in the name of Ri (as quoted above), which requires the justification of a real parental need, not just a parental wish.[18]

In a similar fashion, Rabbi Yeruḥam Perla (d. 1934), in his extensive commentary to Saadya's *Sefer ha-Miẓvot*, advances the possibility that even Naḥmanides and Tosafot would agree that a son must oblige his father in the absence of any benefit to the father—on the grounds of the commandment to "fear."[19] Like the Vilna Gaon, Perla perceives Rashba as permitting disobedience only when the father is contradicted by the Torah, but in the absence of such contradiction, Perla argues, the commandment of fear comes into play, even according to Tosafot and Naḥmanides! He further adds that if it is forbidden to contradict or judge one's father's viewpoint (as stated in *Kiddushin*), even by means of a mere verbal statement, then surely it should be forbidden to act so as to deny the validity of a parental directive. Such behavior, according to Perla, constitutes a snub to the parent that is in direct opposition to the fear that is commanded in the Torah.

Yet in spite of all these considerations, there were two early authorities who favored a lenient interpretation of the tosafists and the Spanish tradition of Naḥmanides and Rashba. R. Yomtov b. Abraham Ashbili (Ritva, d. 1340) states his position forthrightly: Parents are to be obeyed only where there is direct benefit (*hana'ah*) to themselves. In the absence of such benefit, one need not obey them even if their request does not contradict a law of the Torah. Ritva specifically refers to the discussion in *Kiddushin* that lists only such activities as directly benefit the parent. He apparently discounts any appeal to the command to fear, for he adds that if there is no direct benefit, "why *should* he listen to the parent?"[20]

The other halakhist to move in this direction was R. Joseph Colon, known as Maharik (1420–1480).[21] He considered the requirements of honor and fear to be in effect only where the parent had a legitimate interest of direct concern to the parent (*shayakh gaveh*). By invoking the criterion of benefit in this way, Maharik places a significant restriction on the kinds of demands that children need adhere to. Maharik explicitly identifies this view with that of Tosafot, and he explains that when Tosafot accepts the criterion of parental satisfaction as sufficient grounds for filial obedience, that is only where such satisfaction requires no expenditure of money or property belonging to the son. This argument is consistent with the normative halakhic view that a son is not obliged to sacrifice his property to fulfill the commandment to "honor."[22] Maharik expressly includes the commandment to fear under such considerations. As a result Maharik permits a son to disregard his parent's request, as long as the son continues to afford his parent every possible benefit that directly impinges on the parent's well-being.

We can thus see that any attempt to present a fair picture of filial responsibility to adhere to parental directives must recognize that there is a significant variety of opinions in the halakhic literature. It is only on the basis of such an analysis that one can proceed to deal with the specific related circumstances that require resolution.

2. CONFLICT INVOLVING RELIGIOUS OBLIGATIONS OR PERSONAL VALUES

While the discussion in *Kiddushin* remains central, it is necessary to understand a passage in *Yevamot* 6a (J) that deals expressly with a conflict between the command to honor or fear a parent and other laws of the Torah.

The Gemara refers to the statement in *Sifra* (C) that recognizes the juxtaposition of two apparently unrelated commandments in one verse, viz, "and you shall fear every man his mother and his father, and you shall keep My Sabbaths" (Lev. 19:3). The *Sifra* explains this proximity by means of the final phrase in the verse, "I am the Lord your God," which is taken to emphasize the priority of one's duties to God and "His" Sabbath over one's duties to one's parents.[23] The Gemara then questions whether this can be extended into a general principle, i.e., that any positive commandment can be deferred in the face of a negative commandment. In dealing with this question, the Gemara quotes a Beraita that extends the *Sifra* by saying that in addition to the Sabbath prohibitions there are other prohibitions that likewise take precedence over parental wishes. These include a father's wish that his son feed him before returning a lost object to its owner and a request by the father of a priest (who is generally forbidden to enter a cemetery) that the son bring the father's possessions from a cemetery. The Beraita states that in both cases the father is not to be obeyed.

The Gemara then introduces a limiting consideration that would prevent the extension of this Beraita to all commandments. It does so by pointing to the fact that the instances thus far dealt with share one characteristic: The act that violates the negative commandment precedes in time the actual satisfaction of the parental wish. It is therefore conceivable that where the same act simultaneously satisfies the parent and violates the law, the parental wish is to be honored.[24] Tosafot, in commenting on this passage, takes a strong position to say that in spite of the putative distinction offered by the Gemara, the parent's wishes should never be permitted to take precedence over another commandment (K). That this is consistent with Tosafot in *Kiddushin* is obvious from the fact that here too the statement is made in the name of Ri. Furthermore Tosafot makes it clear that this ruling should be followed even where there is some concrete benefit to the parent. It is possible that Ri sensed that the distinction in the Gemara between simultaneous and sequential acts required subtle and rare insight in each individual case, making it a most difficult principle to put into effect. Thus Ri indicates that the minority of truly simultaneous acts is not sufficient reason for upholding the distinction in practice.

On the basis of this passage in the *Sifra*,[25] the Gemara in *Kiddushin* 32a (H) introduces the problem that arises when a parental demand to be served would require the deferral of another commandment. The Gemara concludes with the unanimous view that if it is only the son who can perform the other commandment, the parent's wishes are to be deferred.[26] Naḥmanides and Rashba likewise conclude that parental wishes are to be deferred in the face of competing commandments. All interpretations of Rashba would agree on this point. Another important early authority endorsing this view is R. Asher b. Yeḥiel (Rosh, d. 1327). In a responsum, he counsels a man to disregard his father's insistence that he not make peace with an erstwhile enemy.[27] As Rosh puts it: "The father who commanded his son to hate a man does not have the right to command him to violate the Torah." The violation of the Torah in this case would be by hating a fellow Jew without good reason.

There is thus a consensus that parents should not be obeyed when to satisfy their wishes, a son or daughter would have to sacrifice one or another of the laws of the Torah. This applies whether the parents intend the violation of the law and nonetheless insist on obedience or whether the violation would occur unknown to the parents.

Once this general principle was formulated, it was applied in a variety of ways. One area of application was the issue of choosing a marriage partner considered undesirable by one's parents. Rashba explicitly permitted one man to marry the woman of his choice in opposition to his parents' will.[28] In this case he identified the commandment at stake as marriage *per se* (which, more precisely, is the necessary prerequisite for the commandment to be fruitful and to multiply). Furthermore, as a result of the contemplated union, the son would be precluded from providing the usual range of services to his parents as enumerated in *Kiddushin* (F). By ruling to permit the marriage, Rashba significantly limited even those duties. Rashba also rejects the argument that the parents are opposed not to the son fulfilling the commandment but merely to his fulfilling it with this woman, saying that marriage partners are decreed in heaven even prior to birth, so that if the natural course of things seems to be leading in one direction, it may not be deflected by human intercession.[29]

This approach is developed even further by Maharik in the responsum cited earlier.[30] In his opinion the commandment involved is not merely to marry and raise children but in addition to marry one's beloved. He quotes the Gemara that urges a man to marry only a woman to whom he is attracted,[31] and concludes from this that it must be the son or daughter, and not the parent, who makes the choice of marriage partner. Maharik further invokes the line of reasoning that the commandments to honor and fear parents can be applied only in areas that are of direct benefit to the parents, i.e., in the nature of service activities, as discussed above. As a result Maharik has no reservations about permitting a son to marry the woman of his choice, parental protest notwithstanding.[32]

A similar ruling is found in the writings of R. Elijah Capsali in the sixteenth century.[33] He quotes Maharik approvingly and adds several further considerations in favor of filial independence in matters matrimonial. Among them are the desirability of *shalom bayit*, i.e., loving and peaceful family relations in the home about to be established; the precedent of Samson the judge, who married in opposition to his parents' wishes (Judges 14); and the very practical fact that once a couple is in love it is exceedingly difficult to force the issue anyway. In the context of the last consideration he quotes the verse "many waters cannot quench love, neither can the floods drown it" (Song of Songs 8:7). Capsali concludes by saying that "were the son to marry another woman whom he does not desire, his entire life would be painful and bitter." This statement in itself is eloquent testimony to the presence of great sensitivity to romantic longing as well as human suffering in the halakhic tradition.

This lenient thrust in filial obligation received a major endorsement when R. Moses Isserles (Rema, d. 1572) codified the normative practice by saying: "If a father opposes the marriage of his son to a woman of the son's desire, the son need not accede to the father."[34] As a result of this express and unconditional statement, the lenient view was adopted by most halakhic authorities. A notable reaffirmation is found in the writings of R. Moses Schreiber (Ḥatam Sofer, d. 1839).[35]

At the same time, however, there were later halakhists who took a more restrictive view. R. Naphtali Ẓevi Judah Berlin (known as Neẓiv, 1817–1893) interpreted Rema as still maintaining the integrity of the obligation upon the son to afford the parent every measure of satisfaction (*hana'ah*).[36] But having invoked *hana'ah* as the criterion of honor, Neẓiv provides a new twist by forbidding the converse; i.e., any act that will cause the parent disgrace (*bizzayon*) or anguish (*ẓa'ar*)—which are the antithesis of satisfaction (*hana'ah*)—is to be avoided. Neẓiv concludes that it would be forbidden for a son to marry under such circumstances. He finds biblical sanction for this interpretation in the deuteronomic verse "cursed be he that dishonoreth his father and mother" (Deut. 27:16), where disgrace and dishonor are synonymous. This reading of Rema is not without problems, for Rema does not mention the considerations of disgrace or anguish as qualifying factors. Indeed in one respect Rema is even more lenient than Maharik, in that the latter, in permitting the marriage, describes the woman as "suited to him," whereas Rema does not even specify that qualification.[37]

A similar view is proffered by Ḥazon Ish, who on the basis of his reading of Rashba only permits the son to marry where the parent is not totally opposed to the marriage (it will be recalled that Ḥazon Ish equates parental desire and honor).[38] But where the parents are completely distressed, there is no justification for the son to marry.

In these discussions both Neẓiv and Ḥazon Ish omit consideration of the positive miẓvah of marriage. Apparently their view is that as long as the parents do not oppose marriage *per se*, and therefore would permit his choice of another partner, the parents are to be obeyed. In this view personal predilections and considerations of "love" must take a secondary position in the face of the need to honor and revere a parent.

We encounter another discussion of these sources in a somewhat different context. The eighteenth-century rise of Ḥasidism was, as is well known, accompanied by considerable factionalism and hostility.[39] This in turn engendered conflict within many families when younger people became attracted to Ḥasidism and its popular teachings in opposition to their parents' wishes.[40] Parents forbade their children to engage in such pursuits and thus confronted many of them with a dilemma. The problem came to the attention of R. Shneur Zalman of Liadi (known as the *Baal ha-Tanya*, d. 1813), the leading Ḥasidic master of his day and the author of the *Shulḥan Arukh ha-Rav*, a recognized work of halakhic authority. In a responsum, he firmly upheld the right of a son to disobey his parents in these circumstances.[41] He accepted the reasoning of Maharik, finding it quite consistent with Rashba and Naḥmanides. Furthermore, he adds, from the Jerusalem Talmud it is clear that the five duties enumerated in *Kiddushin* (F) are an exhaustive list and not mere examples, for the Jerusalem Talmud juxtaposes them to the five benefits passed from father to son (physique, strength, wealth, wisdom, and length of years).[42] The *Baal ha-Tanya* thus considers the duties in *Kiddushin* as complete, eliminating any obligation on children to follow the religious "style" of their parents.

It is worthwhile recalling that a major critic of Ḥasidism was the Vilna Gaon. In fact the major confrontation crystalized around the personalities of the Vilna Gaon and the *Baal ha-Tanya* (the latter was rebuffed by the former on several occasions).[43] In the issue of filial obligation we can discern a facet of their differences. As we have seen, the Vilna Gaon understood Rashba to require obedience to parents in these circumstances, whereas the *Baal ha-Tanya* perceived Rashba quite differently, as allowing filial independence in this case, as long as the son continues to fulfill the requirements of the five activities enumerated in *Kiddushin*.[44]

In any case it is significant that the *Baal ha-Tanya* expands the traditional sources to embrace the question of religious posture and affiliation that are at variance with parental preference. This does not mean that the *Baal ha-Tanya* would endorse behavior that is inconsistent with halakhic principles in general, but merely that as long as the behavior remains within halakhic parameters, children may choose their own path.

Such differences of opinion occur in other areas too. Thus on the one hand R. Yair Ḥayyim Bachrach (Ḥavvot Yair, d. 1702) requires obedience in every case unless there is a direct infraction of Halakhah, and he therefore instructs a man to evict a scholar boarding with him, in accordance with his dying mother's will.[45] On the other hand we find a majority of scholars who permit a son to disregard his parents' objections to his studying Torah in one particular place, even though they are not demanding that he cease study altogether.[46] Similarly there is a consensus permitting a son or daughter to emigrate to live in Israel in disregard of parental opposition, so as to fulfill the commandment to settle the land (whether that commandment is viewed as biblical or rabbinic in origin.)[47]

3. *WHEN A PARENT DISPLAYS MENTAL OR EMOTIONAL DYSFUNCTION*

The question arises whether these considerations change in any way when a parent ceases to behave in normal and reasonable fashion toward a child. The Gemara in *Kiddushin* 31b mentions several instances of unusual parental behavior that were tolerated by the children involved. One instance involved the mother of R. Dimi, who publicly tore his clothes and abused his person. Later commentators viewed her as insane and therefore not subject to rebuke.[48] Other such instances are recorded elsewhere,[49] but there was one in particular that attracted the attention of subsequent halakhists.

The case involved the mother of R. Assi, an elderly woman who requested her son to find her a husband as good-looking as himself (I). The Gemara informs us that at that point R. Assi left her to live in the land of Israel. Maimonides understood the mother to be mentally incompetent, and codified R. Assi's response as a valid precedent to be followed in similar situations.[50] Thus he states that the son should try to satisfy the parent, in accordance with the parent's state of mind, but that if unsuccessful because of the severity of the mental condition, the son may take his leave, having entrusted his parent to the care of others (N). R. Abraham Ibn Daud (Ravad, d. 1198) disagrees (O), and says, "Whom could he have take care of the parent?"[51]

Both positions are not without their problems. How did Maimonides know that R. Assi's response was recorded in the Gemara so as to set a normative standard for others? How could Maimonides assume that any destination other than Israel was equally valid (he does not stipulate Israel as the destination, unlike the case of R. Assi)?[52] Furthermore the Gemara does not record that R. Assi in fact entrusted his parent to the care of others?[53] Finally, it is not certain that R. Assi's mother was in fact insane.[54] As for Ravad, how does he account for the precedent provided by the story of R. Assi, which would seem to permit entrusting the care of such a parent into the hands of a stranger?[55]

Those who defend Ravad explain that if a parent can be cared for by a stranger, certainly a child should be able to provide at least as good care.[56] This argument would take Ravad's words to say, "if the child cannot take care of the father, then who can?" Yet Maimonides' defenders respond that it is quite conceivable that a stranger would be more effective in caring for such a person, for a son or daughter might be emotionally involved or otherwise disadvantaged, depending on the circumstances.[57] While a minority of authorities side with Ravad,[58] the majority accept the ruling of Maimonides. The *Shulḥan Arukh* likewise accepts the lenient ruling of Maimonides,[59] in spite of the doubts raised by his particular formulation of the law. Accordingly it is the obligation of children to care for their disturbed parents as long as possible, but once the situation becomes intolerable, they may appoint an agent to care for the parent in their stead.

What of a parent who is not so disturbed as to require constant care but enough to make extreme demands on the son or daughter? Maharshal for one perceived R. Assi's mother to have been such a parent; i.e., by temperament (*meroa ha-lev*) she would make excessive demands upon her son.[60] By thus understanding the relationship, Maharshal appears to permit a son or daughter to take leave of such a parent and, as the saying goes, "live his [her] own life." More generally speaking, however, one could say that a halakhic response to such a situation would be formulated along the lines of the views outlined above. The authorities who identify a parent's will with a parent's honor would tend to the view that a child should respect the parent's wishes even under such circumstances. The authorities who argue that there must be some direct service or benefit accruing to the parent would not insist that the child accede to all parental directives or criticism. Here too it is clear that the particular behavior in question may not involve either the deferral or desecration of other commandments of the Torah and the Halakhah, for such behavior, even if desired by parent or child, would remain prohibited.

4. *HALAKHIC GUIDELINES FOR PARENTS*

The Gemara in *Moed Katan* 17a records the story of a maidservant in the house of R. Judah ha-Nasi, who once saw a man strike his mature son. Said she, "Let that man be placed under a ban, for he violates the prohibition 'thou shalt not put a stumbling block before the blind,' which refers to one who strikes his mature son." There are several views regarding the propriety of physical punishment for a child,[61] and this text figures prominently in the discussions. Of more direct interest to our present concerns, however, are the general lessons gleaned from this and similar passages by later authorities.

Foremost among them was Maimonides, who formulated the general principle that "it is forbidden for a man to impose too heavy a yoke upon his children by being overly insistent on his due honor, for he thereby brings them close to sinning. Instead he should forgive and turn aside, for a father may forgo his honor if he wishes."[62] Moderation in all things, that favorite theme of Maimonidean ethics,[63] applies here too—perhaps especially here in the educational process of the young. Maimonides recognizes the special sensitivity needed if a parent is to maintain the delicate balance between discipline and endearing love. Maimonides' presentation of parent-child relationships preserves the dialectical tensions and nuances by emphasizing the need for mutual respect, forbearance, and perspective on the part of both parent and son or daughter.

Similar words are found in the thirteenth-century *Sefer Ḥasidim*, which states that "the father and mother should not so enrage the son [or daughter] that he cannot restrain himself, but must rebel against them."[64] Clearly even medieval Jewish society knew of the problems associated with rebellious sons and daughters who took issue with their parents' views and methods. Popular conceptions notwithstanding, the phenomenon of intergenerational conflict within the family is not the exclusive domain of the modern era. An adjacent comment found in the *Sefer Ḥasidim* likewise says: "It is best that a father and son separate if they quarrel with each other, for much pain is caused both to father and to son."[65]

To return to the case of the mother and daughter with which this chapter began, it is clear that there are a variety of opinions as to the correct behavior on the part of the daughter, and consequently as to an acceptable therapeutic approach in resolving the conflict. Because what is at issue does not involve the daughter performing any service activities such as those specifically mentioned in *Kiddushin*, but rather involves behavioral patterns that are distressing to the mother, we encounter several approaches.

Tosafot, in the name of Ri and Rabbeinu Tam, as well as Ritva and Naḥmanides, would require the daughter to accede to the mother's request only in order to provide some concrete benefit necessary for the comfort, physical well-being, or public dignity of the mother. One can safely assume that this would hold true even in the present instance, where the mother's health is seriously affected, in that the demands can be illegitimate in the first place (according to this view). Later authorities who agree substantially with this position include Maharik, R. Elijah Capsali, and the *Baal ha-Tanya*.

On the other hand there are those who would require complete obedience by the daughter in this situation. Those holding this view include Meiri, Rashba as understood by the Vilna Gaon, the Vilna Gaon himself, the *Sefer ha-Makneh*, Neẓiv, and R. Yeruḥam Perla. Included also would be Ḥavvot Yair.

In any case, there is no dispute that if the parent demands a violation of the Halakhah, or if by honoring the parent's will the Halakhah will be violated, the child need not obey. On the other hand, it need hardly be pointed out that even the lenient view would not accept filial behavior that violates halakhic norms in their general framework.

Where the mother's expectations of her daughter are obviously extreme, and not satisfiable in any significant way, Maharshal permits the daughter to take leave of her mother, so as to remove further opportunities for friction. Maimonides permits such a course of action only if the mother is judged to be mentally incompetent, although it appears that it is up to the child to make this judgment. This is to be done only if an alternative plan for the care of the mother can be adopted. Ravad rejects even this. A majority of later authorities side with Maimonides, making his view normative.

It would be a truism to say that in such family situations each case is *sui generis*, requiring its own special treatment and resolution. Yet we can see that the Halakhah does offer principles and directives that can assist one who faces this kind of problem. Moreover, the halakhic directives go beyond a mere situation ethic, for the variety of perspectives here reviewed provides a spectrum of approaches in pursuit of *shalom bayit* and the easing of familial conflict.

Notes

1. On the conflicts and problems involving the therapist as counselor, see L. Hankoff, "Psychotherapy and Values: Issues, Conflicts, and Misconceptions," *Journal of Psychology and Judaism* 4, no. 1.

2. A notable exception is G. Blidstein, *Honor Thy Father and Mother* (New York, 1975), an excellent study of much of the literature on the subject.

3. For a detailed discussion of the issues regarding the stubborn and rebellious son, see the *Encyclopedia Talmudit*, s.v. "Ben Sorer u-Moreh." Naḥmanides' commentary to Deut. 21:18 does, however, consider the rejection of parental authority to be equally significant to the rejection of the Torah in determining the infraction of such a youth.

4. The question regarding whether the parent should be obeyed if the directive is clearly not in the child's best interest is discussed below in Section 2.

5. Similarly, Tosafot to *Bava Meẓia* 33a says: "One should restore one's loss before honoring one's father's will, for whereas a father should be honored if he has some benefit from the use of an animal that the son owns, such as when the father says, 'Slaughter your animal for me,' yet when the father says, 'Let your animal get lost, but get me what I desire,' he is not to be obeyed. For in the latter case the loss of the animal is not in the interest of the father either." Cf. also Tosafot to *Zevaḥim* 4b, s.v. *ḥatat ha-of.*

6. Maharshal, *Yam Shel Shelomoh, Kiddushin* 32a, p. 17.

7. *Novellae of Ritva* to *Yevamot* 6a.

8. *Novellae of Ramban* to *Yevamot* 6a.

9. *Novellae of Rashba* to *Yevamot* 6a.

10. The comments of the Gaon are found in his *Beur ha-Gra* to *Sh.A. Yoreh Deiah* 240:36.

11. *Novellae of Ḥazon Ish* to *Kiddushin* 32a, p. 287.

12. Blidstein, *Honor Thy Father and Mother*, p. 196, n. 27, implies that R. Ḥayyim Heller, *Commentary to Maimonides' Book of the Commandments* (Jerusalem, 1946), p. 88, n. 5, has another view of Rashba's opinion. This, however, is not readily apparent from a careful reading of that work.

13. Meiri, *Bet ha-Beḥirah* to *Yevamot* 6a, p. 27.

14. S. Dickman, in his comments accompanying the text of Meiri, appears to identify Meiri's view with Rashba's.

15. This alludes to a related halakhic question: Is a son required to expend his financial resources in honoring his parents? *Kiddushin* 32a discusses the issue, and the normative view is negative (unless the parent is destitute and the son can afford to support the parent). For a fuller discussion, cf. Blidstein, *Honor Thy Father and Mother*, pp. 60–75.

16. *Sefer ha-Makneh*, p. 65c, as quoted by Heller, and Blidstein, *Honor Thy Father and Mother*, p. 196, n. 27.

17. The statement refers to an incident in which R. Ishmael's mother wished to drink the water with which she had washed his feet, against his wishes. The rabbis instructed him to permit her, such being her desire.

18. Perhaps a distinction could be made by pointing to the fact that in the incident of R. Ishmael it is the mother herself who wishes to act, and therefore she is permitted by Tosafot, whereas in the case discussed by Ri it is a question of the parent preventing *the son* from acting to recover his lost article. In the latter case the son's behavior is not subject to parental stricture.

19. Y. Perla, *Commentary to Saadya's Book of the Commandments* (Warsaw, 1914), vol. 1, p. 203.

20. *Novellae of Ritva* to *Yevamot* 6a.

21. *Responsa Maharik* (Warsaw, 1884), no. 164:3, pp. 177–178.

22. Cf. above, n. 15. In this responsum Maharik provides another answer to the problem of the apparent inconsistency in Tosafot (cf. above, p. 204), by saying that the latter lines are expressed in accordance with the view that the son *is* obliged to spend his financial resources, whereas the earlier statement follows the normative view that there is no such requirement.

23. Tosafot to *Yevamot* 5b, s.v. *koolkhem*, explains the *Sifra* by saying that the Sabbath is generally regarded as testifying to God the Creator of the universe, and therefore takes precedence over other commandments. Tosafot does not refer to the use of the possessive ("My Sabbaths"), which implies a special link between God and the Sabbath.

24. This presentation of the discussion in the Gemara follows the interpretation of Tosafot, quoting Rabbeinu Ḥananel, the thirteenth-century Egyptian talmudist. This interpretation takes issue with Rashi, as do most commentators.

25. The linkage of this *Sifra* to the discussion in *Kiddushin* is made explicit in Tosafot to *Yevamot* 5b, s.v. *koolkhem*. Rabbi S. Yisraeli, "Emigrating to Israel against the Will of Parents," *Shanah be'Shanah*, 5725, pp. 143–146, is of the opinion that Maimonides opposed Tosafot's linkage of these two passages in the Gemara, but Maimonides' view is not entirely clear in this regard.

26. Issi b. Judah disagrees when there is someone else who can be delegated to take care of the other commandment, in which case parental honor takes precedence. Blidstein (p. 82) points out that it is generally the ritual commandments that cannot be delegated to another, as they involve man's responsibility to God. However, commandments that stress the ethical dimension, i.e., man's social responsibilities, may be deferred. Apparently one's duties to father and mother precede one's duties to other men but do not precede duties to God.

27. *Responsa Rosh* (Vilna, 1881), 15:5.

28. *Responsa Rashba attributed to Ramban* (Warsaw, 1883), 272.

29. He refers to *Sotah* 2b, which states, "Forty days prior to the formation of the fetus, a heavenly voice says, 'so-and-so will marry so-and-so.' "

30. Cf. above, p. 206.

31. *Kiddushin* 41a. The practice of arranged marriage was widespread, and it commonly was the case that a couple would accept the recommendations of family or marriage agents.

32. Maharik does add the qualifying phrase "a woman suited to him [*hogenet lo*]," from which one could conclude that a parent who claims that the prospective wife is "not suited" would be justified in her claim. Such an interpretation of Maharik would, however, go against the entire tenor of the responsum. Furthermore, as noted by Blidstein (p. 93), it is precisely the question of her suitability that is under debate. In all likelihood Maharik intends the phrase to mean that there is some objective fact disqualifying her, such as her being of another faith or embracing another faith. This is the interpretation of Maharik offered by H. Ben Sasson, "A Jewish Chronicler at the End of the Middle Ages," *Sefer Yovel li-Gedalyah Alon* (Jerusalem, 1970), p. 282, n. 7.

33. Elijah Capsali, *Me'ah She'arim*, as published by Ben Sasson, ibid., pp. 278–283.

34. Rema to *Sh.A. Yoreh Deiah* 240:25.

35. *Responsa Ḥatam Sofer, Ḥoshen Mishpat* 111.

36. *Responsa Meshiv Davar* 50.

37. Cf. above, n. 32. Perla, while raising several objections and qualifying considerations in the course of his discussion of Maharik, seems to accept the authoritative ruling of Rema, specifically in the area of marriage. *Sefer ha-Makneh* (above, p. 205) likewise restricts the applicability of Rema's ruling to the choice of a marriage partner.

38. Cf. above, p. 205.

39. Many of the important documents and events are included in M. Wilensky, *Ḥasidim u-Mitnagdim* (Jerusalem, 1970).

40. For a description of the doctrinal effects of this intrafamilial phenomenon in early Ḥasidism, see L. Jacobs, "Kabed et Avikha," in *Hagut Ivrit be'Eiropa*, ed. M. Zahavi and A. Tratkower (Tel Aviv, 1969), pp. 136–143.

41. This is found in D. Z. Hilman, *Iggerot Baal ha-Tanya u-Venei Doro* (Jerusalem, 1953), pp. 48–49.

42. Jerusalem Talmud, *Kiddushin* 1:7. The Mishnah in *Eduyot* 2:9 lists the five possessions granted by one's father without any parallel reference to the duty toward parents.

43. For a discussion of these events and the history surrounding them, see S. Dubnow, *Toldot ha-Ḥasidut* (Berlin, 1932), pp. 225–257.

44. This issue would provide an interesting case-study for the question, debated in the history of intellectual ideas, whether a given historical situation influences the understanding of a particular concept, or vice versa. Rashba himself was involved in a similar debate in 1305, when he figured prominently in the second phase of the Maimonidean controversy, which saw the banning of the study of philosophy for anyone under the age of twenty-five. Rashba and his followers were apparently concerned about the way in which the younger generation of Jews had been attracted to the pursuit of philosophy, a development that is reminiscent of the rise of Ḥasidism.

45. This responsum is quoted in the *Pitḥei Teshuvah* to *Sh.A. Yoreh Deiah* 240:25.

46. Cf., for example, R. Israel Isserlein (1390–1460), *Responsa Terumat ha-Deshen* (Warsaw, 1882), no. 40. The *Shulḥan Arukh* codifies this as law (*Yoreh Deiah* 240:25).

47. *Responsa R. Meir of Rothenburg* 79, and *Responsa Mabit* 139. With the rise of the modern State of Israel, the issue has once again come to the fore. It has been discussed in several articles, including S. Yisraeli (see above, n. 25) and I. Schepansky, *Or ha-Mizraḥ*, Nissan 5731, pp. 170–172. These are briefly discussed in Bleich, *Contemporary Halakhic Problems* (New York, 1977), pp. 9–13. Yisraeli in this article attempts to show that Maimonides is opposed to Tosafot's view that parental honor applies only where there is benefit to the parent. Yisraeli understands Maimonides as saying that a son must obey parental wishes, whether or not they afford the parent some direct benefit. This would approximate the view of Rashba as understood by the Vilna Gaon. Such an interpretation of Maimonides relies on a subtle analysis of Maimonides' words and literary presentation, one that is not generally perceived by other students of the *Mishneh Torah*.

48. Cf. Maharshal, *Yam Shel Shelomoh* to *Kiddushin* 32a, p. 17.

49. Some of these are mentioned in Blidstein, pp. 116–117.

50. Maimonides, *M.T. Hil. Mamrim* 6:10.

51. The gloss of Ravad ad loc.

52. The commentary of Rabbeinu Nissim (Ran, 14th-cent. Spain) mentions this as a possible explanation of Ravad's opposition to Maimonides, but then he adds, "but I disagree."

53. R. Joshua Falk (d. 1614) points this out in his commentary to the *Tur* ad loc., known as the *Derishah*. It is likewise found in the *Taz* of R. David ha-Levi (d. 1667), commenting on the *Shulḥan Arukh* ad loc.

54. This is noted by Blidstein, p. 118.

55. Cf. the comments of R. Joseph Karo (author of the *Shulḥan Arukh*) in his *Kesef Mishnah* on *M.T. Mamrim* 6:10, and the *Migdal Oz* ad loc.

56. Cf. the *Taz* and the *Derishah*, loc. cit.

57. Thus the *Migdal Oz* notes that it might happen that a parent might not respect or fear the advice offered by a son or daughter as much as that offered by a stranger. Rabbi Y. Epstein (d. 1905), author of the *Arukh ha-Shulḥan* (Warsaw, 1900), says that a son or daughter might be at a disadvantage in situations where a parent needs to be physically restrained or bound, in which case it is a miẓvah to hire another person (commentary to *Yoreh Deiah* 240:32). Cf. similarly R. David Abi Zimrah, *Ridbaz* on *M.T.* ad loc.

58. These include the *Taz* and *Derishah*, as well as Maharshal, *Yam Shel Shelomoh*, loc. cit.

59. *Sh.A. Yoreh Deiah* 240:10.

60. *Yam Shel Shelomoh*, loc. cit.

61. See the discussion in Blidstein, pp. 125–126.

62. *M.T. Hil. Mamrim* 6:8. The *Kesef Mishnah* considers the source for this statement to be the passage in *Moed Katan* 17a.

63. See *M.T. Hil. Deot* 1–2.

64. *Sefer Ḥasidim*, ed. J. Wistinetsky (Berlin, 1891), p. 234 (no. 954).

65. Ibid., p. 233 (no. 949).

9

Homosexuality

Introduction

Recent decades have seen a significant acceptance of a variety of sexually liberal lifestyles. Much has been made of the so-called sexual revolution that has brought about a loosening of traditional attitudes toward sexual relationships that occur outside the bonds of marriage. Prominent among these relationships is both male and female homosexuality, a relationship that can be described as a sexual and emotional interest in members of one's own sex. Studies have indicated that the incidence of homosexuality among males in Western society is significant (Kinsey found that in 1948, in the United States, some 4 to 6 percent of the male population could be considered "hard-core" homosexuals), and a good proportion of men have at least one homosexual experience at some time in their lives (according to Kinsey this was true of about one-third of the men he studied).

The homosexual population of North America has been relatively outspoken in advancing its views and demands for acceptance by society at large. "Gay" activists, as the movement has become known, have lobbied for the acceptance of homosexuality as an "alternative lifestyle," to be treated on an equal footing with heterosexuality. This has in turn generated a debate over the nature of homosexuality, the number of its practitioners, its effect on society (particularly for the young who might come into contact with it), and the rights of homosexuals themselves.

On the one hand, there have been those who have argued for

the complete acceptance of the demands of the homosexual community. The American Psychiatric Association rejected the notion of homosexuality as an illness that requires "treatment," or of the homosexual as "patient." A number of Christian clergymen and organizations have come out in favor of an accepting attitude on the part of organized religion, generally on the grounds that consensual relations between adults that foster a loving relationship should be accepted. In many locales civil libertarians have argued for the passing of ordinances forbidding discrimination against homosexuals in employment and in the holding of public office. And in circles of "enlightened" opinion, there is no shortage of those who would defend the view that homosexual acts are not unnatural; that the fact that many people find homosexuality abhorrent is merely the result of social conditioning; that homosexuals are not any more "maladjusted" than heterosexuals; and that those who argue loudest against homosexuality are probably overcompensating for their own latent homosexual tendencies.

On the other hand, there are those who argue that in the first place homosexuality is against God's law, as clearly stated in the Bible. Furthermore, there can be no gainsaying that most people do consider it to be unnatural and abhorrent, and therefore not socially acceptable. Some who hold this view argue that the primary function of sexuality is procreation, and because that is obviously not possible with homosexual acts, there can be no validation of those acts. Others are of the view that the open acceptance of homosexual behavior is bad for society, particularly for the young, who might be encouraged to imitate such behavior—especially if such contact and activity is initiated by adult homosexuals. Finally, a homosexual "lifestyle" is to be seen as essentially "antifamily," undermining the family institution that is the basis of society as we have come to know it. It should also be added that among mental health practitioners and theorists, there is one view—that of Freudian psychoanalysis—that sees homosexuality as a form of mental disorder, specifically an inability to resolve issues in the Oedipal stages of personality development, through an attachment to the mother and fear of the father, leading to psychotic and phobic symptoms among "fixed" homosexuals.

In responding to these arguments, Reform Jewish spokesmen have tended to approve the major goals of the homosexual movement, while certain Conservative leaders have come out in favor of lenient attitudes that would make room for Jewish homosexuals desiring community involvement as a group. Orthodox leaders have generally opposed any legitimization of the homosexual community, for a variety of reasons. The tensions and problematics inherent in resolving these various attitudes and feelings form the substance of any halakhic response to this painful social issue.

The Question

A young man admits in the course of therapy to having overwhelming homosexual preferences. For a number of years he tried earnestly to overcome these tendencies but was unable to do so. He also derives no lasting satisfaction from heterosexual relationships. For this reason, and because he feels the need to pray, he would like to attend services at a well-known gay synagogue, where he feels he will be accepted and feel comfortable. What approach should be taken in counseling such a person; may such affiliations be encouraged?

Several questions are raised here, requiring clarification:

1. What is the nature of the prohibition against chronic homosexuality, whether male or female?
2. May a homosexual disclaim responsibility for his sexual preferences, on the grounds that they are not the result of choice on his part?
3. Is there a prohibition against associating in public or in private with individuals who profess homosexuality?
4. Is there a place in the traditional Jewish community for avowed homosexuality in public or private life?

Sources

A. Leviticus 18:22

Thou shalt not lie with mankind as with womankind, it is an abomination.

B. Leviticus 20:13

And if a man lie with mankind as with womankind, both of them have committed an abomination: they shall surely be put to death; their blood shall be upon them.

C. Leviticus 18:3

After the doings of the land of Egypt wherein ye dwelt, shall ye not do . . . neither shall ye walk in their statutes.

D. Deuteronomy 23:18

There shall be no harlot of the daughters of Israel, neither shall there be a Sodomite of the sons of Israel.

E. Genesis 19:5

And they called unto Lot and said unto him: "Where are the men that came in to thee this night? Bring them out unto us, that we may know them!"

F. Mishnah, Kiddushin 82a

Said. R. Judah: "A bachelor should not be shepherd to a cow, and two bachelors should not sleep under one cover." But the sages permit this.

G. Kiddushin 82a

It is stated in a Beraita: "They said to R. Judah: Israelites are not suspected in matters regarding homosexuality or zoophilia."

H. Mishnah, Sanhedrin 54a

The punishment for practicing homosexuality or zoophilia . . . is stoning.

I. Sanhedrin 54a–b

Where is the prohibition of homosexuality? Because it says (B) "if a man," i.e., a man and not a minor. And it says "lie with mankind," i.e., whether the passive partner be an adult or a minor. And it says "as with womankind," from which we learn that there are two modes of lying with a woman. . . . This verse speaks of the punishment for this act; whence comes the prohibition? It is Leviticus 18:22 (A). That verse speaks only of the "active" partner; what of the passive one? R. Ishmael said that it is referred to in Deuteronomy 23:18 (D), as well as 1 Kings 14:24, "and there were also Sodomites in the land." R. Akiva said: "Those verses are not necessary; instead, there is an alternative reading in our verse, for by changing the pointing to read *tishakhev*, it would read 'thou shalt not be lain with mankind as with womankind.' "

J. Yevamot 53b

Rava said: "A man may not claim that he committed a prohibited sexual act involuntarily, for there cannot be an erection against his will."

K. Yevamot 86a

Said Rava: "The law is not in accordance with Rav Huna, who said that a lesbian may not marry a *kohen* [priest]. For even according to R. Eliezer, who considers an unmarried couple who have cohabited as performing an act of *zenut* [harlotry, which disqualifies the woman from ever marrying a *kohen*], this does not apply to two women who lie together; in their case, it is simply sexual licentiousness."

L. Maimonides, M. T. Hilkhot Issurei Biah 22:2

Israelites are not suspected in matters regarding homosexuality or zoophilia, therefore it is not forbidden to sequester oneself with another Jewish male. If, however, one does take special precaution to avoid being alone with another male, such an attitude is praiseworthy.

M. Shulḥan Arukh, Even ha-Ezer 24

[Quotes (L) verbatim, then adds:] But in these times, when there is so much licentiousness, one should indeed take special precautions to avoid being alone with another male.

N. Sefer ha-Ḥinukh 209–210

The view of Maimonides is that "there shall be no harlot" (D) adds a negative command to the prohibition of homosexuality, similar to a number of prohibitions in the Torah that duplicate other prohibitions using different words. I have noted also that according to Naḥmanides, (D) forbids us to permit in our holy nation the existence of a *kadesh*, which refers to a male who is available for homosexual acts, in the manner commonly found in Islamic lands to this day. . . . At the root of this command is that God wanted the world to be populated, and so He commanded us not to waste our seed in the manner of Gentile sexual practices. For homosexuality is in truth destructive of the seed, not leading to offspring, nor providing conjugal fulfillment. Besides, such an act is detestable and vile in the extreme to any intelligent person. A person who was created to serve his Creator should not debase himself by such vile acts.

Discussion

1. THE NATURE OF THE PROHIBITION AGAINST HOMOSEXUALITY

The fundamental fact regarding any discussion of Jewish approaches to homosexuality is that the Torah considers homosexuality to be an abomination, and therefore categorically prohibited (A). It is an act which, if all the legal conditions are satisfied, is punishable by death (B) for both the active ("male") and passive ("female") partners who intentionally commit such an act. The Talmud (H, I) establishes the textual prohibition as well as punishment for them both, even though there is some difference of opinion between R. Ishmael and R. Akiva as to the exact verses involved. Such views are occasioned by the fact that a second verse, found in Deuteronomy (D), prohibits what appears to be homosexuality. The term in Deuteronomy is *kadesh*, used in juxtaposition to the female *kedeshah*, which is likewise prohibited. The term *kadesh* is taken by the preponderance of authorities, such as Maimonides and Naḥmanides (see N), to refer to any male who is available for homosexual acts, a state of affairs not uncommon in the ancient Near East.[1] For Maimonides, however, this is not a separate prohibition but merely an enlargement upon the levitical prohibition, simply echoed and emphasized a second time.

Beyond these purely legal contexts, Scripture conveys its abhorrence of homosexuality through a variety of narrative settings, at least as understood by the rabbinic tradition. The paradigmatic instance of such aberrant behavior is found in the demand of the men of Sodom to "know" the men visiting Lot, the nephew of Abraham (E), thus lending their name to the practice of "sodomy" (homosexuality).[2] A somewhat similar episode is encountered in Judges 19, this time involving the tribe of Benjamin. Homosexual as well as incestuous overtones are detected by the amora Samuel in the narrative of the drunken Noah and his son Ham—an act sufficient to cause Noah to curse Ham's posterity.[3] There is also a hint of homosexual intent on the part of Potiphar, master of Joseph. According to Rav, Potiphar purchased Joseph on account of his physical beauty, intending to maintain a homosexual relationship, but was thwarted by divine intervention.[4] The Midrash likewise identifies one of the contributory factors leading to the flood that destroyed Noah's generation as the common practice of issuing formal "marriage" contracts legitimizing homosexual liaisons in public.[5]

In later generations, sodomy is encountered in the scriptural account of such practices during the days of the kings Rehoboam, Asa, and Jehoshaphat—and only finally erased by Josiah.[6] From such descriptions as these, referring to "houses of the sodomites that were in the house of the Lord" (2 Kings 23:7), it would appear that they played the role of ritual male homosexual prostitutes until finally eradicated by Josiah.[7]

In postbiblical times, recorded instances of homosexual activity in Jewish communities are rare in the extreme. The Jerusalem Talmud records one such incident, accidentally encountered by R. Judah b. Pazzi,[8] while according to Josephus, King Herod's son Alexander had homosexual tendencies.[9]

Clearly what emerges from the biblical and postbiblical sources is an attitude that considered homosexuality an anathema to be abhorred. The exact class of the prohibition involves a difference of opinion among the *rishonim*: Maimonides is of the opinion that homosexuality is prohibited because it is considered to be one of the *arayot*, the severe sexual transgressions, like incest, forbidden to both Jew and Gentile.[10] Other early authorities, such as Rashba, Meiri, and Ritva, are in substantial agreement with Maimonides in classifying homosexuality as *arayot*.[11] On the other hand, a minority view is that of Tosafot, which considers the act to belong in the more conventional category of generally prohibited acts, even though punishable by death.[12] The distinction is not merely casuistic; it determines whether or not one may submit to performing a homosexual act at the risk of one's life. If homosexuality is *arayot*, one has no choice but to be killed rather than commit such an act. If it is merely "forbidden" (a *lav*), then submission becomes possible. In any case, it is the majority, and stricter, view that became normative.[13] Hence this viewpoint can be seen to be quite consistent with the talmudic dispensation to prevent an act of homosexual rape, if necessary, by killing the rapist.[14]

Similarly, because the act is viewed as one of the *arayot*, it is forbidden to the Gentile as well.[15] Indeed, since rabbinic literature presumes Gentile society to be particularly open to homosexual tendencies, extreme care is to be taken in situations where such tendencies might lead to homosexual activity.[16] The punishment for Gentile acts of homosexuality is likewise the death penalty, although in certain details this punishment differs from that of a Jewish sodomite.[17]

Having examined the parameters of the prohibition against homosexuality, we may well ask why the Torah and the tradition are so emphatic in their condemnation of the act. What is the reason for the prohibition? In the Talmud, Bar Kapparah is recorded as seeing a play on words in the very term *to'evah*, or "abomination," as used in the levitical prohibition. To his mind the term is the equivalent of *to'eh atah bah*, i.e., "by such an act you go astray."[18] The import of this interpretation is taken by the classical commentaries (such as Rashi, Rosh, and Tosafot ad loc.) to refer to the undermining of marital life by the homosexual abandoning his familial responsibilities to pursue such illicit relationships.

More direct, however, is the view that sees in homosexuality a violation of the command to be fruitful. Thus *Pesikta Zutarta* points out that it is of the very nature of such relations that no children can result from them.[19] Accordingly, sexual activity of this kind must be seen as a violation of the prohibition of the wasting of seed (*hashḥatat zera*), otherwise known as onanism.[20] This approach is adumbrated by the *Sefer ha-Ḥinukh* (N) as in contravention of God's will to populate the world, and simply a barren exercise in momentary pleasure "in the manner of Gentile sexual practices."[21]

The *Sefer ha-Ḥinukh* also reasons that the act is "detestable and vile in the extreme to any intelligent person," irrespective of a particular prohibition that might be assigned to the act. Clearly this view is echoed in the Talmud itself when it comments on the unnaturalness of the homosexual act, i.e., the anatomical reality that attests to the more natural union of heterosexual activity.[22] As Rabbi Barukh Halevi Epstein put it in his *Torah Temimah*, such activity goes astray from the foundations of creation and of nature.[23] Such views are well summarized by Rabbi Norman Lamm when he says that "an act characterized as an abomination is *prima facie* disgusting and cannot be further defined or explained. . . . It is, as it were, a visceral reaction, an intuitive disqualification of the act, and we run the risk of distorting the biblical judgment if we rationalize it."[24] Hence, no matter how popular or accepted an act, it remains biblically abhorred and anathema—and, as Rabbi David Ẓevi Hoffmann explains, that is the ultimate meaning of the term *to'evah:* "it is abominable."[25]

But the most recent, and repercussive, comments elucidating the gravity of the homosexual act are found in a responsum dated 1976, and published in 1981, by Rabbi Moshe Feinstein. He understands Bar Kapparah's comment ("by such an act you go astray") to be motivated by the following question: There are numerous forbidden sexual acts that are considered *to'evah*, or an abomination, in Leviticus—but why is homosexuality alone singled out to be referred to *twice* as an abomination (both in A and B)? R. Moshe answers that whereas the other forbidden acts can be seen as deviant expressions of a basically legitimate and natural sexual urge implanted in man's nature, the homosexual act is devoid of any natural sexuality in any form, and does not derive from the divinely implanted sexual urge. It is instead a fundamental expression of rebellion against the biblical norm, almost a deliberate flaunting that is carried out *because* the act is forbidden (*le'hakh'is*). Accordingly, the homosexual act has no justification whatsoever; by its nature it is an act of defiance, and it is therefore the abomination par excellence.[26]

The discussion to this point, while speaking of "homosexuality" (lit., "preferring the same sex") in general terms, has not attempted to distinguish between male and female homosexuality. The latter, i.e., lesbian activity, commands separate attention in the halakhic context and is not viewed with the same stringency as male homosexuality, albeit it is considered a prohibited act. The Torah forbids the Israelite from imitating the "doings of the land of Egypt" (C), and the *Sifra* takes this to be referring to Egyptian lesbianism.[27] Since its biblical basis does not invoke mention of *arayot*, lesbianism does not assume the proportions of incest or adultery or other severely prohibited *arayot*. It remains within the category of the "merely" forbidden activities.

According to Rav Huna in the Gemara, the act of lesbianism is sufficient to render a woman a *zonah* (harlot), which in its technical application would disqualify her from ever marrying a priest (K). Apparently, Rav Huna considers the act to involve genital intercourse, and therefore to change the sexual status of the women involved.[28] The more accepted view of the Talmud, however, is more lenient, in asserting that such an act is not harlotry (*zenut*) at all, but merely sexual licentiousness (*priẓut*) (K). Consequently, Maimonides and R. Jacob b. Asher (author of the *Tur)* codify the law as forbidding lesbian liaisons, even though there is no biblically mandated punishment on technical grounds. (Corporal lashes are administered only where there is a specific prohibition directed to that activity, whereas the "doings of Egypt" includes other activities.)[29] At the same time, because there is no *zenut*, the lesbian may subsequently marry a priest.[30] Nonetheless, efforts to prevent lesbian activity are required. Thus, for example, the Talmud records the practice of the father of the amora Samuel, who prevented his daughters from sleeping together in one bed, so as not to become accustomed to such patterns of behavior.[31] Maimonides likewise counsels care in having women avoid other women known to have lesbian preferences.[32]

Why the Halakhah distinguishes in this way between male and female homosexuality is not absolutely clear. While Maimonides speaks in terms of lesbianism not being an act of genital intercourse (*biah*), it would appear that a more fundamental reason would be the absence of destruction of the male seed, the consideration that figures so prominently in the prohibition of male homosexuality. Thus lesbianism is forbidden as an act of sexual license, in that it is perceived as weakening the fabric of family life and the normative patterns of permitted sexual expression.

One final question in dealing with the nature of the prohibition can now be dealt with: Is it the homosexual act *per se* that is prohibited and is the exclusive concern of the Torah, or is there a prohibition even of homosexual preferences, thoughts, or friendships that do not involve the act of sexual intercourse or sodomy? Moshe Halevi Spero has argued that the latter are likewise prohibited in the Torah by implication.[33] Starting with the verse in Genesis 2:24, "therefore shall a man leave his father and his mother, and shall cleave unto his wife, and they shall be one flesh," and the talmudic inference that "cleaving" by implication is opposed to homosexuality (in that the physical union in homosexuality is not complete),[34] Spero concludes that the verse is an indictment even of homosexual thoughts. This follows from the verse's emphasis on achieving a stable and healthy sexual life by detaching oneself from any sexual attraction to one's parents, whether hetero- or homosexual. Accordingly, what the Torah seems to be requiring is a normal heterosexual outlook, one that has resolved any latent parent-child conflicts that might lead to a homosexual orientation. Spero concludes that the homosexual, even without engaging in homosexual acts, fails to achieve the scriptural mandate of heterosexual maturity or completeness (in accordance with the talmudic statement that "any man who has no wife is not a man").[35] Thus, irrespective of the consequences for family life or social stability, the homosexual is to be regarded as defective, whether or not he engages in homosexual acts.

2. CAN THE HOMOSEXUAL DISCLAIM RESPONSIBILITY FOR HIS CONDITION?

From the preceding discussion it is obvious that the biblical-rabbinic tradition considers homosexuality to be forbidden under any circumstances, when undertaken as a deliberate, conscious act. That is to say, one may not freely choose to engage in homosexual relations as an "alternative sexual preference." But what if one is a so-called genuine homosexual, who has made serious efforts to overcome that orientation, but to no avail. Is he to be held responsible for his condition, even though it is not by choice?

The question is not merely technical, for it gets to the heart of the issue as to how the homosexual is to be treated within the halakhic community: Is he a sinner, or merely "sick"; is he immoral, or simply the victim of circumstances and forces beyond his control?

The fundamental halakhic principle touching on this problem occurs in tractate *Yevamot* (J), where Rava states that a male who commits a prohibited sexual act cannot claim to be acting under duress, for by virtue of having achieved sexual erection, he is deemed to have desired that act. This is not the case with a woman, who, even though she too might have been sexually stimulated, might well claim that her response was involuntary and under duress, as the result of a rape situation.[36] In the case of a man, in Rava's view, there cannot be an erection against one's will. This principle was formulated and codified into law by Maimonides.[37] The only mitigating consideration occurs when such sexual arousal occurred in an initially legitimate context but was deflected by external coercion to a forbidden act.[38] The severity of this principle is clearly consistent with the normative view, encountered earlier,[39] and articulated by Maimonides, that would prohibit a man from performing a forbidden sexual act under duress.

It is this principle which must govern the attitude taken toward the genuine homosexual. Accordingly, he cannot claim internal "duress," or the inability to control his sexual drives. If he is sexually aroused, it must be assumed that this is an act of his own autonomous desire, and hence he is responsible for his condition. This is particularly true when, as is normally the case, the homosexual derives pleasure from the act, for as R. Moshe Feinstein has argued in a slightly different context, any pleasure derived from a prohibited act performed under duress increases the level of prohibition.[40]

And yet, having affirmed that the homosexual cannot disclaim responsibility for his condition, there is room to argue for a more lenient judgment of homosexuality if it is perceived as a disease. Rabbi Norman Lamm has argued for the view of homosexuality as pathology, based on findings that indicate certain developmental traits, such as passivity, dependence, and phobic tendencies.[41] Responding to the majority view of the American Psychiatric Association, which declares homosexuality "normal," Lamm believes strongly that such a view is politically motivated, and the result of societal pressures brought to bear. In his view there are sufficient clinical traits that would render homosexuality to be a pathology that simply cannot be turned into health by majority vote. Invoking the principle that "no man sins unless he is overcome by a spirit of madness" (*Sotah* 3a), he argues for leniency in formulating a halakhic response to genuine homosexuality. Lamm finds a rough parallel in the response of the Halakhah to a suicide: The suicide is generally presumed, unless there is strong evidence to the contrary, to have acted out of a measure of insanity or incompetence, even though the Halakhah retains the strongest possible anathema against the act of suicide.[42] Similarly, homosexuality can be viewed as absolutely prohibited even while the homosexual himself is to be sympathetically understood with a view to treatment and rehabilitation. Lamm similarly argues against judicial punishment for such activities, as being at best ineffective and at worst counterproductive.

Reinforcing this view is a responsum by R. Ḥayyim Pelaggi, in the nineteenth century.[43] Dealing with the status of an admitted homosexual, Pelaggi accepts the possibility of genuine repentance and rehabilitation of the individual concerned, even though he cautions against anyone secluding himself with that individual. Apparently, even when repentance is genuine, the possibility of subsequent failure remains and requires additional precaution. The first Chief Rabbi of Israel, Rabbi A. I. Kook, likewise assumes the possibility of repentance of a homosexual in a responsum dealing with an individual suspected of such activity.[44]

To summarize, then, the homosexual is held responsible for his actions, no matter how much they may be the result of inner forces which he feels are beyond his control. But at the same time, such behavior, when genuinely impervious to sincere efforts to change, is to be viewed with compassion and sympathetic concern that is intended to overcome the effects of this pathology. Repentance must always be a possibility, even though homosexuality constitutes a sickness of profound proportions.

3. ASSOCIATION OR SECLUSION WITH THE HOMOSEXUAL

The Mishnah in *Kiddushin* (F) records two opinions regarding latent homosexuality and the problems involved in two men sleeping under one cover. R. Judah forbids such intimacy, evidently on the grounds that homosexual tendencies might come to the fore, whereas the sages, constituting the preponderance of tannaim, did not share this concern and permitted two Israelite men to share a blanket. The Gemara records the basis for their leniency in the face of R. Judah's concern: Israelite men are not suspected of harboring homosexual tendencies (G). Hence, no special precautions are required as a matter of course. An adjacent passage similarly records two views regarding seclusion with another person who is sexually forbidden because of the prohibition of *arayot*. In that passage, R. Judah reports the view of R. Assi permitting such seclusion and allowing a man, for instance, to live with his mother or daughter. The amora Samuel, however, is opposed to any seclusion involving two people whose union is prohibited as *arayot*.[45]

Regarding both passages, Maimonides accepts the more lenient view; i.e., he agrees with the sages and R. Assi that, as a rule, seclusion, and even sharing a blanket with another male, is permissible.[46] Nevertheless, Maimonides does add that extra precaution is praiseworthy and to be admired, even though not strictly required by law (L). Such precautions would seem to be prompted by the concerns of R. Judah and Samuel.[47] In addition, the same passage in the Gemara records the personal precautions of Abbaye and Rava, as an act of personal piety, to avoid any hint of such seclusion. The Tosafot likewise accepted the view of R. Assi, against the view of Samuel.[48] Maimonides' decision and formulation (L) was adopted verbatim by the *Tur*.[49]

Such agreement notwithstanding, subsequent generations saw a measure of debate. R. Joseph Karo, in formulating the law in his *Shulḥan Arukh* (M), first quotes Maimonides but then adds the important qualifier that in times of widespread sexual license, such as in his own day, the extra precautions were not merely "personal piety" but required by law. This view, as explained by the Vilna Gaon,[50] understood the lenient view of the sages to be conditional upon the perceived behavioral patterns of a given age, and not a blanket principle with universal validity through time. Hence a more strict application of R. Judah and Samuel becomes possible in another era.

However, there were those who insisted on retaining the earlier, more permissive view regarding such seclusion. R. Joel Sirkes (known as the *Baḥ*), about a century after the *Shulḥan Arukh*, considered the ruling of the *Shulḥan Arukh* to have been the result of conditions and practices peculiar to its own time and place, but not valid in seventeenth-century Poland, where homosexuality was unheard of among Jews, according to him.[51] Accordingly it was his view that avoiding seclusion with another male Israelite, while praiseworthy, was certainly not required by law. An even more lenient position was taken by R. Solomon Luria (Maharshal). In his view, not only is such seclusion permitted, but one who deliberately avoids seclusion with another male (or an animal, for that matter) is guilty of acting presumptuously (*miḥzi ke'yuhera*).[52] He bases this view on a passage in Rabbeinu Asher (Rosh) that speaks of permissible avoidance of seclusion with conventional *arayot*, without mentioning homosexuality or zoophilia, and from this he concludes that there is no warrant for deliberately avoiding seclusion with another male. Luria's position, however, was criticized by later authorities for not recognizing other passages by Rosh, as well as those by Maimonides and R. Jacob b. Asher, that explicitly include homosexual concerns as legitimate reason to avoid seclusion.[53]

Subsequent authorities tended to the view of R. Joel Sirkes, i.e., as a rule the law does not require special precautions to avoid seclusion, for such action can be left to the personal piety of the individual, unless there is widespread practice of homosexuality in a given time or place, such as that of the *Shulḥan Arukh.* Thus, for instance, R. Jacob Emden (Ya'aveẓ) mentions in passing that no special precautions are required when two Israelite men are secluded together.[54] R. Ḥayyim Pelaggi, in the above-mentioned responsum,[55] prohibits seclusion only where one of the individuals involved has shown homosexual tendencies or experiences in the past.[56] In the twentieth century, Rabbi Abraham Isaac ha-Kohen Kook, in the above-mentioned responsum, added a novel explanation: The differences between Karo and Sirkes can be explained with reference to the respective climates of Israel and Poland, whereby colder lands such as Poland see less homosexual activity, while the warmer Middle Eastern countries are more conducive to homosexual proclivities. Hence Sirkes in Poland is more lenient, and Karo (in Israel) is more strict. On the basis of this distinction, Rabbi Kook considers the view of Karo in the *Shulḥan Arukh* to be operative at least in Israel, and he thus finds fault with an individual for having permitted himself to be secluded with another male.

The outcome of views such as these is that the permissibility of seclusion with another male is a function of the climate—whether physical or moral—of one's times, and this is so whether we adopt Rabbi Kook's criterion of hot or cold weather patterns, or the more conventional approach of determining what kind of sexual practices are prevalent in a given society. Where homosexuality is widespread and openly practiced in many quarters, and where sexual licentiousness is the hallmark of the time, it would appear that even the lenient school would prohibit seclusion with another male, even without his having evinced homosexual tendencies in the past. Such precautions would apply *a fortiori* to sleeping under one blanket.[57]

4. *HOMOSEXUALITY IN THE JEWISH COMMUNITY*

It is clear from the foregoing that no responsible traditionalist could seriously consider homosexuality to be an "alternative sexual preference" to be accepted side by side with heterosexuality.[58] Whether it be viewed simply as "abomination" or more analytically as in contravention of divine intentions vis-à-vis human fulfillment and the begetting of progeny, homosexuality remains anathema. In the Torah it is a capital crime, associated with the most corrupt societies, such as Sodom and decadent Egypt. The view of Maimonides is that homosexuality is forbidden as *arayot*, i.e., comparable in seriousness to incest, while Tosafot considered it "merely" prohibited. In this dispute, Maimonides' stricter view became normative, with one result being the acceptance of the permissibility of killing a homosexual who is about to rape another male, assuming there is no other way to prevent the act.

As to the reason for the Torah regarding homosexuality as an abomination, there are three major views: Some, like Rashi, see homosexuality primarily as a threat to family life; others, like the *Sefer ha-Ḥinukh*, find the rationale in the "wasting of male seed," otherwise referred to as onanism. A third approach could be characterized as nonreductionist, i.e., the homosexual act is simply detestable. It is not important how we formulate the rationale, for the act remains "unnatural" and simply unacceptable. Such a view is associated with Bar Kapparah in the Talmud.

Lesbianism is not viewed by the Halakhah with the same degree of seriousness, even though female homosexuality remains strictly forbidden. While all are agreed that it is not one of the *arayot*, there is some difference of opinion about whether it is a form of harlotry or merely sexual licentiousness. The latter, more lenient, view was accepted by most authorities, including Maimonides and R. Jacob b. Asher. Nonetheless, they urged extreme caution in avoiding women known to have homosexual predilections lest associations with them lead to lesbian activities.

This, however, is not to say that all halakhists would insist on punishment of the genuine homosexual. Some, such as Rabbi Norman Lamm, have argued for a more realistic approach that, while recognizing the heinousness of the act, perceives homosexuality as a form of disease or psychological disability and pathology, requiring treatment and not incarceration, understanding and not harsh judgment. An approach of this kind could be a parallel to the attitude of Halakhah to the suicide, which condemns the act even while taking a humane and conciliatory approach to the agent himself. This view is consistent with the few responsa on the topic in general that speak of repentance and rehabilitation (R. Ḥayyim Pelaggi and Rabbi A. I. Kook).

One further area of concern in developing an overall approach to the place of homosexuality in the Jewish community occurs in the halakhic discussion pertaining to seclusion with another male, with or without a homosexual history. The Talmud records two opinions, one permitting two Jewish men to be secluded with each other, the other forbidding this. The former view predominated, in that Israelite men were not to be suspected of homosexuality. Nonetheless, while most authorities permitted this seclusion, they also viewed any special precautions preventing it to be a desirable step, even though not required by law. Such was the view of Maimonides and R. Jacob b. Asher, and later of R. Joel Sirkes. A more restrictive position is taken by R. Joseph Karo in the *Shulḥan Arukh.* It is his position that if in fact lewdness is socially widespread, then such seclusion would be forbidden by law. On the other hand, however, Maharshal took a very lenient view regarding seclusion: One who avoids seclusion is guilty of presumptuous behavior and is not to be tolerated. This latter view did not become widespread. The generally accepted view was to permit seclusion where neither individual thus secluded has a history of homosexuality—except in places or times where sexual license and depravity are widespread. In such cases extra care would be required by law. This is the thrust of remarks by the Vilna Gaon, R. Ḥayyim Pelaggi, Ya'aveẓ, and Rabbi A. I. Kook. Similar positions have been enunciated by other traditionalist spokesmen within the Orthodox community.[59]

Attempts to come to terms with the problem of homosexuality that argue for its acceptance because it is so widespread seem to put the cart before the horse. The Halakhah, as we have seen, classically has responded to sexual depravity by raising, not lowering, acceptable standards of behavior, and by demanding additional precautions and care. The answer to the "gay liberation" movement in halakhic terms cannot be by meeting it halfway, but rather by an unequivocal rejection of such practices, while seeking to help in every way those genuine homosexuals who wish to overcome their unfortunate condition.

To return to the case with which this chapter began, the young man should not attend services or programs at homosexual synagogues or organizations. Instead, he should make every effort to find a conventional synagogue where he might feel socially accepted. He should certainly attempt to overcome his condition by psychological therapy and genuine religious introspection leading to a more normal sexual life.

Notes

1. Cf. Rashi to Deut. 23:18. Onkelos, however, takes the term *kadesh* to be referring to marriage with a Canaanite bondwoman—cf. *Sefer ha-Ḥinukh* 209, and *Minḥat Ḥinukh* ad loc., sec. 3.

2. Cf. *Genesis Rabbah* 50:5, on Gen. 9:22 ff. More generally see M. Kasher, *Torah Shlemah*, vol. 3, to Gen. 19:5.

3. *Sanhedrin* 70a. Rav's view, however, is that Ham castrated Noah, thereby preventing the birth of a fourth son, and accounting for the curse of Ham's own fourth son, Canaan.

4. *Sotah* 13b, with reference to Gen. 39:1. Rav derives this from the subsequent listing of Potiphar as Potiphera (Gen. 41:45), the latter term implying mutilation (by the angel Gabriel, according to Rav). Cf. *Targum Yerushalmi* to Gen. 39:1, and Rashi ad loc.

5. *Leviticus Rabbah* 18:13.

6. 1 Kings 14:24, 15:12, 22:47; 2 Kings 23:7.

7. This is the conclusion reached by *Sanhedrin* 24b. See also Louis M. Epstein, *Sex Laws and Customs in Judaism* (New York, 1948), pp. 135–136.

8. Jerusalem Talmud *Sanhedrin* 6:3 (p. 28a).

9. Josephus, *Wars* I, 24:7, as well as his *Antiquities of the Jews* 15:25–30, in referring to the Roman ruler Anthony, whose homosexuality was evidently well known. Cf. Epstein, *Sex Laws*, p. 137. A passing reference to Roman sexual depravity is found in *Lamentations Rabbah* 4:4.

10. Maimonides, *M.T. Hil. Melakhim* 9:5–6. This is based on *Sanhedrin* 58a. Cf. also *M.T. Hil. Roẓeiaḥ* 1:11.

11. *Responsa Rashba* 1237, Meiri to *Sanhedrin* 9b, and Ritva to *Pesaḥim* 26b, in the name of Ra'ah. These and other sources are discussed at length in Meir Krauser, *Devar ha-Melekh* (Jerusalem, 1962), vol. 1, pp. 22–23.

12. Tosafot, *Sanhedrin* 73a, and Tosafot, *Yevamot* 54b. The *Penei Yehoshua* (Responsa on *Even ha-Ezer* 44) agrees with this minority view.

13. For further discussion of this point, see below regarding the status of one forced to perform a homosexual act.

14. See *Sanhedrin* 73a.

15. *Sanhedrin* 58a, and Maimonides, *M.T. Hil. Melakhim* 9:5–6. The biblical source is Gen. 2:24.

16. See Maimonides, *M.T. Hil. Issurei Biah* 22:5. Also see *Sefer ha-Ḥinukh* (N).

17. Maimonides, *M.T. Hil. Issurei Biah* 14:18, *Hil. Melakhim* 10:1–2 and 9:6.

18. *Nedarim* 51a.

19. Cf. *Torah Temimah* to Lev. 18:22

20. For a general discussion of the prohibition of the wasting of male seed, see above Chapter 1.

21. A preponderance of views agree that the prohibition is biblical and not merely rabbinic in nature. Cf. the exchange in *Tradition* 9, nos. 1–2 (1967): 205–212, no. 4 (1967): 140–147.

22. *Sanhedrin* 58a.

23. *Torah Temimah* to Lev. 18:22 and Gen. 2:24.

24. Norman Lamm, "Judaism and the Modern Attitude to Homosexuality," *Encyclopaedia Judaica Yearbook*, 1974, and reprinted in M. Kellner, ed., *Contemporary Jewish Ethics* (New York, 1978), p. 383. Many of Lamm's points were made earlier in his "The New Dispensation on Homosexuality: A Jewish Reaction to a Developing Christian Attitude," *Jewish Life* 35, no. 3 (January–February 1968): 11–16.

25. *The Commentary of D. Ẓ. Hoffmann to Leviticus* (Jerusalem, 1972), to Lev. 18:30 (vol. 2, p. 54).

26. See Moshe Feinstein, *Iggerot Moshe* (New York, 1973), *Oraḥ Ḥayyim* 4:115.

27. *Sifra Lev.* 9:8.

28. Cf. Rashi to *Yevamot* 76a, and Tosafot ad loc.

29. Maimonides, *M.T. Hil. Issurei Biah* 21:8, *Tur Even ha-Ezer* 20.

30. Ibid.

31. *Shabbat* 65a.

32. Maimonides, *Hil. Issurei Biah* 21:8.

33. Moshe Halevi Spero, "Homosexuality: Clinical and Ethical Challenges," *Tradition* 17, no. 4 (Spring 1979): 57–59.

34. *Sanhedrin* 58a, *Torah Temimah* to Gen. 2:24.

35. *Yevamot* 63a.

36. The classic illustration is Esther in the Purim story, as explained by Tosafot to *Yevamot* 63a, as well as *Ketuvot* 51b and *Sanhedrin* 73a.

37. Maimonides, *M.T. Hil. Sanhedrin* 20:3, *Hil. Issurei Biah* 1:9.

38. Tosafot, loc. cit., as well as *Kesef Mishnah* to *M.T. Sanhedrin* 20:3, and *Maggid Mishnah* to *Hil. Issurei Biah* 1:9.

39. Cf. above, p. 183.

40. R. Moshe Feinstein, *Iggerot Moshe, Yoreh Deiah* 2:59. Likewise *Responsa Atvan de'Oraita* 24. Similar considerations are to be applied in avoiding therapy that requires therapeutic sexual arousal; see Spero, "Challenges," pp. 59–65.

41. Lamm, "Homosexuality," p. 393. Cf. also David Feldman, in *Sh'ma* 2, no. 33 (1972): 100–102.

42. J. M. Tykocinski, *Gesher ha-Ḥayyim* 1:25. Cf. also Y. Greenwald, *Kol Bo al Avelut* (New York, 1965), pp. 319–321.

43. This appears in his *Ruaḥ Ḥayyim*, as quoted in *Oẓar ha-Poskim, Even ha-Ezer* 24:1, sec. 2.

44. *Responsa Da'at Kohen* 3, as quoted in *Oẓar ha-Poskim*, loc. cit.

45. *Kiddushin* 81b

46. Maimonides, *M.T. Hil. Issurei Biah* 22:2.

47. *Maggid Mishnah* to ibid.
48. See the comments of the *Bet Yosef* on the *Tur*, who quotes Rosh to this effect.
49. See *Tur Even ha-Ezer* 24 (a printer's error in the *Tur* is noted in the *Oẓar ha-Poskim*, ibid., whereby the word *aviv* ["his father"] should be amended to read *zakhor* ["a male"], yielding the conventional prohibition of secluding oneself with another male).
50. *Beur ha-Gra* to *Shulḥan Arukh*, ibid.
51. *Bayit Ḥadash* to *Tur Even ha-Ezer* 24.
52. *Yam Shel Shelomoh* to *Kiddushin* 4:23.
53. Cf. *Oẓar ha-Poskim* quoting Ra'avan, *Yosef Omeẓ*, and others.
54. *Responsa Ya'aveẓ* 171.
55. Cf. above, n. 43.
56. See also his *Responsa Ḥikkekei Lev, Yoreh Deiah* 46.
57. Yeḥiel Michael Epstein, *Arukh ha-Shulḥan, Even ha-Ezer* 24:6.
58. This is to be contrasted with the response of the Reform movement, which has by and large legitimized the Gay movement, or at least the establishment of Gay synagogues. See the *CCAR Journal*, Summer 1973, which contains several essays on the subject from a Reform point of view. Certain Conservative rabbis have likewise argued for the legitimacy of Gay synagogues and even homosexual rabbis. See H. Matt, "Sin, Crime, Sickness, or Alternate Life Style? A Jewish Approach to Homosexuality," *Judaism* 27, no. 1 (1978): 13–24. See also B. Schwartz, in *Jewish Week/American Examiner*, April 9, 1978, and idem, "The Jewish View of Homosexuality," (diss., Jewish Theological Seminary, 1979), in which he argues for his own view that would support a more accommodating stance toward homosexuality in the Jewish community.
59. See W. Wurzburger, in the *Jewish Examiner* February 5, 1978.

Business Ethics

10

The Limits of Truth and Deception in the Marketplace

Introduction

In business, contemporary promotional activities have raised a number of questions as to what constitutes acceptable practice. How may products be aggressively advertised without violating the truth; what constitutes deceptive behavior on the part of the seller or buyer; what disclosure requirements ought to be imposed on merchants at the time of sale; who is responsible after the sale for goods that are defective or unsatisfactory?

Questions such as these, and the apparent failure of government agencies to adequately protect the consumer, have given rise to the movement dedicated to what has become known as "consumer protection." Concerned at the unwillingness or inability of industry or government to police the goods or services provided in the broad marketplace, and in order to protect the "consumer," groups and associations have in recent years proliferated, in a concerted effort to foster the interests of consumers as opposed to those of businessmen. Such efforts include independent testing services, the proliferation of malpractice lawsuits, lobbying for truth in advertising, popular magazines and radio and TV programs devoted to the topic of "better business," and other similar public-interest groups.

These developments have led to a significant change in the way business is carried out. Whereas in the past the philosophy of *caveat emptor* ("let the buyer beware") served to insulate the "seller" from responsibility for goods sold or services provided, the current emphasis on consumer protection seems to have tilted the scale in the opposite direction. As a result advertising is more carefully monitored, the number of lawsuits, and monetary awards therefrom, have mushroomed, disclosure of product information has accelerated, and there are widespread efforts to educate the public to these issues.

Yet there is another side to this issue. While everyone is, as a matter of preference, in favor of truth and high quality, at what cost are these to be achieved? What if demands for ever better quality control result in ever higher costs to the consumer? What if the costs of malpractice awards result in significantly higher costs to the consumer himself, or even a cutback in desired goods or services because of high insurance premiums?

But even assuming that the vendor or manufacturer is indeed responsible for the quality and reliability of all goods and services that he provides, very practical questions still remain: Where precisely does the responsibility of the manufacturer or merchandiser end, and that of the purchaser or patient/client begin? How much are they duty-bound to disclose? What kind of advertising is to be considered misleading? When can they assume that the buying public is sufficiently informed as to the quality or risks involved in the product? What responsibility must the purchaser bear in ascertaining these facts?

But our question can be put in even broader, and more inclusive, terms. In the larger picture of financial transactions, what is the lowest level of disclosure that is to be considered proper? When must analysts, executives, or Wall Street traders and insiders properly divulge information that might cause loss to others? Such considerations of honesty, integrity, and good faith have always been matters of concern, but in recent years they have become even more pronounced, given the violations and fraudulent activities that have come to light. Yet there are opposing considerations that enter into the moral calculus, in that the modern entrepreneurial business model is built on privileged information and at times concealment of value or intent. Where is the line to be drawn?

The issue, it need hardly be said, reaches beyond the world of business. Honesty and integrity are the sine qua non of societal well-being. And everyone pays lip service to these virtues as morally axiomatic and fundamental. Yet even here it is necessary to clarify what precisely constitutes deception or misrepresentation. What if, as a result of one person's misrepresentation, others are not materially harmed? What of students who engage in questionable behavior to improve their grades? Or of people who create social facades so as to benefit themselves in the eyes of others?

On all of these issues the Halakhah contains important ethical and moral principles and concepts that attempt to balance all of these competing claims and considerations, in a manner that combines abstract principles and practical implementation, without losing sight of the realities "on the ground." It is to an examination of some of these fundamental halakhic parameters that the present chapter is devoted.

The Question

The widow of a lung cancer victim sues for damages from the manufacturer of the cigarettes which the victim smoked for over forty years. She claims that even though the company through its research was aware of the health dangers of its product, it failed to provide adequate warning to its customers as to the medical risks involved (until forced to do so by law, at a relatively late juncture). Furthermore, she contends that the company misled the public by advertising that indirectly suggested that it was safe to smoke.

The tobacco company in turn argues that the victim had chosen to continue to smoke despite awareness of the risks, because he enjoyed smoking. In addition it is its contention that the company was not obliged to fully reveal all the results of its own research into the nature of smoking, insofar as its customers are themselves responsible to determine the safety and effects of the products they purchase. In advertising its products, the company claims, it simply attempted to present them in their most favorable light.

Is the company guilty of improper and misleading promotional activities? Did the customer bear any responsibility to establish for himself the dangers of the product purchased?

The following issues are raised in this situation:

1. According to the Halakhah, what is the nature of the prohibition to misrepresent oneself or one's product, and is it forbidden to mislead another party, even where there is no financial loss involved?
2. Are there any circumstances under which the seller or provider is not required to make full divulgence of pertinent facts? Put differently, what responsibilities must a purchaser

or consumer bear in determining the value, the condition, or the risks of the goods or services that are purchased?

3. What are the limits of legitimate promotional and advertising activity, and according to the Halakhah, what kind of claims or statements can be considered to be misleading and improper?

Sources

A. Leviticus 19:11

Ye shall not steal, neither shall a man deal falsely, nor lie to his fellow.

B. Leviticus 19:36

Just balances, just weights, a just ephah, and a just *hin* shall ye have: I am the Lord your God, who brought you out of the land of Egypt.

C. Leviticus 25:17

And ye shall not wrong [*lo tonu*] one another; but thou shalt fear thy God; for I am the Lord your God.

D. Numbers 32:22

And you shall be guiltless [*nekiyyim*] before the Lord and before Israel.

E. Mekhilta, Mishpatim, chap. 13; Tosefta, Bava Kamma 7:3

There are seven categories of fraud [*ganavim*]: the first among them is one who misrepresents himself to others [*gonev da'at ha-beriyot*], one who insincerely invites another to his home, one who plies another with gifts that he knows he will not accept, one who impresses his guest by opening a barrel of wine that is already sold to a vendor, one who has improper measures, one who lies regarding his weights, one who adulterates his merchandise. . . . Whence do we know that misrepresentation is a form of stealing? Because it says, "so Absalom stole the hearts of the men of Israel" [II Sam. 15:6].

F. Mishnah, Bava Meẓia 4:12 (58b)

Just as there is unfair advantage [*ona'ah*] in pricing, so is there unfair verbal exploitation [*ona'at devarim*]. Thus one should not say "how much is this item" when one has no intention of purchasing it.

G. Bava Meẓia 60a–b

Mishnah: R. Judah said: A shopkeeper must not distribute parched corn or nuts to children, because he thereby accustoms them to come to him. The sages permit it. [And R. Judah said:] Nor may he reduce the price. But the sages say such a practice is to be commended. One must not sift pounded beans [to remove the refuse]. This is the view of Abba Saul. But the sages permit it. Yet they admit that he must not pick out the refuse only from the top of the bin, because such activities are like engaging in deceptive appearances. Men, cattle, and utensils may not be painted.

Gemara: The sages have taught: An animal may not be given an appearance of stiffness, entrails may not be inflated, nor may meat be soaked in water. What is meant by "an appearance of stiffness"? Here, in Babylon, it is explained as referring to bran broth [which bloats the animals fed on it]. Ze'iri said in R. Kahana's name: brushing up an animal's hair [to make it look more valuable]. Samuel permitted fringes to be put on a cloak. R. Judah permitted a gloss to be put on fine cloths. Rabbah permitted hemp cloths to be beaten [to appear of finer texture]. Rava permitted arrows to be painted. R. Pappa permitted baskets to be painted. But doesn't our Mishnah say that men, cattle, and utensils may not be painted? The answer is that painting new utensils is permitted, whereas old ones [to make them appear new] is forbidden.

What is the purpose of painting men? It is like the case of the aged slave who dyed his hair and beard. He came before Raba and said, "Buy me." [He refused.] So he went to R. Papa b. Samuel, who bought him. One day he said to him, "Give me some water to drink." Thereupon he went, washed his head and beard white again, and said, "See, I am older than your father [and you should not order me to do such things]!"

H. Bava Meẓia 49a

Where a verbal agreement is reached [and subsequently the price fluctuates, leading one party to revoke the terms as agreed to], it is the view of Rav that this does not constitute improper reneging [*meḥusrei amanah*]. R. Yoḥanan says that this is improper reneging.

The following statement contradicts Rav: R. Yossi b. Judah asked why in (B) does the verse include the requirement of a just *hin* in addition to the requirement of a just *eifah*, when a *hin* is one sixth of an *eifah*? It must refer to the requirement that one's *hain* ["yes"] and one's *lav* ["no"]—i.e., one's word—should be righteous (*Rashi:* live up to your word, and justify it).

Abbaye answers for Rav as follows: This statement forbids only the practice of saying one thing while intending another (*Rashi:* at the time he makes his verbal commitment he should not intend to change the terms, but this does not address the situation where the prices subsequently change).

I. Ḥullin 94a

Samuel has stated that it is forbidden to deceive anyone—even an idolater. And although Samuel never actually made this statement, it can be deduced from his actions. For it once happened that he used a ferry, and instructed Shemaya to pay the Gentile ferryman, but subsequently Samuel rebuked Shemaya. Why was he angry? Abbaye said that it was because Shemaya paid him with an unkosher chicken, which the ferryman presumed to be kosher. Rava said he was angry because he told Shemaya to pay him with [undiluted] wine, whereas he gave diluted wine (*Rashi:* and the ferryman thought it to be undiluted).

R. Meir would say: One should not repeatedly invite one's fellow to one's home knowing full well that he will refuse (*Rashi:* in so doing one receives the undeserved appreciation of the invitee who thinks that one genuinely expects him to accept the invitation). Likewise one should not ply another with gifts knowing full well that they will not be accepted. One should also not honor a guest by opening a new barrel of wine that was already sold to a vendor unless he informs him that it is already sold [in that the guest mistakenly believes that his host has on his account risked a financial loss, given that an open barrel of wine might spoil until such time as a vendor comes along to purchase it]. And if one knows that a person will not accept the offer, one should not present him with an empty container of oil, unless the effect is to bring public honor to the one so approached.

How is this possible—did it not happen that Ulla once visited with R. Judah, who opened a new barrel of wine for him, one that was already sold? There are two answers: either R. Judah so informed him, or even if he did not it was because Ulla was so beloved of R. Judah that even were it not already sold he would have opened the barrel for him.

. . . The sages have taught: a person should not sell shoes of leather from an animal that died of natural causes on the pretense that the leather is from a healthy animal that was slaughtered, for two reasons: because he is deceived, and because it might be dangerous (*Rashi:* perhaps it died of a snakebite, and the leather is poisonous).

. . . For two reasons they said one should not sell unkosher meat to an idolater: firstly because he is thereby deceived, and secondly because he may resell it to another Jew.

J. Ḥullin 94b

How is the public pronouncement [that nonkosher meat has been sold to a Gentile] formulated [to prevent Jews from purchasing it in error]? Said R. Isaac b. Joseph: "It is formulated to say, 'Meat has been sold to Gentiles.' " Why do we not say, "Nonkosher meat has been sold to a Gentile"? Because then the Gentiles will not buy it at all (*Rashi:* they will not want to be shamed by purchasing meat that the Jews do not want). But by not so identifying it as nonkosher, are we not misleading them? The answer is that really they are misleading themselves.

It is similar to the case where Mar Zutra b. Naḥman was once going from Sikara to Maḥoza, while Rava and R. Safra were going to Sikara, and they met on the way. Believing that they had come to meet him, Mar Zutra said: "Why did you take this trouble to come so far to meet me?" R. Safra replied: "We did not know that the master was coming; had we known it we would have put ourselves out even more than this." [Later] Rava said to R. Safra: "Why did you say that, you upset him." Said R. Safra: "We would be deceiving him otherwise." "No," said Rava, "he would be deceiving himself."

K. Pesaḥim 13a

It is stated in a Beraita: where collectors of brass coins for charity have no poor people on hand to whom to distribute the coins, and they must consequently exchange them for silver ones [that do not corrode as easily], they should not use their own silver coins, but those of others. Likewise those who collect food for the poor, and having no poor on hand must sell the food, should not buy the food themselves (*Rashi:* because people might suspect them of paying less than the market price), as it is said (D) "and you shall be guiltless."

L. Maimonides, M. T. Hil. De'ot 2:6

It is forbidden to accustom oneself to smooth speech and flatteries. One must not say one thing and mean another. Inward and outward self should correspond; only what we have in mind should we utter with the mouth. We must deceive no one, not even an idolater. A man, for example, must not do the following: [as in (I)]. . . . Even a single word of flattery or deception is forbidden. A person should always cherish truthful speech, an upright spirit, and a pure heart freed of all pretense and cunning.

M. Maimonides, M. T. Hil. Mekhirah 18:1–4

It is forbidden to mislead [*le'ramot*] people in business or to deceive them [*lignov et da'atam*]. This is equally true whether it involves Gentiles or Jews. Thus when one knows that there is some defect in one's merchandise, one must so inform the purchaser. And it is even forbidden to deceive people in words only.

One may not display old persons, animals, or vessels that are for sale so that they appear young or new. But one may display new ones by polishing, ironing, or beautifying them all they require.

One should not feed a man bran broth or the like to fatten him and thus make his face appear robust; nor should one paint his face with red clay. One should not inflate animal intestines nor soak meat in water. All similar acts are likewise forbidden. One must not sell to a Gentile meat of an animal not slaughtered according to ritual law under the impression that it is meat from an animal slaughtered according to ritual law, though to the heathen the two are the same.

It is permitted to sift pounded beans—but not when the sifting is only at the top of the bin, because the latter serves to deceive the eye into thinking that the whole container is similarly sifted. And a storekeeper may distribute parched corn or nuts to children and maid-servants to accustom them to frequent his store. And he may reduce the price to increase his customer share. And his competitors cannot prevent this, for it does not constitute deception.

N. Rabbeinu Yonah, Sha'arei Teshuvah 3:184

The seventh category [of liars] consists of those who deceive their neighbor by telling him that they have done him a favor or spoken well of him, when in reality they have not done so. Our sages of blessed memory have said, "it is forbidden to deceive others, even Gentiles." The sages of Israel account this sin as more severe than that of robbing a Gentile, because lying lips bear great guilt. We are obliged to remain within, and uphold, the bounds of the truth, because it is one of the foundations of the soul.

O. Tur H.M. 228

Just as it is forbidden to defraud, so it is forbidden to deceive. And deception is a greater transgression than fraud, for the proceeds of fraud can be returned, whereas deception cannot; fraud affects one's possessions, whereas deception affects one's self. . . . It is likewise forbidden to deceive another by making it appear that one acts to his benefit when that is not the case. . . . thus one should not open barrels for one's guest that are already sold, without informing the guest that he does not open them only for him. . . . But this is not the case where it should occur to the other party that this act was not done only for him—in such a case he deceives himself, and one does not have to correct him, e.g., where one meets another en route, and he thinks one has come to meet him.

Discussion

1. PROHIBITIONS INVOLVED IN MISREPRESENTATION BY THE SELLER

Elsewhere we have examined the question whether it is permissible to avoid the truth and even speak an outright lie where the intent is to benefit the person so deceived.[1] Our conclusion was that according to the Halakhah such deception is indeed sometimes permitted. Our present concern is to clarify what precisely is involved in deceptive behavior intended to benefit oneself, in a variety of settings, including business and career advancement.

Where anyone has recourse to an outright lie or false statement, it is quite clear that such behavior is forbidden under the rubric of the biblical exhortation to "keep thee far from a false matter" (Exod. 23:7). But the question is whether this verse applies as well to statements that carefully avoid or conceal the truth. For certain statements can be technically true even while they misrepresent the reality of a situation.

Similarly it is unclear precisely what is involved in deception or misrepresentation that does not cause financial loss for the other party. In other words, while the various prohibitions against stealing (A) or fraudulent behavior of various kinds seem clear enough, it still remains to be clarified whether it is permissible under any circumstances to misrepresent the quality or condition of goods or services, even if the other party receives full value for its money.

---

1. See *Jewish Ethics and Halakhah*, vol. 1, chap. 2, addressed to the question of confronting dying patients with the truth as to their condition. Some recent general halakhic analyses of the topic include Rabbi M. Dratch, "Nothing But the Truth," *Judaism* 37, no. 2 (Spring 1988): 218–229, and Rabbi Gary Lavit, "Truth Telling to Patients with Terminal Diagnoses," *Journal of Halakhah and Contemporary Society* 15 (Spring 1988): 94–125.

Ona'ah

In examining these questions, we can deal first with the prohibition of *ona'ah*, or "exploitation." The prohibition derives from the passage in Leviticus (C) that forbids "wronging one another" (*lo tonu*). As understood by the oral tradition, this prohibition takes two forms. The first involves unjust enrichment in regard to the price paid for goods or services, whether from the point of view of the seller (setting too high a price) or from that of the purchaser (where the price is unconscionably low). Such practices violate the prohibition against brazen stealing (*gezel*), even though not force but a business transaction is involved.[2] Thus a significant body of halakhic discussion and law is devoted to the various aspects of pricing policy, and means of redress on either side.[3]

But the prohibition of *ona'ah* exploitation goes beyond considerations solely of profit margins. Even if the other party receives full value for monies paid, it remains necessary that the seller provide proper disclosure as to the nature of the goods or services provided. As Rabbi Eliav Shoḥatman puts it, the moment one party conceals from the other the precise quality and character of the goods, or by his words and actions creates the impression that they possess a superior quality which they in fact do not have, then the prohibition of *ona'ah* is triggered.

What precisely is involved? The Mishnah in *Bava Meẓia* (F) delineates both kinds of *ona'ah*, referring to the latter as *ona'at devarim*, or verbal exploitation. One example offered by the Mishnah is that of a person who has no intention of purchasing an item from a particular vendor, yet nonetheless inquires as to the sale price involved. Here, as the fourteenth-century R. Menaḥem Meiri points out, what is involved is an insensitivity to the feelings of the vendor, whose emotions are needlessly manipulated in the expectation—and then disappointment at the loss—of a successful sale.[4] Of course where there is a genuine interest on the part

2. See E. Shoḥatman, "Haganat Ẓarkhan Mipnei Te'ur Kozev be'Halakhah," *Dine Israel* 3 (5732): 227–228.

3. See *Encyclopedia Talmudit* 1:328–343. A most comprehensive discussion of the implications of this principle for modern-day economic systems is to be found in I. Warhaftig, "Haganat ha-Ẓarkhan le'Or ha-Halakhah," *Teḥumin* 2 (5741): 444–488.

4. *Beit ha-Beḥirah*, *Bava Meẓia* 59a.

of the customer to price the article, so as to purchase it if the price is suitable, such an inquiry would be entirely permissible.[5] A second instance in this Mishnah involving economic activity occurs when a person directs a potential customer to a third party, knowing full well that the third party does not deal in such merchandise. Such advice is forbidden, according to R. Joseph Karo, because it will likely compromise the dignity of either the customer or the third party—a blatant case of emotional insensitivity.[6] These instances of *ona'at devarim* are equated in the Mishnah with similar noncommercial circumstances,[7] all of them sharing the characteristic of needless emotional pain inflicted on another human being. As R. Shneur Zalman of Liadi (the eighteenth century author of the *Shulḥan Arukh ha-Rav*) put it, such activities are a source of genuine heartache (*ẓa'ar ha-lev*) to the other party—and are thus forbidden.[8]

A rather revolutionary explanation of the principle of *ona'at devarim* has been suggested by Rabbi J. David Bleich.[9] Rather than the rationale of *ona'at devarim* as inflicting shame or emotional pain, Rabbi Bleich believes that the prohibition should be understood as forbidding behavior that shows disrespect for another, and deprives him of his essential honor and dignity, irrespective of how that other person actually feels. In other words it is not the feelings of the injured party, but rather the insensitivity of the sinner, that is the operative factor. If, for instance, the other party was not even aware of the disrespect intended and hence felt no pain whatsoever, even so, says Rabbi Bleich, *ona'at devarim* is committed. While this explanation is based on a careful analysis of Tosafot and Maimonides, it has little explicit

5. Rabbi A. Levine, *Economics and Jewish Law* (New York, 1987), pp. 8–9 (hereafter cited as *Economics*), concludes from this that consumers who deliberately use the showroom and sales personnel of nondiscount stores in order to select the merchandise that they intend to purchase at a discount store are in flagrant contravention of the biblical prohibition of *ona'ah*. See the same author's treatment of this matter in his *Free Enterprise and Jewish Law* (New York, 1980), pp. 119–120 (hereafter cited as *Free Enterprise*).

6. *Kesef Mishnah* to Maimonides, *M.T. Hil. Mekhirah* 14:12.

7. Other prohibited behaviors listed by this Gemara include references to another's sinful past, raising the matter of a convert's Gentile past, any attempt to justify another's sufferings by imputing that they must be deserved, or referring a questioner to a third party whom one knows to be unable to provide an answer.

8. *Shulḥan Arukh ha-Rav, Hil. Ona'ah u-Geneivat Da'at* 27, 28.

9. *ha-Darom* 35 (Nissan 5733): 140–143.

precedent in halakhic literature, and seems to be contradicted by the above authorities.

The gravity with which the sages viewed this transgression is demonstrated by the fact that while behavior involving *ona'at devarim* is not punishable by the statutory lashes given for a negative commandment (being a transgression of a merely verbal nature), the Gemara here considers it to be even more reprehensible than instances of financial exploitation. For unlike the latter, the emotional trauma of the former cannot be fully undone. In addition, the perpetrator's intention cannot be easily uncovered or proven (hence the verse refers to the fear of God as the primary motivating factor).[10] And, according to Naḥmanides, even though the purchaser may have paid no more than the actual value of what he received, still he can claim that the transaction was conducted under false pretenses, not having received what was contracted for, and be allowed to void the sale altogether.[11]

Subsequent authorities extended the list of *ona'ah* prohibitions: needlessly hurtful criticism, cursing another to his face, the use of shameful nicknames even though the person so named be accustomed to them, and even inflicting an *ayin ha-ra*, or "evil eye."[12] And several early authorities (notably R. Eliezer of Metz and the *Sefer ha-Ḥinukh*) permitted an individual who is thus abused to respond vigorously so as to avoid debasement—but to remain at all times dignified and respectful, "for it is permitted to answer a fool, just as the Torah permits one to kill someone who breaks into one's property before being killed oneself, for there is no doubt that a person is not obliged to suffer at the hand of another, but can rather save oneself."[13]

Geneivat Da'at

In addition to *ona'ah*, there is an even more inclusive prohibition involved in misrepresentation, and it is that referred to in the

10. *Bava Mezia* 58b and Maimonides, *M.T. Hil. Mekhirah* 14:18. Rabbi Zalman Halevi Uri, *ha-Pardes*, 35:5, pp. 21–22, has argued that verbal abuse is a lesser infraction than others because it is "merely" verbal, and hence requires no confession on Yom Kippur. But while the absence of lashes is clearly because of the exclusively oral nature of the transgression, this characteristic by itself does not appear to vitiate the need for divine forgiveness.

11. *Naḥmanides' Commentary to the Torah*, Lev. 25:15. See I. Warhaftig, "Haganat ha-Zarkhan le'Or ha-Halakhah," pt. II, *Teḥumin* 3 (5742): 356.

12. See the sources quoted in the *Encyclopedia Talmudit* 1:344.

13. *Sefer Yerayim ha-Shalem* 180; *Sefer ha-Ḥinukh* 338.

expression *geneivat da'at*, literally "stealing another's mind." Under the rubric of this prohibition, it is forbidden to engage in any activity that misrepresents any fact or situation to the mind of another person, Jew or Gentile. The Midrash *Mekhilta*, as well as the Tosefta (E), lists seven categories of theft, and the very first of them is the one by which a person steals the mind of another via misrepresentation—and it goes on to specify several commonly encountered behaviors that do just that. Such illicit activity is described by these early sources not as stealing the mind, but as stealing the heart (in reference to a phrase describing the devious actions of Absalom). But the difference in phraseology is inconsequential. What is forbidden by the term *geneivat da'at* is the very act of concealing the truth to the detriment of another person. The definitive formulation of the prohibition of *geneivat da'at* is that of Samuel, who said (I), "it is forbidden to deceive anyone—even an idolater."

What is the source of the prohibition? According to the Ritva, quoting "certain sages in the name of the Tosafot," it is of biblical origin, and included in the Levitical verse "ye shall not steal, neither shall a man deal falsely, nor lie to his fellow" (A). He explains that the verse prohibiting stealing is intentionally nonspecific, so as to incorporate all forms of stealing, including purloining the mind.[14] Ritva, in referring to Tosafot, is in all likelihood referring to the above-mentioned R. Eliezer of Metz, author of the *Sefer Yerayim ha-Shalem*, who in that work also derives this principle from (A), as do several additional early authorities.[15] A different biblical source is identified by Rabbeinu Yonah of Gerondi (N), in that he perceives *geneivat da'at* to be entirely subsumed under the category of lying. Yet others, notably the *Sefer Miẓvot Katan*, R. Joel Sirkes (the Baḥ), and R. Shneur Zalman of Liadi, see no biblical source or dimension at all, but rather a prohibition of purely rabbinic provenance.[16] As for Maimonides' position on this question, R. Menaḥem Krakowski, author of the *Avodat ha-Melekh*, is of the view that he too considered it merely rabbinic, in that Maimonides omits any

14. *Novellae of the Ritva, Ḥullin* 94a.

15. *Sefer Yerayim ha-Shalem* 124; *Sefer Miẓvot Gadol* (R. Moses of Coucy), Neg. 155; *Kiryat Sefer* (Mabit) to *M.T. Hil. Mekhirah* 18.

16. *Sefer Miẓvot Katan* 261; Baḥ to *Y.D. H.M.* 228; *Shulḥan Arukh ha-Rav, Hil. Ona'ah u-Geneivat Da'at* 12 ("*mi-divrei sofrim*").

mention of such a biblical prohibition in enumerating the commandments in the *Sefer ha-Miẓvot*.[17] It should be noted, however, as we will see below, that Maimonides does mention a prohibition against *geneivat da'at* in the context of the prohibition against the *me'onen*.[18]

Notable in this regard is the inclusive nature of Samuel's formulation, in that even idolaters must not be the victims of Jewish deception (I). The Ritva finds support for such broad inclusion in the very verse in Leviticus (A). As he explains, while a superficial reading of the verse seems to restrict the prohibition of *geneivah* to actions against one's "fellow," i.e., one's fellow Jew, in fact the limiting phrase "to his fellow" (*ba-amito*) qualifies only the latter half of the verse, i.e., dealing falsely or lying—but not stealing. This is so, says the Ritva, for two reasons: (a) the prefix *ba* ("to") cannot be used in conjunction with stealing (*tignovu*); (b) the authoritative rabbinic cantillation notation places a break (*etnaḥta*) under *tignovu* ("stealing") as if to separate it from what follows. Consequently the prohibition against *geneivah* or stealing, unlike the rest of the verse, is not restricted to deceiving a fellow Jew, but prohibits deceiving a Gentile as well. And the Ritva goes one step further than his teachers Naḥmanides and the Rashba when he states that from Samuel one should conclude that the prohibition also applies when giving a Gentile an outright gift—even then absolute candor is required.

Now there are two primary talmudic texts that detail what is, and is not, forbidden in *geneivat da'at*. The first of these occurs in *Ḥullin* 94a (I) in discussing Samuel's aphorism. Samuel himself, according to the Gemara, disapproved of Shemaya's misleading a Gentile ferryman, even though there was no blatant deception (payment in the form of nonkosher chicken instead of kosher; wine diluted in accordance with common practice). And in the name of R. Meir the Gemara goes on to forbid a variety of similar actions: repeatedly inviting a guest in the full knowledge that he will not accept the invitation; offering a gift knowing it will not be accepted; opening a large container of food for a guest to give the mistaken impression that the uneaten balance will constitute a significant financial loss.[19]

17. *Avodat ha-Melekh* to Maimonides, *M.T. Hil. Deot* 2:6.
18. Maimonides, *Sefer ha-Miẓvot*, Negative 32, and see below.
19. It should be noted that the Gemara qualifies these rules by adding that they

Further notable cases of improper deception involve the sale of leather shoes where the purchaser is not informed that the leather is from an animal that had succumbed to natural causes. For even though there is no prohibition against such leather, still the customer is marginally misled, and might have avoided the purchase on the grounds that the animal skin was diseased or poisoned. And likewise it is improper to sell unkosher meat to a Gentile who believes that it is kosher, for even though it should not really make any difference to him, and he pays no more for it than for any nonkosher meat,[20] it is nonetheless morally wrong, in that he may have his own reasons for preferring kosher meat. Hence he should not be deceived into thinking that this vendor benefits him in this fashion.[21]

Similarly R. Isaac Bar Sheshet Perfet (the Rivash) forbade a Jew to sell a Gentile meat from a healthy animal that had been improperly slaughtered, without properly informing the purchaser, so as not to receive unearned gratitude.[22] These examples are quoted and approved by all subsequent codifiers.[23] A similar example of illicit *geneivat da'at* is proffered in the Jerusalem Talmud when a person is forbidden to bring a gift of wine to a house of mourning in a bottle made of colored glass, giving the impression that it is wine of greater value than it is in fact.[24]

The second passage is found in *Bava Meẓia* (G). The Mishnah specifies that one who wishes to sell his slaves, cattle, or utensils may not paint or disguise them so as to make them appear better than they in fact are. In discussing this statement, the Gemara records a number of complementary views, all of which serve to reinforce and provide specific application to this principle: including artificially stuffing, inflating, or fattening animals by feeding or grooming them to give a temporary appearance that

---

may be suspended where the effect is to bring public honor and recognition to the one so treated, or where in fact such treatment reflects a genuine desire to honor him. See the many sources referred to in *Encyclopedia Talmudit* 6:229.

20. Baḥ to *Sh.A. H.M.* 228:6.

21. See Warhaftig, "Ẓarkhan," pt. II, p. 357, n. 134. For a discussion of the rest of this talmudic passage, see below.

22. *Responsa Rivash* 403. See *Encyclopedia Talmudit* 6:226, n. 23.

23. Maimonides, *M.T. Hil. Deot 2:6, Hil. Mekhirah* 18:3; Rosh to *Ḥullin* 7:18; *Tur H.M.* 228:6; *Sh.A. H.M.* 228:6; *Shulḥan Arukh ha-Rav, Hil. Ona'ah* 12; *Arukh ha-Shulḥan, H.M.* 228:3.

24. J.T. *Demai* 4:3, as explained in the comments of R. Elijah of Vilna and the *Pnei Moshe*.

belies their true condition. The Gemara then goes on to list a number of vendor activities that are permissible, even though they change the appearance of the merchandise: fringes on a garment, polishing or rubbing textiles, and even repainting hardware. But does this latter case not contradict the Mishnah that forbids painting an item that is for sale as a deceptive practice? The Gemara answers that what is forbidden is the dressing of old items to appear new; whereas it is permitted to freshen new, unused items so as to give them their finest appearance. This passage was regarded as normative by Maimonides, the *Shulḥan Arukh*, and other codifiers.[25]

The *Shulḥan Arukh* likewise forbids a vendor to mix fruits or vegetables so as to disguise the true condition of some of them—whether it be a minority that are of lower grade among a majority of higher grade, or even to include some higher-grade older specimens in a lower-grade group that is fresh, for perhaps the purchaser wishes to keep his purchase over a longer period, and the higher grade will spoil.[26] The general rule, as expressed by Hai Gaon, is that a vendor may not intentionally conceal the true quality of his merchandise, but he may so display it that its best qualities are most favorably projected.[27] (Later, in section 2, we will take up the question whether a vendor has any responsibility to correct a purchaser's misconceptions, as well as the issue of which facts he may or may not assume to be "known" to the consumer.)

These two talmudic passages formed the basis for the larger application of the principle of *geneivat da'at* as it might apply across the board.

What kinds of activity are included in the prohibition? In its broadest formulation, what *geneivat da'at* forbids is any attempt to foster or allow an impression that one is acting so as to benefit another person when such benefits are either absent or unintended.[28] Among early authorities, several classic formulations of the prohibition are encountered. Maimonides for one, in his

---

25. Maimonides, *M.T. Hil. Mekhirah* 18:2; *Tur/Sh.A. H.M.* 228:9; *Sh.A. ha-Rav, Hil. Ona'ah* 18. See similar practices in the Tosefta *Bava Meẓia* 3:12.

26. *Tur/Sh.A. H.M.* 228:10.

27. Hai Gaon, *Sefer ha-Mekaḥ ve'ha-Memkar* 59:14. See the summary in Shoḥatman, pp. 230–232.

28. *Encyclopedia Talmudit* 6:225.

Mishneh Torah (L), after quoting these talmudic passages, goes on to forbid all flattering speech, any inconsistency between sentiments that are spoken and those uttered, and any action that diminishes "truthful speech, an upright spirit, and a pure heart freed of all pretense and cunning." Moreover, he says, it makes no difference whether the addressee is Jew or Gentile. And Rabbeinu Yonah of Gerondi (N) includes any behavior by which one allows the impression that one has done a neighbor a favor, or spoken well of him, when in fact this has not been the case. He likewise extends the prohibition to Gentiles, and adds that this sin is even worse, and bears greater guilt, than robbery, in that truth is one of the "foundations of the soul." In other words, it is not only injury to the other party that is of concern, but also damage to the deceiver himself, whose soul is compromised. Similar sentiments are put forth by R. Judah he-Ḥasid in the *Sefer Ḥasidim* in forbidding anything less than the truth. He specifically forbids a Jew to secretly curse a Gentile when he greets him while pretending otherwise (as he puts it, "for there is no deception greater than this"), and he also excoriates those who show external signs of piety to impress others, knowing full well, as they do, that their spirituality is less than appearances would suggest.[29] These demands for absolute truthfulness do not, however, prevent the *Sefer Ḥasidim* from permitting a righteous man (he refers to a *ẓaddik*) to purchase a Torah scroll or some other religious item from a corrupt person (referred to as a *rasha*), using subterfuge so as to acquire it from him.[30] Apparently such deception is warranted in that it is not intended to benefit the purchaser personally, but rather to safeguard the honor or safety of the religious item itself.[31]

Such formulations of the prohibition of *geneivat da'at* were subsequently applied in concrete fashion by these and later authorities. We can examine three such areas.

---

29. *Sefer Ḥasidim* 51, 7.
30. This is quoted in the *Da'at Zekeinim mi-Ba'alei ha-Tosafot* to Gen. 25:34.
31. In referring to this quotation, Levine (*Economics*, p. 21) understands it as permitting one to pay less than the commercial fair market value for such religious items, and Levine consequently has difficulty understanding such a ruling. But the text does not speak of a price below market value, it merely permits deceptive means to ensure that the item is transferred to more honorable ownership. It is quite possible that *Sefer Ḥasidim* does, even under these circumstances, require payment of full market value.

Sleight of hand. In his *Sefer ha-Miẓvot*,[32] Maimonides refers to
the scriptural prohibition against the *me'onen* (Lev. 19:26, Deut.
18:10) and takes it refer to two practices: one is astrological
speculation devoted to giving practical advice, and the other is
the practice of "beguiling the eyes" (*ha-oḥez et ha-einayim*).[33] In
the latter sense, *me'onen* is etymologically related to *ayin*, or
"eye" (in the former sense it is related to *onah*, or "time period/
phase"). Maimonides explains that this latter group includes
practitioners of sleight of hand, who through manual dexterity
lead people to believe that they have performed magic, whereas in
fact they merely deceive them (the examples he gives are ropes
allegedly transformed into snakes, and coins that seem to disap-
pear into thin air and then reappear). Such a person, says Maimonides, in contravening the prohibition of *me'onen*, is guilty of
geneivat da'at ha-beriyot, i.e., deceiving his fellow men. By thus
extending the principle of *geneivat da'at*, Maimonides takes this
principle far beyond the merely commercial sphere.

This view of Maimonides was reinforced by one of his descendants, known as R. Joshua b. Abraham Maimoni ha-Nagid, a
leader of Egyptian Jewry in the fourteenth century.[34] In answering a question regarding an apparent inconsistency in the *Mishneh Torah*, R. Joshua discusses the Maimonidean view of the
me'onen. Maimonides in the *Mishneh Torah* writes that any
person who "beguiles the eyes" (*ha-oḥez et ha-einayim*) is considered a *me'onen* who is punished with the biblical lashes.[35] R.
Joshua defines this act of beguiling by referring to the Arabic
term *al-no'argi*,[36] which probably refers to the medieval doctrine
(associated with the Moslem Avicenna and with Ibn Ezra) by
which certain men claim to be able to perform miracles and
unnatural feats through the interaction of their souls with higher

---

32. *Sefer ha-Miẓvot*, Neg. 32.
33. For a good summary of the various definitions of the concept of *aḥizat einayim*, see the entry in the *Encyclopedia Talmudit* 1:460–463.
34. See "Teshuvot ha-Rav Yehoshua ha-Nagid," *Kobeẓ al Yad* (5700): 85–86. The responsum is also mentioned in the *Kesef Mishnah* to M.T. *Hil. Avodah Zarah* 11:15.
35. M.T. *Hil. Avodah Zarah* 11:9.
36. Interestingly, this same term appears in the original Arabic text of the *Sefer ha-Miẓvot* quoted above, as the act that is prohibited under the rubric of *me'onen*. See the *Sefer ha-Miẓvot*, ed. R. Ḥayyim Heller, loc. cit., n. 23.

supernatural forces.[37] It is clear from the *Sefer ha-Mizvot* that Maimonides himself considers all such acts to be pure deception, without any real spiritual substance or standing, and he nowhere accepts the Avicennian doctrine as true.[38] R. Joshua then goes on to refer to the Mishnah and Gemara in *Sanhedrin* 67a that speak of witchcraft (*kishuf*) as opposed to beguiling (*ha-oḥez et ha-einayim*). He also quotes Maimonides' own nonextant commentary to *Sanhedrin*, in which witchcraft is punishable by death, while beguilement is that in which "a person makes it appear that he has performed some outcome but in fact has done nothing." The punishment for the latter is lashes. Clearly, according to Maimonides, the actions of *me'onenim* are biblically prohibited, not because there is any reality to what they purport to show, but rather because it essentially violates the prohibition against *geneivat da'at*, being deceptive and misrepresentative of the truth. It is worthwhile noting that such a "naturalism" on the part of Maimonides is consistent with his overall opposition toward astrology, magic, and all similar recourse to supernaturalism. Thus it is to be expected that Maimonides would consider such practitioners to be charlatans, guilty in principle of pure deception.

In a lengthy responsum dealing with the subject, R. David b. Abu Zimra (the Radbaz) discussed Maimonides' approach.[39] Radbaz does indeed accept the possibility of real supernatural effects (as opposed to mere deception), and he takes issue emphatically with Maimonides' refusal to accept such a possibility. The very prohibition against sorcery, he argues, is proof positive that there is some reality to the claims of its practitioners. And the Torah would not punish with lashes the mere sleight of hand practiced in order to deceive. Nonetheless, he too recognizes that, besides the concern for illegitimate supernaturalism, part of the reason for the Torah's prohibition against the actions of the *me'onen* is indeed *geneivat da'at*.[40]

37. *Kobez al Yad*, n. 6, as stated by Prof. D. Z. Baneth. For a comprehensive treatment of this subject in medieval Jewish philosophy, see Aviezer Ravitsky, "The Anthropological Theory of Miracles in Medieval Jewish Philosophy," *Studies in Medieval Jewish History and Literature*, vol. 2, ed. I. Twersky (Cambridge, 1984), pp. 231–251, esp. n. 14.

38. Ravitsky, p. 241.

39. *Responsa Radbaz* 1695.

40. For a discussion of this responsum, and some of the problems it raises, see R. Ḥayyim Heller's comments to his edition of the *Sefer ha-Mizvot*, ad loc.

Self-evaluation in offsetting discrimination. The passage in *Ḥullin* 94a (I) includes, among the list of improper deceptive practices, the case of a host who opens a new barrel of wine for his guest without informing him that the balance of the barrel is already sold. The act is forbidden because the guest, believing that the remainder represents a real financial loss incurred on his behalf, is misled and unduly indebted to his host. The Gemara then records that R. Judah once entertained Ulla under such circumstances but did not so inform him, in spite of this disclosure requirement. The Gemara provides one answer to the effect that R. Judah did not have to inform him because R. Judah felt that he would have opened the barrel under any circumstances for his honored guest. In other words, a person is capable of judging his own motives in his dealings with others, so that he can legitimately behave in ways that under other circumstances would be deceptive.

Yet while Maimonides (L) and the *Tur* (O) both codify the prohibition against opening a wine barrel without such disclosure, neither of them includes this leniency that relies on honest self-evaluation. Why the omission? One answer is provided in the nineteenth century by R. Aryeh Judah b. Akiva.[41] He feels that Maimonides and the *Tur* consider R. Judah's character and ability to practice honest self-evaluation to be exceptional. It is simply not applicable to most people, who cannot be expected to demonstrate such moral fiber and objective self-knowledge, and are likely to confuse self-serving gestures with true selflessness. If the story of R. Judah and Ulla is included in the Gemara, it is merely to illustrate their moral greatness, but not in order to make such behavior universally permissible. Thus the law requires a host to disclose the prior sale of the wine. Indeed the Gemara itself provides a second explanation of R. Judah's behavior, saying that he did actually make full disclosure to his honored guest and correct any false impressions that he might have had.[42]

Yet in spite of the views of Maimonides and the *Tur*, later authorities seem to take a more lenient position, at least regarding self-evaluation to offset job discrimination. A case in point involves a man who wishes to gain employment in a particular

41. *Lev Aryeh*, *Ḥullin* 94a.
42. See the analysis of this question in Levine, *Economics*, pp. 23–24.

position and is certain that he is fully able to discharge all the duties involved. Yet he feels that he might encounter age discrimination on account of his graying beard, in that such beards generally give a man the appearance of being advanced in years. May this man, to offset such potential discrimination, dye his beard? More specifically, does the Halakhah consider him capable of honestly evaluating his ability to fulfill the job requirements, so that he does not improperly deceive his potential employer? Or do we say that he cannot be expected to show such high moral judgment concerning his own motivations, and therefore must present himself as he is, i.e., with full disclosure?

In the twentieth century several authorities considered this question. R. Moshe Mordecai Epstein of Slabodka considered an average man capable of objective self-evaluation as to his ability to perform a given job, and he thus gave permission to dye one's beard under such circumstances.[43] Similarly permissive is a responsum by R. Eliezer Meir Preil.[44] Both of these views are mentioned by Rabbi Moshe Feinstein, and he too concurs, permitting self-evaluation and the dying of one's beard under such circumstances.[45]

Rabbi Aaron Levine attempts to reconcile these latter views with the more stringent rulings of Maimonides, the *Tur*, and R. Aryeh.[46] In his opinion it all depends upon the situation: thus even Maimonides and the *Tur* can agree that self-assessment can be considered sufficiently reliable in ordinary, predictable life-situations, such as the ability to function on a given job on a day-to-day basis. This is not the case for circumstances that are extraordinary, in that most people cannot extrapolate with any degree of certainty how they would react to special or rare situations; in such cases even these modern authorities would concur with the more restrictive view, and require the fullest disclosure.

This discussion would appear to dovetail with the express position found in the Gemara in *Bava Meẓia* 60a–b (G). There the Mishnah forbids dying of a beard to give a mistaken impression of youthfulness, and the Gemara explains that such improper actions are sometimes carried out in marketing a slave, so

43. *Levush Mordecai* 24.
44. R. Eliezer Meir Preil, *ha-Maor* 1:26–27.
45. *Responsa Iggerot Moshe, Y.D.* 2:61.
46. Levine, *Economics*, p. 25.

as to give the appearance of youth. The Gemara illustrates the point by referring to R. Papa, who purchased an elderly slave, misled by his appearance, and subsequently was ill-served by him. Clearly what is forbidden is intentional misleading of the potential buyer, whose expectations will not be met. It does not, however, forbid honest self-evaluation as to one's ability, or readiness, to perform expected work, and then acting in good faith.

The written word: Publishing and academic liberties. In 1980, Rabbi Eliezer Waldenberg wrote a responsum to a young doctor who had inquired whether it is halakhically permissible to alter details of medical research when it comes to publication, so as to further the career of the author—without, however, endangering the life of others.[47]

Rabbi Waldenberg finds that such activity violates the prohibition against *geneivat da'at.* It makes no difference, he says, that the vast majority of the readers are Gentiles—and he refers to Maimonides' formulation of the prohibition (L). He also quotes Rabbeinu Yonah (N), who extends the prohibition to a concern beyond the intended audience to the effect on the inner life of the person responsible for an act of deception. Such reflexive concern, says Rabbi Waldenberg, is similar to Maimonides' novel interpretation of the prohibition against cursing another, i.e., not that the curse has some supernatural effect, but that it undermines the wholesome character of the curser.[48] This is certainly true of written material, in that any modification of the truth "uproots the parameters of truth from foundations of the soul." Thus any alteration in the data or presentation of such a paper violates *geneivat da'at.*

In addition, Rabbi Waldenberg considers such "tampering" to be prohibited under the rubric of the prohibition against lying ("keep thee far from a falsehood," Exod. 23:7). Based on another passage in Rabbeinu Yonah, he concludes that it is prohibited to "embellish the truth" to benefit oneself, even where it does not lead to financial loss for someone else. He further quotes the twentieth-century Ḥafeẓ Ḥayyim, who included under the rubric of forbidden lying, loose talk that takes liberties with truth in

47. *Responsa Ẓiẓ Eliezer* 15:12.

48. *Sefer ha-Miẓvot,* neg. 317. For further discussion of this aspect of Maimonides' philosophy, see my *Joseph Ibn Kaspi's "Gevia Kesef"* (New York, 1982), pp. 119 ff.

order to enhance the social standing of its speaker.[49] This, says Waldenberg, is essentially identical with the case of a researcher who publishes a "doctored" paper to advance his career. Moreover, hiding one's rationale in this fashion is quite analogous to the case of a man who faithfully reports events as they happened, but conceals his own motivation and intent for reasons of his own (he might get pleasure from keeping his own counsel.) This latter situation is prohibited by the *Sefer Yad ha-Ketanah*.[50]

There is, however, one early view that appears to differ with this negative conclusion. The *Sefer Yerayim* of R. Eliezer of Metz, quoted earlier, states that the lying that is prohibited refers to lying that causes damages to another person, "whereas falsehood that causes no injury to others is not forbidden by the Torah."[51] As explained by the To'afot Re'eim in commenting on this passage, this distinction serves to explain the well-known view of Beit Hillel, found in *Ketuvot* 17a, that it is permitted to lie in describing a bride at her wedding, just as one may falsely praise a friend's new purchase.[52] Beit Hillel apparently considers a lie forbidden only where it causes definite loss (financial or otherwise) or material misrepresentation, but not where it serves merely to set another's mind at rest. Beit Shammai, on the other hand, considers *any* lie *geneivat da'at*, constituting an act of forbidden deception. According to the *Sefer Yerayim*, therefore, if we accept Beit Hillel's view, it is permissible to tamper with nonessential information, if as a result there is no measurable harm to others.

Yet, as Rabbi Waldenberg points out, it is likely that even this minority view speaks only of the absence of a Torah prohibition. On a rabbinic level, as suggested by the To'afot Re'eim, such activity represents improper behavior.

A somewhat different, although essentially similar, question is posed by the common practice of students who cheat in one form or another, so as to inflate their grades, albeit without apparent "damage" to either their fellow students or their teachers. Is this too *geneivat da'at?*

---

49. *Sha'arei Teshuvah* 3:186, *Sefer Shemirat ha-Lashon*, chap. 6.
50. *Sefer Yad ha-Ketanah, Deot* 10:9, as quoted in *Ẓiẓ Eliezer* 15:12.
51. *Sefer Yerayim ha-Shalem* 235.
52. For a discussion of this Gemara and some of its ramifications, see *Jewish Ethics and Halakhah*, vol. 1, pp. 55–56.

R. Menasheh Klein was asked this question, and he answered that such actions are definitely forbidden.[53] Which prohibition is involved? It depends on the purpose of the studies undertaken. Where they are intended to be used to gain subsequent employment, such cheating constitutes outright theft against a future employer, who is misled into a mistaken evaluation of this employee, including payment of salary beyond his or her actual qualifications or expertise. But where the purpose of the studies is merely to become a diplomate or for self-enrichment, and the grades are fraudulently manipulated by means of such cheating, while this is not theft per se, it is deceptive, and therefore constitutes *geneivat da'at*, according to Rabbi Klein.

Very similar thoughts were expressed in a short essay authored by a young Israeli yeshivah student, dismayed at the incidence of cheating by her classmates in school examinations.[54] Pointing to the ramifications of *geneivat da'at*, she also holds teachers and proctors who tolerate such behavior equally guilty of unacceptable indulgence. Rabbi David Bleich, reviewing this issue, adds the further consideration of *ḥillul Hashem*, by which a religious student who cheats in this fashion can bring dishonor to the Torah and religious life, and ultimately to the God who commanded the *miẓvot*. Widespread cheating in religious institutions would certainly discredit all these, and for this additional reason be prohibited.[55]

It might be added that the halakhic concerns relative to the problem of plagiarism and infringement of copyright are also of significance to this issue. Beside the specific prohibitions involving theft or unauthorized use of material belonging to another—bans that are not within our present purview[56]—it would appear that considerations of deception should come into play. After all, when one person gains unearned and unwarranted respect or other rewards by passing off the work of others as his own, he has surely committed an act of deception upon his fellows, whether or not there is a financial cost to them. Such considerations are raised by a number of halakhists in dealing with the question of Torah scholars who repeat the scholarship or creative

53. *Responsa Mishneh Halakhot* 7:275.
54. Zipporah Wieder, *Shma'atin* (Tammuz 5736): 80–81.
55. Bleich, *Contemporary Halakhic Problems*, 2:109–111.
56. For a good summary, see ibid., 2:121–130.

thought of other scholars whom they have heard, or whose work they have read, but without proper attribution. The Maharam Schick considers this an infringement of *geneivat da'at*,[57] and a number of others, including the Magen Avraham (R. Abraham Gombiner) and the *Noda bi-Yehudah*, largely concur.[58]

Before concluding this section, we can examine two other principles that occur in the context of deceptive behavior. Besides considerations of *ona'ah* and *geneivat da'at*, principles that are essentially negative and prohibitive, there are two positive exhortations that are derived from the Torah.

Hain Ẓedek

In Leviticus (B) the Torah requires that commercial transactions be carried out with honest weights and balances. The prohibition, as the Torah formulates it, even extends to the mere possession of inaccurate weights. Now the Gemara in *Bava Meẓia* (H) contains the following discussion, pertinent to this scriptural verse:

Where there is a verbal agreement as to the terms of a commercial transaction, and prior to the formal consummation of the deal, the market value of the goods fluctuates, may either party renege on its oral obligations? The Gemara records two views: Rav permits such action and perceives no real lack of good faith, whereas R. Yoḥanan considers such action reprehensible in that it indicates an improper failure to live up to one's word. In questioning the lenient view of Rav, the Gemara quotes R. Yossi b. Judah in the *Torat Kohanim* to *Kedoshim*. R. Yossi notes that in (B) there is an apparent redundancy—if the Torah requires precise weights in the case of an *eifah*, why must it repeat the requirement in the case of a *hin*, which is merely one-sixth the size of an *eifah*? He answers that the term *hin* in this context has an additional connotation, notably as it is etymologically related to *hain*, meaning "yes" or "agreed." Hence *hin ẓedek* in this context teaches the obligation of treating one's "word," or verbal agreement, with utmost seriousness, i.e., as binding and sacred,

57. *Responsa Maharam Shick, Y.D.* 156.

58. *Magen Avraham* to *O.H.* 156; *Noda bi-Yehudah, Mahadura Tinyana O.H.* 20. These and other sources are quoted by R. Shelomoh Zalman Braun, *She'arim ha-Meẓuyyanim be'Halakhah*, vol. 4, p. 200, n. 4.

even in the absence of a written agreement. If so, says the Gemara, how can Rav permit a man to renege on his solemn word or agreement?

Abbaye answers on behalf of Rav that a distinction is to be made. What R. Yossi refers to is the obligation to remain true to one's word, so that one does not agree or commit to a transaction without every intention of living up to the terms agreed upon. R. Yossi requires solemn consistency between one's word and one's heart. But he does not, according to Rav, insist that a man must honor his word even if in the interim (prior to formalization of the transaction) the market fluctuates and new conditions prevail. Pulling out of a verbal agreement under such conditions does not automatically qualify as bad faith.

Even so, it is not the view of Rav which became normative, but that of R. Yoḥanan.[59] Thus even where circumstances change, a man should feel obligated to honor his word and his verbal undertakings. And even Rav agrees that where circumstances remain constant, the Halakhah requires complete consistency between the spoken word and one's inner intentions.[60] And Maimonides makes it quite clear that this standard is certainly applicable to the dealings of a *talmid ḥakham*, a student of the law, as he comports himself with "truth and good faith."[61]

The obligation to live up to one's word emerges in yet another context. The Mishnah in *Bava Meẓia*,[62] in discussing various forms of acquisition, states that one party to a transaction can renege up until the moment that actual possession of the goods is taken. This is true even where payment has been made, insofar as it is not the payment per se which renders the transaction final, but possession alone. But having said this, the Mishnah then adds, quoting what is apparently a tannaitic consensus, that "they said that the God who punished [*mi she-para*] the

---

59. *M.T. Hil. Mekhirah* 7:8. See *Shulḥan Arukh ha-Rav*, *Hil. Mekhirah* 2.

60. In the subsequent literature, two views emerged as to the primary sense of the verse in Leviticus, whether it be the principle of consistency between one's words and one's heart (Naḥmanides, Rashba, and Rosh), or the importance of sticking by a verbal commitment (Baal ha-Ma'or, Ittur, Sema, and the Shelah). For a full treatment of these various views in the halakhic literature relative to the sources, biblical status, and application of *hain ẓedek*, see the entry in the *Encyclopedia Talmudit* 9:463–466.

61. *M.T. Hil De'ot* 5:13.

62. *Bava Meẓia* 4:1 (44a).

generation of the great flood and the generation of those who built the tower to heaven, will likewise punish anyone who is not true to his word." In other words, while in the strictly legal sense it is quite permissible to renege on one's verbal commitment of purchase or sale, even up to the last moment, nonetheless it is wrong and morally reprehensible to act in such a fashion.

With this Mishnah as the foundation, the Halakhah subsequently incorporated the so-called *mi she-para* curse to be invoked upon any Jew who reneged on his verbal commitment, whether as buyer or seller. Indeed the one guilty of such a moral offense is obliged to "accept" the malediction at the hands of the rabbinical court. As Maimonides put it, such behavior is unworthy of a Jew, for in so doing "he has not acted in the way that a Jew should act [*lo asah ma'aseh Yiṣrael*]." In Maimonides' version, the curse includes additional references to the divine punishment of Sodom and Gomorrah, and of Egypt at the Red Sea.[63]

Clearly, the Halakhah in this prescription demands fealty to one's solemn undertakings well beyond the letter of the law, and takes great care to instill the fear of heaven in favor of honesty and fairness.

From these passages it is clear that not merely honesty, but good faith too, is required in one's business dealings. Again we can refer to Maimonides' inclusive statement (L) that the Halakhah requires that "one must not say one thing and mean another . . . only what we have in mind should we utter with the mouth."[64]

vi'Heyitem Nekiyyim

When the Torah in Numbers (D) exhorts one to be held guiltless (*nekiyyim*) before God *and* Israel, the Halakhah took this as an obligation not only to do the right thing, but also to *be seen* as doing the right thing.[65] Sometimes known as *mar'it ayin*, or "mistaken appearance," this refers to situations in which one is likely to be suspected or perceived by others as acting improperly.

---

63. Maimonides, *M.T. Hil. Mekhirah* 7:1.

64. Regarding the relationship of this passage in *Hil. De'ot* to the concept of *hain ẓedek*, see the respective views of *Minḥat Ḥinukh* to 259 and the *Or Sameaḥ* to *Hil. De'ot* 2:6.

65. An exhaustive treatment of the entire topic, known as *ḥashad*, can be found in *Encyclopedia Talmudit* 17:567 ff.

Now in the realm of commerce and finances, this principle of *vi'heyitem nekiyyim* has some very specific applications. A case in point, found in *Pesaḥim* (K), affects collectors of charity. For such collectors, it is not sufficient that they be scrupulously honest in handling and disposing of charity funds. This Gemara requires them to invite outside participants to ensure that no questions can be raised by others. Thus they may not exchange their own coins for those in the charity fund, and they may not themselves purchase charitable perishables, even at market price, lest they be suspected of taking advantage of such funds.[66] According to *Responsa Beit Ya'akov*, the only exception involves very small quantities, where it is unlikely that people will harbor such suspicions.[67]

Other situations where the Halakhah specifically calls for avoiding all appearances of impropriety include the use of monies, goods, or food in one's possession as security on loans;[68] a widow who disposes of her children's assets to ensure her own *ketubah* rights; the proper disposal of lost and found property to ensure that the value of the goods is preserved in case the owner is located;[69] and the proper payment of money pledged to charity and payable in a distant city.[70]

In all such cases, it is not merely suggested, but required, that a Jew make every effort to treat the property and person of others with complete fairness, openness, and integrity. Only in that way can one be held guiltless and irreproachable, as the verse puts it, both in the eyes of God (for the objective reality of one's actions) and in the eyes of men (who can, after all, only judge based on subjective reactions to a given situation).

2. *THE RESPONSIBILITIES AND ONUS DEVOLVING UPON THE PURCHASER*

The discussion to this point has concentrated exclusively upon the halakhic expectations that relate to the seller, or vendor, in

66. *Encyclopedia Talmudit* 17:596–597. See also Levine, *Economics*, p. 16. See Maimonides, *M.T. Hil. Matanot Aniyyim* 9:11.
67. *Responsa Beit Ya'akov* 70, as quoted in *Pitḥei Teshuvah, Sh.A. Y.D.* 257:1.
68. *Bava Meẓia* 38a.
69. *Bava Meẓia* 28b.
70. *Megillah* 27a.

commercial transactions. Clearly, these standards are considerable. Yet there are also limitations on these duties and responsibilities, as will soon become clear, insofar as the consumer must assume certain responsibilities for ascertaining the condition of the goods involved in the transaction.

The passage in *Ḥullin* 94a (I) that formed the basis for our discussion of *geneivat da'at* lists, inter alia, the prohibition against the sale of nonkosher meat to a Gentile, for the reason that he is thereby deceived, and furthermore that he might resell it to a Jew as kosher meat. Thus, as Rashi explains, the Gentile must be informed at the time of sale, so that there is no deception, and furthermore such meat can only be sold to him in a community where Jews know not to purchase any meat from Gentiles (and in such a community it is unnecessary to alert other Jews to this sale by public pronouncement). The Gemara (J) then asks as follows: in those communities where Jews do indeed purchase kosher meat from Gentiles, and in so doing rely on their fellow Jews to make a public announcement in cases where nonkosher has been sold to Gentile suppliers, how is that announcement to be made? R. Isaac b. Joseph permits a nonspecific statement that "meat" has been sold to Gentiles, without specifying "nonkosher meat," for we can presume that the Gentile only buys it because he believes it to be kosher, hence a more specific announcement will result in his not purchasing the meat altogether.

But, the Gemara asks, does this not constitute *geneivat da'at* and deception? The Gemara answers that in such a case, the purchaser is not misled by the seller—rather he misleads himself (which is but another way of saying that he has been negligent). Rashi explains this answer as saying that it was his responsibility to inquire whether the meat be kosher or not, and not to assume it to be kosher. This, says Rashi, is to be distinguished from the earlier-mentioned sale of nonkosher meat forbidden by the Gemara, for in the earlier case the seller intimated clearly that the meat was kosher (*be'ḥezkat kesheirah*). Likewise, says Rashi, the earlier-quoted case of a host opening wine barrels for his guest forbids the host to say, "I am opening these specifically for you." Thus, according to Rashi, *geneivat da'at* occurs when one party falsely describes the nature of the goods or states in so many words that he is acting to benefit the other party. To Rashi, mere silence is not *geneivat da'at*. Tosafot, however, finds this explanation of Rashi problematic.[71] In the case of the wine barrels, the Gemara (I) had said that the host acts improperly "unless he so informs him that it is already sold." Apparently, says Tosafot, the host practices deception when he does not fully inform his guest, and he violates *geneivat da'at* by passively permitting his guest to get the wrong impression. Furthermore, says Tosafot, R. Judah would never have lied to his honored guest; thus the Gemara must mean that R. Judah disclosed all the facts fully to him. From this we can learn, says Tosafot, that even silence in such a case is forbidden, for "a guest should not be expected to know that the barrels are already sold." This is to be distinguished from the case of selling meat to a Gentile, for there it should indeed occur to the purchaser that the meat might not be kosher.

It would appear that Rashi and Tosafot differ as to the essential definition of forbidden deception. According to Rashi, the vendor should not make a false statement, but he does not have to correct an unwarranted misconception on the part of the purchaser, where the vendor did not deliberately create the misunderstanding. Tosafot, on the other hand, requires that the seller actively disabuse his customer of any such error, whenever he recognizes the purchaser (or guest) as likely to be laboring under some misconception, either as to the circumstances or the quality of the goods.

The Gemara goes on to record an incident in which Mar Zutra mistakenly believed that Rava and R. Safra had set out in his honor to welcome him as he approached their town. R. Safra hastened to correct Mar Zutra's wrong impression, telling him that they were indeed on their way elsewhere, and their meeting had been entirely fortuitous. Rava, on the other hand, disagreed with R. Safra, saying that it had not been necessary to correct Mar Zutra's error. R. Safra claimed that to have acted otherwise would have constituted *geneivat da'at*. "No," said Rava, "he would be deceiving himself." Here, too, Rashi says, "we did not tell him

71. Tosafot, *Ḥullin* 94b, s.v. *inhu*. In the preceding Tosafot (s.v. *amar*) Rabbeinu Tam seems to agree with Rashi, and a similar view is attributed to Rabbeinu Tam by the Rosh (to *Ḥullin* 7:18.). It also appears that Rashi is in agreement with his teacher, Rabbeinu Gershom ("*Me'or ha-Golah*"). Tosafot is quoted verbatim in the *Beit Yosef* to the *Tur H.M.* 228.

'we have come to meet you,'" i.e., for Rashi they would be blameless for remaining silent, just as long as they did not make a false statement to mislead him. Whereas Tosafot explains, "It should have occurred to Mar Zutra that they might not be journeying to meet him," i.e., in this case there was no need for them to correct his mistaken impression, for he should have known better. But under other circumstances, it is implied by Tosafot, they would have had to set the record straight, in word or in deed. Among later medieval authorities, Nahmanides and the Rashba side with Rashi,[72] while the Rosh,[73] R. Joseph Karo (in the *Beit Yosef*),[74] and the Sema agree with Tosafot.[75]

Maimonides' position in this regard is not quite clear. In *Hilkhot De'ot* (L), in forbidding various kinds of *geneivat da'at*, he does not expressly include the concept of self-deception that emerges from the talmudic discussion. This alone would indicate that there is a categorical obligation, à la Tosafot, to correct a wrong impression, no matter that it was unwarranted in the circumstances.[76] Maimonides' all-inclusive formulation of the need to embrace complete honesty would also lead to this conclusion. This, at any rate, is how Maimonides was understood by a number of interpreters, including the *Knesset ha-Gedolah*.[77] R. Abraham de Boton (the *Leḥem Mishneh*), however, feels that Maimonides agrees with Rashi, based on Maimonides' terminology that "even a single *word* of . . . deception is forbidden," i.e., what is forbidden are explicit words that mislead, but in the absence of any such misleading words, where it is self-deception by the other party that is involved, then one can conclude that the first party is not obligated to correct him.[78] Even so, as the *Leḥem Mishneh* himself admits, the problem with this interpretation of Maimonides' text is that Maimonides should have made the distinction more explicit than it appears in his formulation.

In any case, this dispute between Rashi and Tosafot, involving

72. See their Novellae to *Ḥullin* 94b.
73. Rosh, *Ḥullin* 7:18, explicitly differs with Rashi.
74. *Beit Yosef* to *Tur H.M.* 228.
75. *Sefer Me'rat Einayim* (Sema), *Sh.A. H.M.* 228:9.
76. See *Encyclopedia Talmudit* 6:230.
77. *Knesset ha-Gedolah* to *Sh.A. H.M.* 228:3. Likewise R. Masud Hai Rekaḥ (the Ma'aseh Rokeaḥ) understood Maimonides in similar terms, in his *Ma'aseh Rokeaḥ*, *M.T. Hil. Mekhirah* 18:4 (4). See Shoḥatman, pp. 232–233.
78. *Leḥem Mishnah*, *M.T. Hil. Deot* 2:6. See also the *Kesef Mishnah* ad loc.

the issue of the purchaser who comes to mistaken conclusions for lack of his own careful consideration, seems to be decided in favor of Tosafot. Thus the *Tur* (O), in formulating the law of *geneivat da'at*, starts out by emphasizing the gravity of the transgression, due to the difficulty of undoing the negative effects that follow such tactics. He then goes on to refer to the case of the wine barrels, and states that it is necessary for the host to make it quite clear to his guest that the barrels are already sold; i.e., mere silence is not sufficient, in that the guest might well assume the barrels to be opened exclusively for him. Clearly this position reflects the view of Tosafot. A similar position is codified by the *Shulḥan Arukh*, as well as the *Shulhan Arukh ha-Rav*.[79] The *Arukh ha-Shulḥan*, however, sides with Rashi's minority view.[80]

Related to this question of the responsibility of the purchaser to exercise care in making certain assumptions regarding goods or services purchased is another issue: where the goods are defective, how specific must the seller be in describing the condition of the goods in question? Does the purchaser bear any responsibility to clarify the condition of the goods at the time of purchase?

R. Vidal Yomtov of Tolosa, the *Maggid Mishnah*, is of the opinion that where the purchaser could have checked the condition of the goods at the time but did not, he has no further claim on the vendor.[81] Other authorities, however, differ with him. Thus the *Mishneh la-Melekh* disagrees, in view of the fact that the major codifiers do not include such a law. And R. Jacob Moses Lorberbaum (the *Netivot ha-Mishpat*) assigns such responsibility only where the purchaser uses the goods, in that such usage can be taken as a readiness to overlook the defect.[82] The view of the Radbaz is that the purchaser does not have to check if the seller assured him that the goods were free of all defects.[83] Regarding the purchase of a building,.two views are expressed. R. Joshua Falk in his *Prishah* is of the opinion that if the purchaser does not check the facility at the time of purchase, he cannot claim to

79. *Sh.A. H.M.* 228:6; *Shulḥan Arukh ha-Rav*, *Hil. Ona'ah* 13.
80. *Arukh ha-Shulḥan*, *H.M.* 228:3.
81. *Maggid Mishnah*, *M.T. Hil. Mekhirah* 15:3. The section that follows here is based on the article by Warhaftig, pp. 350 ff.
82. *Netivot ha-Mishpat* to *Sh.A. H.M.* 232:1.
83. *Responsa Radbaz* 4:1206.

be misled if he subsequently discovers obvious defects.[84] But the twelfth-century R. Joseph Ibn Migash has an opposing view.[85]

If the defect was obvious to the purchaser at the time of purchase, he cannot subsequently claim to have been misled. Thus the Gemara *Ketuvot* 57b states that when a man purchases a slave with an obvious blemish, it can be assumed that he purchased him knowing, and accepting, the defect. And where it is common for purchasers of wine or other foods to taste prior to purchase, they cannot subsequently claim to be misled, for they should have tasted it at the time.[86] The same is true, says the Rema, where the nature of the goods is obvious to the purchaser, even though the seller describes them in a manner that is clearly incorrect (e.g., describing wood as gold).[87] When the purchaser continues to use the goods even after the defective nature of the item is known to him, this can be taken as clear indication that he has accepted such defects in their entirety, and cannot subsequently return the goods in question.[88] Once the purchaser informs the seller of the problem, he remains responsible for the item until it is returned.[89]

If the seller does indeed point out defects or possible problems with the item in question, the purchaser cannot subsequently return the goods with a claim to have been misled.[90] Maimonides in particular requires not simply a general disclaimer as to possible defects, but a detailed enumeration of every defect known to the seller—otherwise the purchaser may claim to have been misled, and in any case could not have waived his rights, given such a vague disavowal.[91] The *Tur* differs with Maimonides on this point, and does not require a detailed disclaimer on the part of the seller.[92]

A further consideration occurs where there are certain widespread assumptions as to the condition of goods purchased. Thus, it is permissible, according to the *Shulḥan Arukh*, for a

84. *Prishah* to *Tur H.M.* 232:5.
85. *Responsa Ri Migash* 51.
86. *Bava Meẓia* 60a.
87. Rema, *Y.D. H.M.* 232:7.
88. Maimonides, *M.T. Hil. Mekhirah* 15:3; *Tur/Sh.A. H.M.* 232:3.
89. Warhaftig, p. 352.
90. *Sh.A. H.M.* 232:19.
91. Maimonides, *M.T. Hil. Mekhirah* 15:6.
92. *Tur/Sh.A. H.M.* 232:7.

distributor of grain to mix the product using various types and qualities, without explicitly informing his customers of such mixing, because it is generally understood by buyers that this is the usual procedure.[93] The fact that a given customer may not be aware of this conventional practice does not require the seller to assume the responsibility of informing him. Furthermore, says Warhaftig, where the quality of the product is likely to be doubtful or ambiguous, it is the responsibility of the purchaser to take the initiative and ask the appropriate questions.[94] This can be deduced from *Ḥullin* (J), where the Gemara permits the ambiguous announcement that "meat" has been sold, putting the onus on the purchaser to clarify the precise nature of the meat, because he should realize that there is a reasonable possibility that what is being sold is nonkosher meat. Thus, if the purchaser does not question or seek to establish its status, the seller has no obligation to inform him.

The responsibilities of clarification devolving upon the purchaser emerge in yet another area, treated earlier, where the seller presents the goods in the best possible light, using a variety of nonverbal promotional techniques. Thus we have seen, based on *Bava Meẓia* (G), that the seller may indeed resort to a number of strategies to put the best appearance on new goods. It is understood by purchasers that the merchandise is deliberately spruced up to promote its sale. What is forbidden, as we saw, is the deliberate attempt to mislead or to cover up defects of one kind or another.

A discussion, and difference of opinion, involving precisely such a case arose in the twentieth century, in a way that served to reflect the respective opinions of Rashi and Tosafot (and possibly even of Rava and R. Safra in [J], or for that matter Samuel and Shemaya themselves in [I]), as well as the later discussants, seen above. In 1937 Rabbi Yehoshua Baumol was asked to rule whether it be permissible for kosher butchers to soak liver in blood, which in its congealed state serves to preserve the appearance of freshness.[95] A number of kashrut considerations are raised by this practice, but in addition a key concern is whether this action

93. *Sh.A. H.M.* 228:16.
94. Warhaftig, p. 358.
95. *Responsa Emek Halakhah* 2:4, 5, 6.

improperly misleads customers, who might think that the meat is fresher than it is. Rabbi Baumol refers to the Gemara *Bava Meẓia* (G) that forbids a vendor from soaking meat in water, the reason being, as Rashi explains, that the meat thereby appears fatter and more succulent—hence more valuable. Maimonides (M) accepts this stricture as normative. This, says Rabbi Baumol, is clearly analogous to blood-soaked liver, in that both intend to conceal the true state or quality of the meat. Furthermore, he argues, it makes no difference whether the selling price for fresh liver is higher than for preserved liver or not; even if the price is identical, *geneivat da'at* is involved.

This responsum generated an exchange of views among some of the leading authorities of the day. Rabbi Moshe Feinstein authored two responsa on the topic.[96] In the first, he dismisses the kashrut concerns, but does concede that where the customer is unaware of the butcher's conserving tactic, the prohibition of *ona'ah* is triggered. While Rabbi Feinstein does not explain precisely, it would appear that the *ona'ah* is of the nature of deceptive and misleading business practices. A short while later, in his second responsum, Reb Moshe returned to the topic, this time at greater length. Again he dismisses the kashrut questions raised (in the interim several other rabbis had added their concerns). Furthermore, in this responsum he pulls back from his earlier concession with regard to *ona'ah*. Thus he refers to the Gemara *Ḥullin* 8b, in which Rav Pappa forbids a butcher to display his meat in such a way that forbidden fats (*ḥelev*) lie on top of the permitted cuts of meat, because (as Rashi explains) some of the fat might be absorbed into the meat beneath it. Now Maimonides, in accepting this rule, adds one word of clarification—*le'na'oto*, "to make it appear attractive."[97] Rabbi Feinstein concludes from this that what is forbidden is not the attractive display or presentation per se, but rather any action that might mix nonkosher fat with kosher. Apparently, says Rabbi Feinstein, this case is to be distinguished from the sale of nonkosher meat to a Gentile (I), otherwise Maimonides would certainly have forbidden the activity on the grounds of it being a deceptive business practice as well.

96. *Responsa Iggerot Moshe, Y.D.* 30, 31. The second of these appeared originally in *ha-Pardes*, Elul 5697.

97. Maimonides, *M.T. Hil. Ma'akhalot Asurot* 7:19.

But what of the prohibition in *Bava Meẓia* (G) that forbids soaking meat so as to make it appear more desirable? Reb Moshe answers that there is a difference: soaking meat to fatten it, as with painting old merchandise to look new, is forbidden on grounds of *ona'ah* because "the purchaser has no reason at all to suspect" such a tactic, "and there is no reason for him to have to ask" if the product be fat or fresh. The customer, says Reb Moshe, properly relies on his eyes in judging the quality or freshness of the meat, which the butcher in so displaying implies to be consistent with its appearance. This is to be distinguished from the case of blood-soaked liver, which is like the case in *Ḥullin* 8b of meat displayed to best advantage: in both instances the customer should consider the possibility that the meat is not as fresh or tasty as it appears, insofar as it is common for liver to be soaked or meat to be displayed (in the absence of kashrut considerations) in this fashion, and the butcher merely presents it to its best advantage. In this latter case the onus is on the customer to consider the possibility that it has been so soaked, and thus to ask the appropriate questions. And if he does not ask at the time, then it is apparent that he is not particular in this regard, or if he is particular but omitted to ask, then he has in fact misled himself (or at any rate has been negligent). The seller, says Rabbi Feinstein, does not have to prompt such a question, when it is a question that the customer himself should be asking, given the common occurrence of such merchandising practices.[98]

Proof for this contention, says Rabbi Feinstein, is the Gemara in *Ḥullin* (J), where it is quite permissible for the butcher to sell nonkosher meat to a Gentile under the pretense that it is kosher, without alerting him as to its real status. For it should have occurred to the Gentile purchaser that he was getting nonkosher meat, and by not asking he was negligent and remiss in his own interest. The butcher, in that case, is no more than an indirect cause of self-deception by the purchaser, as is made clear by the analogous case in the Gemara, whereby Mar Zutra deceived himself too.

Thus, says R. Moshe, in the case of the liver the soaking does

98. The *Arukh ha-Shulḥan*, *H.M.* 228:5, seems to support such a position too, in that he indicates that the prohibition against soaking meat does not apply where butchers resort to such procedures and "everyone knows that they do this."

not establish its freshness, it merely preserves or establishes a neutral appearance, on the basis of which it is for the customer to establish the facts. By not inquiring, it is the customer who is at fault, and the butcher is not guilty of any misleading behavior. Rabbi Feinstein concludes that butchers do nothing wrong in so displaying their merchandise.

In his second responsum, Rabbi Baumol set out to further clarify his views. It is clear, he says, that fresh liver is more desirable, and therefore more costly, than liver that is even a few days old. Hence any activity that has the effect of concealing the age of liver, so that a customer might unwittingly pay for fresh liver while getting the preserved variety, must be considered deceptive, and an infraction not only of *ona'ah*, but of real theft (*gezel*). Rabbi Baumol also questions Reb Moshe's proof from Maimonides' formulation of the law in *Ḥullin* 8b. For he takes Rabbi Feinstein to understand Maimonides as saying that the butcher in this case acts with the intention of taking advantage of the customer (*ona'ah*), and thus Rabbi Baumol takes issue with him, saying that Maimonides means only that the butcher intends to display his wares in the best fashion.[99] In any case, he states, even if the responsibility devolves upon the customer to ask pertinent questions, still that does not permit the butcher himself to exploit such negligence and charge more than the market price of the liver.

In considering these two views, they appear to correspond in rough measure to the views of Rashi and Tosafot in commenting on *Ḥullin* 94a–b (I, J). Reb Moshe, like Rashi, finds room to permit the seller a passive response to a mistaken impression on the part of the purchaser, just as long as the seller does not resort to outright lies or deception. Rabbi Baumol, on the other hand, is closer to the view of Tosafot, in requiring a more activist stance to dispel any misconception, whether the result of negligence on the part of the purchaser or not. For Reb Moshe the key criterion is to establish what is the common and accepted practice in the case at hand, and then to require that each party conform to such expectations. But for Rabbi Baumol what is prohibited is

---

99. Frankly, however, a careful reading of Rabbi Feinstein's responsum (reflected in our presentation of his views above) yields the conclusion that he too understands Maimonides to be describing the butcher's action as *le'na'oto* ("to make it attractive"), and not as *le'honoto* ("to take advantage of him").

any misleading presentation that contributes to a misunderstanding of the true nature of the goods in question; and it makes no difference that accepted practice requires one party to satisfy certain criteria before it can claim to have been misled. Apropos of these two views, it would appear that R. Shneur Zalman of Liadi offers a hybrid solution: he says that if indeed it is the case that local butchers commonly soak meat to make it appear fatter, and their customers generally are aware of this, then there are those who permit such soaking;[100] nonetheless, he adds, one who is careful will not do such a thing, for certain purchasers might actually believe that what they see is in fact the higher-grade meat when it is not.[101]

Parenthetically, this view of Reb Moshe, with its overtones of halakhic sensitivity to common practice and assumptions, is fully reflective of his position on the presence—or absence—of a prohibition against cigarette smoking and nonmedical drugs.[102] There too it is at least partially a question of what is socially understood, practiced, or sanctioned that heavily influences the halakhic attitude to such activities.

There is one further situation that should be examined, but this time involving a lack of knowledge on the part of the seller and not the buyer. This is the case where the purchaser conceals not the objective condition or value of the item at hand, but rather its potential or subjective value to him. Must he disclose to the other party all the circumstances that motivate him to enter into this transaction, or may he conceal them as long as the seller gets fair market value? One such situation occurs where an entrepreneur wishes to purchase land for development; were he to disclose all pertinent information regarding his intentions, or the subsequent value of the real estate as a result of the implementation of his plans, he would be at a distinct disadvantage in negotiations with the seller, or sellers, of various parcels of the land in question. May he mislead the seller as to his intentions?

Rabbi Aaron Levine answers that in cases such as this, concealment of information can only be viewed as improperly deceptive if it in some way misrepresents the nature of the property

---

100. He is probably referring to the Sema, *Sh.A. H.M.* 228:16. See Warhaftig, p. 359.

101. *Shulhan Arukh ha-Rav, Hil. Ona'ah* 19.

102. See *Jewish Ethics and Halakhah*, vol. 1, chap. 9, esp. pp. 232–235.

right being transferred. But the purchaser is under no obligation to reveal his motives or entrepreneurial intent unless the other party explicitly requests its disclosure.[103] Even so, the purchaser should not lie, but he is permitted to distract the other party.

Rabbi Levine finds support for his view in the rabbinic understanding of two incidents in Genesis. In the first, when Abraham purchased the cave of Makhpelah for a burial plot (Gen. 23) he was careful not to reveal to the seller the special significance of that particular parcel of land for himself and his family, it being the ancestral burial ground, according to his family tradition, of Adam and Eve. Had the seller known this fact, he would have demanded vastly more for the land in question. The second incident involved Jacob in his purchase of the birthright from his brother Esau (in Gen. 25). Taking advantage of Esau's hunger, Jacob gets Esau to agree to sell the birthright for a mess of pottage, surely less than what its value to Jacob would subsequently be. Is this not deception or exploitation? The answer, according to Rabbi Levine, is no, in that Esau felt that he was likely to die before his father anyway (as explained by Naḥmanides), hence to him the offer by Jacob represented a fair exchange given his needs and expectations, and in any case he could sell the birthright to no one other than Jacob. Thus Jacob was fully entitled to make his low offer, and even to reinforce in subtle (but not false) fashion Esau's anticipation of his own early death.[104]

Thus it would be similarly permissible for a purchaser to conceal the eventual value to him of the transaction involved, just as long as he (a) pays the current market value to avoid the prohibition of *ona'ah*, (b) does not make a false statement, and (c) if asked directly does in fact disclose all the pertinent facts or motives.

A variation on this theme, leading to a similar conclusion, occurs when one party (e.g., a day laborer) contracts to perform certain work, (i.e., "sells" his services) for his employer, but then is guilty of a breach of contract that would lead to a financial loss for the employer. While as a general rule it is forbidden for either to engage in bluffing or deceptive behavior (for reasons of *ona'ah* and *hain ẓedek*, as above), in this case the Halakhah does permit

103. Levine, *Economics*, p. 17.
104. Ibid., pp. 19–20.

the employer to promise the worker the additional salary to induce him to complete the terms of the contract, but then to withhold the promised differential once the work is actually completed.[105] This is yet another instance in which the "purchaser" may conceal his intentions, given the breach of contract and lack of good faith of the "seller," in order to complete the terms of their agreement and avoid improper financial loss.

3. *THE LIMITS OF LEGITIMATE ADVERTISING*

The preceding discussion raises many fundamental questions regarding the ethics of mass advertising and promotion as these activities are carried out in the modern consumer society. Given the strict rules and guidelines that we have thus far encountered, we may well ask what be the limits on claims and statements made in support of one product as opposed to another. When may misleading or ambiguous advertising be undertaken? Is it at all proper to allure and entice others to purchase items or services which they had originally no intention to purchase?

In addressing these questions, it seems clear from our foregoing analysis that in merchandising and promoting products it is forbidden to make false claims—both on the grounds of *ona'ah*, insofar as the customer will be disappointed once the purchase is made and claims made on its behalf are proven wrong, as well as on the grounds of *geneivat da'at*, the very act of deception and misrepresentation, whether or not the purchaser gets full value for money paid.

But little, if any, advertising makes blatantly false claims or statements, if for no other reason than that such outright deception would backfire over the long run, in customer dissatisfaction and loss of product credibility. Thus our real question occurs in the context of advertising ploys or statements that (a) are misleading or insincere, or (b) use subtle means to motivate and persuade potential customers to purchase any given product.

We have seen already that the Mishnah (G) forbids painting or disguising old products to appear new. But the Gemara to that

105. *Bava Meẓia* 75b; Maimonides, *M.T. Hil. Sekhirut* 9:4; *Sh.A. H.M.* 333:18–22; Levine, *Economics*, p. 22. For a fuller treatment of this case, see Levine, *Free Enterprise*, pp. 44–49.

Mishnah *does* permit sprucing up new products to project their finest, most appealing image. And the Mishnah in *Arakhin*, as understood by Rashi, states explicitly that it is permitted to dress slaves in their finest clothing prior to their being sold, in order to maximize their salability and market price.[106] In commenting on this Mishnah, R. Israel Lipschutz, the Tiferet Yisrael, makes the pointed observation that while such activity would be forbidden when intended to disguise defects such as aging, it *is* permitted "in order to heighten the desire of customers to make a purchase."[107]

A pertinent passage is encountered in the Mishnah and Gemara in *Bava Meẓia* 60a–b (G). The Mishnah records several tannaitic disputes. In the first, R. Judah forbids storekeepers from promoting sales either by giving away promotional samples to minors or by discounting the price, whereas the sages permit both ploys. In the second, Abba Saul forbids any sifting of a mixture to improve its appearance by more than the value of the refuse removed, whereas the sages permit it as long as the entire mixture (and not just the visible exterior) is sifted. In both cases, the sages favor what might be called "creative merchandising," just as long as no customer is deliberately misled so as to harbor a mistaken impression. Apparently it is permitted, in their view, to promote one's product, but not at the expense of the truth. Significantly, this permissive view of the sages became normative, as codified almost verbatim by Maimonides (M), the *Tur*, and the *Shulḥan Arukh*.[108] In his formulation of the law, Maimonides explains that such activities are simply not considered *geneivat ayin* or visual deception of the customer. It would appear that even though the customer may not be fully conscious of the psychological means used to get him to purchase particular goods at a particular time and place, nonetheless the customer is not improperly misled as to the nature of the product under consideration. One can therefore draw the conclusion that there is nothing improper per se in resorting to subtle yet effective strategies to encourage a purchase, even those that take advantage of any emotional vulnerability on the part of the consumer, just as long as there is neither

106. *Arakhin* 6:5 (24b).
107. *Tiferet Yisrael* to *Arakhin* 6:5. See Warhaftig, p. 359, n. 145.
108. *Tur/Sh.A. H.M.* 228:15–17, *Sh.A. H.M.* 228:17–18.

an intent nor a result of concealing the true nature of the item at hand. Indeed the *Shulḥan Arukh ha-Rav* expressly permits a storekeeper to inflate the price of his spruced-up and attractive products beyond the cost differential involved in the product improvement, because, as he puts it, "someone who is prepared to pay more for attractive items can be considered to have intentionally forgone the additional cost."[109] Likewise the *Arukh ha-Shulḥan* permits a slight additional premium for produce that is sifted or polished, on the assumption that certain purchasers will gladly pay a little extra to avoid additional work for themselves.[110]

Yet even here, there are those who see a clear limit as to the boundary of such motivating strategies. Thus Warhaftig quotes the *Tosafot Yomtov* to this Mishnah, who states that when the sages forbid a seller to sift beans unless the entire mixture is consistent, this applies even where the seller informs the purchaser that it is only the exterior that is sifted.[111] This is based on the mishnaic phrase *ke-gonev et ha'ayin*, "like deceptive appearances"; were the Mishnah describing a case where the purchaser had no idea that the rest of the produce was not of this quality, it would not merely be "like" deception, it would *be* deception, plain and simple. He concludes therefore that the case under discussion involves full intellectual awareness by the customer, but still a lack of customer self-control, given the visual appeal of the item. In other words, the purchaser may be "seduced" by what he sees, and end up purchasing what he knows to be inappropriate or of inferior quality, at a price beyond its market value, and it is this which the sages forbid. If this be the intent of the sages, then clearly an advertiser or promoter must take into consideration that certain consumers or customers will be unfairly exploited, and he is therefore forbidden to promote his product under such circumstances, even though he is, in the narrow sense, quite truthful in his claims or statements.

As outlined by Rabbi Levine, several common promotional strategies fall into this category of halakhically questionable tactics.[112] Thus the so-called weasel-word stratagem, which deliberately creates false or exaggerated claims (e.g., "cleans like a white

109. *Shulḥan Arukh ha-Rav, Hil. Ona'ah* 18.
110. *Arukh ha-Shulḥan, H.M.* 228:13.
111. Warhaftig, p. 364.
112. Levine, *Economics*, pp. 46 ff.

tornado"), would be forbidden where it creates impressions or expectations that cannot be fulfilled by the product. The same is true of any claim that improperly implies that the sale price is a genuine bargain. While, as we have seen, the sages consider price-cutting to be quite permitted, and even to be encouraged, it is forbidden to misrepresent the circumstances surrounding the lower prices.[113] Such a case involves a merchandiser who has dated or overstocked products, and wishes to dispose of such inventory at clearance prices. In advertising the lower prices, he may not characterize them as "discounted" or "in the public interest," implying thereby that he is selling them for less than what is available elsewhere. In short one should not imply that one offers a bargain (defined as a price below "fair market value") when in fact the price merely reflects changed market conditions.

In the realm of advertising a "bargain," similar dishonesty can occur when a retailer claims to be selling an item below the "manufacturer's suggested list price." For if indeed that suggested price is so inflated that hardly any retail stores can charge that amount while remaining competitive, then the "bargain" is no bargain at all, but merely the "going" rate. Hence the advertiser is guilty of seeking to garner undeserved good will by misrepresenting his merchandise or the conditions surrounding its sale.[114] This would not be the case, however, where it is generally understood that the "suggested list price" is merely for reference purposes.

Another common advertising ploy is "puffery," by which the qualities of a product are exaggerated out of proportion to reality. Levine finds that where such claims relate to the realm of subjective feelings or purely aesthetic judgment (e.g., that a certain product evokes a mood of romance, serenity, or glamour), they are not forbidden, as long as they do not misrepresent the extent of popularity of the item in question.[115] But where such puffery occurs in the performance domain, promising results that are

---

113. A curious caveat is made by the *Arukh ha-Shulḥan, H.M.* 228:14, when he states that price-cutting is permitted only in the case of produce (*tevuah*), for it will lead to a general marketwide reduction of the price, but not in the case of merchandise (*seḥorah*), insofar as it will lead to economic breakdown and financial ruination. The *Arukh ha-Shulḥan* likewise forbids any deliberate deception intended to cause additional purchases by the customer.

114. Levine, *Free Enterprise*, p. 123.

115. Levine, *Economics*, pp. 53–54.

objectively measurable, the law of *ona'ah* requires that such promises or implied benefits must be consistent with what the purchaser can expect to enjoy as a result of the advertising.

Rabbi Levine also finds grounds to object to the tactic known as "bait and switch," by which stores advertise a product which they do not have in stock (or do have, but do not disclose that it is in very limited quantity). By pricing that article at an extraordinarily low price, they hope to attract customers, who, upon being informed that the item is no longer available, might be convinced to purchase some other, more expensive, product. Such activity can be classified as *ona'ah*, in that the seller deliberately intends the customer to experience disappointment, followed by intentional manipulation to purchase other merchandise at more normal prices. Hence "bait and switch" activities are clearly forbidden. It is not, however, forbidden to feature a "loss leader" to attract customers who might subsequently purchase other goods at normal prices, as long as the underpriced item is available in ample quantity and presented in good faith.[116] In this case, the discounted item represents a true bargain, available for less than what it might cost elsewhere.

One final advertising tactic that we can examine is the use of testimonials or statistics. Here, too, Levine points out that use of such data in promoting sales can trigger the *geneivat da'at* prohibition if the source being used is less than absolutely objective, and the advertising fails to reveal that fact. The situation is similar to the halakhic demand for absolute neutrality on the part of a judge in cases that come before him. Thus, for instance, when the effectiveness of a product is measured and attested to by a source that is retained and supported by the marketer itself, and such a relationship is not revealed in advertising the product, then the public has been effectively misled.

In all such cases, according to Levine, it is necessary to clarify how specific advertising or presentations are perceived by the target group. Thus it would be necessary to pilot-test and measure the impressions and inferences the consumer draws; and should the product or the advertised price differential fail to fulfill the benefits stated or implied in the advertising, such promotional activity must be said to be forbidden as *ona'ah* (exploita-

116. See ibid., pp. 45–47; Levine, *Free Enterprise*, pp. 120–121.

tion, leading to disappointment) as well as *geneivat da'at* (deceptive business practices).[117]

SUMMARY AND CONCLUSIONS

In examining the issues involved in possible misrepresentation in the business setting, we have examined a number of prohibitions. The first of these is *ona'ah*, or exploitation, involving not so much price fraud as insensitivity to the emotions and feelings of others. As explained by the Meiri, any pretense that necessarily leads to disappointment in the business sphere is forbidden insofar as it needlessly manipulates the feelings of the other party. And insensitivity to the emotional pain thus inflicted is likewise condemned as redundant *ẓa'ar ha-lev*, or heartache, by the *Shulḥan Arukh ha-Rav*.

The second prohibition is *geneivat da'at*, or the intentional misrepresentation of the facts of a situation. According to the *Mekhilta* this behavior is the highest form of thievery, and it was given its definitive formulation by the amora Samuel, to include deception of even a Gentile victim. While there is some disagreement as to the source of the prohibition (the Ritva finds a biblical source that forbids stealing, Rabbeinu Yonah derives it from the biblical prohibition against lying, while the Semak, the Baḥ, and R. Shneur Zalman consider it purely rabbinic in origin), all agree, following Samuel's dictum, that the prohibition applies equally to the treatment of Jew or Gentile.

From the Gemara *Ḥullin* 94a–b are derived the major parameters of forbidden deception: e.g., offering favors or gifts that one knows will not be accepted; allowing a guest the mistaken impression of expenses incurred on his behalf; the failure to reveal to a purchaser the true source of shoe leather; and the sale to a Gentile of nonkosher meat as if kosher—all improper actions because they give the false impression of favors proffered. And from *Bava*

117. There are other halakhic concerns raised by modern promotional activities, as discussed by Levine (including providing inappropriate advice, disparagement of competitors or their products, incitement of envy, price gouging, the dissuasion responsibility, and the like) or by Warhaftig (improper value formation, consumerism, and creating artificial needs). But these concerns are extraneous to the specific issues of deception, misrepresentation, and integrity that are the concerns of this chapter.

Meẓia 60 a–b are derived several other facets of *geneivat da'at:* e.g., the impropriety of disguising aging products to appear young or new, and the prohibition against dressing meat to appear of higher quality. On the other hand, it is permissible to spruce up items to their best appearance, as long as there is no deliberate attempt to conceal their true age or defective condition. Such forbidden activity was extended to include mixing of various qualities of merchandise, where done in such a way as to mislead the customer.

Among the medieval authorities, a few formulations of *geneivat da'at* stand out as comprehensive and repercussive. The first is Maimonides, who in *Hilkhot De'ot* of the *Mishneh Torah* requires at all times "truthful speech, an upright spirit, and a pure heart freed of all pretense and cunning." The second is Rabbeinu Yonah of Gerondi, who emphasizes the psychological damage of misrepresentation, in that, as he puts it, truth is one of the "foundations of the soul." Another notable passage is encountered in the *Sefer Ḥasidim*, which decries those who knowingly pretend to false piety.

The principle of *geneivat da'at* finds expression in a number of areas: one, according to Maimonides, and his descendant Joshua ha-Nagid, is the biblical prohibition against the *me'onen*, or "beguiler," which is based on his deceptive sleight of hand that fools his audience, i.e., *geneivat da'at*. The Radbaz echoes this rationale for the prohibition. A second application of *geneivat da'at* is in the realm of self-evaluation. The Gemara in *Ḥullin* records that a certain amora (R. Judah) honored an important guest without informing him of all the circumstances surrounding his generosity in opening a barrel of wine, and the Gemara indicates that evaluation of his motivations could be left to himself. Yet both Maimonides and the Tur, as explained by R. Aryeh Judah b. Akiva, do not consider such self-knowledge and evaluation possible for most people, whose motives, whether they recognize it or not, can be considered to include a measure of deception. Thus complete disclosure of intent and circumstance to one's guests is, as a rule, necessary. Yet in other circumstances, later authorities (R. Moshe Mordecai Epstein of Slabodka, R. Eliezer Meir Preil, R. Moshe Feinstein) were more lenient, permitting a man to evaluate his own ability to perform certain work given his age, and as a result to resort to some deception (dyeing his beard) to offset possible age discrimination against him. A third area in which we saw the principle of *geneivat da'at* implemented was that of publishing and academic grading. Rabbi Waldenberg thus prohibits any alteration of research findings in order to advance the author's career, both on grounds of *geneivat da'at* and of falsehood, whether or not others incur financial loss as a result. A minority view (R. Eliezer of Metz) sees no biblical prohibition as long as no other people are harmed by such tampering, although Rabbi Waldenberg feels that even this view would agree that there is a rabbinic ordinance against it. A related concern is that of students who cheat on examinations; according to Rabbi Menasheh Klein this too is forbidden under the rubric of *geneivat da'at*, whether or not the student subsequently uses those grades to obtain employment. The same is true, according to the Maharam Schick, of those who do not properly acknowledge the sources of creative scholarship which they pass off as their own.

In addition to *ona'ah* and *geneivat da'at*, we also saw that the principle of *hain ẓedek* (to treat one's word as binding) requires good faith and complete consistency between intent, verbal assurance, and fulfillment of even verbal commitments. The Halakhah also curses the man who reneges on a deal at the last moment, after verbal agreement has been reached, considering such behavior unbefitting a Jew. The same is true of the principle of *vi'heyitem nekiyyim*, which requires that one not only do what is right, but also ensure that one is perceived by others as doing it, as for instance in properly disposing of charitable funds, taking proper care in safeguarding items one held either on deposit or as security, protecting lost property, and making full payment of charitable pledges. In all these cases it is important to be held guiltless both in the eyes of God and of man.

Yet the Halakhah does not overlook the responsibilities of the purchaser either. Clearly the purchaser bears a certain onus of inquiring as to the nature of the goods purchased. The major text for this duty is the passage in *Ḥullin* that speaks of self-deception, the case in point being the Gentile who purchases meat without inquiring whether it be kosher or not. Here the Gemara implies that it should occur to him that the meat is not kosher, insofar as the laws of kashrut do not apply to him, and therefore it is up to him to inquire; and the Jew is not obliged to inform him that it is not kosher. In examining this passage, we encountered the opposing views of Rashi and Tosafot. Rashi's view is that while the seller is not permitted to make a false statement at the time of sale, he is also not required to actively correct the purchaser's unwarranted misconception. Tosafot, on the other hand, requires of the seller that he completely disabuse the purchaser of any erroneous notion. All are agreed that where the other party had no reason at all to assume a certain intent (e.g., thinking that a fortuitous meeting with others was planned in his honor), there is no need to correct such a mistaken impression. Maimonides' view is debatable: most understand him to agree with Tosafot, but a minority view (the *Leḥem Mishneh*) takes him to agree with Rashi. The majority of subsequent halakhists (e.g., *Tur*, *Shulḥan Arukh*) side with Tosafot in requiring that the seller actively correct the purchaser's unwarranted misconceptions.

On the matter of defective goods, we encountered a number of views. The *Maggid Mishnah* holds the purchaser responsible for not checking the condition at the time of purchase, but the *Mishneh la-Melekh* disagrees. The Radbaz indicates that the purchaser can rely upon the seller's assurances and does not have to check himself. From the Gemara *Ketuvot* it is clear that where the defect was fully evident at the time of purchase, it must be assumed that the buyer accepted the goods "as is," and has no subsequent claim on the vendor. This is equally true where it is common for purchasers to taste (or test) the product at the point of purchase and obvious defects are present. Likewise, continued use of the goods is clear indication of the purchaser's readiness to overlook such defects, and invalidates any subsequent claim. And once it is clear that the seller did inform the buyer of the presence of defects at the time of sale, the buyer has no further claim in their regard. How detailed must such disclosure be? Maimonides requires complete specificity, whereas the *Tur* is more flexible.

A much-discussed question occurs where there are certain broad assumptions made by the market or purchasers as a class. The *Shulḥan Arukh* permits a distributor to mix grains from various sources, because such recourse is widespread and generally known. This is analogous to the sale of nonkosher meat to the Gentile, who is expected to inquire under such circumstances. Implicit herein, as explained by Warhaftig, is that it is up to the purchaser to inquire whenever the quality is likely to be ambiguous or in doubt, and the seller is not required to inform him if he happens to be ignorant of what is widely known. This is certainly the case where vendors customarily display their goods to best advantage, seeking to paint or spruce up the merchandise in question—as indicated in *Bava Meẓia*—just as long as they do not intentionally mislead or hide defects or aged items.

Just such a situation led to an exchange of views in the twentieth century regarding the practice of butchers who soak livers in blood to preserve a fresh appearance. While Rabbi Yehoshua Baumol and several others were categorically opposed to such practices, on the ground that they improperly disguised meat to hide its age, causing the customer to pay more than its worth, or at any rate to be misinformed, Rabbi Moshe Feinstein saw no reason to forbid it. While the stricter view saw this case as analogous to the talmudic prohibition against soaking meat to make it appear fatter, the lenient view of Rabbi Feinstein refers to the talmudic dispensation, as understood by Maimonides, to display meat "to make it appear attractive." What is permitted, says Rabbi Feinstein, is visual improvement and display that is undertaken with the general knowledge of purchasers at large, whereas what is forbidden is where customers as a rule are not aware of such steps, and have no reason to question the condition or freshness of the item at hand. Thus the butcher is not duty-bound to explicitly notify the customer on each occasion of purchase, insofar as the customer bears the responsibility to inquire whether the meat be fresh or not, given the pervasive custom among butchers. On this issue, it would appear that Rabbi Feinstein takes a position that largely reflects the view of Rashi, whereas Rabbi Baumol seems closer to the position of Tosafot.

Where it is not the purchaser, but the seller, who may be ignorant of the subjective or entrepreneurial value of an item being negotiated, it is the view of Rabbi Levine that the purchaser is not required to disclose that subjective value or intent (unless specifically questioned by the seller), just as long as he does not in some way misrepresent the nature of the property right being transferred, and the seller receives fair market value for his goods. Levine draws support for this position from Abraham's purchase of the Cave of Makhpelah (in which he hid from the seller its subjective value to him), and from Jacob's bargain purchase of the birthright from Esau (given Esau's anticipation of his own early death, and the relatively low value of the birthright to Esau). One further instance involving concealment of intent by the "purchaser" occurs where a day laborer reneges on his work commitment, and the employer deceptively promises to pay a premium to the worker to get him to finish the job. In this case, Rabbi Levine argues, the employer is fully within his rights to conceal his intentions, as long as he pays the original figure, given the breach of contract on the other side.

The implications of the foregoing for product advertising are considerable. Certainly it is true that misleading or false claims would be prohibited by the Halakhah. But what of more subtle means to motivate the purchase of a given product? The Mishnah in several places permits putting the best appearance on products that are for sale (e.g., slaves, produce, clothing), to make them as attractive as possible. It likewise records the majority view allowing the use of promotional samples and price discounting, as well as careful, and consistent, sifting of one product, as long as there is no deliberate deception. This view became normative, and even Maimonides, otherwise so careful, allows such subtle motivating tactics that utilize psychological incentives leading to such sales. Similar dispensations are offered (by the *Shulḥan Arukh ha-Rav* and the *Arukh ha-Shulḥan*) to require a premium for specially packaged or treated goods.

Yet here too there are limits, and competing views. *Tosafot Yomtov* interprets the sages as forbidding any selective sifting that belies the true nature of the mixture, even where the purchaser is fully informed of the practice, because the purchaser will be emotionally vulnerable to the attractive appearance. The effect of this prohibition is to curtail promotional activities that strictly speaking are truthful, but nonetheless are insincere and exploitative. This includes so-called weasel-word tactics, improperly implying a bargain or discount price, when the asking price actually reflects no discount from fair market value. Other forbidden tactics include puffery in the performance domain that promises more than the purchaser can expect to receive by purchasing the product; "bait and switch" that entices a customer under false pretenses, while deliberately steering him to more profitable items (whereas the use of a loss-leader strategy is itself permitted); and the use of testimonials or statistics that are either not fully disinterested or measurable by the purchaser. In all these cases, it is necessary to establish (by pilot-testing advertising or the relevant copy) whether in fact customers or consumers draw inaccurate or unwarranted inferences from the advertising. If this is in fact the case, such advertising must be seen as deceptive, and therefore forbidden.

To answer the questions with which we began this chapter, one would have to say that if indeed the cigarette manufacturer knew, or had good reason to suspect, that its products were faulty or posed a risk, while at the same time there was no widespread public knowledge of such a risk, then the company acted improperly—and deceptively—by misrepresenting the nature of its product. But once it was publicly known that this product was at the very least suspected of causing health problems, the company can properly claim that it was under no special obligation to inform the consumer of what was already widely known. Of course, even at that point, if the company advertised (either explicitly or implicitly) that its product was safe even while it knew the hazards involved, it would certainly be guilty of improper deception. If, on the other hand, the company had no idea as to the hazards involved, it would not be guilty of misrepresentation or deception, but it could be held responsible for damages caused by its product.

In advertising, while the vendor is permitted to project its product in the best light, and even to make it appear as alluring and attractive as possible, nonetheless the company is duty-bound to avoid any implication that the product is safe or without peril, contrary to what it knows to be true. Failure to do so would make the company guilty of irresponsibility, misrepresentation, and deceptive business practices.

Table of Authorities Cited

This alphabetized list consists of generally recognized authorities whose names are found in the chapters and discussions that follow. It provides in each case a few facts relative to their name(s), time, place, and major halakhic publications, without referring to their nonhalakhic works, but including, where applicable, any well-known teachers or students that they might have had.

Abu Zimrah. See *Radbaz*.
Abulafia, Ḥayyim b. David. 1700–1775. Smyrna, Turkey. Codifier.
Abulafia, Meir ha-Levi. See *Ramah*.
Adret. See *Rashba*.
Agudat Ezov. See *Maharam Zev*.
Aḥi'ezer. Ḥayyim Ozer Grodzinski. 1863–1940. Vilna. Responsa.
Alfasi. See *Rif*.
Alshikh, Moses. d. after 1593. Safed, Israel. Bible commentaries. Student of Joseph Karo.
Arukh la-Ner. See *Ettlinger, Jacob*.
Arukh ha-Shulḥan. Yeḥiel Mikhel ha-Levi Epstein. 1829–1908. Russia. Novellae and rulings to *Shulḥan Arukh*.
Asheri. See *Rosh*.
Avodat ha-Leviyyim. See *Jonathan b. David of Lunel*.
Avodat ha-Melekh. Menaḥem Krakowski. 1870–1929. Commentary to Maimonides' *Mishneh Torah*.
Azulai. See *Ḥida*.
Babad. See *Minḥat Ḥinukh*.
Baḥ. Joel Sirkes. 1561–1640. Poland. Commentary on the *Tur* (the *Bayit Ḥadash*, acronym "Baḥ"). Responsa (*Bayit Ḥadash*). Teacher and father-in-law of the Taz.

Baḥya b. Asher, Rabbeinu. 13th century. Saragossa, Spain. Commentary to Torah. Student of Rashba.

Baumol, Yehoshua. 1879–1947. Russia and New York. Responsa (*Emek Halakhah*).

Beit Ya'akov. Jacob b. Samuel of Zausmer. 17th century. Responsa.

Beit David. Joseph David. 1667–1736. Salonika. Responsa.

Benveniste. See *Knesset ha-Gedolah*.

Berlin. See *Neẓiv*.

Binyan Ẓion. See *Ettlinger, Jacob*.

Bleich, J. David. Contemporary. New York. Essays, articles, reviews.

Braun, Shelomoh Zalman. Contemporary. New York. Commentary/compendium on *Kiẓur Shulḥan Arukh* (*She'arim ha-Meẓuyyanim be'Halakhah*).

Chayes, Ẓvi Hirsch (Mahariẓ Chayes). 1805–1855. Galicia. Responsa (*Mahariẓ Chayes)*, various studies on halakhic topics.

Darkhei Noam. Mordecai b. Judah ha-Levi. d. 1684. Cairo. Responsa.

Divrei Malki'el. Malki'el Ẓvi ha-Levi Tannenbaum. 19th century. Lomza, Lithuania. Responsa (publ. 1891–1901).

Duran. See *Tashbaẓ*.

Efrati, Shimon b. Yekutiel. 1909–. Poland and Israel. Responsa (*me-Emek ha-Bakha, mi-Gei ha-Harigah*).

Eibeschutz, Jonathan. 1690–1764. Prague. Commentaries on the *Shulḥan Arukh* (incl. *Kreiti u-Fleiti*).

Eiger, Akiva b. Moses. 1761–1837. Posen, Germany. Talmudic commentaries (incl. *Gilyon ha-Shas*) and glosses to *Shulḥan Arukh*.

Eiger, Solomon. 1786–1852. Germany. Talmudic commentaries (incl. *Gilyon Maharsha*). Son of R. Akiva Eiger.

Elberg, Simḥah. Contemporary. Warsaw and New York. Commentaries and novellae (*Shalmei Simḥah*).

Eliezer b. Samuel of Metz. 1115–1198. France. Tosafist, compendium and elaboration of *miẓvot* (*Sefer Yerayim*). Student of Rabbeinu Tam and Rashbam.

Elijah of Vilna, the Gra. 1720–1797. Commentaries and glosses to the Talmud, the *Shulḥan Arukh* (incl. *Be'ur ha-Gra*), Scripture, Midrash, and others.

Emden, Jacob b. Ẓvi, Yaveẓ. 1697–1776. Altona, Germany.

Responsa (incl. *She'elat Yaveẓ*). His father and teacher was the Ḥakham Ẓvi.

Emek Halakhah. See *Baumol, Yehoshua*.

Epstein, Barukh ha-Levi. See *Torah Temimah*.

Epstein, Moshe Mordecai. 1866–1933. Lithuania and Israel. Talmudic discussions (*Levush Mordecai*).

Epstein, Yeḥiel Mikhel ha-Levi. See *Arukh ha-Shulḥan*.

Ettlinger, Jacob. 1798–1871. Altona, Germany. Talmudic commentaries (incl. *Arukh la-Ner*) and responsa (*Binyan Ẓion*).

Falk, Joshua ha-Kohen. See *Sema*.

Feinstein, Moshe. 1895–1986. Luban, Russia, and New York. Responsa (*Iggerot Moshe*) and talmudic commentaries.

Gershom b. Judah Me'or ha-Golah, Rabbeinu. 960–1028. Mainz, Germany. Commentaries to Talmud, responsa. Taught the teachers of Rashi.

Gershuni, Yehudah. Contemporary. New York and Israel. Essays and articles (included in *Kol Ẓofayikh*).

Gesher ha-Ḥayyim. See *Tucatzinsky, Yeḥiel*.

Gombiner, Abraham. See *Magen Avraham*.

Goren, Shelomoh. Contemporary. Israel. Essays, articles, monographs.

Gra. See *Elijah of Vilna*.

Greenwald, Yekutiel. 1889–1955. Columbus, Ohio. Compendium of Laws of Mourning (*Kolbo al Aveilut*).

Grodzinski, Ḥayyim Ozer. See *Aḥi'ezer*.

Grossnass, A. L. Contemporary. England. Essays and articles.

Gulevsky, Ḥayyim Dubber. Contemporary. New York. Essays and articles.

ha-Meiri. See *Meiri*.

ha-Rah. Aaron ha-Levi. 1235–1300. Barcelona, Spain. Talmudic commentaries.

Hadaya, Ovadiah. 1891–1969. Jerusalem. Responsa (*Yaskil Avdi*).

Ḥafeẓ Ḥayyim. Israel Meir ha-Kohen Kagan. 1838–1933. Radun, Poland. Commentary to *Shulḥan Arukh* (*Mishnah Berurah*); ethical treatises.

Hagahot Maimoniyyot. R. Meir ha-Kohen. 13th century. Rothenburg, Germany. Maimonidean commentator, with additional responsa (*Teshuvot Maimoniyyot*). Student of Maharam Rothenburg.

Hai b. Sherira Gaon. 939–1038. Pumbedita. Various halakhic treatises, most particularly *Sefer ha-Mekaḥ ve'ha-Memkar.*

Ḥakham Ẓvi. Ẓvi Hirsch b. Jacob. 1660–1718. Altona, Germany. Responsa. Father of Jacob Emden.

Ḥananel b. Ḥushi'el, Rabbeinu. d. 1055. Kairouan. Talmudic commentary.

Ḥatam Sofer. Moses Sofer (Schreiber). 1762–1839. Pressburg, Hungary. Responsa (*Ḥatam Sofer*), Talmudic commentaries. Son-in-law of Akiva Eiger.

Ḥavvot Yair, Yair Ḥayyim Bachrach. 1638–1702. Germany. Responsa

Ḥayyim ha-Levi Soloveichik. 1853–1918. Volozhin, Russia. Novellae on the Talmud and Maimonides.

Ḥazon Ish. Avraham Yeshayahu Karelitz. 1878–1953. Vilna and Bnei Brak. Commentary on *Shulḥan Arukh.*

Heller, Ḥayyim. 1878–1960. Poland, Berlin, and New York. Author of studies in Scripture, Targumim, Peshitta, and Maimonides' *Sefer ha-Miẓvot.*

Heller, Yomtov Lipman. 1579–1654. Prague, Nikolsburg, and Poland. Commentary on Mishnah (*Tosafot Yomtov*), responsa.

Henkin, Yosef Eliyahu. 1880–1973. Responsa.

Ḥida. Ḥayyim Joseph David Azulai. 1724–1806. Jerusalem. Glosses to *Shulḥan Arukh.*

Ḥeshek Shelomoh, Solomon b. Mordecai. 1269–1340. Smyrna, Turkey. Commentary to the *Tur.*

Hubner, Shmuel. Contemporary. Israel. Responsa (*Nimmukei Shmuel*).

Ibn Ezra, Abraham. 1089–1164. Spain and Rome. Biblical commentator, poet, grammarian, philosopher.

Ibn Migash, Joseph b. Meir ha-Levi. 1077–1141. Spain. Talmudic commentaries. Student of Alfasi and teacher of Maimonides' father.

Iggerot Moshe. See *Feinstein, Moshe.*

Isaac b. Joseph of Corbeil. See *Semak.*

Isaac of Molena. Died before 1580. Spain and Cairo, Egypt. Responsa.

Israel Meir ha-Kohen Kagan. See *Ḥafeẓ Ḥayyim.*

Isserles, Moses. See *Rema.*

Jacob b. Asher. See *Tur.*

Jacob of Orleans. d. 1189. England. One of the authorities among the Tosafot. Student of Rabbeinu Tam.

Jaffe, Mordecai b. Abraham. See *Levush*.

Jakobovits, Immanuel. Contemporary. London. Essays and articles.

Jonathan b. David ha-Kohen of Lunel. 12th century. Commentary to Rif (*Avodat ha-Leviyyim*). Student of Ravad.

Joshua b. Abraham Maimoni, ha-Naggid. 1310–1355. Cairo. Responsa. Descendant of Maimonides.

Judah he-Ḥasid. See *Sefer Ḥasidim*.

Judah b. ha-Rosh. 1270–1349. Toledo, Spain. Responsa (*Zikhron Yehudah*).

Karelitz, Avraham Yeshayahu. See *Ḥazon Ish*.

Karo. See *Shulḥan Arukh*.

Kasher, Menaḥem. 1895–1983. Poland, New York, and Israel. Compendium/commentary on the Torah (*Torah Sheleimah*), essays and articles.

Klein, Menasheh. See *Mishneh Halakhot*.

Kluger, Solomon (Maharshak). 1785–1869. Brody, Poland. Responsa (incl. *Tuv Ta'am ve'Da'at*).

Knesset ha-Gedolah. Ḥayyim b. Israel Benveniste. 1603–1673. Smyrna, Turkey. Commentator and codifier. Student of Maharit.

Kolbo. See *Greenwald, Yekutiel*.

Kook, Abraham Isaac ha-Kohen. 1865–1935. Latvia and Israel. Halakhic monographs related to Israel and redemption.

Krakowski. See *Avodat ha-Melekh*.

Lamm, Norman. Contemporary. New York. Essays and articles.

Landau, Ezekiel b. Judah. See *Noda bi-Yehudah*.

Landsofer, Jonah b. Elijah. 1678–1712. Prague. Responsa (*Me'il Ẓedakah*).

Leḥem Mishneh. Abraham b. Moses di Boton. 1545–1588. Salonika, Greece. Maimonidean commentator. Student of Maharashdam.

Levush. Mordecai b. Abraham Jaffe. 1535–1612. Poland. Commentary on codes (the *Levushim*). Student of Maharshal and Rema.

Lieberman, Saul. 1898–1983. Poland, Jerusalem, and New York. Studies on Tosefta, Jerusalem Talmud, and history of halakhic literature.

Liebes, Yiẓḥak. Contemporary. New York. Responsa (*Beit Avi*).

Lipshutz, Israel. See *Tiferet Yisrael*.

Lorberbaum, Jacob b. Moses. 1760–1832. Poland. Commentaries on *Shulḥan Arukh*, Scripture (*Netivot ha-Mishpat*).

Luria, Solomon. See *Maharshal*.

Mabit, Moses b. Joseph. 1500–1580. Safed. Responsa (*Mabit*). Father of Maharit.

Magen Avraham. Abraham Gombiner. 1637–1683. Poland. Commentary to *Shulḥan Arukh*.

Maggid Mishnah. Vidal Yomtov of Tolosa. Late 14th century. Spain. Commentary on Maimonides' *Mishneh Torah*.

Maharam Zev. Zev Naḥum Bernstein. 1839–1910. Biale, Poland. Talmudic commentary (*Agudat Ezov*).

Maharam Schick. Moses b. Joseph. 1807–1879. Hungary. Responsa. Student of Ḥatam Sofer.

Maharam Padua. Meir b. Isaac Katzenellenbogen. 1473–1565. Italy. Responsa.

Maharam Lublin. Meir. b. Gedaliah. 1558–1616. Poland. Talmudic commentaries and responsa (*Manhir Einei Ḥakhamim*).

Maharam Rothenburg. Meir b. Barukh. 1215–1293. Germany. Talmudic commentaries, responsa. Students were Rosh, Mordecai, Hagahot Maimoniyyot, Tashbaẓ.

Maharashdam. Samuel b. Moses de Medini. 1506–1589. Salonika. Responsa (*Maharashdam*).

Mahari ben Lev. See *Maharival*.

Maharit Ẓahalon. Yomtov b. Moses. 1559–1620. Safed. Responsa, Talmudic commentaries. Student of Joseph Karo.

Maharit. Joseph b. Moses Trani. 1568–1639. Safed and Turkey. Talmudic commentaries and responsa (*Maharit*). Son of Mabit.

Mahariv. Jacob Weil. d. before 1456. Germany. Responsa (*Mahariv*); manual on laws of slaughtering.

Maharival. Joseph b. David Ibn Lev. 1505–1580. Salonika. Responsa.

Mahariẓ Chayes. See *Chayes*.

Maharsha. Samuel Adels. 1555–1631. Poland. Commentary to Talmud.

Maharshak. See *Kluger, Solomon*.

Maharshal. Solomon b. Yeḥiel Luria. 1510–1574. Poland. Talmudic commentaries (*Yam shel Shelomoh, Ḥokhmat Shelomoh*). Teacher of Levush and Sema.

Maharsham. Shalom Mordecai b. Moses Shvadron. 1835–1911. Galicia. Responsa.

Maimonides. Moses b. Maimon. 1135–1204. Fostat, Egypt. Codifier and author of *Mishneh Torah*, responsa, *Sefer ha-Mizvot*, Commentary on Mishnah.

Mareh ha-Panim. Moses b. Simon Margaliyot. Died 1781. Lithuania. Commentaries on Jerusalem Talmud (*Mareh ha-Panim*, *Pnei Moshe*). Student was the young Elijah of Vilna.

Margaliyot, Moses. See *Mareh ha-Panim*.

Meir Simḥah ha-Kohen of Dvinsk. 1843–1926. Russia. Commentary to Maimonides and Talmud (*Or Sameaḥ*) and Torah (*Meshekh Ḥokhmah*), and responsa.

Meiri. Menaḥem b. Solomon. 1249–1316. Perpignan, France. Commentaries on Talmud (*Beit ha-Beḥirah*) and parts of Scripture.

Meisels, Ẓvi Hirsch. Contemporary. Poland and Chicago. Responsa (*Mekadeshei Hashem*).

Mekadeshei Hashem. See *Meisels, Ẓvi Hirsch*.

Minḥat Yiẓḥak. See *Weiss, Yiẓḥak Ya'akov*.

Minḥat Ḥinukh. Joseph b. Moses Babad. 1800–1875. Poland. Expositions and novellae to *Sefer ha-Ḥinukh*.

Mishneh la-Melekh. Judah b. Samuel Rosannes. 1657–1727. Turkey. Commentary on Maimonides' *Mishneh Torah*.

Mishneh Torah. See *Maimonides*.

Mishneh Halakhot. Menasheh Klein. Contemporary. New York. Responsa.

Mizraḥi, Elijah. 1450–1526. Turkey. Responsa, talmudic commentaries, supercommentary to Rashi on the Torah (the *Mizraḥi*).

Molena, Isaac of. See *Isaac of Molena*.

Mordecai b. Hillel ha-Kohen. Known as "the Mordecai." 1240–1298. Germany. Student of Maharam Rothenburg, brother-in-law of Hagahot Maimoniyyot. Compendium/commentary (the *Mordecai*).

Mordecai b. Judah ha-Levi. See *Darkhei Noam*.

Moses b. Isaac Lima. 1605–1658. Lithuania. Commentary on *Shulḥan Arukh* (*Ḥelkat Meḥokek*.) Student of Sema, colleague of Shakh.

Naḥmanides. Moses b. Naḥman. 1194–1270. Gerona, Spain.

Talmudic commentaries, responsa, monographs, glosses. First cousin of Rabbeinu Yonah and teacher of Rashba.

Nathanson Joseph Saul. 1810–1875. Lemberg, Poland. Responsa (*Sho'el u-Meshiv*) and commentaries (*Divrei Sha'ul*).

Netivot ha-Mishpat. See *Lorberbaum*.

Neẓiv. Naftali Ẓvi Yehudah Berlin. 1817–1893. Volozhin, Russia. Talmudic and biblical commentaries, responsa (*Ha'amek She'elah, Ha'amek Davar, Meishiv Davar*).

Nimmukei Yosef. Joseph Ibn Ḥabib. Early 15th century. Talmudic commentary.

Nissim b. Reuben Gerondi, Rabbeinu. Known as the Ran. 1310–1375. Spain. Talmudic commentaries (*Ḥiddushei ha-Ran*), ethical works (*Sha'arei Teshuvah*).

Noda bi-Yehudah. Ezekiel b. Judah Landau. 1713–1793. Prague. Responsa (*Noda bi-Yehudah*) and various commentaries.

Or ha-Meir. Judah Meir b. Jacob Shapiro. 1886–1934. Lublin. Responsa.

Or Zarua. Isaac b. Moses of Vienna. d. 1260. Compendium and commentary (*Or Zarua*). Responsa.

Oshry, Efraim. Kovno. Responsa (*mi-Ma'amakim*).

Ovadiah Yosef. Contemporary. Egypt, Israel. Responsa (*Yabia Omer, Yeḥaveh Da'at*).

Pick, Isaiah b. Judah Leib. 1725–1799. Breslau, Germany. Glosses and commentaries (incl. *Masoret ha-Shas*).

Pitḥei Teshuvah. Abraham b. Ẓvi Hirsch Eisenstadt. 1813–1868. Lithuania/Poland. Responsa digest in form of commentary to *Shulḥan Arukh*.

Preil, Eliezer Meir. d. 1934.

Rabbeinu Asher. See *Rosh*.

Rabbeinu Nissim. See *Nissim*.

Rabbeinu Tam. Jacob b. Meir. 1100–1171. Ramerupt, France. Responsa and talmudic commentaries (together in his *Sefer ha-Yashar*), also recorded in his pivotal position in Tosafot. Grandson of Rashi and teacher of (inter alia) Eliezer of Metz.

Radbaz. R. David b. Abu Zimra. 1479–1573. Alexandria and Cairo, Egypt. Responsa and talmudic/Maimonidean commentaries.

Ramah. Meir ha-Levi Abulafia. 1170–1244. Toledo, Spain. Commentaries to Talmud (*Yad Ramah*) and Maimonides.

Rambam. See *Maimonides*.

Ran. See *Nissim*.

Rashba. Solomon b. Abraham Adret. 1235–1310. Barcelona, Spain. Talmudic commentaries and responsa. Student of Rabbeinu Yonah of Gerondi.

Rashi. Solomon b. Isaac. 1040–1105. Troyes, France. Primary talmudic commentaries, responsa. Teacher of Rashbam and Rabbeinu Tam (his grandsons).

Ravad. Abraham b. David of Posquières. 1125–1198. Spain. Maimonidean critic. Commentaries and responsa. Student of Meshulam b. Jacob of Lunel.

Recanati, Menaḥem. Early 14th century. Italy. Commentary on Torah, halakhic compendium (*Piskei Halakhot*).

Reischer, Jacob b. Joseph. 1670–1733. Prague, Worms, Metz. Responsa (*Shevut Ya'akov*) and various commentaries.

Rema. Moses Isserles. 1530–1572. Cracow. Glosses to *Tur* and *Shulḥan Arukh*, responsa, and various commentaries.

Rif. Isaac b. Jacob Alfasi. 1013–1103. Fez. Talmudic codes, commentaries. Student of Rabbeinu Ḥananel.

Ritva. Yomtov b. Abraham Asbili. 1250–1330. Commentaries to the Talmud, responsa. Student of Aaron ha-Levi of Barcelona and Rashba.

Rivash. Isaac b. Sheshet Perfet. 1326–1408. Barcelona, Spain. Responsa (*Rivash*). Student of Nissim b. Reuven Gerondi.

Rosannes, Judah b. Samuel. See *Mishneh la-Melekh*.

Rosh. Asher b. Yeḥiel. 1250–1327. Worms, Germany, and Toledo, Spain. Talmudic commentaries, responsa. Student of Maharam Rothenburg.

Saadia b. Joseph Gaon. 882–942. Egypt, Israel, Babylon. Monographs on various topics, *Sefer ha-Miẓvot*, responsa.

Samuel b. Moses de Medini. See *Maharashdam*.

Schick, Maharam. See *Maharam Schick*.

Sdei Ḥemed. Ḥayyim Hezekiah b. Rephael. 1832–1904. Crimea. Halakhic compendium.

Sefer Yerayim. See *Eliezer b. Samuel of Metz*.

Sefer Ḥasidim, Judah he-Ḥasid. d. 1217. Regensburg, Germany. Compendium of ethical and halakhic teachings.

Sema. Joshua ha-Kohen Falk. 1555–1614. Poland. Commentaries on *Shulḥan Arukh* (*Sefer Me'irat Einayim*, *Perishah*, and *Derishah*). Student of Rema and Maharshal.

Semak. Isaac b. Joseph of Corbeil. d. 1280. French Tosafist. Compendium of contemporary Halakhah (*Sefer Mizvot Katan*).

Seridei Esh. See *Weinberg, Yeḥiel.*

Sha'arei Teshuvah. See *Yonah b. Abraham of Gerondi.*

Shakh. Shabbetai b. Meir ha-Kohen. 1621–1662. Lithuania. Commentaries to *Shulḥan Arukh* (*Shakh, Nekkudot ha-Kesef*).

She'iltot. Aḥa of Shabḥa. 680–752. Pumbedita and Israel. Early collection of halakhic discussions.

Shevet mi-Yehudah. See *Unterman, Isser Yehudah.*

Shevut Ya'akov. See *Reischer, Jacob b. Joseph.*

Shivat Ẓion. Samuel b. Ezekiel Landau. d. 1834. Sudilkov, Poland. Responsa.

Shneur Zalman of Liadi. See *Shulḥan Arukh ha-Rav.*

Shternbuch, Moshe. Contemporary. South Africa and Israel. Responsa (*Teshuvot ve'Hanhagot*).

Shulḥan Arukh ha-Rav. Shneur Zalman of Liadi. 1745–1813. Code based on *Shulḥan Arukh.*

Shulḥan Arukh. Joseph b. Ephraim Karo. 1488–1575. Turkey, Greece, and Safed, Israel. Codifier (*Beit Yosef, Shulḥan Arukh*), Maimonidean commentator (*Kesef Mishnah*), and responsa.

Shvadron, Shalom Mordecai. See *Maharsham.*

Sirkes, Joel. See *Baḥ.*

Soloveichik, Ḥayyim ha-Levi. See *Ḥayyim ha-Levi Soloveichik.*

Soloveichik, Aaron. Contemporary. Lithuania, New York, and Chicago.

Soloveitchik, Joseph Dov (The Rav). Contemporary. New York and Boston. Student of his father, Moses Soloveitchik. Oral discourses and responsa.

Tam, Rabbeinu. See *Rabbeinu Tam.*

Tashbaẓ. Simon b. Ẓemaḥ Duran. 1361–1444. Majorca and Algiers. Responsa and commentaries to Talmud, Scripture, and others.

Taz. David b. Samuel ha-Levi. 1586–1667. Various communities in Poland. Commentary to *Shulḥan Arukh*. Son-in-law, and student, of Joel Sirkes.

Tendler, Moshe David. Contemporary. New York. Essays and articles. Son-in-law of Moshe Feinstein.

Teshuvot Maimoniyyot. See *Hagahot Maimoniyyot.*

Tiferet Ẓvi. Ẓvi Hirsch b. Benjamin Baschko. 1740–1807. Brod, Poland. Responsa.

Tiferet Yisrael. Israel Lipschutz. 1782–1860. Poland. Commentary on Mishnah (*Yakhin u-Boaz*).

Torah Temimah. Barukh ha-Levi Epstein. 1860–1942. Russia. Torah commentary. Student of his father (the *Arukh ha-Shulḥan*) and uncle (the *Neẓiv*).

Tosafot Yomtov. See *Heller, Yomtov Lipman*.

Tosafot. Collections, printed together with the Talmud itself, of comments and commentaries by French and German scholars in the 12th–14th century, arranged according to the order of talmudic discussions, usually reacting to Rashi.

Tucatzinsky, Yeḥiel. 1872–1955. Jerusalem. Responsa and compendium of Laws of Mourning (*Gesher ha-Ḥayyim*).

Tur. Jacob b. Asher, Ba'al ha-Turim. 1270–1340. Toledo, Spain. Codifier (the *Tur*), commentator on Torah. Son, and student, of the Rosh.

Tuv Ta'am ve'Da'at. See *Kluger, Solomon*.

Unterman, Isser Yehudah. 1886–1976. Lithuania and Israel. Responsa (*Shevet mi-Yehudah*).

Uziel, Ben Ẓion. 1880–1953. Jerusalem. Responsa (*Mishpetei Uziel*).

Vidal Yomtov of Tolosa. See *Maggid Mishnah*.

Vilna Gaon. See *Elijah of Vilna*.

Waldenberg, Eliezer. See *Ẓiẓ Eliezer*.

Weil, Jacob. See *Mahariv*.

Weinberg, Yeḥiel. 1885–1966. Lithuania, Berlin, Switzerland. Responsa (*Seridei Esh*), as well as studies and essays.

Weiss, Yiẓḥak Ya'akov. Contemporary. England and Jerusalem. Responsa (*Minḥat Yiẓḥak*).

Yad Eliyahu. Elijah Rogoler of Lublin. d. 1900.

Yaveẓ. See *Emden, Jacob*.

Yismaḥ Lev. Solomon Gagin. 19th century.

Yisraeli, Shaul. Contemporary. Jerusalem. Essays and articles.

Yomtov b. Abraham Asbili. See *Ritva*.

Yonah b. Abraham of Gerondi, Rabbeinu. 1200–1263. Spain. Ethical treatises (*Sha'arei Teshuvah*) and commentaries.

Yosef, Ovadiah. See *Ovadiah Yosef*.

Ẓahalon, Maharit. See *Maharit*.

Zevin, Shelomoh Yosef. 1890–1978. Encyclopedist (editor of *Encyclopedia Talmudit*), essayist, and reviewer.

Zimrah, Abu. See *Radbaz*.

Ẓiẓ Eliezer. Eliezer Yehudah b. Ya'akov Waldenberg. Contemporary. Jerusalem. Responsa.